Y0-DWZ-237

Portraits of Pioneers in Psychology

VOLUME V

Portraits of Pioneers in Psychology

VOLUME V

Edited by

Gregory A. Kimble
Michael Wertheimer

AMERICAN PSYCHOLOGICAL ASSOCIATION
Washington, DC

LEA LAWRENCE ERLBAUM ASSOCIATES, PUBLISHERS
2003 Mahwah, New Jersey   London

Published by

Lawrence Erlbaum Associates, Inc., Publishers
10 Industrial Avenue
Mahwah, New Jersey 07430

American Psychological Association
750 First Street, NE
Washington, DC 20002

Cover design by Kathryn Houghtaling Lacey

Library of Congress Cataloging-in-Publication Data

Portraits of pioneers in psychology / edited by Gregory A. Kimble and Michael Wertheimer
      p. cm.
   "Sponsored by the Division of General Psychology, American Psychological Association."
   Includes bibliographical references and index.
   ISBN 0-8058-4413-9 (cloth : alk. paper) — ISBN 0-8058-4414-7 (pbk. : alk. paper)
   1. Psychology – biography. 2. Psychology – History. I. Kimble, Gregory A. II. Wertheimer,
Michael. III. American Psychological Association. Division of General Psychology.

BF109.A1P67 2003
150′.92′2—dc20

[B]   91-7226
                                                                                          CIP

Portraits of Pioneers in Psychology: Volume V has been published under the following ISBNs:

LEA: 1-8058-4413-9
         1-8058-4414-7 (pbk.)
APA: 1-59147-016-1
         1-59147-017-X (pbk.)

Printed in the United States of America
10 9 8 7 6 5 4 3 2 1

British Cataloging in Publication Data
A CIP record is available from the British Library

First edition

Contents

Preface

The chapters in this book, like those in the previous four volumes in this series, offer glimpses into the personal and scholarly lives of some of the giants in the history of psychology. They should be of interest to psychologists and scholars in many fields, but particularly to students and teachers in courses on the history of psychology. As in the earlier volumes, prominent scholars were invited to prepare chapters on pioneers who have made important contributions in their areas of expertise. Almost all of them accepted.

Taken together, these five volumes contain a wealth of materials that bring some of the pioneers in psychology and related sciences more vividly to life. The following paragraphs show how the more than 100 chapters in *Pioneers I–V* relate to important topics in the field. Teachers of courses on these topics may wish to assign them as supplementary readings.

Philosophical, Methodological, and Statistical Foundations: Pioneers I: Galton, Tryon. *Pioneers II*: Fechner, Rhine. *Pioneers III*: Binet, Ebbinghaus, Hickok, Thurstone. *Pioneers IV*: Eysenck, Hathaway, Heider, Koch, Müller, Schneirla, Spearman, Terman, Upham. *Pioneers V*: Brunswik, Leibniz, Lord, McDougall, Washburn.

Schools and Systems: Pioneers I: Carr, Freud, Heidbreder, Jung, Köhler, Pavlov, Titchener, Tolman, Watson, Wertheimer. *Pioneers II*: Dewey, Guthrie, Sechenov. *Pioneers III*: Duncker, Hickok, Lewin, Piaget, Rogers, Skinner, Spence, Wundt. *Pioneers IV*: Heider, Horney, Müller, Stumpf, Upham. *Pioneers V*: Angell, Brunswik, Goldstein, Harlow, McDougall, Metzger, Washburn.

Biological/Genetic/Evolutionary/Physiological Psychology: Pioneers I: Galton, Hunter, Lashley, Pavlov, Tryon. *Pioneers II*: Blatz, Burks, Graham, Hebb, Schiller, Yerkes. *Pioneers III*: Darwin, Festinger, Krech, Kuo, McGraw, Nissen. *Pioneers IV*: Beach, Helmholtz, Schneirla, Sperry. *Pioneers V*: Hall, Goldstein, Harlow, McDougall, Ratliff, Washburn.

Sensation and Perception: Pioneers I: Köhler, Wertheimer. *Pioneers II*: Fechner, Gibson, Graham, Hebb, Rhine. *Pioneers III*: Duncker, Festinger, Piaget, Wundt. *Pioneers IV*: Heider, Helmholtz, Müller, Sperry, Stumpf. *Pioneers V*: Brunswik, Metzger, Michotte, Ratliff.

Comparative Psychology and Animal Behavior: Pioneers I: Hull, Hunter, Köhler, Lashley, Pavlov, Thorndike, Watson. *Pioneers II*: Schiller, Yerkes. *Pioneers III*: Darwin, Kuo, Nissen. *Pioneers IV*: Beach, Schneirla, Sperry. *Pioneers V*: Harlow, McDougall, Washburn.

Learning and Conditioning: Pioneers I: Calkins, Hull, Hunter, Köhler, Lashley, Pavlov, Thorndike, Tolman. *Pioneers II*: Blatz, Guthrie, Hebb, Sechenov. *Pioneers III*: Duncker, Ebbinghaus, Krech, Skinner, Spence, Underwood. *Pioneers IV*: Bartlett, Beach, Hovland, Müller, Schneirla. *Pioneers V*: Harlow, Washburn.

Cognitive Psychology: Pioneers I: Calkins, Köhler, Lashley, Tolman, Wertheimer. *Pioneers II*: Dewey, Stern. *Pioneers III*: Duncker, Ebbinghaus, Hickok, Piaget, Underwood, Wundt. *Pioneers IV*: Bartlett, Heider, Müller, Stumpf, Terman. *Pioneers V*: Brunswik, Harlow, Leibniz, Michotte.

Motivation and Emotion: Pioneers I: Freud, Hull, James, Jung, Sullivan, Tolman. *Pioneers II*: Milgram, Schiller, Tomkins, Yerkes. *Pioneers III*: Erickson, Festinger, Lewin, Spence. *Pioneers IV*: Beach, Heider, Horney. *Pioneers V*: Asch, Harlow, McDougall.

Developmental Psychology: Pioneers I: Freud, Leta Hollingworth, Puffer, Watson. *Pioneers II*: Blatz, Doll, Murchison, Witmer. *Pioneers III*: Binet, McGraw, Piaget. *Pioneers IV*: Horney, Schneirla, Terman. *Pioneers V*: Ainsworth, Bayley, Hall, Harlow.

Individual Differences: Pioneers I: Galton, Leta Hollingworth, Pavlov, Tryon. *Pioneers II*: Burks, Doll, Milgram, Stern. *Pioneers III*: Allport, Binet, Thurstone. *Pioneers IV*: Eysenck, Hathaway, Horney, Spearman, Terman. *Pioneers V*: Ainsworth, Bayley, Downey, Hall, Lord, Tyler.

Personality: Pioneers I: Calkins, Freud, Jung. *Pioneers II*: Tomkins. *Pioneers III*: Erickson, Rogers, Thurstone. *Pioneers IV*: Eysenck, Hathaway, Horney. *Pioneers V*: Ainsworth, Downey.

Applied Psychology: Pioneers I: Jastrow, Puffer, Titchener, Watson. *Pioneers II*: Dix, Gilbreth, Hollingworth. *Pioneers III*: Skinner, Thurstone. *Pioneers IV*: Bartlett, Hathaway, Münsterberg. *Pioneers V*: Bingham, Lord.

Psychopathology and Clinical Psychology: Pioneers I: Freud, Leta Hollingworth, Jastrow, Jung, Sullivan. *Pioneers II*: Dix, Doll, Tomkins, Witmer.

Pioneers III: Binet, Duncker, Erickson, Rogers. *Pioneers IV*: Eysenck, Hathaway, Horney. *Pioneers V*: Ainsworth, Goldstein, Harlow.

Social Psychology: Pioneers I: Puffer. *Pioneers II*: Milgram, Murchison. *Pioneers III*: Allport, Festinger, Krech, Lewin. *Pioneers IV*: Cook, Heider, Hovland. *Pioneers V*: Asch, Harlow, McDougall.

Psychology and Gender, Politics, Poverty, and Race: Pioneers I: Calkins, Heidbreder, Leta Hollingworth, Puffer. *Pioneers II*: Burks, Dix, Doll, Milgram, Murchison. *Pioneers III*: Allport, Darwin, Krech, Lewin, McGraw. *Pioneers IV*: Hooker, Horney, Münsterberg, Schneirla, Spearman, Sumner, Terman. *Pioneers V*: Hall, Wolfe.

This book owes its existence to the contributions of many people. Primary among them, of course, are the authors of the chapters, to whom we extend our heartfelt thanks. We acknowledge the financial support of the Society for General Psychology, Division 1 of the American Psychological Association. At Duke and Colorado, respectively, Hazel Carpenter and Donna Huckaby helped manage the details involved in corresponding with authors and in preparing the manuscripts for publication.

Gregory A. Kimble
Michael Wertheimer

Portraits of the Authors and Editors

David B. Baker, coauthor of the chapter on Walter Van Dyke Bingham, is director of the Archives of the History of American Psychology and associate professor of psychology at The University of Akron. Baker received his Ph.D. in counseling psychology from Texas A&M University in 1988. His initial academic appointment was at the University of North Texas, where he was active in child clinical research, practice and training, and the history of psychology. In 1999, he assumed the directorship of the Archives of the History of American Psychology. He has written on the history of school and counseling psychology and coauthored and coedited a special section of the *American Psychologist* in February 2000 that examined the 50th anniversary of the Conference on Graduate Education in Clinical Psychology, better known as the "Boulder Conference." Baker has a long-standing interest in the rise of professional psychology in America and is coauthor with Benjamin of a forthcoming book on that subject that will be published by Harcourt.

Ludy T. Benjamin Jr., author of the chapter on Harry Kirke Wolfe and coauthor of the portrait of Walter Van Dyke Bingham, is the Fasken Professor of Distinguished Teaching and professor of psychology and educational psychology at Texas A&M University, where he has been on the faculty since 1980. He received his doctorate in experimental psychology from Texas Christian University in 1971. His initial academic appointment was at Nebraska Wesleyan University for 8 years. He then served for 2 years as director of education for the American Psychological Association (APA) before going to Texas A&M. He has served as president of two of APA's divisions: Division 26 (History of Psychology) and Division 2 (Society for the Teaching of Psychology). He also served as president of the Eastern Psychological Association. Much of Benjamin's work as a historian of psychology has focused on applied psychology. He contributed chapters to two of the earlier volumes in this series—Harry Hollingworth and Hugo Münsterberg. Currently Benjamin is writing a book with David Baker on the origins and development of the psychology profession in America.

Inge Bretherton, author of the chapter on Mary Ainsworth, was born and grew up in Germany. Her initial training was as translator and interpreter. She obtained her B.A., M.A., and Ph.D. in developmental psychology at the Johns Hopkins University after she, her husband, and three children emigrated from Britain to the United States. After completing her Ph.D. with Ainsworth, she collaborated with Elizabeth Bates at the University of Colorado, resulting in two books on language development and an edited volume on symbolic play. As associate professor at Colorado State University, she became a member of the MacArthur Network on Early Childhood Transitions and, in collaboration with Everett Waters, edited "Growing Points of Attachment Theory and Research" (in the *Monographs of the Society for Research in Child Development* series). After moving to the University of Wisconsin–Madison, where she is Rothermel-Bascom Professor of Human Ecology, she developed a widely used "Attachment Story Completion Task" for preschoolers and expanded Bowlby's theoretical work on internal working models. She is associate editor of the new journal *Attachment and Human Development*.

Laura Burlingame-Lee, coauthor of the chapter on Margaret Floy Washburn, graduated summa cum laude with an A.B. degree in psychology from Whitman College in 1998. She is currently working on a Ph.D. in counseling psychology at Colorado State University. Her areas of interest include the contributions of women to psychology, contemporary gender issues, and problems of peace and violence.

Donald A. Dewsbury, author of the chapter on James Rowland Angell, is a professor of psychology at the University of Florida. Born in Brooklyn, New York, he grew up on Long Island and attended Bucknell University. His doctorate is from the University of Michigan and was followed by postdoctoral work at the University of California, Berkeley. Through much of his career he worked as a comparative psychologist with an emphasis on social and reproductive behavior. But in recent years his work has shifted so that his primary focus is on the history of psychology, with comparative psychology remaining a secondary interest. He is the author or editor of 14 books, including *Comparative Animal Behavior And Comparative Psychology in the Twentieth Century*. He also edited a series of volumes on the histories of the APA division, *Unification Through Division*, published by APA. In addition, he has published more than 300 articles and chapters.

Raymond E. Fancher, coauthor of the chapter on Leibniz, is professor of psychology at York University in Toronto, Ontario. He was a founding member of York's unique graduate program in History and Theory of Psychology in 1981 and has served as president of APA Division 26 (History of Psychology) and as executive officer of Cheiron: The International Society for the History of Behavioral and Social Sciences. He is the author of *Psychoanalytic Psychology: The Development of Freud's Thought*, *The Intelligence Men: Makers of the IQ Controversy*, *Pioneers of Psychology*, and a chapter on Alfred Binet in Volume III of the present series. Currently he serves as editor of the *Journal of the History of the Behavioral Sciences*.

Ruth E. Fassinger, author of the chapter on Leona Tyler, is an associate professor in the Counseling Program at the University of Maryland and an affiliate faculty member in Women's Studies. She grew up on Long Island in New York and, like Tyler, is a former English teacher, having taught for a decade before earning her Ph.D. in psychology from the Ohio State University in 1987. She joined the University of Maryland faculty after holding staff psychologist positions at the University of California–Santa Barbara and Arizona State University. Her primary scholarly work is on the psychology of women and gender, career development, and issues of sexuality and sexual orientation. Like Tyler, her work integrates methodological, psychometric, therapeutic, developmental, and historical issues in psychology. Also like Tyler, she is deeply involved in professional activities. She is a Fellow of two divisions of APA: Division 17 (Society of Counseling Psychology) and Division 44 (Society for the Psychological Study of Lesbian, Gay, and Bisexual Issues). She currently serves as vice president for Scientific Affairs of Division 17. She is on the editorial board of *Psychology of Women Quarterly* and is an instructor for the National Academy of Feminist Practice. She also maintains a psychotherapy and consultation practice, specializing in issues related to gender, work, and sexuality. She has been the recipient of many awards for her scholarship, teaching, and service, but her real dream is to be honored someday with the coveted Leona Tyler Award, Division 17's most prestigious recognition of lifetime contributions to the field of counseling psychology.

Eileen A. Gavin, author of the chapter on Albert Michotte, was born in Chicago and reared in the Twin Cities of Minnesota where she attended public schools through graduation from high school. As a child and adolescent she helped her next-door neighbor, University of Minnesota School of Education professor Guy L. Bond, identify and adapt stories for his series of children's readers. She received her A.B. degree from the College of St. Catherine in St. Paul, an M.A. in psychology from the University of Minnesota, and a Ph.D. from Loyola University in Chicago. She taught psychology for 40 years and served four terms as chair of the Psychology Department at the College of St. Catherine. Gavin is past president and treasurer of APA's Division 36 (Psychology of Religion), past secretary-treasurer of Divisions 24 (Theoretical and Philosophical Psychology) and 26 (History of Psychology), and former convention program chair of Divisions 24 and 26. Her professional work has included the organization of many symposia for colleagues in psychology. She has published articles in psychology and related fields, largely in encyclopedias and reference books. In 2000 she received the Walter Mink Undergraduate Teacher Award from the Minnesota Psychological Association. In earlier years, she received the Distinguished Service Award and the Mentoring Award from APA's Division 36. She is presently professor emerita of psychology at the College of St. Catherine.

Herbert Götzl, author of the chapter on Wolfgang Metzger, was born in Moravská Tøebová in Czechoslovakia and attended Oberschule there. After that he studied at the humanistic gymnasiums in Münnsterstadt (Bavaria) and Bielefeld (Westphalia). Later, he learned theology, philosophy, psychology, and mathematical logic in Münster and Bochum, Germany. Götzl became first a student of Wolfgang Metzger in 1955, and then his coinvestigator. This collaboration lasted until 1965. Thereafter, he became a colleague of Heinz Heckenhausen and Kurt Schneider, relationships that continued until the deaths of these two men. Presently, Götzl is a collaborator of the biopsychologist Marlies Pinnow at Ruhr University in Bochum. His research includes studies of the influence of motivational and volitional states on attention; information processing and performance; the effects of theatrical performances on the arousal and expression of aggression; the generation of emotional states including affection; and the effects of propaganda on affect and behavior, especially the motivational and habitual determiners of anti-Jewish prejudice.

Bert F. Green, author of the chapter on F. M. Lord, was born in Pennsylvania and attended high school in New York. After receiving his A.B. degree from Yale, he obtained his Ph.D. from Princeton. After graduation he joined a group of psychologists at MIT's Lincoln Laboratory, working on human factors problems in man–computer systems. In 1962, after a year at the RAND corporation, he became head of the Psychology Department at Carnegie Mellon University. In 1969, he joined the Johns Hopkins University as professor of psychology, where he is now professor emeritus. Green has been editor of the journal *Psychometrika*. He served on a technical panel that advised the U.S. Navy on the development of the computer-based vocational aptitude battery and advised the Department of Defense on the assessment of performance of military personnel. More recently, he was a member of a committee that revised *Standards for Educational and Psychological Testing*. He has authored one book and more than 100 research articles in human factors, multivariate statistics, and computer applications in psychology and statistics. His recent research concerns computer-based adaptive testing. Green's awards include the Maryland State Psychological Association's award for outstanding scientific contributions to psychology; the APA Division 5 award for lifetime contributions to evaluation, measurement, and statistics; a career achievement award in computer-based testing from the Association of Test Publishers, and the Lindquist Award for Excellence in Research in Measurement from the American Educational Research Association.

John D. Hogan, author of the chapters on Anne Anastasi and G. Stanley Hall, and coauthor of the chapter on June Downey, received his Ph.D. from the Ohio State University in developmental psychology. He is now professor of psychology at St. John's University in New York. The major areas of his writings are the history of psychology, international psychology, and developmental psychology. He is particularly interested in the history of American psychology and developmental psychology. He is a board member and historian of the Eastern Psychological Association. Recently, he received the Excellence in Teaching and Scholarship Award from St. John's University.

Nancy K. Innis, author of the chapter on William McDougall and coauthor of the chapter on Egon Bruswik, is a professor in the Department of Psychology at the University of Western Ontario (UWO). She was born in Toronto and grew up in Peterborough, Ontario. Innis received her B.A. and M.A. from the University of Toronto and her Ph.D. from Duke University for research on animal timing. Returning to Canada, she worked briefly at the Addiction Research Foundation in Toronto and then did postdoctoral research in Werner K. Honig's laboratory at Dalhousie University, in Halifax, Nova Scotia. Following an additional year at Dalhousie as a visiting faculty member, she accepted a position at UWO. Her interests in animal learning and the history of psychology came together during a sabbatical leave when she began research for a biography of Edward C. Tolman. To increase her expertise in the history of psychology, she was awarded a study leave, which was spent with the history of science group in the History Department at Duke University. As her work on the biography continues, she has been publishing book chapters and articles on the activities and ideas of Tolman and some of his colleagues.

Gregory A. Kimble, senior editor of Volumes I–V of *Portraits of Pioneers in Psychology* and coauthor of the chapter on Harry Harlow in this volume, was born in Iowa and grew up in Minnesota. His A.B., M.A., and Ph.D. degrees were from Carleton College, Northwestern University, and the University of Iowa, respectively. He also has an honorary degree, Doctor of Humane Letters, from the University of Colorado. Kimble's major academic appointments have been at Brown University, Yale University, the University of Colorado, and Duke University. He is currently professor emeritus of Psychological and Brain Sciences at Duke. Kimble has been president of APA Divisions 1 (General Psychology) and 3 (Experimental Psychology). He was the last editor of the now-discontinued *Psychological Monographs* and the first editor of the *Journal of Experimental Psychology: General*. His books include *Principles of General Psychology* (which appeared in six editions, the last five with Norman Garmezy and Edward Zigler as coauthors), *Hilgard and Marquis' Conditioning and Learning*, *How to Use (and Misuse) Statistics*, and *Psychology: The Hope of a Science*. He was the 1999 recipient of the APA Award for Distinguished Contributions to Education and Training in Psychology. In 2001, he received the Arthur W. Staats Award for Unifying Psychology.

Elke Kurz-Milcke, coauthor of the chapter on Egon Brunswik, is a research scientist working at the University of Tuebingen, Germany, and at the Georgia Institute of Technology, Atlanta. Born in Germany, she grew up in Stuttgart. She received her diploma in psychology from the University of Konstanz with a thesis on Karl Popper's early studies in psychology. Subsequently, she moved to the United States to study cognitive psychology and the history of psychology with Ryan D. Tweney at Bowling Green State University, Ohio. Her Ph.D. thesis dealt with the representational practices of the differential calculus. The American Psychological Foundation supported this work with a graduate research scholarship. Returning to Germany, she joined the research group Adaptive Behavior and Cognition at the Max Planck Institute for Human Development in Berlin. As a postdoctoral fellow she received a Schloessmann Fellowship awarded by the Max Planck Society for the Advancement of Science, which has allowed her to continue her career at the University of Tuebingen and at the Georgia Institute of Technology. In collaboration with Gerd Gigerenzer, she is currently editing *Experts in Modern Societies*. She has published several papers on Egon Brunswik's work, collaborating with Ryan Tweney, Michael Doherty, Ralph Hertwig, and Gerd Gigerenzer. Her interest in the history of psychology and the history of science continues to be informed by a cognitive–historical approach.

Helen A. LeRoy, senior author of the chapter on Harry Harlow, is a lifelong resident of Madison, Wisconsin. She received her B.S. in journalism from the University of Wisconsin, where she is currently the assistant director of the Harlow Primate Laboratory. She initially joined the Primate Laboratory staff in October, 1958, as a part-time student employee, majoring in sociology at Wisconsin. She soon became involved in assisting Harlow in his capacity as editor of the *Journal of Comparative and Physiological Psychology* and, for a time, sent out acceptance or rejection letters and consulting editors' comments to contributing authors. One thing led to another and she became Harlow's right-hand person and editorial assistant, working closely with him day to day in all his diversified roles until his retirement from Wisconsin in 1974. She continued to maintain a close relationship with both Harry and Clara Harlow after they moved to Tucson, Arizona, and until their deaths in 1981 and 1989, respectively. LeRoy is the overseer of the Harlow archive collection.

Clark McCauley, coauthor of the chapter on Solomon Asch, is professor of psychology at Bryn Mawr College and codirector of the Solomon Asch Center for Study of Ethnopolitical Conflict at the University of Pennsylvania. His undergraduate B.A. (1965) is from Providence College and his Ph.D. (1970) in social psychology is from the University of Pennsylvania. He has worked on a variety of topics, including the psychology of disgust, stereotyping, group dynamics including the psychology of terrorist groups, identification with ethnic and national groups, and intergroup conflict. He is editor or coeditor of *Terrorism Research and Public Policy, Stereotype Accuracy: Toward Appreciating*

Group Differences, and *Personality and Person Perception Across Cultures*. His recent publications have focused on the psychology of peace education programs, especially the use of diversity workshops on U.S. campuses.

Wade Pickren, author of the chapter on Kurt Goldstein, grew up with his 11 siblings in then-rural central Florida, where he roamed the forests and orange groves. After an early adulthood marked by communal living, cross-country hitchhiking, and serving as a Christian minister, he went to college and completed a B.S. degree in psychology at the University of Central Florida. Pickren left the ministry when he entered the University of Florida's graduate program in clinical and health psychology, intending to become a clinical psychologist. After completing an M.A. in clinical health psychology, however, he enrolled in a course in the history of psychology taught by Donald A. Dewsbury and found his true intellectual interest there. He now serves as APA's director of archives and library services and as editor of the obituary section of *American Psychologist*. Pickren's current scholarly interests include the history of post-World War II medicine and psychology and the public imagination.

Judy F. Rosenblith, author of the chapter on Nancy Bayley, was born in Utah, grew up in California, and attended Occidental College and the University of California at Los Angeles. During World War II, she lived in Rapid City, South Dakota, where she taught high school, lectured, had two children, and collected data on prejudice. Her M.A. (1958) and Ph.D. (1958) degrees were from Harvard University. Rosenblith's teaching positions have been at Simmons College, Harvard University, Brown University, Wheaton College, and Florida International University. She was senior editor of three editions of *Readings in Child Development and Educational Psychology* and of the first edition of *In the Beginning: Development in the First Two Years*. Six of her papers and monographs are on prejudice, imitation, and perception; seven are on the follow-up of the newborns, a topic on which she has 13 publications in medical journals. She has book chapters on two now-deceased female psychologists—Nancy Bayley and Pauline Sears.

Paul Rozin, coauthor of the chapter on Solomon Asch, is Edmund J. and Louise W. Kahn Professor for Faculty Excellence in Psychology at the University of Pennsylvania. He is also codirector of the new Solomon Asch Center for Study of Ethnopolitical Conflict at the University of Pennsylvania. Rozin and Asch were colleagues at the University of Pennsylvania during Asch's last academic position, 1972–1979, and remained close until his death in 1995. His B.A. (1956) is from the University of Chicago and his Ph.D. (1961) jointly in biology and psychology is from Harvard University. Rozin's major interests include the psychology of food choice (often using a cultural approach), cultural evolution, disgust and magical thinking, the development of preferences and values, forgiveness, and identification.

Heather Schmidt, coauthor of the chapter on Gottfried Leibniz, is a graduate student in social psychology at York University with strong interests in cross-cultural psychology, social justice, and minority voices. For her master's thesis, she recently conducted a qualitative study on Islamic perceptions of justice. She received her undergraduate degree from the University of Victoria (in British Columbia, Canada) and plans to specialize in applied social justice projects.

Lothar Spillmann, coauthor of the chapter on Floyd Ratliff, was born in Silesia (now Poland), went to gymnasium in Hannover (Lower Saxony), and studied in Würzburg, Münster, and Freiburg. He spent 2 years at MIT and 5 years at the Retina Foundation and Massachusetts Eye and Ear Infirmary in Boston. Spillman is interested in the neurophysiology of visual perception as it relates to visual illusions, light and dark adaptation, color vision, figure–ground segregation, and the clinical consequences of dysfunction of the visual system. He has published extensively in those areas. Spillman is the editor, with Bill R. Wooten, of *Sensory Experience, Adaptation, and Perception*, and, with John S. Werner, of *Visual Perception: The Neurophysiological Foundations*. In 1976, he founded the European Conference on Visual Perception. Since 1971, Spillmann has been head of the Visual Psychophysics Laboratory, Brain Research Unit, at Freiburg University, Germany.

Dennis N. Thompson, coauthor of the chapter on June E. Downey, is professor of educational psychology at Georgia State University in Atlanta. Born in Youngstown, Ohio, he received his Ph.D. degree in developmental psychology from the Ohio State University. One of his current projects is to locate archival 16 mm and 35 mm film of early psychologists and their work. The project, undertaken with Prentice Hall, will attempt to identify representative film and make it more widely available and in modern format to teachers and researchers. In addition to his interest in the history of psychology, he conducts empirical research in the area of cognitive aging.

Wayne Viney, senior author of the chapter on Margaret Floy Wahsburn, is professor of psychology at Colorado State University where he teaches graduate and undergraduate courses in the history of psychology. He served as head of the Department of Psychology (1967–1973) and as associate dean of Natural Sciences and director of the Biology Core Curriculum (1973–1976). Viney earned a Ph.D. at the University of Oklahoma in general-experimental psychology with a minor in the history and philosophy of science. He has also engaged in sabbatical work in the history of psychology with Michael Wertheimer at the University of Colorado. Viney is coauthor with D. Brett King of *History of Psychology: Ideas and Context* now in its third edition. He has served as president of APA's Division 26 (History of Psychology) and as president of the Rocky Mountain Psychological Association. The major focus of his historical work is on the philosophy and psychology of William James.

John S. Werner, coauthor of the chapter on Floyd Ratliff, was born on the plains of Nebraska, attended the University of Kansas as an undergraduate, and received a Ph.D. in psychology from Brown University. He was a postdoctoral fellow at the Institute for Perception—TNO (Soesterberg, The Netherlands) and in the Department of Neurophysiology of Freiburg University (Germany). From 1979 to 1999, he was a member of the Psychology Department faculty at the University of Colorado, Boulder. Werner is an experimental psychologist who studies vision and its variations across the life span. He is currently a professor at the University of California, Davis, in the Department of Ophthalmology and Section of Neurobiology, Physiology, and Behavior.

Michael Wertheimer has coedited all five volumes of *Portraits of Pioneers in Psychology*. The fourth volume appeared in 2000, the year of publication of the fourth edition of his *Brief History of Psychology* and (coauthored with Stephen F. Davis), an oral history of Psi Chi, the national honor society in psychology. Wertheimer has received the Lifetime Achievement Award for Sustained, Outstanding, and Unusual Scholarly Contributions to the History of Psychology from APA's Division 26 (History of Psychology). He has been president of Psi Chi, of the Rocky Mountain Psychological Association, and four divisions of APA: General Psychology, Teaching Psychology, Theoretical and Philosophical Psychology, and History of Psychology. Wertheimer received his bachelor's degree from Swarthmore College, his master's degree from The Johns Hopkins University, and his doctorate from Harvard. He has taught at Wesleyan University and the University of Colorado, Boulder, becoming full professor there in 1961 and professor emeritus in 1993. He directed the undergraduate honors program in psychology at Colorado and was director of doctoral programs in experimental and sociocultural psychology. Author, coauthor, editor, or coeditor of dozens of books (mostly on the history of psychology), he is also author or coauthor of about 200 articles in journals. A grandparent, parent, spouse, gardener, cook, and hiker, he also enjoys extensive foreign travels.

Chapter 1

Gottfried Wilhelm Leibniz: Underappreciated Pioneer of Psychology

Raymond E. Fancher and Heather Schmidt
York University

The German philosopher Gottfried Wilhelm Leibniz (1646–1716) was not popular in England in his lifetime, and a certain tendency to deprecate him in the English-speaking world has continued ever since. Bertrand Russell, for example, conceded that Leibniz was "one of the greatest intellects of all time" but gratuitously added: "As a human being he was not admirable. . . . He was wholly destitute of those higher philosophic virtues that are so notable in Spinoza" (Russell, 1945, p. 581). Edward G. Boring's classic history of psychology baldly described Leibniz as "less important for experimental psychology than Descartes or Locke" (Boring, 1950, p. 166) and accordingly devoted less than half the space to him than the two others. Gordon Allport (1955) attempted to counter this attitude by proposing that a "Leibnizean" emphasis on an active and purposive mind ought to be given equal weight to the "Lockean" conception of the mind as a *tabula rasa* passively awaiting and recording the impressions of sensory experience. But Allport's has remained a minority view within anglophone psychology. Most history textbooks follow Boring's example and give more emphasis to Locke. When one of the authors of this chapter was recently invited to contribute articles for the APA-sponsored *Encyclopedia of Psychology*, 1,500 words were allocated for Locke as against 750 for Leibniz. Negotiations led to an increase of the latter to 1,000 words (Fancher, 2000). We shall argue here that in all justice the balance should have been at least equal, as Allport had suggested.

We begin by providing a summary of Leibniz's life and career, followed by an account of those specific works and accomplishments that had particular importance for the history of psychology.

LEIBNIZ'S LIFE AND EARLY CAREER

Gottfried Wilhelm Leibniz was born in Leipzig, Germany, on July 1, 1646, the youngest child of Friedrich Leibnütz,[1] an aging professor of moral philosophy at the city's famous university. His young mother Catherine was Friedrich's third wife. Well known for her tranquil, patient, and kindly manner, she seems to have passed on to her son a lifelong sense of optimism as well as a strong sense of social responsibility. The more intellectual Friedrich also took a strong interest in his precocious youngest child, teaching him to read and love books while just a toddler.

Education

Following Friedrich's death in 1652, 6-year-old Gottfried was sent to school where he astonished his teacher by accurately translating a Latin text normally used by university students. This opened a debate as to whether a child so young should be kept away from books so advanced, or instead should be provided unlimited access to his dead father's well-stocked library. Fortunately, the latter plan prevailed and Leibniz embarked on a career of encyclopedic learning by devouring his father's substantial collection of books on poetry, law, philosophy, history, mathematics, and theology.

Meanwhile, at school he eventually received formal instruction in classical philosophy and became particularly interested in Aristotle's logic. He amazed his teachers with his ability to apply Aristotelian rules to concrete cases, to recognize some of the limitations of Aristotelian logic, and to develop original ideas of his own. One of the earliest of these was a scheme for a universal system for organizing all known truths and propositions. He thought that a certain "alphabet" of human thought might be developed, and that "from the combinations of the letters of this alphabet and analysis of the words built from them, everything could be discovered and also demonstrated" (Aiton, 1985, p. 13). The realization of this wonderful idea would remain a lifelong, if ultimately unfulfilled, dream for Leibniz.

At 14 Leibniz matriculated at Leipzig's renowned university, where he pursued the classical curriculum while simultaneously completing studies for a doctorate in law. His law dissertation, written when he was 19, dealt with combinatorial logic and developed further his dream for a "language of human thought." Here he imagined a universal language similar to Chinese, in which ideas would be represented by combinations of pictorial signs corresponding to their component parts, arranged systematically to allow reasoning and demonstration by cal-

---

[1] As a young man Leibniz changed the spelling of the last syllable of his name from *-ütz* to *-iz*; he never himself used the spelling "Leibnitz," although this was commonly used by commentators about him until recently.

culations analogous to those involved in arithmetic and algebra. Leibniz hoped that ultimately such a universal system could be used to spread peace and understanding among the various people of the world (Aiton, 1985, p. 21). Coincidentally, this work marked the beginning of a lifelong fascination with China and its culture.

Leibniz's youth now became a disadvantage because the University of Leipzig awarded just 12 doctorates in law each year, with priority determined by age if there were more qualified candidates than that. Angered at being told he would have to wait for his degree, Leibniz went to the smaller University of Altdorf where he got his degree in 6 months and so impressed the faculty that they offered him a professorship. Wanting to put his knowledge to more practical use, Leibniz politely declined and began a quest for work that would satisfy his broad intellectual interests while earning him a living. In an age when paid positions for intellectuals outside the universities were rare, this was not so easy to do.

Career

After a brief and unsatisfying stint as secretary to an alchemical society in Nuremburg, Leibniz hatched a plan for world travel "to Holland and beyond" (Aiton, 1985). But while still in Germany and passing through the city of Mainz, he met the Baron Johann Christian von Boineburg, an influential statesman in the service of the Elector of Mainz.[2] Struck by the young man's enthusiasm and erudition, Boineburg introduced Leibniz to the elector, who was similarly impressed and appointed him a judge in the High Court of Appeal. Even this important and impressive appointment proved insufficient to meet Leibniz's intellectual needs, but fortunately he met other members of his new patrons' circle who were able to broaden his outlook and interests. One, Athanasius Kircher, was a scholar and priest with broad contacts who acted as a kind of one-man intellectual clearinghouse for cultural and scientific information obtained by Jesuit missionaries throughout the world. Kircher introduced Leibniz to the work of Father Matteo Ricci, a skilled mathematician and the first missionary to immerse himself in Chinese culture. Another new friend, the mathematician Adam Kochanski, also regularly corresponded with leading Jesuits in the China mission. Within this group of mature and broad-minded intellectuals, Leibniz worked on an assortment of "extracurricular" projects, including the development of new methods of teaching law, a scheme for the systematic review of scholarly books, a study of doctrinal differences between Catholics and Protestants, and a book on China.

---

[2]There were just eight German princes with the right to elect the Holy Roman Emperor, hence their titles as "electors."

Inventions in Paris

After 2 years in Mainz, Leibniz was sent to Paris on a delicate diplomatic mission. In hopes of deflecting Catholic France's bellicosity away from the Protestant German states, Leibniz was to present King Louis XIV with a detailed battle plan for invading Egypt. The French king did not rise to this bait, despite the fact that the plan closely resembled the one successfully carried out much later by Napoleon, but the mission allowed Leibniz to spend 4 years in a great intellectual capital, with ample free time to pursue his own interests and to meet new people. Among his eminent new friends were the great mathematician Christian Huygens and the Cartesian philosopher Nicholas de Malebranche. Through contacts such as these men, Leibniz gained access to the unpublished as well as published works of Descartes and his French followers, and greatly expanded his mathematical and philosophical sophistication.

No passive learner, Leibniz put his new knowledge to immediate use in a remarkable display of intellectual virtuosity. During his 4 years in Paris he burst onto the world stage with three major inventions. Only one of them, a calculating machine, was mechanical in nature. Some 30 years before Leibniz's visit, Blaise Pascal had amazed Paris by inventing the "Pascaline," a machine that could accurately add and subtract. It employed a series of adjacent, 10-toothed cogwheels arranged so that a complete revolution of one wheel effected a rotation of 1 tooth in a wheel next to it—essentially the mechanism still used in modern-day automobile odometers and utilities meters. Although simple from today's perspective, Pascal's invention was dependent on recent improvements in precision clock-making technology and amazed those who saw it in operation.

The Pascaline's mathematical functions were limited, however, to addition and subtraction. Multiplication and division could only be accomplished through numerous repetitions. For example, to multiply 5 times 6 the operator would have to crank the rightmost wheel through six cogs on five separate occasions. Leibniz saw that this limitation could partially be overcome by the introduction of a new, "stepped," cylindrical gear that could mechanize the extent of the cog's rotation at any value between 1 and 10 teeth. Leibniz took his calculator on a visit to London in 1673. At least at this early point in his life Leibniz and his machine made a favorable impression in Britain, leading to his election as one of the first foreign members of the British Royal Society. Later, he arranged to have a calculator sent to the Emperor of China as an example of Western technical virtuosity, and somewhat immodestly suggested it could be emblazoned with the phrase, "Superior to Man" (Ross, 1984, p. 12).

The other two Parisian inventions were mathematical in nature: the fundamental ideas for binary arithmetic and the infinitesimal calculus. The former arose from Leibniz's recognition that all numbers could be represented by linear sequences of just 1s and 0s, with each successive digit to the left representing increasing powers of 2, instead of 10 as in the standard decimal notation. Accordingly, in binary the numbers 1 through 8 are represented, respectively, as 1, 10, 11, 100, 101, 110, 111, 1000. Leibniz was pleased with the fundamental simplicity of this system, but in his day any advantages following that simplicity were outweighed by the difficulties in apprehending long strings of digits (e.g., 43 is easier to take in at a glance than its binary equivalent 101011). Furthermore, the kind of gear and cog technology then available for the construction of mechanical calculators was much more suited to a decimal than to a binary mode of representation. It was only with the subsequent development of electronics and the recognition that ones and zeroes could be represented mechanically by open or closed switches, that modern digital computers and calculators could be developed. Thus, for young Leibniz, binary arithmetic was fascinating but lacked any immediate practical usefulness.

Far different was the case with the calculus, which had immediate and unquestioned practical usefulness and established Leibniz among the world's most influential mathematicians. Although Isaac Newton had already devised techniques for the infinitesimal calculus several years earlier, he had kept its details secret. Now Leibniz developed similar answers to problems that came from the limitations of Cartesian analytical geometry. In the previous century, Descartes had represented algebraic equations graphically by lines and curves drawn on systems of geometric coordinates. These methods were limited, however, to curves and lines definable as conic sections: the circles, ellipses, parabolas and straight lines that can be produced by slicing through cones at differing angles. Many of the most important phenomena in nature, from the motions of pendulums to the vibrating of musical strings or the orbits of planets, cannot be represented by such forms.

Leibniz and Newton sought a mathematical technique for dealing with such examples of continuous change. They succeeded in doing so by conceptualizing continuously varying quantities as infinite series of constantly but imperceptibly changing instants or "infinitesimals." As a falling object accelerates in speed from 0 to 20 feet per second, for example, there has to be an instant when it is falling exactly 1 foot per second, 2 feet per second, and indeed every intermediate speed between 0 and 20. Yet because the acceleration is constant, each of these instants when it is falling at any particular speed is infinitessimally brief. Traditional mathematics could not deal with such concepts because speed was calculated as distance traveled divided by the time elapsed, yet for each one of these infinitesimals the time elapsed was 0, and division by 0, was not permissible. This is not the place for details, but essentially Leibniz and Newton developed procedures to calculate the sums of infinite series of infinitesimals (the integral calculus), or to extract the properties of individual infinitesimal instants from particular curves of variation (the differential calculus).

Unlike Newton, Leibniz published his work on the calculus almost immediately. Although similar in concept to the Englishman's calculus, he employed a different and more flexible notation system, which in the long run became the standard. It is common practice among historians today to credit both men as independent co-inventors of the calculus, with Newton first to conceive it and Leibniz first to publish and to present it in a more useful and flexible format. Unfortunately, as we shall see, the principals themselves could not agree to this sharing of credit.

We conclude this section by noting that Leibniz's calculus had not just practical applications, but also created in him a fundamental attitude that would extend into his later philosophical and even psychological theorizing. This attitude had two components, the first of which stemmed from the fact that the calculus deals with supremely important natural phenomena that undergo constant and continuous change. Henceforth, Leibniz would see the linked characteristics of continuity and change as essential features of the world in general. Furthermore, the calculus had demonstrated that these essential qualities of continuity and change are most usefully analyzed in terms of infinitesimal units that are literally mental "fictions," incapable of being concretely or individually experienced. Any material entity, however small, could still be infinitely subdivided. This led Leibniz to be highly skeptical of cosmological schemes such as those proposed by Galileo, Descartes, and Locke, in which the "primary qualities" or "ultimate" units of the universe are held to be extended material particles in motion. Because both the particles and their paths of motion could be infinitely subdivided, Leibniz did not believe they could be ultimate.

Encounters in Amsterdam

Leibniz loved the stimulating Parisian atmosphere and would gladly have stayed there permanently. Unfortunately, however, Boineburg and the Elector of Mainz both died within a few months of each other, and in 1676 Leibniz found himself without a patron and in search of a new means of livelihood. He briefly hoped to fill a vacated spot in the Paris Academy of Sciences, but was told that with the Dutch Huygens and the Italian astronomer Cassini already there, the Academy had no more room for foreigners in salaried posts. Finally and reluctantly, Leibniz accepted an offer to leave Paris and become a Court Councillor at Hanover, one of the smaller German states.

En route to Hanover Leibniz accomplished his earlier goal of visiting "Holland and beyond." When he stopped in Amsterdam, he encountered two further important influences on his thought. He visited the lens-grinding philosopher Benedict Spinoza shortly before Spinoza's death and learned of the Dutchman's pantheistic and "double aspect" view of the universe, which rejected Descartes's mind–body dichotomy in favor of the belief that materiality and thought are but separate attributes of a single universal substance equated with God. Another Amsterdam lens grinder, Anton van Leeuwenhoek (1632–1723), allowed Leibniz to peer through his recently developed microscope and to observe at first hand the amazing spectacle of microorganisms swimming in ordinary pond water. This gave rise to a vision of a universe composed of hierarchies of living organisms within organisms:

> Each portion of matter may be conceived as like a garden full of plants, and like a pond full of fishes. But each branch of every plant, each member of every animal, each drop of its liquid parts, is also some such garden or pond. Thus there is nothing fallow, nothing sterile, nothing dead in the universe; no chaos, no confusion save in appearance. (quoted in Klein, 1970, p. 456)

At the age of 30, Leibniz had now encountered the major formative influences on his subsequent philosophy and career. Vastly intellectually ambitious and curious about almost everything, his major goal was to encourage a universal language of philosophical and ethical discourse that would undercut all current national and cultural differences. Mathematics provided a partial model for such a language, and from his own original mathematical work Leibniz inferred certain basic characteristics of the world in general. The crucial physical phenomena so miraculously illuminated by the new calculus are characterized by continuity and change, but do not seem ultimately molecular in nature—that is, composed of "ultimate" material particles in motion. Instead, the ultimate units seem to be infinitesimals literally beyond individual concrete apprehension but capable of acting in the aggregate to produce concrete experience. And from his Amsterdam experiences Leibniz learned to see the universe as organic rather than mechanical and populated with hierarchies of organisms within organisms, all presumably governed by an overriding pantheistic intelligence identifiable with God.

Serving the House of Hanover

Leibniz undertook his new position at Hanover with some trepidation, fearing that he would be intellectually isolated in the small city. The first few years proved to be unexpectedly pleasant, however, because his new patron Duke Johann Friedrich turned out to be an ambitious and intellectually curious man who appreciated those same traits in his new councilor. The duke shared Leibniz's ambition to reunite the churches, and together they crafted an essay about Leibniz's hope for a universal language of logic that the duke delivered to the pope in hopes (futile, it turned out) that he might be persuaded to initiate the reconciliation. The duke also provided Leibniz with ample time to pursue his own studies, among which the pursuit of a universal language figured highly.

Leibniz subscribed to the biblical theory of a single origin for all of humankind and therefore supposed that there must have been an original language, whose remnants are widely scattered among existing languages. Thus, Leibniz tried to conduct a wide-ranging study of all languages, including those in many relatively unknown cultures. He sought through correspondence and research almost encyclopedic ethnographic information on the Islamic Arabs, the Hindu South Asians, and particularly the Chinese. Some of his correspondents believed that the Chinese language had been invented all at once to establish communication between many different peoples, or alternatively that it was the original primitive language of all humankind. In due course Leibniz rejected these theories, but in the meantime he developed a full and sympathetic understanding of Chinese life and culture.

Even while pursuing these pet projects, Leibniz assumed official duties as a court librarian, political advisor, and technological advisor. When the duke died in 1680 his title was assumed by his younger brother Ernst Augustus, a man with little interest in academic questions of theology and philosophy, but who still respected Leibniz and sought out more practical projects for his versatile councilor. After Leibniz devised a plan to use windmill power to extract water from the Harz mountains, the new duke promised him a lifetime pension if he could develop it successfully. Leibniz plunged obsessively into the work, but unfortunately overestimated the average winds in the region and none of his ingeniously designed pumps, windmills, and siphons worked as planned. As he ever more desperately pressed the mining engineers to alter their designs, he began for the first time to gain a reputation as a nuisance and object of ridicule. A book appeared entitled *Foolish Wisdom and Wise Folly*, satirizing him as a designer of impossible contrivances such as a coach capable of traveling at the incredible speed of 35 miles per hour.

During these difficult years Leibniz found some solace in his conversations with Ernst Augustus's intellectually curious wife, the Duchess Sophia, and her equally clever daughter, Sophie Charlotte, who would later become Queen of Prussia. These able women became Leibniz's greatest friends and supporters at Hanover and provided some relief from the general intellectual emptiness of the court. Finally, in 1685 Leibniz and the duke struck a new bargain about his pension, which was now to be awarded for a historical rather than a technological project. Leibniz agreed to write an extended history of the House of Hanover's family tree, tracing it to its earliest recorded origins. Ernst Augustus hoped that this project would not only enhance the family's social glory, but also establish legal claims to a connection with, and thereby an inheritance from, the famous and wealthy Italian house of Este.

For Leibniz this job provided a major fringe benefit in the opportunity to travel extensively between 1687 and 1690 to the major archives in southern Germany, Austria, and Italy. At Modena he succeeded in documenting the connection between Hanover and Este, and in other European capitals he expanded his general range of intellectual acquaintances. Coincidentally, several of the new friends that Leibniz made in these journeys had firsthand knowledge of China and the Orient. Particularly well received in Rome, Leibniz was granted unlimited access to the Vatican and Barberini libraries and made a member of the Accademia Fisico-Matematica. Offered a paid position at the Vatican library, he declined because of the condition that he first would have to join the Catholic Church.

Returning to Hanover in 1690, Leibniz chafed in his relative isolation and complained, "All my difficulties derive from the fact that I am not in a great city like Paris or London, which have a plethora of learned men from whom one can obtain instruction and assistance" (Mates, 1986, p. 23). Nevertheless, even in this rather backwater location he managed to accomplish a breathtaking number of things. He completed nine volumes of his commissioned Hanoverian history—although these only brought the family record up to 1024 and the unfinished parts hung like a black cloud over him in his declining years. He promoted public health and fire-fighting services for the general population and worked toward the creation of a state bank and a silk-producing industry. He corresponded indefatigably with hundreds of individuals throughout Europe, on every manner of scientific, philosophical, and cultural matter. And during the late 1690s he undertook two intellectual projects with particular implications for the future development of psychology and the social sciences.

First, he read and was much stimulated by Locke's recently published *Essay Concerning Human Understanding*, the strong empiricist explanation of human knowledge as primarily the result of sensory experience. Although impressed by much of Locke's argument, Leibniz entertained strong reservations about its relative neglect of innate rational faculties and its fundamental belief that the physical world is ultimately explainable in terms of physical particles in motion and interaction. Leibniz sketched out some of his reservations and sent them to Locke in 1697, with a polite covering note assuring Locke that "it is not possible to express in a letter the great character Monsieur Leibniz has of you." Locke, however, dismissed Leibniz's discussion as "a sort of fiddling" and did not condescend to respond (Cranston, 1957, p. 417). Now stimulated to express himself at greater length, Leibniz wrote a book-length manuscript in French entitled *Nouveux Essais sur L'Entendement Humain* (New Essays on Human Understanding), in which he commented on Locke's work on a section-by-section basis. Unfortunately, however, Leibniz was never one to rush into print and he put off publishing this work until word came of Locke's death in 1704. Not wishing to dispute with a dead author, Leibniz put the manuscript aside and it was not published until a half century after his own death. We return to this later, because it constituted his most direct and supremely important contribution to psychology.

A second project with more immediate fruition was the *Novissima Sinica* (News from China), a compilation of letters and essays that Leibniz had received during his correspondence with the Jesuit missionaries in China, introduced by a preface that he wrote himself. Published in 1697, with a second and enlarged edition 2 years later, this marked the culmination of Leibniz's lifelong fascination with China and gave him the opportunity to transcend Eurocentric thinking and to promote his hopes for a truly universal understanding. We also return to this work in the next section.

In the meantime, Leibniz's patrons, never a boring family, were seeking his advice on almost every political question that arose in Hanover during the

1690s, ranging from their petition to become a ninth German Elector state to conspiracy plots, murders, weddings, a divorce, and even the imprisonment of a princess. Ironically, his greatest political achievement ultimately produced unhappy personal consequences. When the possibility arose that the English crown might pass to Ernst Augustus's eldest son Georg Ludwig, a great-grandson of England's James I, Leibniz prepared the legal case and conducted many of the negotiations that eventually led to its realization. Georg Ludwig, who succeeded his father as head of the House of Hanover in 1698, was not grateful for these efforts. Unlike his glory-loving father who would have been thrilled by the prospect of acquiring the English throne, Georg Ludwig had no desire for such heavy responsibilities or to move so far away from his native Germany. Also unlike his father, Georg had no interest in scholarly pursuits and, accordingly, no appreciation of Leibniz's abilities. Thinking him just an eccentric old man, Georg publicly ridiculed his advisor, once describing him as "an archeological find" likely to be mistaken for a clown, and complaining that he strove excessively to ingratiate himself with female members of the aristocracy (Ross, 1984, p. 26).

Georg Ludwig's attitude, which he continued to express openly after he became King George I of England in 1714, undoubtedly contributed to Leibniz's disrepute in that country. Matters were made worse when Newton and his English followers falsely accused Leibniz of plagiarizing Newton's ideas for the calculus, and a nasty priority dispute erupted that cast credit on neither side.[3] Unfairly reviled by the English and unsupported by his patron, Leibniz was required to remain in Hanover and work on the interminable family history. He continued to correspond widely and write private philosophical manuscripts, but published nothing of significance. Finally, his health declined and in November 1718 he died in Hanover. Although Georg Ludwig and his court were on a hunting party nearby and could easily have attended Leibniz's burial, they opted not to. Neither the British Royal Society nor the Berlin Academy of Sciences marked Leibniz's death with a memorial address or publication, and no monument was commissioned; indeed, his grave remained unmarked until half a century after his death.

In fact, the full and astonishing range of Leibniz's activity remained unknown to the public until long after his death. Interested in almost everything, he had conducted an enormous correspondence with people all over the world, and more than 15,000 of his letters remained behind. Many of his more formal works remained unfinished or, like his response to Locke, unpublished, and would only be known to posterity. One leading Leibniz scholar has accordingly summarized his career as follows:

---

[3]As a side effect of this dispute, English mathematicians continued for more than a century to use the notation system devised by Newton whereas those on the continent followed Leibniz. The latter proved to be much more flexible, and English mathematics languished as a result.

Leibniz's life was dominated by an unachievable ambition to excel in every sphere of intellectual and political activity. The wonder is not that he failed so often, but that he achieved as much as he did. His successes were due to a rare combination of sheer hard work, a receptivity to the ideas of others, and supreme confidence in the fertility of his own mind. . . . On the other hand, his desire to produce monuments to his genius, which would be both complete and all his own work, made it impossible for him to finish anything. Despite all his notes, letters and articles, he never wrote a systematic treatise on any of his special interests. (Ross, 1984, p. 26)

Thanks to the archivists and historians who uncovered his unpublished work, Leibniz's successors have been able to benefit from it. Among those beneficiaries have been psychologists—and we turn now to those of Leibniz's contributions that have had particular significance for our field.

LEIBNIZ'S PSYCHOLOGICAL CONTRIBUTIONS

Leibniz deserves credit as a psychological pioneer for three contributions, two of them relatively indirect but the third of supreme importance for the very emergence of our discipline. In the first category, he anticipated many of the attitudes and ideas that underlie the current fields of artificial intelligence and cross-cultural psychology. In the second, he promoted a moderate nativism in which the properties of the mind itself became significant objects of investigation, providing a rationale for a science of the mind.

Artificial Intelligence

Although Leibniz's mechanical calculator was limited in its functions to arithmetic, he believed with characteristic exuberance that the potential for such machines extended far beyond number crunching. He knew that Thomas Hobbes had already suggested in 1651 that arithmetical calculation provides a model for reasoning in general, writing: "Reason is nothing but reckoning (that is, the adding and subtracting of consequences)" (Hobbes, 1651, Pt. I, chap. 5). The visionary Leibniz dreamed of a way in which this concept might be developed further with the establishment of his long-sought universal language. He imagined that in this language different words or concepts might contain one another hierarchically, in the way that "living things" contains the concept of "animals," which in turn contains "human beings." Concepts would also exclude one another in the sense that "animal" excludes "plants" (which in turn would contain a large number of more specific, hierarchically arranged concepts with their own containments and exclusions). Leibniz believed that, potentially, numerical values could be applied to all of these varying degrees of embeddedness and exclusion and, once that was done, all possible logical relations among all concepts could be calculated by standard arithmetical procedures (for further details about this scheme, see Pratt, 1987, chap. 5). This meant that with the new universal language, people of all backgrounds could not only converse with one another but that they could also calculate with mathematical precision solutions to all of the problems of reasoning or even of ethics that divide them. And, because machines could calculate more reliably and accurately than human beings, they could reduce error even further. As Ross (1984, p. 13) put it: "Instead of fruitless arguing, people would say, 'Let us calculate'—and they could do so by setting the dials and cranking the handle of [Leibniz's] machine."

Of course Leibniz's universal language never came to fruition in the particular form in which he conceived it. Still, the 19th century developments of Boolean algebra and symbolic logic finally did succeed in extending mathematical and computational procedures into the realms of reasoning and logic. And in the 20th century Leibniz's other Parisian invention, binary arithmetic, would be developed as a language for representing Boolean and logical operations, represented by the on or off states of electronic switches in digital computers. With his general conception that reasoning processes are reducible to mathematical-like computations, which in turn could be performed by machines, and with his anticipation of the binary notation that underlies the workings of modern digital computers, Leibniz deserves at least the title of intellectual grandfather to the modern movement of artificial intelligence.

Cross-Cultural Psychology

We have seen that throughout his life Leibniz was intensely interested in non-Western cultures, particularly that of China. His *Novissima Sinica* was specifically intended to educate Europeans about Chinese civilization, and about past, present, and potential future relations between Europe and the Chinese. Leibniz argued that the Chinese possessed knowledge that could be of great use to the war-torn and constantly battling Europeans. In his preface he spoke with awe of China's superiority in matters of "civil life" or "practical philosophy," and expressed his desire for Chinese missionaries to come to Europe and teach the art of harmonious living and good-natured courtesy. He believed that European mathematics, sciences, and the Christian religion would be a fair trade in return for this lesson in civility.

To improve relations between the East and the West, Leibniz eagerly sought out evidence that might prove a shared distant past between the two civilizations. Thus, he expounded on historical and archeological evidence that he believed offered proof that Christian concepts had previously been introduced to China and (although forgotten in name) were embedded in Chinese beliefs. He strongly supported the Jesuit missionaries and their "accomodationist" philosophy, which expressed the belief that Confucianism and Christianity could be synthesized into a culturally acceptable variant of the religion. Leibniz composed several essays and his preface to the *Novissima Sinica* to defend this position, employing logical deduction to elucidate the similarities between Chinese and European beliefs about the nature of spirits, matter, the soul, God, and the afterlife. Leibniz also saw similarities between his own theory of metaphysics and that of the Chinese. Both hypothesized the existence of immaterial basic principles from which everything else in the universe is derived. Both also agreed on the existence of a pre-established harmony and an organic universe in which everything is posited to be alive and imbued with a common spiritual force. As part of his evidence, Leibniz cited the Fuxi hexagrams found in the *Yi Jing*, or *Book of Changes*. Analogous to his own binary arithmetic, the Chinese hexagrams consisted of two basic elements: a broken line "yin" and a straight line "yang," which were found in groups of six. Leibniz saw binary arithmetic and the hexagrams as a metaphor for the origin of the universe. In binary terms: from nothing (0) and God (1) everything else in the universe is derived. Leibniz hoped that by emphasizing such similarities instead of differences, the cultural exchange between China and the West could be facilitated.

From today's perspective, Leibniz's detailed ethnographic studies of China and other cultures are notable for their openness and cultural sensitivity. His cautionary edict that "their customs should not be judged by ours" (Leibniz, 1994/1699, p. 70) is useful advice to the relatively recent field of cultural psychology, as well as to psychologists working within our increasingly multicultural societies. Leibniz was surprisingly unchauvinistic in his belief that non-European cultures could have valuable knowledge, which implies that Westerners are not necessarily the "most developed" or the "most progressive" people in the world. The accomodationist philosophy that he endorsed affirms the value in keeping indigenous cultural traditions alive and the belief that change and development can happen without discarding the past.

Mental Philosophy

Leibniz's tremendously influential mental philosophy emerged hand in hand with a more general cosmological viewpoint he called his "monadology." As previously noted, Leibniz emerged from his mathematical explorations in Paris with a profound distrust of the Cartesian mechanistic analysis of the material world in terms of extended physical particles in motion and interaction with one another. Locke, to the contrary, had enthusiastically endorsed this view, accepting extended particles in motion as the ultimate "primary qualities" out of which all physical explanations should be constructed. But Leibniz cited the infinitesimals of the calculus as demonstrating that any material particle, no matter how small, can still be infinitely subdivided further; accordingly, one can never reach an ultimate material particle as a building block of the universe.

But although denying ultimate status to material particles, Leibniz believed two properties were worthy of the claim. One was the notion of force or energy. The second derived from a part of Descartes's philosophy that Leibniz did agree with, the assertion of the unquestionable reality of one's own conscious experience. As Descartes had famously pronounced, "I think, therefore I am." That is, although one may doubt the reality of the contents of any experience, which may be dreams, hallucinations, or the figments of imagination, one cannot deny the immediate reality of having those experiences. Accordingly, some degree of consciousness or awareness seemed to Leibniz to be a candidate for the status of an ultimate explanatory unit. Leibniz combined these two qualities in his conception of the "monad" as the fundamental unit of the universe, a term derived from the Greek *monos*, for "unit."[4] All monads, according to Leibniz, are characterized by (a) a charge of energy or drivenness, a teleological urge to fulfill tendencies innate within themselves, and (b) some degree of perceptiveness or awareness.

Leibniz hypothesized that monads vary in the strength and breadth of their perceptive capacities, and fall into four hierarchically ordered classes. First, at the lowest level are the bare or *simple monads*, whose perceptions, although real, are indistinct and subconscious. Leibniz called these "petites (minute) perceptions" and likened them to the impression created in a human being by a single drop of water in a crashing surf. In and of itself the perception is indiscernible, although it is obviously real because in the aggregate with thousands and millions of other minute perceptions it produces the crashing sound of the surf. Second, at the next higher level of Leibniz's scheme, *sentient monads* have the capacity for basic conscious perception. Third, at the level above the sentient monads came *rational monads*, with a further capacity for awareness of themselves and their own perceptual activity, as well the ability to comprehend their experience in terms of logical, mathematical, or other rational categories. Writing in French, Leibniz designated ordinary perceiving with the verb *apercevoir* ("to perceive"), and the higher form with the reflexive *s'apercevoir*, literally "to perceive oneself," but traditionally translated into English as "to apperceive."

Leibniz argued that these three classes of monads constitute the world as human beings are capable of knowing it. Aggregations of exclusively simple monads make up "inorganic" matter. Sometimes, however, an aggregation of simple monads comes under the influence of a sentient monad, thus constituting a living organism with its own conscious awareness and motives. As suggested by Leibniz's experience with Leeuwenhoek's microscope, aggregates of sentient micro-organisms may be hierarchically contained within larger ones to create the higher animals. And finally, when a complex aggregation of sentient monads comes under the domination of a rational monad, we have a human being.

Overriding all of these monadic aggregations constituting the world as humans know it, Leibniz postulated, fourth, a *supreme monad* equated with God.

---

[4]Aristotle had distinguished between the "monadic," in which each individual constitutes a species, and the "sporadic," in which several individuals are members of the same species. Leibniz may also have encountered a general concept of monads in the writings of the Englishwoman Lady Anne Finch Conway (1631–1679).

Just as the simple perceptive capacities of an animal reacting to its environment are put in the shade by a human being who can further apperceive it with self-awareness and in terms of logical and mathematical laws, so are the apperceptive capacities of human beings overshadowed and subsumed by those of the supreme monad. Human apperception provides only vague glimpses and partial intimations of the overall grand scheme as formulated by the omniscient Creator, although Leibniz assumed that that scheme was grand indeed and formulated according to the most perfect possible system of organizing principles. Indeed, all inferior grades of monads operate in accordance with the principles of the supreme monad, and thus have a "pre-established harmony" with respect to one another. That is, they do not mutually influence or interact with each other, as the Cartesian system would have it, but rather pursue independent courses that are "preset" to be parallel and harmonious, somewhat in the way that a set of perfectly constructed clocks, all set to the same time, would be in perfect harmony.

It was from this basic metaphysical viewpoint that Leibniz addressed Locke's *Essay on Human Understanding* soon after its publication in 1690. In that work Locke famously likened the human mind at birth to a blank slate, or *tabula rasa*, and argued that all knowledge is the result of experiences that leave impressions on it. Accordingly, as an old saying goes, "There is nothing in the mind which was not first in the senses." Leibniz believed this to be an oversimplification, one which might possibly account for the learning of animals who merely perceive the world, but not for the higher processes of human apperception. The thought processes of animals, he wrote, represent just "a shadow of reasoning," and are comparable to those "of simple empirics who maintain that what has happened once will happen again in a [similar] case, . . . although that does not enable them to judge whether the same *reasons* are at work" (Leibniz, 1982/ 1765, p. 51, emphasis added). Human beings, whose higher functions are determined by rational monads that can apperceive as well as perceive the world, can comprehend those underlying reasons in terms of inherent "necessary truths" such as mathematical axioms and logical laws. Although these laws and necessary truths may be revealed by individual instances of sensory experience, they are not created by it. As Leibniz put it, their truth "does not depend on instances nor, consequently, on the testimony of the senses, even though without the senses it would never occur to us to think about them" (1982, p. 50).[5]

Accordingly, Leibniz rejected Locke's metaphor of the newborn human mind as a blank slate and likened it instead to a block of veined marble whose internal lines of cleavage predispose it to be sculpted into some shapes more easily than others. The sculptor's hammering and chiseling, like the specific sensory experi-

---

[5]Leibniz recognized and acknowledged that he was here following in the tradition of Plato, who had taught that human beings have an innate knowledge of the ideal "forms," but that this knowledge is not immediately accessible and must be "recollected" through appropriate sensory experiences.

ences encountered by the human mind, are necessary to bring out the statue's form and in part to mold it. But marble and mind alike contain certain innate inclinations and dispositions that are an essential part of the process. Thus, Leibniz added a tag line to the saying: "There is nothing in the mind that was not first in the senses—*except the mind itself.*"

Leibniz further described the human mind as guided not only by its innate "higher" capacities for apperception and logical analysis, but also by a susceptibility to the influences of subconscious *petites perceptions*, or minute perceptions. The only kind of perception of which the bare monads are capable, Leibniz believed these also occur constantly in human minds: "At every moment there is in us an infinity of perceptions, unaccompanied by awareness or reflection" (Leibniz, 1982/1765, p. 53). Sometimes a minute perception may rise to the level of an ordinary perception or apperception, as when an originally unremarked background noise rises to the center of our conscious awareness. Other minute perceptions may remain beneath the threshold of consciousness individually, but produce a conscious sensation when acting in an aggregate with countless others, like the multitude of falling individual water drops within a crashing ocean wave. In his *New Essays*, Leibniz argued that these aggregated minute perceptions can be "more effective in their results than has been recognized," contributing to one's sense of continuity as an individual, distinctive *self*, and adding to one's experience "that *je ne sais quoi*, those flavours, those images of sensible qualities vivid in the aggregate but confused as to the parts." In a brief but significant anticipation of later dynamic psychology Leibniz added, "It is these minute perceptions which determine our behavior in many situations without our thinking of them, and which deceive the unsophisticated" (1982, pp. 54–56). He added that they are like "so many little springs trying to unwind and so driving our machine along. . . . That is why we are never indifferent, even when we appear to be most so, . . . for the choice that we make arises from these insensible stimuli, which, mingled with the actions of objects and our bodily interiors, make us find one direction of movement more comfortable than the other" (1982, p. 166).

In sum, Leibniz offered a strong argument that the human mind cannot be understood simply as a passive reflector or recorder of the things it experiences, but rather is itself an important contributor to its experience. The mind has its own tendencies and predispositions to experience the world in certain ways, as well as certain limitations in the extent and acuity of its awareness. With the assistance of its own apperceptive abilities, however, the mind has at least the potential ability to understand its own predispositions, and in some cases to overcome its limitations. Here, in a nutshell, was a rationale for the establishment of a discipline devoted to the systematic study of the mind. Accordingly, it was no historical accident that the generally acknowledged founders of psychology as an independent discipline were not the British successors of Locke and the associationistic tradition, but German-speaking followers of Leibniz. Kant,

Helmholtz (chap. 2, *Pioneers IV*), and Wundt (chap. 3, *Pioneers III*), among others, who advanced the idea that human experience is determined by the interaction between an external world of sensory stimulation and an active mind or perceptual apparatus that processes that stimulation. And Herbart and Fechner (chap. 1, *Pioneers II*) both emphasized the phenomena of unconscious and subliminal ideation, before those concepts were raised to supreme importance in the psychoanalytic theories of Freud (chap. 4, *Pioneers I*). Each of these individuals attempted in his own way to specify the rules and laws by which the human mind participates in the creation of its own experience, and thus helped to fulfill a program previously envisaged by Leibniz.

REFERENCES

Aiton, E. J. (1985). *Leibniz: A biography*. Bristol, UK: Adam Hilger.

Allport, G. (1955). *Becoming: Basic considerations for a psychology of personality*. New Haven, CT: Yale University Press.

Boring, E. G. (1950). *A history of experimental psychology* (2nd ed.). New York: Appleton-Century-Crofts.

Cranston, M. (1957). *John Locke: A biography*. London: Longmans.

Fancher, R. E. (2000). Leibniz, Gottfried Wilhelm. In A. E. Kazdin (Ed.), *Encyclopedia of psychology* (Vol. 8, pp. 42–44). Washington, DC, and New York: American Psychological Association and Oxford University Press.

Hobbes, T. (1651). *Leviathan*. London. Printed for Andrew Crooke.

Klein, D. B. (1970). *A history of scientific psychology*. New York: Basic Books.

Leibniz, G. W. (1982). *New essays on human understanding* (P. Remnant & J. Bennett, Trans.). Cambridge, England: Cambridge University Press. (Originally published 1765)

Leibniz, G. W. (1994). *Writings on China*. (D. J. Cook & H. Rosemount Jr., Trans.). Chicago: Open Court. (Originally published 1699)

Mates, B. (1986). *The philosophy of Leibniz: Metaphysics and language*. New York: Oxford University Press.

Pratt, V. (1987). *Thinking machines: The evolution of artificial intelligence*. Oxford, England: Basil Blackwell.

Ross, G. M. (1984). *Leibniz*. Oxford and New York: Oxford University Press.

Russell, B. (1945). *A history of western philosophy*. New York: Simon & Schuster.

Chapter 2

G. Stanley Hall: Educator, Organizer, and Pioneer Developmental Psychologist

John D. Hogan
St. John's University, NY

Granville Stanley Hall was one of the dominant figures of early American psychology but his contributions were different from those of other pioneers in the field. Moreover, he was a controversial figure, in both his professional and his personal life. As a result, the value of his contributions has not always been fully appreciated.

Hall is usually remembered for his organizational work. In 1892, he was the major force in founding the American Psychological Association (APA) and was its first president. In 1887, he established the *American Journal of Psychology* (*AJP*), the first psychology journal in America, and one that still exists today. He is also remembered for inviting Sigmund Freud (chap. 4, *Pioneers I*) to Clark University to lecture in 1909 and, by so doing, giving Freud his first academic recognition anywhere in the world.

Hall played a pivotal role in the founding of developmental psychology. Beginning in the 1880s, he was the leader of the child-study movement that created the climate in which many important educational reforms took place. His monumental two-volume work *Adolescence* (Hall, 1904) was about much more than adolescence. It was a milestone in developmental psychology, with significant social and scientific impact.

Despite the magnitude of these contributions, they were frequently overshadowed by Hall's personal style. He has been described as abrasive, overly ambitious, and more than a bit grandiose. Freud said there was something of the "king maker" about him. And his relationship with many of his professional colleagues soured through the years. Even at his funeral, the presiding minister caused a minor scandal by criticizing Hall for his attitude toward institutional-ized religion (Ross, 1972).

Hall's scholarly ideas also got him into trouble. He proposed dramatic evolu-tionary theories of development that were not well received. He thought that central topics for study by scientific psychology should include sex, psycho-pathology, and childhood, topics that were unpopular in the psychology of his day. He upset his critics with the argument that the science of psychology could help to transform religion. And, adding to their unhappiness, he sometimes—as in his two volumes on *Adolescence*—combined several of his unpopular ideas in the same work. In a letter written after reviewing this work, E. L. Thorndike (chap. 10, *Pioneers I*) said that Hall's book was: "chock full of errors, masturba-tion and Jesus. He is a mad man" (quoted in Ross, 1972, p. 385).

EARLY YEARS

Hall was born in the small farming community of Ashfield in northwestern Mas-sachusetts in 1844. His parents were farmers but both of them had some higher education and had taught school for several years. His mother, Abigail Beals Hall, was deeply religious and hoped that her oldest son, Stanley, as he was known, would become a minister. His father, Granville Bascom Hall, was a suc-cessful farmer and a local leader, but he was full of insecurities and not always happy as a farmer. During the Civil War, before Stanley left for college, his fa-ther obtained a military exemption for him, a source of great embarrassment for the younger Hall. Stanley admitted that he was afraid of war but the exemption remained a sore spot for the rest of his life.

Stanley was very close to his mother. He described her as his only confidant during his youth, and he idealized her in a way that Victorian women were fre-quently idealized—as both maternal and pure. He was astonished to learn late in life, from a packet of letters, that his mother had had a warm and intimate rela-tionship with his father (Ross, 1972, p. 9).

In his autobiography, Hall tells of being ambitious but not being able to share his ambitions with his family or community. He writes of being interested in in-tellectual issues, but unable to find local contemporaries with similar interests. Most of all he writes of being alone and isolated, a feeling that remained with him and dominated his entire life—he was an outsider, virtually from the begin-ning (Hall, 1923, p. 594).

COLLEGE AND YOUNG ADULTHOOD

Hall left Ashfield for nearby Williston Academy for 1 year to prepare for col-lege and then went to Williams College. After graduation, in 1867, he traveled to New York City and enrolled at Union Theological Seminary for study to become a minister, an act that greatly pleased his mother. Despite being at the seminary, however, he already suspected that he was not going to pursue conventional ministry as a career. Even so, he remained very much interested in religion, and attended religious services for many different denominations.

In his autobiography, Hall described this incident at the seminary: "After preaching our trial sermon before the institution we visited the president for criticisms. When I entered his study for this purpose, instead of discussing my sermon with me he at once knelt and prayed that I might be shown the true light and saved from mortal errors of doctrine, and then excused me without a word" (Hall, 1923, p. 178). This description may owe a bit to Hall's penchant for self-dramatization, but it also fit the facts. Hall may have been a profoundly religious man, but not in the traditional way, and he certainly was not a follower of organized religion.

Hall interrupted his seminary studies to visit Europe, traveling on borrowed money. After more than a year abroad, he returned to complete his studies, receiving his degree in 1870. Following a brief stint as a visiting preacher, he decided that he was not made for the life of a minister and, instead, that he would teach philosophy. While waiting for a job opening, he became a tutor to a family in New York, an arrangement that lasted for 2 years. Finally, he learned of a position available at Antioch College in Yellow Springs, Ohio, and applied for it. He was hired and at the age of 28 began his first full-time academic position.

Hall's responsibilities at Antioch were daunting. In addition to teaching French, German, rhetoric, and English literature, he was the librarian, forensic coach, and drillmaster (Ross, 1972, pp. 50–51). Soon he added choirmaster to his duties. He also began lecturing at nearby Wilberforce College, a traditional Black college. He had a reasonably good salary, was active and popular, and attracted a group of young women about him, one of whom he married later in Germany.

Beginning in the fall of 1873, Hall began to include psychology in his philosophy classes. But Antioch College was struggling with change, and although Hall was well respected, his prospects for the future there were not promising. He decided to resign and go to Harvard to hear some lectures and then determine if he should return to Germany to study psychology. Arriving at Harvard in 1876, Hall met William James (chap. 2, *Pioneers I*) who, the year before, had begun teaching the first course in America on the new psychology.

Hall obtained an instructorship to pay his way and enrolled at Harvard to study for a doctorate degree in philosophy. He took most of his psychology courses under James. In June 1878, Hall received a doctorate degree in psychology. His doctorate was the first to be awarded by the Department of Philosophy at Harvard, and the first in psychology to be given in the United States.

GERMANY AGAIN

In the late summer of 1878, Hall returned to Germany. In Berlin, he heard lectures by Hermann von Helmholtz (chap. 2, *Pioneers IV*) and had the opportunity to explore his interests in psychopathology. He moved on to Leipzig in the fall of 1879, where he attended lectures by Wilhelm Wundt (chap. 3, *Pioneers III*) and was a student in one of Wundt's seminars. He was present at the inauguration of the psychological laboratory at the University of Leipzig that year and served as one of two participants (the other was Wundt himself) in the first experiment conducted in the laboratory. But Hall was not impressed with Wundt, and although he is sometimes identified as Wundt's first American student, Hall never did any important work or publish anything with him.

During this period, when Hall was beginning to commit himself to a lifetime as a psychologist, he was also exposed to the work of Ernst Haeckel that was controversial in Germany at the time. Haeckel had expanded the ideas of Charles Darwin (chap. 2, *Pioneers III*) to include the notion of recapitulation, the idea that, in development, the individual repeats the course of evolution taken by the species ("ontogeny recapitulates phylogeny"). Hall had reservations about Haeckel's approach and about evolutionary theory in general. But, later in his autobiography, he wrote: "As soon as I first heard it in my youth I think I must have been almost hypnotized by the word 'evolution,' which was music to my ear and seemed to fit my mouth better than any other" (Hall, 1923, p. 357).

While Hall was exploring career choices, he was also courting Cornelia Fisher, a former student from Antioch College, who had come to Europe to study art. They were married in Berlin in October 1879. Hall was 35 years old; Cornelia was 2 years younger. Throughout his life, Hall talked very little about their courtship and marriage—even after the great tragedy that later befell them. Thus, little is known about their relationship.

On his return to America, Hall's job prospects were dim because psychology was too new to be included in the programs of most colleges and universities. Hall thought that a position at the Johns Hopkins University was his best hope but, even with letters of endorsement to the Johns Hopkins president from James, he was not offered a job there. Initially, he was discouraged and considered studying medicine. Finally, however, he settled on a different course, one that he had begun thinking about in Germany—to apply the principles of psychology to education. This decision was to have profound implications for both psychology and education.

THE CHILD-STUDY MOVEMENT

When the "child-study movement" began, sometime in the 1870s, it did not arise from psychology. Instead, it originated in a variety of fields, particularly education, medicine, and social-service work. The movement had important goals, including mandatory schooling, shifting children out of the workforce, stopping the exploitation of children, and promoting the welfare of exceptional children (Siegel & White, 1982). The expression of these perspectives was the creation of a "child-care industry," consisting of juvenile courts, orphanages, and schools.

Not surprising, the new "industry" was hungry for information, particularly regarding developmental norms, child care, and theories of development. Hall entered this movement at precisely the right time to meet this need. He argued that education should be based on the scientific study of child development. Ross (1972) maintained that Hall was probably the first scientist or educator to make this argument in a sustained way.

Hall conducted one of the first scientific studies in the child-study movement. Using questionnaires, he sought to explore "the contents of children's minds." He began his research, his first with children, in September 1880, using more than 400 children from Boston schools. The questionnaire consisted of 134 questions, an extension of questions asked in German studies conducted earlier (Siegel & White, 1982).

In this research, Hall reached conclusions that were consistent with those of certain German studies—children do not know much when they entered school, but those raised in the country know more than those raised in the city (Siegel & White, 1982). But Hall went beyond the results, offering advice to parents and teachers regarding the best way to prepare children for school and proposing that all children should be evaluated for their knowledge once they arrive there.

Hall's use of the questionnaires was not intended simply to sample children's knowledge and, thereby, to alert parents and teachers to their children's intellectual gaps. Hall also hoped to demonstrate patterns of emergence for particular thoughts, consistent with his evolutionary ideas regarding children's development. When the article based on this research was published in 1883, it became one of the cornerstones in the founding of developmental psychology (Dennis, 1949).

HARVARD AND JOHNS HOPKINS UNIVERSITY

Hall had applied for a few positions unsuccessfully and had asked friends to speak in his behalf to influential people. With their help, he finally received the offer that set his career in motion. In the fall of 1880, President Eliot of Harvard offered him lectureships in pedagogy and the history of philosophy, and Hall accepted. Hall's lectures on both topics were well received, but the lectures on pedagogy were more successful. Although this success made the prospects for a permanent position in education brighter, Hall was more interested in scientific psychology and looked for other opportunities.

After giving the Harvard lectures, Hall delivered a series of 10 lectures on psychology at the Johns Hopkins University. These, too, were very successful and, in March 1882, he was offered a 3-year appointment in the Philosophy Department as a lecturer in psychology and pedagogics. In 1884, he was elevated to the level of full professor.

At Johns Hopkins, Hall established a laboratory, usually regarded as the first "working" laboratory for psychology in the United States. The few experimental studies that Hall conducted there were the last he ever did. He continued his interest in psychopathology, often taking students to local asylums, and he established psychology classes for psychiatrists. One of the things that Hall did not do during this period was to promote child psychology. For him, experimental psychology, with its laboratory base, had greater scientific rigor, the goal he wanted to pursue.

CLARK UNIVERSITY

Hall resigned from Johns Hopkins in the spring of 1888 to become president of the newly founded Clark University in Worcester, Massachusetts, named for its major supporter, Jonas Clark. The university was to be a graduate center, much like Johns Hopkins, and Hall immediately set about hiring an extraordinary group of faculty. Clark University opened in the fall of 1889, and for a few brief years it was considered one of the most remarkable institutions of higher learning in the country, but the honeymoon was not to last.

Hall's difficulties began with a personal tragedy. While he was away from home, recovering from a bout with diphtheria, his wife and daughter were accidentally asphyxiated in a home accident. His son Robert, 9 years old, was in a different part of the house and survived. In his autobiography, Hall wrote only briefly of his great misfortune and there is no record of his sharing his thoughts with friends. He considered leaving his position at Clark but, by fall, he seemed determined to work even harder. His religious beliefs apparently deepened during this period. But additional difficulties would soon follow.

It was about this time that Clark began to withdraw his support from the university. Clark had anticipated more support from the town of Worcester, particularly from its wealthiest citizens, but that support did not materialize and expenses were greater than anticipated. In addition, local newspapers were critical of the university, citing its aloofness from the community. In April 1891, Clark largely withdrew from the university and left Worcester, with his plans for the future of the university indefinite.

In an attempt to resolve some of the town–gown issues, Hall began a summer school for teachers and introduced a new journal, *Pedagogical Seminary*, now considered the first journal of developmental psychology in the United States. That journal is still in existence as the *Journal of Genetic Psychology*. This new journal was intended to have a practical and popular bent (Hall, 1891). The university's board of trustees also considered adding an undergraduate college to help in the relations with the community, but Hall was not in favor of it. As a result, Clark University did not change quite yet, and Clark stopped his contributions to the university.

Hall did not fare well during this difficult period. He had deceived Clark about the expense of running a university, and now he began to deceive his faculty about the financial condition of the university. The faculty increasingly began to see him as devious and untrustworthy. Some of them began negotiations with the University of Chicago, then in its formative stages and having difficulty recruiting science faculty. By the time the dust had settled, two-thirds of the faculty and even more of the student body had left Clark for Chicago (Ross, 1972, p. 227). With this exodus, Hall's great plan for the university came to an end, and Clark was left with only one strong department—psychology.

At about this time, Hall's leadership role in American psychology also began to deteriorate. He lost some influence in the discipline because of the decline of his university, but his own actions contributed to his diminished power. He published particularly brutal attacks on books by James and Ladd in the *AJP*, and he was seen as using the journal for his own selfish purposes. Some colleagues thought they would be better served by buying *AJP* from him or founding another journal. In 1893, APA printed the proceedings of its convention independently, instead of in the *AJP*, as it had done in the past. Hall did not attend the APA meeting that year because of the conflict and, after that, his attendance at APA conventions for the rest of his life was spotty.

RETURN TO THE CHILD-STUDY MOVEMENT

In the period between the exodus at Clark and 1895, Hall reached his 50th birthday and spoke of the "great fatigue" that accompanies this segment of life. Clearly, he was in crisis. His way out of the crisis was to become more active in the child-study movement that he had put aside a decade earlier. He announced his interest in writing a book on adolescence and declared that child study was part of scientific psychology. The return to child study appeared to free Hall. He had never been a very successful laboratory man, no matter how much he talked of its importance. Now he could devote himself to omnivorous reading and use his talent for organizing information from different fields.

In 1899, the 10th anniversary of the founding of Clark University, Hall held a conference, inviting five distinguished foreign scientists to speak and awarding them honorary degrees. This event seemed to put Hall in a more favorable position with the community and with some of his professional colleagues. In 1899, he also married for a second time a teacher, Florence Smith, who had attended summer school at the university. She was present when Freud (chap. 3, *Pioneers I*) and C. G. Jung (chap. 11, *Pioneers I*) stayed at the Hall home during the famous 1909 conference at Clark. Shortly after that, however, Hall and his wife separated. She had become increasingly eccentric and eventually had to be institutionalized, diagnosed with advanced arteriosclerosis of the brain (Ross, 1972, p. 275).

In July 1892, Hall held a 2-week summer school at Clark on "higher pedagogy and psychology," an event that was repeated for the next 10 years. Many teachers now believed that child study should be made part of every teacher's training. In 1894, the National Education Association formed a Child Study Department within the association and Hall was elected its first president. Hall also became involved in the Child Study Congresses that were held in Chicago beginning in 1894. The child-study movement was spreading to England and other parts of Europe around this time, with direct connections to the movement in America and to Hall.

Hall's child-study program did not receive a great deal of support for his child study among psychologists. Both James Mark Baldwin and John Dewey (chap. 4, *Pioneers II*) were interested in the subject but apparently were suspicious of Hall and supported him reluctantly. Consequently, most of the scientific personnel needed to maintain the movement were graduates of Clark University and followers of Hall. By 1895, a half dozen of his graduates had assumed chairs of psychology and pedagogy at normal schools or universities in the Midwest and West. Others would follow.

Although support in psychology languished, women's clubs and parent-teacher associations took up the cause of child study. Hall gave many talks on children and education, and traveled across the country to deliver them. By all accounts, he was a very impressive speaker, and his talks continued to stimulate general interest in child study. Toward the end of his life, he estimated that he had given about 2,500 such talks (Ross, 1972, p. 288).

THE RETURN OF QUESTIONNAIRES

Soon after the initial publication of the *Pedagogical Seminary*, Hall returned to the use of questionnaires, this time with renewed energy. During 1894 and 1895, he mailed out a series of 15 questionnaires to approximately 800 correspondents, covering such topics as anger, fear, and moral and religious experience. The practice of mailing questionnaires continued, at varying rates, until 1918. The data from them were frequently used for theses at Clark and resulted in many publications (White, 1990).

These questionnaires came under considerable criticism. Some members of the child-study movement felt they were receiving too much attention and were diverting focus from other important aspects of the movement. Many prominent psychologists of the day, including Dewey (chap. 4, *Pioneers II*), Hugo Münsterberg (chap. 7, *Pioneers IV*), and Edward Thorndike (chap. 10, *Pioneers I*) objected to the questionnaires because of their shortcomings as objective measures (White, 1990). James, who saw them as an intrusion on privacy, was particularly unkind. He objected to the "circulars of questions sent out by the hundreds to those supposed able to reply. The custom has spread, and it will be well for us in the next generation if such circulars not be ranked among the common pests of life" (James, 1890, p. 194). In addition, Hall was prone to engage in far-fetched speculation, and this tendency, combined with the other problems of his research, had a negative impact on his reputation. Still, except for Dewey's work at the University of Chicago, Hall's program at Clark was the only Ph.D. program before 1900 to consider the study of the child to be an important part of psychology's mission (Koelsch, 1984).

FOUNDING THE APA

In the spring of 1892, Hall sent letters to a group of colleagues proposing the establishment of a psychological association. On July 8, 1892, a meeting took place in the study of his home at Clark University to discuss the newly proposed society. By the time the meeting was concluded, the APA had been formed and Hall was chosen as its first president.

The creation of the APA came about for several reasons. Clearly, there was a need for such an association, and Hall was aware of the establishment of other scientific organizations around this time. It is also likely that the founding was related to Hall's desire to regain some of his lost influence in the national community of psychologists (Sokal, 1992).

Twenty-six individuals accepted membership in the association, including some of those present at the meeting, and another five were approved for membership. Since then, the organization has grown to become the largest organization of psychologists in the world. It has more than 100,000 members and an annual budget of more than $80 million. It is also the largest publisher of psychological books and journals in the world. The organization held the first of its annual meetings on December 27, 1892, at the University of Pennsylvania. Eighteen people were present for that meeting (Sokal, 1992). These days, the conventions routinely attract between 10,000 and 20,000 registrants.

Over the years, the APA has played a crucial role in the development of psychology as a science, a profession, and as a means of promoting human welfare. The importance of its founding cannot be overestimated. The association gave psychology a core, a focus, and a voice—important qualities that were lacking before it came into being. Although Hall did not play a strong role in the later development of the organization—he did not even attend the second annual meeting—his pivotal role in its founding has never been in doubt. It is significant that he was honored with the APA presidency again in 1924, the year of his death—the only APA president to die in office—and one of only two people to be president of the APA twice (the other was James).

ADOLESCENCE

In 1904, 10 years after he began writing it, Hall published his two-volume study on *Adolescence, Its Psychology and Its Relations to Physiology, Anthropology, Sociology, Sex, Crime, Religion and Education*. It was his first and most important book, and the crowning achievement of his work in the child-study movement. It revitalized the use of the somewhat archaic term "adolescence" and sectioned off a particular period of the life span for study. The appearance of the book was a milestone; the beginning of the psychological study of adolescence is usually identified with it.

Adolescence was about development—not just adolescent development—and it included a clearer description of Hall's evolutionary ideas concerning development than had appeared before. For Hall, adolescence is a critical stage of development. During this period, the individual has the potential to take the next small step in the journey toward human perfection. But it is up to the environment to provide the kind of stimulation necessary to help the individual to help the species move onto a higher evolutionary stage.

For Hall, childhood prepares the adolescent for potential change. In his view, it is particularly important for parents and educators not to interfere with nature. Each of the childhood periods must be accorded its own timing, neither stymied nor rushed. Only in this way can the full potential of the adolescent be assured. Hall argued, as he had before, for the need to discover the natural pattern of development for the child. He maintained that parents and teachers must provide "the most favorable environment and eliminate every possible cause of arrest or reversion" (1904, p. 89). For Hall, child rearing and education are the central tasks of life.

Hall's treatment of adolescence was probably the first systematic portrayal of this stage of life in the modern world (Ross, 1972, p. 333). The two-volume set is reputed to have sold more than 25,000 copies, at the time a surprisingly large number for a scholarly work. But the book was not consistently well received. The copies owned by both Freud and James survive, but their pages are uncut (Koelsch, 1984). Hall's view of evolution, already antiquated by the time *Adolescence* was published, stood at the center of his convictions on development. He believed that by applying evolutionary ideas to development, he would "unlock the complexities of human development, accelerate evolutionary processes, and even reveal the purpose and destiny of life itself" (Grinder, 1969, p. 356).

Hall's volumes on adolescence are frequently criticized for ignoring the influence of culture, emphasizing physical aspects of adolescence, and focusing on stages of growth rather than emphasizing the continuous nature of development (Grinder & Strickland, 1963). Some of the criticism is due to a misinterpretation of Hall. Hall believed strongly in the power of the environment, particularly during adolescence. It was, in fact, this outlook that gave him such optimism about the future of the race. Nonetheless, his rigid position on recapitulation undercut his influence on the scientific movement in adolescence. His thoughts on cognitive and social development were equally arcane, although, oddly enough, his discussions of moral development seem quite modern and very much in line with those of Piaget and Kohlberg (Grinder, 1969).

Eventually, his contributions to the scientific study of adolescence became largely a historical oddity.

Some psychologists had begun to speak out against the child-study movement long before Hall published his book on adolescence. They called the movement unscientific and included attacks on Hall's questionnaire studies. Hall's railing against the direction that the movement was taking did not help its status. In addition, many teachers found that the movement was of little practical use to them. Attendance at Clark's summer school for teachers began to drop off, and the program was discontinued in 1903.

THE FREUD VISIT

Hall planned a celebration in 1909 to commemorate the 20th anniversary of the founding of Clark University, an event similar to the one he had held 10 years earlier. The 1909 conference was planned around a number of disciplines, including psychology. Several prominent psychologists, for example, Wundt and Binet (chap. 5, *Pioneers III*), were invited, but they declined. The centerpiece of the conference would turn out to be the visit of the Viennese physician, Freud.

Freud was not well known in America at this time. James had reviewed some preliminary work by Freud and Breuer in *Psychological Review* in 1894, probably the first reference to Freud's work to appear in America (Koelsch, 1984). Hall had begun to refer to Freud's work in his graduate lectures at Clark as early as 1901–1902. They shared several common interests in psychology, including a belief in the important role of early experience and in an evolutionary, developmental model. Hall's volume on adolescence contained several references to Freud's work.

Late in 1908, Hall wrote to Freud, offering him the opportunity to give a series of lectures. Freud declined. Later, when the date was changed to September, and the honorarium was increased, Freud accepted. Carl Jung, Freud's new friend, was quick to grasp the potential significance of the invitation. He realized that, although Freud would be speaking in America, his talks were likely to have an impact in Europe. Eventually, Freud reached the same conclusion. He sailed for the United States in August 1909, accompanied by Jung and Sandor Ferenczi, a Romanian psychoanalyst. They arrived in New York August 29, 1909 (Evans & Koelsch, 1985).

The first of Freud's five lectures was given, in German, on Tuesday, September 7, at 11 a.m.; his subsequent lectures were on consecutive days at the same time. The lectures were not written in advance but were constructed during early morning walks with Ferenczi. Although some historians have argued that too much has been made of Freud's visit, his lectures, which were later published, have been characterized as the most concise and lucid account of the birth of psychoanalysis (Koelsch, 1984).

Hall continued to lecture about Freud's work in his classes at Clark and to refer to him in his writings. As a result, Clark University produced some of the first psychologists to apply psychoanalysis to child guidance and educational psychology (Hale, 1995). Hall's last Ph.D. student, Francis C. Sumner (chap. 11, *Pioneers IV*), the first African-American to receive a Ph.D. in psychology in the United States, wrote his thesis on a comparison of Freudian and Adlerian psychoanalytic thought. Later, when Sumner became chair of psychology at Howard University, he required the study of Freud as part of the psychology curriculum (Koelsch, 1984).

HALL'S VIEWS ON RACE

Hall is frequently described as racist. He spoke of Negroes, Jews, southern Europeans, and Anglo-Saxons as distinct races, a common way of thinking in his day. But Hall argued against colonialism, the establishment of the authority of one nation in the land belonging to another. He said that we know too little about foreign people and that we should not impose our beliefs on them. In general, "Hall believed in the right of each race to be left alone to develop its indigenous culture in its own way" (Ross, 1972, p. 413).

For the most part, Hall's writings consider only two "racial" minorities, Jews and Blacks. Hall was favorably disposed to Jews, perhaps because of his work as a tutor in a Jewish household early in his career. There was much prejudice against Jews in Hall's time, but he encouraged his Jewish graduate students and he hired at least three Jewish faculty members when he organized his original faculty at Clark (Winston, 1998, p. 33). As anti-Semitism arose in Germany and in America, Hall frequently spoke out against it. When he spoke to Jewish groups, he urged them to retain their religious and cultural identities.

Hall's writings on Blacks were less favorable. Although he regarded himself as liberal on race, his writings on Blacks do not always reflect that position. He thought that Whites and Blacks were as far apart as races could be, in both physical and psychological characteristics. His biographer describes him as stuck in a 19th century mode of thinking about race (Ross, 1972, p. 416). But there was another side to Hall's attitude toward Blacks. According to Guthrie (1998), Clark University under Hall was one of the few universities that actively encouraged the enrollment of Blacks and allowed entrance examinations to be given at Black colleges. Clark University not only enrolled Black graduate students in the early part of the last century, but it graduated more Black scholars in the behavioral sciences than all other White colleges combined. Guthrie concluded that although Hall expressed views that would have to be judged as racist by contemporary standards, his actions toward Blacks would have to be considered liberal, even by today's standards.

HALL AND WOMEN

L. A. Diehl has written several articles on Hall and women at Clark University during Hall's tenure. She called Hall a paradox, a foe of coeducation and, yet, an educator of women (Diehl, 1986). This paradox is similar to the one presented by the discrepancy between his words and actions with respect to Blacks. Hall was clear in stating his belief that women belong in the home. When it became evident that women were entering higher education, however, he insisted that those at Clark be treated fairly. Originally, he had encouraged Clark, the founder of the university, to support a graduate university with no undergraduate students. In his autobiography, Hall stated that when he submitted a proposal to Clark in 1895 for an undergraduate college, his proposal (reluctantly) was for a coeducational college (Hall, 1923, pp. 306–308). By the terms of Clark's will, made available on his death in 1900, however, the admission of female students was forever barred.

Many of Hall's ideas concerning women derived from his beliefs about evolution and recapitulation. A belief in psychological sex differences based on evolutionary principles was common at the time but Hall, unlike many of his colleagues, was not shy about expressing his ideas. In the early 1900s, he gave many talks and wrote several papers on recapitulation theory as it should be applied to the home and school. For Hall, these biological differences require educational differences beginning in adolescence. Many feminists believe that Hall's work was an impediment to social change for women, particularly at a time when some psychologists, for instance Dewey and James Rowland Angell (chap. 4, this volume), were willing to consider gender roles as social constructions rather than as biological inevitabilities.

Eventually Hall became a spokesman for the anticoeducation movement that sprang up again in the early 1900s. He wrote that if women were to be educated at all, they should be educated for motherhood. But his behavior at Clark University regarding the education of women was not consistent with his "scientific" position. Between 1896 and 1920, when Hall stepped down as president of Clark, approximately 150 women were enrolled in courses there (Diehl, 1986, p. 874).

In 1909, Hall proposed the establishment of an educational department that would grow out of the Saturday morning classes that had been previously established for teachers. Women were to receive masters degrees from this program but would be excluded from other masters degree programs. But then Hall ignored his own proposal and placed women in any graduate program they wished. The first graduate degrees were given in 1907, and the first Ph.D. was granted in 1908. Most of the degrees were in education, but they were in other fields as well. After reviewing Hall's presidential papers, Diehl (1986, p. 874) found no evidence that Hall treated inquiries from prospective female students any differently from letters from prospective male students. Some feminist scholars have concluded that, at the beginning of the 20th century, the two schools most open to women were Cornell and Clark (Rosenberg, 1982, cited in Diehl, p. 876).

HALL AND THE PSYCHOLOGY OF RELIGION

Vande Kemp (1992) argued that Hall's first love was the psychology of religion, and that, along with James, he must be considered the cofounder of religious psychology in America. As one observer said, "It is indisputable that Hall launched . . . the classical psychological interpretation of religion" (Hopkins, 1937/1959, p. 52, quoted in Vande Kemp, 1992, p. 290).

In his introductory lecture at Johns Hopkins University in 1884, Hall maintained that psychology and theology had common concerns, that psychology is "connected in the most vital way with the future of religious belief in our land" and that the "Bible [is] slowly being re-revealed as man's great text book in psychology" (Hall, 1885, pp. 247–248). Twenty years later in *Adolescence* (1904), he wrote: "One of the great tasks of the psychology of the future . . . must be to reinterpret its Lord and Master to the Christian world" (p. viii). There, he also wrote that psychology "is slowly taking the place once held by theology as the intellectual expression of the religious instinct" (p. 324).

Between 1900 and 1920, Hall taught a course in religious psychology almost every year. In 1904, the year *Adolescence* appeared, Hall announced a new *American Journal of Religious Psychology and Education.* Among its editors were two of his former students. In one article in that journal, he claimed that psychology could bring to Christianity "a new revival of a kind and degree that the Christian world has not known in recent centuries" (Ross, 1972, p. 417). Among its other articles, not written by Hall, were some that interpreted world religions within a framework of recapitulation.

It has been estimated that approximately 10% of Hall's publications were in religious psychology. Almost a third of the doctoral dissertations he supervised were concerned with the topic (Vande Kemp, 1992), and the journal served as an outlet for many of these dissertations. Hall did not take a great deal of interest in the journal, however, and passed control of it to an editor who died in 1914. Hall claimed he could not find another editor and discontinued the journal soon after.

In 1917, Hall published *Jesus, the Christ, in the Light of Psychology*, which several commentators called the most ambitious book of its genre. The book was strongly criticized by conservative religious groups, but it was accepted, if not exactly praised, by others. In the book, Hall called Jesus a mythic creation, who incorporates all the good tendencies in man. The purpose of the story of Jesus is to aid us in our search for personal fulfillment. For Hall, that fulfillment is to be found in the service of others.

THE FINAL YEARS

In June 1920, Hall resigned from Clark University. He was 76 years old and had been president of the university for 31 years. After retirement, he found himself becoming increasingly isolated, in a state of near helplessness (Ross, 1972, p. 430). In typical fashion, he fought back from this depressed state through intellectual activity, and in the process he gathered together all the information he could find on old age. As he tried to find meaning in his new life, he returned to a project he had abandoned earlier and published *Senescence: The Latter Half of Life* in 1922, the first major American work on gerontology (Cole, 1993).

As in so much of his writing, Hall did not confine himself to psychological literature, but covered a wide range of sources from the scientific to the literary. In addition, he included substantial material on personal reminiscences. The mix produced a work that was at the very least "frustrating" (Troyansky, 1993). But his central ideas were similar to those that he had expressed earlier in his career. He called for a scientific understanding of old age, both physical and psychological. He asked for recognition of this period as a separate stage of life and for greater appreciation of the value of the aged. He also called for social understanding and an acknowledgment of the "wisdom" of old age.

In his autobiography, *Life and Confessions of a Psychologist*, Hall (1923) made it clear that he had deliberately remained silent on some personal aspects of his life and said virtually nothing about his wives and children. In one passage, he wondered why he was so alone and isolated, why he was comfortable with his students but not with his colleagues.

SOME CONCLUDING THOUGHTS

Hall died on April 24, 1924, of pneumonia. The bulk of the estate was willed to Clark University, where it was used to establish a professorship in genetic psychology in his name. Hall's death "marked the final close of the pioneer period in American psychology" (Sanford, 1924, p. 317).

Hall's contributions to psychology, education, and related fields are enormous, yet they tend to be undervalued. Perhaps his most important legacy can be found in the people he influenced, particularly his students. Although many of his students went on to administrative positions in education and did not become well known, several of them achieved substantial visibility and influence.

Among the most important of Hall's students was Arnold Gesell, a central figure in American developmental psychology for decades, best known for his work on developmental norms for children. Gesell's work can be seen as a fulfillment of many of the promises Hall made to the child-study movement.

Another of Hall's students, Lewis Terman (chap. 8, *Pioneers IV*), famous for his landmark study of genius and for the development of the Stanford Revision of the Binet–Simon Scales, earned his doctorate degree from Clark in 1905. Terman remarked: "My greatest debt is to Stanley Hall. . . . No one else ever so stimulated my thinking or fired me with so much enthusiasm with regard to the importance of psychology and its applications" (quoted in Wallin, 1968, p. 152).

Henry H. Goddard, who received his doctorate degree from Clark in 1899, is best known for bringing the Binet–Simon Scales to America, and for promoting their use. Zenderland (1986, as cited in Sokal, 1990) noted that Goddard always spoke highly of Hall and remained grateful to him throughout his life.

Among Hall's less-known contributions was his work in the history of philosophy and psychology. His great passion for the subject prompted others to pursue work in the field. For instance, 2 years after leaving Clark, E. G. Boring wrote *A History of Experimental Psychology* (1929), which contains many of the anecdotes mentioned in Hall's writings. In addition, Boring's personalistic approach to the history of psychology was originally proposed by Hall (Bringmann, Bringmann, & Early, 1992, pp. 287–288).

A few of Hall's other influences are even more obscure. At the turn of the century, some authors of vocal instruction programs and music-appreciation textbooks followed Hall's suggestion to coordinate teaching methods and materials with stages of childhood development (Humphreys, 1985). Hall's work had an impact on medical education. Abraham Flexner, who established the modern standards of medical school education in 1910, argued that medical school education should have a solid scientific foundation. This view was influenced by the two psychology courses Flexner took with Hall at Johns Hopkins from 1884 to 1886 (King, 1978).

Hall's recapitulation theory was a significant influence in the growing popularity of the Boy Scout movement during the early 20th century (Reaney, 1914). Hall had an indirect influence in the establishment of the national Parent Teachers Association (PTA) (White, 1983). Hall's influence was also felt outside the United States, for example, in the work of Yujiro Motora, a student of Hall at Johns Hopkins, who helped introduce modern psychology to Japan. Even Binet, the famed French psychologist, acknowledged the contributions of Hall to his work (Wolf, 1973).

Should Hall receive more credit for his contributions? To some degree, his personal style and controversial views interfered with his acceptance. Critics also point to his rigid adherence to the theory of recapitulation, his difficult writing style, and his failure to develop a coherent psychological theory. It should be remembered that, despite his voluminous writings, Hall is not associated with a successful theory or empirical finding. Yet, when his contributions are looked at in their totality, their range and depth are dazzling. He played so many crucial roles in the early years of psychology, it is difficult to imagine the path American psychology would have taken without him.

REFERENCES

Berndt, T. J., & Zigler, E. G. (1985). Developmental psychology. In G. A. Kimble & K. Schlesinger (Eds.), *Topics in the history of psychology* (pp. 115–150). Hillsdale, NJ: Lawrence Erlbaum Associates, Inc.

Boring, E. G. (1929). *A history of experimental psychology*. New York: Appleton-Century.

Bringmann, W. G., Bringmann, M. W., & Early, C. E. (1992). G. Stanley Hall and the history of psychology. *American Psychologist, 47*, 281–289.

Cole, T. R. (1993). The prophecy of Senescence: G. Stanley Hall and the reconstruction of old age in twentieth-century America. In K. W. Schaie & W. A. Achenbaum (Eds.), *Societal impact on aging: Historical perspectives* (pp. 165–181). New York: Springer.

Dennis, W. (1949). Historical beginnings of child psychology. *Psychological Bulletin, 46*, 224–235.

Diehl, L. A. (1986). The paradox of G. Stanley Hall: Foe of coeducation and educator of women. *American Psychologist, 41*, 868–878.

Evans, R., & Koelsch, W. (1985). Psychoanalysis arrives in America. *American Psychologist, 40*, 942–948.

Grinder, R. E. (1969). The concept of adolescence in the genetic psychology of G. Stanley Hall. *Child Development, 40*, 355–369.

Grinder, R. E., & Strickland, C. E. (1963). G. Stanley Hall and the social significance of adolescence. *Teachers College Record, 6*, 390–399.

Guthrie, R. V. (1998). *Even the rat was white* (2nd ed.). Boston: Allyn & Bacon.

Hale, N. G., Jr. (1995). *Freud and the Americans*. New York: Oxford University Press.

Hall, G. S. (1883). The contents of children's minds. *Princeton Review, 11*, 249–272.

Hall, G. S. (1885). The new psychology. *Andover Review, 3*, 120–135, 239–248.

Hall, G. S. (1891). Editorial. *Pedagogical Seminary, 1*(1), iii–viii.

Hall, G. S. (1904). *Adolescence, its psychology and its relations to physiology, anthropology, sociology, sex, crime, religion and education* (2 vols.). New York: Appleton.

Hall, G. S. (1917). *Jesus, the Christ, in the light of psychology* (2 vols.). New York: Doubleday.

Hall, G. S. (1922). *Senescence: The last half of life*. New York: Appleton.

Hall, G. S. (1923). *Life and confessions of a psychologist*. New York: Appleton.

Humphreys, J. T. (1985). The child-study movement and public school music education. *Journal of Research in Music Education, 33*, 79–86.

James, W. (1890). *Principles of psychology* (Vols. 1–2). New York: Holt.

King, D. J. (1978). The psychological training of Abraham Flexner, the reformer of medical education. *Journal of Psychology, 100*, 131–137.

Koelsch, W. (1984). *Incredible day-dream: Freud and Jung at Clark, 1909*. Worcester, MA: Friends of the Goddard Library.

Reaney, M. G. (1914). The psychology of the Boy Scout movement. *Pedagogical Seminary, 21*, 407–411.

Ross, D. (1972). *G. Stanley Hall: The psychologist as prophet*. Chicago: University of Chicago Press.

Sanford, E. C. (1924). Granville Stanley Hall 1846–1924. *American Journal of Psychology, 35*, 313–321.

Siegel, A. W., & White, S. H. (1982). The child study movement: Early growth and development of the symbolized child. In H. W. Reese (Ed.), *Advances in child development and behavior* (Vol. 17, pp. 233–285). New York: Academic.

Sokal, M. M. (1990). G. Stanley Hall and the institutional character of psychology at Clark. 1889–1920. *Journal of the History of the Behavioral Sciences, 26*, 114–124.

Sokal, M. M. (1992). Origin and early years of the American Psychological Association 1890–1906. *American Psychologist, 47*, 111–122.

Troyansky, D. G. (1993). Commentary: Aging and prophecy: The uses of G. Stanley Hall's Senescence. In K. W. Schaie & W. A. Achenbaum (Eds.), *Societal impact on aging: Historical perspectives* (pp. 198–203). New York: Springer.

Vande Kemp, H. (1992). G. Stanley Hall and the Clark School of religious psychology. *American Psychologist, 47*, 290–298.

Wallin, J. E. W. (1968). A tribute to G. Stanley Hall. *Journal of Genetic Psychology, 113*, 149–153.

White, S. H. (1983). Is it really all going to go away? Looking behind and beyond the 1960s. *Young Children, 38*, 56–65.

White, S. H. (1990). Child study at Clark University: 1894–1904. *Journal of the History of the Behavioral Sciences, 26*, 131–150.

White, S. H. (1992). G. Stanley Hall: From philosophy to developmental psychology. *Developmental Psychology, 28*, 25–34.

Winston, A. S. (1998). "The defects of his race": E. G. Boring and antisemitism in American psychology 1923–1953. *History of Psychology, 1*, 27–51.

Wolf, T. H. (1973). *Alfred Binet.* Chicago: University of Chicago Press.

Chapter 3

Harry Kirke Wolfe:
A Teacher Is Forever

Ludy T. Benjamin Jr.
Texas A&M University

In 1929, 40 years after the first International Congress of Psychology met in Paris, more than 100 foreign psychologists joined their American colleagues at Yale University for the ninth congress, and the first to be held on American soil. James McKeen Cattell, the dean of American psychologists at age 69, addressed the congress as president (Cattell, 1929). He traced the development of psychology in America and in the course of his remarks noted that the University of Nebraska had been among the leaders in the production of psychologists. That claim was based on two surveys of American psychologists published in the 1920s (Fernberger, 1921, 1928). In each of the surveys psychologists were asked where they had received the initial stimulation for their interest in psychology. In both surveys the University of Nebraska ranked third, a fact that Samuel Fernberger (1928), the author of the two surveys, labeled "curious." In searching for an explanation of Fernberger's curious finding, one does not have to look far. The answer to the question "Why Nebraska?" is Harry Kirke Wolfe (1858–1918). He was the central figure in an educational program that sent more than 20 students to other universities for their doctorates in psychology and into important careers in psychology. Three of his undergraduate students would become presidents of the American Psychological Association, a figure not matched by any of his contemporaries.

THE MAKING OF A TEACHER

Wolfe was born in Bloomington, Illinois, on November 10, 1858, the first of seven children. His parents had met when both were professors at a small women's college in Ohio. Eventually both parents left education, Wolfe's mother to assume full-time duties as a mother and homemaker, and Wolfe's father to pursue interests in law. In 1872 when Harry Wolfe was 13 the family moved to a farm on the outskirts of Lincoln, Nebraska, where Wolfe's father also was involved in politics and land development. Wolfe attended the University of Nebraska, less than a decade old when he began his studies there, principally in the classics with an emphasis in philosophy. After graduation he taught public school in Nebraska for 3 years. Given his family background and the family emphasis on education (five of his six brothers and sisters also earned college degrees, and the sixth completed 2 years of college), it is not surprising that Wolfe chose a career in teaching.

In 1883 Wolfe resigned his teaching post in Edgar, Nebraska, a small town about 90 miles southwest of Lincoln, and traveled to what must have seemed like the other side of the world for a Nebraska farm boy. That fall he enrolled at the University of Berlin, intending to earn a doctorate in classics. In the second semester he took two courses in the newly emerging science of psychology, both taught by a 34-year-old lecturer, Hermann Ebbinghaus (chap. 4, *Pioneers III*). This experience changed Wolfe's educational plans. By the fall semester of 1884 he had transferred to the University of Leipzig where he pursued his doctorate in psychology in Wilhelm Wundt's (chap. 3, *Pioneers III*) laboratory. It seems likely that Wolfe would have preferred to have remained with Ebbinghaus at Berlin, but Ebbinghaus's faculty status would not have allowed him to supervise doctoral students in 1884. Thus, Wolfe's opportunity for psychology lay in Leipzig.

Upon arriving in Leipzig, Wolfe found another American student studying psychology there as well. It was James McKeen Cattell, then in his second year of study. Cattell graduated with his doctorate in April 1886 (Wolfe was a subject in Cattell's dissertation research), and Wolfe earned his degree in August of the same year. Both dissertations were supervised by Wundt and both were published in Wundt's journal, *Philosophische Studien*. Wolfe's dissertation, a series of experiments on the memory for tones, was perhaps stimulated by Ebbinghaus's interest in memory but more likely was the result of a methodological disagreement between Wundt and Carl Stumpf (chap. 4, *Pioneers IV*) about how best to study the perception of tones (Wolfe, 1886).

Cattell returned to the United States to a faculty position at the University of Pennsylvania. Wolfe returned to Nebraska where he lived with his parents for a year before locating a position as principal of a high school in California. He was in his second year of that job when an invitation came from his alma mater to assume the chair of philosophy there. So in the fall semester of 1889, Wolfe returned to Lincoln with his new bride, Katharine Brandt, a physician whom he had met in California.

THE NEW PSYCHOLOGY IN NEBRASKA

When Wolfe began his tenure on the faculty at the University of Nebraska he was the sole member of the Philosophy Department. He was obligated to teach the traditional philosophy courses, but in his initial year he added two new courses, an introduction to the new scientific psychology and a course in experimental psychology. The latter course had a weekly laboratory session in which students conducted experiments. Several students also began working in the rudimentary psychology laboratory that he established, a laboratory equipped with some of the instruments of the day that defined the new psychology—a metronome; a stop clock that measured time in quarter-seconds; a Hipp chronoscope, the showpiece of the laboratory that measured time in thousandths of a second; tests for color perception; and an "acoumeter," a device for producing sounds of differing intensities. There were also anatomical models of the brain, eye, and ear, and drawings of the nervous system and various sensory systems. It was a respectable collection for an early psychology laboratory, establishing the Nebraska lab as one of only seven in the United States by 1889 (Benjamin, 2000).

At the end of his first year on the faculty, Wolfe campaigned for support of his laboratory, in terms both of necessary equipment and space. He wrote to the chancellor that teaching psychology should be a scientific enterprise but that the lack of needed equipment had forced him to use an approach that was largely literary. In addition to his desire to expand the laboratory, Wolfe also asked for support to start a program in pedagogical psychology, arguing that psychology is the most relevant of the sciences to education and that teachers need to know the facts of psychological research to succeed at their jobs. After hearing the requests, the university's regents approved the plans for a pedagogy program, but no additional staff as had been requested. They increased the library budget for the Philosophy Department to cover purchases of books for the pedagogy program. They also gave Wolfe an additional room in the basement of University Hall (the campus's sole building) for his laboratory, but they rejected the request for equipment funds.

To expand the laboratory in his second year, Wolfe borrowed equipment from some of his colleagues in the other sciences, built some of it himself with the aid of the university's "mechanic," and, in a move that angered some of the regents, used $80 of his library funds to buy needed equipment. At the end of his second year he wrote again to the chancellor and regents about the need for a better equipped laboratory. In an effort to educate the agriculturally minded regents, Wolfe wrote:

> The scientific nature of Psychology is not so generally recognized; hence I feel justified in calling attention to two points. 1st The advantages offered by experimental Psychology, as a discipline in scientific methods, are not inferior to those offered by other experimental sciences. The measurement of the Quality, Quantity, and Time Relations of mental states is as inspiring and as good discipline as the determination of, say the percent of sugar in a beet. . . . The exact determination of mental processes ought to be as good mental discipline as the exact determination of processes taking place in matter. 2nd The study of mind is the most universally applied of all sciences. . . . Whatever is known of mind is especially valuable in

professional life, and particularly so in that profession whose object is the training of mind [namely, teachers]. (Wolfe, 1891)

Wolfe followed his rationale with a request for 29 pieces of laboratory equipment at a cost of approximately $1,300 plus an additional $500 for other needs in the lab. The regents remained unconvinced about the value of scientific psychology, and no additional funds were granted. So while the university's sugar beet research program flourished, the science of mind limped along on borrowed batteries, misappropriated library funds, and overspent departmental budgets.

Wolfe's struggles for the laboratory became an annual theme in his end-of-year reports to the chancellor and regents. His classes grew in popularity, especially his psychology offerings, which now included new courses on child study; sensation and perception; and attention, memory, and will. The last two courses were added principally to serve the pedagogy program. The introductory psychology class grew to 70 students by the third year, and finding a room to accommodate such a large class was a problem. Wolfe had added a required laboratory section to that course, which he taught by dividing the class in half and meeting each half for a 2-hour weekly laboratory. By his third year the courses he had added in psychology and pedagogy, plus the laboratory sections, increased his contact hours to 35 hours per week. Wolfe received no teaching credit for his laboratory sections, nor did the students. Yet they still flocked to his classes, despite the extra work for no extra credit hours. As one of Wolfe's students later remarked, students were "willing to venture the work for the sake of the zest" (Alexander, 1918a, p. 1).

For Wolfe, the laboratory experience was paramount in his philosophy of teaching. He believed it is the key to mental growth. He wrote:

> If we go back to childhood it is plain that research is the sole method of growth. Watch the child in his cradle investigating his fingers, his toes, his toys, the wall paper, anything that attracts his interest. Try the lecture method with him and observe his disgust! No worse, his indifference. The beginning of interest and of development is in self-initiated movements. (Wolfe, n.d.b, p. 9)

Thus, Wolfe made research a part of all of his courses. Students were encouraged to seek out their own answers to questions. He wanted them to wrestle with complex problems, to question rather than blindly accept the views of their teachers. He warned students against submitting too easily to the authority of their instructors. Wolfe also argued for the value of research for lifelong learning. A college education is not a vaccination that lasts for a lifetime or even several years. He wrote, "The growing mind should be reinoculated with the virus of independent research for facts and new relations every week" (Wolfe, n.d.a, p. 14).

ACADEMIC POLITICS

To understand the importance of research in Wolfe's educational philosophy is to understand his frustration in not being able to develop his laboratory as he envisioned it should be. His annual requests for money and equipment were annually denied. He was warned about spending his library budget for equipment and asked to justify the small deficits in his department's budget (which he reimbursed the university out of his own pocket). Yet his classes remained enormously popular and his dedication to his students was unquestioned, and so the university administration tolerated his occasional indignation and what could be construed as mild insubordination.

In 1895, the university hired a new chancellor, George MacLean, an individual who viewed his authority as supreme. Whereas Wolfe encouraged his students to challenge authority, his own clashes with MacLean would not be tolerated. In late April 1897, as the semester was drawing to a close, MacLean called Wolfe to his office. Wolfe assumed it was to discuss the department's budget, following up a successful meeting he had had with MacLean a few weeks earlier. MacLean opened the meeting by telling Wolfe that the regents had decided that his services at the university were no longer required. He would be allowed to resign and if he did not, he would be fired. Wolfe was stunned. Apparently he had no inkling that such an action was even being considered. He refused to resign and, as promised, was fired.

Word of Wolfe's firing reached students the next morning. By the end of the day they had collected nearly 1,000 signatures (from a student body numbering approximately 1,650) on a petition calling for his reinstatement. The student leaders of the petition drive encouraged other students to attend the chapel services where they chanted Wolfe's name again and again as MacLean and some members of the regents took their places on the platform. When MacLean spoke he applauded the students for their loyalty to their professor and noted that "Dr. Wolfe was all right in many ways" ("Dr. Wolfe is Removed," 1897, p. 7). The remark elicited hissing from the students, an action for which they would later be required to apologize. In an effort to quiet the student protesters, MacLean promised a meeting with some of the students and some members of the board of regents who were in Lincoln for their final meeting of the academic year. But the regents left town and the meeting with students never took place.

The regents were scheduled to meet in Lincoln again in late June and Wolfe assumed he could gain reinstatement at that time. He asked MacLean for a statement of the charges against him but was denied. Through the academic rumor mill he heard that he had been fired for meddling in the affairs of other departments, a charge likely related to his questioning the distribution of funds to departments based on enrollments. Wolfe had questioned, in particular, the enrollment figures used by the chemistry department and had accused that department chair of inflating his numbers by counting students separately in lectures and laboratory sections. He was right and the chemistry department was forced to lower its student count by almost half. MacLean and the chair of the chemistry department were friends, so it is quite possible that Wolfe's charges irritated MacLean. Yet there was never good chemistry between Wolfe and MacLean, and the chancellor would have been willing, perhaps eager, to dismiss Wolfe whether valid charges existed or not.

Even though he had no official knowledge of the reasons for his dismissal, Wolfe wrote to the regents asking for reinstatement. His letter was considered at the June meeting of the board, but the earlier decision for dismissal was allowed to stand. It was then too late to apply for other academic jobs. Wolfe, and his wife and daughter, moved in with his parents once more.

A PUBLIC SCHOOL INTERLUDE

After a year of unemployment, Wolfe accepted a position as superintendent of the schools of South Omaha, then a separate city. It was a community on the wrong side of the tracks, home to the railroads and the acrid smells of the stockyards and meat packing plants that were built in the latter part of the 19th century. Life revolved around the packing plants, which employed more than 4,000 workers in 1898 when Wolfe arrived in the community. The city was also known for its many saloons and had been called, by one Methodist minister, Nebraska's worst city (Wenger, 1971). Compared with its larger neighbor to the north, South Omaha was a poor city whose citizens regularly endured the derision of the social-class sophisticates of Omaha. The schools of South Omaha were poorly funded, truancy was a significant problem, and dropping out of school was more common than graduation. Yet there was, among the leadership of the school board, a strong belief in the importance of education. Some members of the board viewed Wolfe's hiring as a crucial step in improving the schools (Benjamin, 1991).

Wolfe began by meeting with parents in neighborhood and church groups to ask for their help in getting their children to attend school regularly. At two campuses he established night schools for adult students. He appealed especially to those recent dropouts who required only a few credits to graduate. He staffed these night schools with some of his best teachers, using them half days in the regular classes and adding salary bonuses for their evening work. When it was evident that science teaching was not up to par, Wolfe established summer classes for science teachers to increase their knowledge and enhance their pedagogy, and provided incentives for teachers to take these classes. Not surprising, he persuaded the school board to appropriate funds for laboratory equipment, including microscopes.

The reforms began to show immediate effects. Attendance improved, dropout rates declined, new night school classes had to be added because of increased demands, and teacher salaries and teacher morale were said to have improved. Yet the reforms were not easily undertaken. Whereas the community expressed a desire to improve schools, the funds needed for significant changes were not forthcoming. Wolfe found himself fighting once more with administrators, this time school board members who were reluctant to provide what was needed for the students. After 3 years of these battles, Wolfe returned to Lincoln and to a principal's job at Lincoln High School.

The Lincoln High School job was a clear success. There were 1,200 students in a building built for 800. Every room in the school was in use as a classroom. Behavioral problems were rampant, perhaps because of overcrowding or perhaps because of a lack of discipline. Wolfe installed a system of self-government among the students. Controversial at first, it worked. Student behavior improved in the hallways, classrooms, and assemblies. Special programs were initiated for failing students, with mandated extra school time before and after regular school hours. Whether it was because of the extra study time or the desire to avoid the extra hours of school, the number of students with failing grades decreased dramatically.

In his third year in the Lincoln High School job, Wolfe received an offer from the University of Montana to become professor of psychology and pedagogy. The offer created a difficult decision for him. It meant leaving Lincoln High in midyear because Montana wanted him to begin the job in January 1905. And it meant leaving Lincoln and Nebraska where he had so many friends, made through his years of teaching and his involvement with child-study groups all over the state. On the positive side, his sister, Jessie, lived in Missoula, Montana, where the university was located, and her husband was superintendent of schools there. Most of all, it was an opportunity to be back in a university setting, teaching the courses he loved most. So, in late December the Wolfes left the rolling plains of southeastern Nebraska for the mountains of Montana.

Wolfe was at Montana for a little more than a semester when events transpired in Lincoln that would bring him home. The University of Nebraska had a new chancellor, Benjamin Andrews, who wrote to Wolfe in October 1905, offering him a position at Nebraska as professor of educational psychology beginning in January. Thus, after only two semesters at the University of Montana, Wolfe prepared to return to Lincoln. That he was admired and respected, despite his brief stay in Montana, is evident in a report in a Missoula newspaper, published on his departure.

[Wolfe] left tonight on the Burlington for his new field of labor. At the train he was given a rousing sendoff by the students, who were at the train in large numbers to bid him adieu as he left for the east [sic]. The members of his classes, in recognition of his services to them, presented him at the train with a solid silver dish, of handsome pattern and suitably engraved. They speak of him in the highest praise as a teacher and regret exceedingly that he has left. . . . The students of his classes passed resolutions speaking in the highest terms of his work with them, a copy of which was presented to him at the train this evening. ("Sendoff for Dr. Wolfe," 1906, p. 2)

HOME AGAIN

The *Omaha World Herald* welcomed Wolfe home with an editorial entitled "A Blot Wiped Out" (1905), congratulating the university on bringing him back and deploring the politics that had cost such an inspirational professor his job. In Lincoln, Wolfe's friends held a special homecoming party for him. At the party was Thaddeus Lincoln Bolton, who had taken Wolfe's place in teaching the psychology and philosophy courses. Wolfe was located within the College of Education where he taught courses in child study, educational psychology, and methods of teaching.

Wolfe resumed his position as professor of philosophy after Bolton was dismissed. The dismissal was one of great irony. In taking Wolfe's vacant position in 1900, Bolton, who had trained in the very well-equipped psychology laboratory of G. Stanley Hall (chap. 2, this volume) at Clark University, began immediately to lobby for a state-of-the-art laboratory. Eventually he was successful and was promised seven well-equipped rooms that would be in the new physics building scheduled for completion in 1905. Bolton proudly described his laboratory-to-be in an article in *Science* entitled "The Changing Attitude of American Universities Toward Psychology" (Miner, 1904). Although some American universities may have changed their attitudes, in the end, Nebraska did not. Several months after the article appeared, the Nebraska administration informed Bolton that the rooms had been reassigned to the physics department. Bolton was furious and vigorously protested the breach of promise. At the end of the 1907–1908 academic year he was dismissed. For Wolfe, this affair must have looked painfully familiar. During the next year Wolfe stayed in the College of Education but taught some of Bolton's classes. The following year he moved back into the Philosophy Department as department head, joining two other colleagues there.

Wolfe's second period of employment at Nebraska was largely a successful and happy one. In addition to his many classes and laboratory hours, he also worked closely with the state's teacher groups, holding workshops for them, helping them organize themselves into child-study groups to contribute observations, research, and testing results to the national efforts in child study centered at Clark University under Hall's direction. Of course he was not about to forget his quest for a laboratory that would provide his students with the educational opportunities they deserved. He pressed his needs with the new chancellor, Samuel Avery. In 1917, Avery told Wolfe that there would be a new social sciences building to be completed in 1919. It was to contain a psychology laboratory, and Avery wanted Wolfe to design one that would be a source of pride for the university. The long-held professional dream was about to become a reality (Benjamin, 1991).

PATRIOTISM ON TRIAL

In 1916 with war raging in Europe, Woodrow Wilson campaigned for a second term as president of the United States on a platform of maintaining America's neutrality. Like many Americans, Nebraskans were divided on the "right" course of action. There were those who believed the United States's involvement in the war was long overdue and there were others who urged the continuance of neutrality. Among the latter group was Wolfe. He was 1 of 89 signers of a petition sent to President Wilson on April 2, 1917. Known as the "peace petition," it called for the federal government to engage in preparations to ensure the defense of the United States and its commerce abroad but to keep American troops out of the European war. Four days later, at Wilson's request, the Congress of the United States declared war on Germany.

The entire text of the peace petition, along with the names of the 89 signers, was published in the *Nebraska State Journal* on April 10. The article also quoted from a follow-up letter written by the signers that stated "It is of course to be understood that all the signers are now ready to support the president and congress in their conduct of the war" ("All Will Support the War," 1917). The follow-up letter suggests that the peace petition signers already recognized that they were in trouble for having declared their pacifist goals in the hours before war was declared. Newspaper editorials and letters to the newspapers made accusations of disloyalty. Chancellor Avery tried to diffuse the situation in an April 14 speech in which he admitted that some faculty members had been slower than others to recognize the justness and necessity of the war, but that all were now united in their support of the government. But the matter would not go away. Newspaper editorials criticized the University of Nebraska for harboring individuals who were wishy-washy at best or cowards at worst. The university was urged to purge itself of these disloyal professors who surely should not be allowed to influence the minds of young Nebraskans.

What was happening in Nebraska in 1917 was happening all over the United States in what some historians have labeled America's "reign of terror." It was a time "when strident voices filled the air, when mobs swarmed through the streets, when violence of all kinds was practiced upon the opponents of the war" (Peterson & Fite, 1957, p. 194). Those strident voices continued in Nebraska, calling for the suspect professors to be brought before tribunals. Avery did what he could to protect his faculty, defending the university for more than a year. But the opposition forces constituted a juggernaut of patriotism in its ugliest forms; it would not be denied. On April 19, 1918, a little more than a year after the declaration of war, the Nebraska State Council for Defense, a wartime government entity charged with investigating disloyal activities, sent a letter to the regents of the university. It read, in part,

> These are the days when every one connected with the State University should be measured absolutely by an active, outspoken fealty to the nation, and that notions of academic freedom which permits or excuses lack of wholehearted aggressive support of the nation at this critical time, should be severely frowned upon and dealt with. Nebraska's leading educational institution should and must be one hundred per cent agressively [*sic*] American. Behavior which is negative, halting or hesitating by anyone on the University staff, in support of the government, should not be tolerated and especially all teaching which is covertly insidious in its influence upon the minds of students would be made impossible. The boards of many universities and colleges of the country have taken vigorous action to purge themselves of such pernicious influences and on behalf of the patriotic people of the University and state we ask you to do likewise in support of the government. (Nebraska State Council for Defense, 1918)

The Nebraska State Council for Defense, with the help of a number of informants, including students and professors at the university, assembled a list of a dozen faculty and staff members who were charged with disloyalty. Faced with the direct charges against university employees and under enormous pressure from Nebraska public opinion, the board of regents agreed to hold hearings on May 28, presided over by its members. Those accused had approximately 48 hours to prepare their defense.

Wolfe was not among the dozen initially charged with disloyalty (11 of whom were faculty members) but he was called before the hearing board on the second day, having been given 24-hours notice that he was being charged. He was charged with refusing to sign a card indicating his subscriptions to various wartime activities. The council had also received an anonymous letter, signed "A taxpayer," that accused Wolfe of expressing pro-German views in his classes and of arguing for the validity of the German educational system. When he appeared before the hearing board the charges were read as follows: "That he had not signed a wartime activity subscription card, that he had not displayed a Red Cross emblem in his office or home, and that when he had made a donation to the Red Cross Fund, he had asked that his name not be recorded" (Benjamin, 1991, p. 117). Wolfe answered the charges by saying he did not recall anyone asking him to sign a subscription card or to display a Red Cross emblem. He said he had made his Red Cross donation through a friend at the university and had asked that it be made anonymously. Records of donations produced during the hearings showed that Wolfe's contribution to the Red Cross and his purchase of war bonds were "in proportion to his means and if anything beyond his quota" (Benjamin, 1991, p. 119).

Eventually 24 university faculty and staff members were formally charged by the board. Initially the charges were "disloyalty"; however, after it was decided that such a claim might be difficult to prove, the charges were changed to "hesitating, halting, and negative support of the government" (Benjamin, 1991, p. 120). The hearings lasted for 2 weeks. At their conclusion, charges against 15 individuals were dismissed. Recommendations for dismissal were made against the remaining 9, 1 of those being Wolfe. The board deliberated the findings for more than a week before returning its verdict on June 18. Six of the professors were exonerated. Three were found guilty and subsequently dismissed from the university. Wolfe was among the exonerated.

The hearings marked the end of an arduous and exhausting year for Wolfe. Not only was he under suspicion for much of that time, but several of his closest friends were embroiled in the witch hunt as well. One of those was George Luckey, who had been instrumental in bringing Wolfe back from Montana; Luckey was among the three professors dismissed from the university. Reactions from the press were generally not supportive of the verdicts. Editors and letter writers believed that the university had lacked the courage to rid itself of its traitors. They called the hearings a "whitewash" and argued that there were many exonerated faculty members who deserved dismissal. Thus, it is likely that Wolfe felt no vindication.

Five weeks after the verdicts were announced, Wolfe and his family took a much needed vacation to Wheatland, Wyoming, to visit one of his brothers. While there, Wolfe began to complain of chest pains. Two hours later he was dead at the age of 59. His body was brought back to Lincoln by train. The funeral service was held at the Wolfes' home and had to be moved into the yard because of the crowd. Colleagues at the university called for a memorial service at the university but were stalled in their efforts by administrators who feared, with probably good cause, public backlash given Wolfe's tainted status. The on-campus service was eventually held, during the December break when faculty and students were gone.

The war had disrupted much of life, including the university's building program. The planned social sciences building opened a little behind schedule in 1920. Its residents included the Philosophy Department, and it housed the state-of-the-art psychology laboratories Wolfe had designed. Some of his friends and former students had hoped the new labs would be named in his honor, and a proposal to do so was formulated. But apparently it was never considered by the administration, who no doubt wanted to avoid the continued fallout from the disloyalty hearings.

THE LEGACY OF A TEACHER

Wolfe was part of the pioneering generation of American psychologists, one who brought the new psychology to the prairies of his adopted state, Nebraska. His academic pedigree was especially impressive. He had trained with two of the field's founders in Ebbinghaus and Wundt, earning the second Leipzig doctorate in experimental psychology by an American student. He opened one of the earliest psychology laboratories in America. He was a member of the editorial board of America's first psychology journal, the *American Journal of Psychology*, and 1 of 31 charter members of the APA. He published more than 50 articles, most of those in child study, a field in which he was especially active in the Midwest. Yet he is not among the members of American psychology's hall of fame. The history books tell of William James (chap. 2, *Pioneers I*), G. Stanley Hall, James McKeen Cattell, E. B. Titchener (chap. 7, *Pioneers I*), John B. Watson (chap. 12, *Pioneers I*), and countless others. But Wolfe's name is typically nowhere to be found in those histories. Such is the lack of fame that befalls those who would dedicate their lives to teaching.

Wolfe spent 30 years as a teacher, 9 of those as a teacher and administrator in the public schools and 21 as a college professor. In his university years he taught mostly undergraduates. Only in his final few years at Nebraska did he supervise a few master's degree students and one doctorate in education. As noted earlier, more than 20 of his undergraduate students went on to earn doctorates in psychology. Three of those—Walter Pillsbury, Madison Bentley, and Edwin Guthrie (chap. 10, *Pioneers II*)—achieved distinguished academic careers and would become presidents of the APA. Others achieved some measure of fame as well. Horace English is remembered for writing one of the great reference works in psychology, *A Comprehensive Dictionary of Psychological and Psychoanalytical Terms* (English & English, 1958). Carl J. Warden spent his career at Columbia University, where he was recognized as one of America's leading comparative psychologists, writing four books on that subject, three of them with Thomas Jenkins, another of Wolfe's undergraduate students. Jenkins also developed a personality test that was used in colleges and businesses for selection purposes. Frederick Kuhlmann published a translation of the Binet–Simon intelligence test in 1912 and later created a version of the test that could be used for testing infants. His mental testing work culminated with the publication of the Kuhlmann–Anderson Intelligence Test, coauthored with Rose Anderson, another of Wolfe's undergraduates. Margaret Wooster Curti wrote a popular textbook on child psychology. Frederick Lund wrote two important books on the psychology of emotion that established him as one of the leaders in that field in the 1930s. Not surprising, several of Wolfe's students—Frank Bruner, Grace Munson, and Bertha Luckey (daughter of dismissed professor George Luckey and Wolfe's one doctoral student)—spent their careers working in the public schools in positions of research, assessment, and curriculum development.

All of these students, and others, had discovered their love of psychology in Wolfe's courses and laboratory. Madison Bentley, who published more than 200 books and articles in his career at the University of Illinois and Cornell University, described the influence of Wolfe's laboratory:

During the teaching years I have often tried to recover the best things in my own early instruction that I might use them for inspiring junior [undergraduate] students. . . . Interesting exercises in the primitive but resourceful laboratory which I first encountered accompanied the lectures and discussions of the initial course. The exercises were impressive and they formed associative nodes. But it was, as I now recover the course, the dissection at first-hand of the sheep's brain which seemed most definitely to put me sympathetically inside psychology. That I was then acquiring sound and relevant knowledge, and not being merely entertained, I have had frequent occasion to realize. And so far from inclining toward a mere anatomy of the brain, those simple but absorbing dissections seem now to have done more than anything else to form a working conception of the organism which is strictly psychology. . . . That early teacher—to revert to primary influences— was a very engaging man. It may well be that the experiments and dissection were impressive and instructive mainly because they were the modes of Wolfe's teaching. (Bentley, 1936, p. 58)

Wolfe's laboratory was a place for demonstrating the phenomena and principles of psychology; however, its greater purpose was, as happened with Bentley, to get his students "inside psychology" to involve them in research. And as he wrote, "[Research] is the sole method of growth" (Wolfe, n.d.b, p. 1). It was by research that the infant in the cradle learns about the world, and it is no different for adults. For Wolfe, mental growth comes from questioning, working through complex problems, and self-initiated exploration. The laboratory was designed to provide those opportunities.

As an educator, Wolfe was an unqualified success. His popularity as a professor was evidenced in many ways. One was the growth of his classes. In his initial year at the University of Nebraska he had 21 students in his psychology classes. When he was dismissed in 1897, that number had increased to 225, a tenfold increase in a university that underwent a fourfold increase in enrollment during the same period. Wolfe's enrollments are even more impressive when one remembers that the students were spending all those hours in the lab without receiving any course credit.

Consistent with his views on mental growth, Wolfe consistently prodded his students to think for themselves. They were taught to question "givens" and to recognize the fallibility of authoritative sources. He did not view obedience as a virtue. Students were encouraged to work through issues on their own. He had a knack, according to some of his students, for leading students to the path of intellectual discovery and then making them proceed on their own. He believed that knowledge gained by self-discovery holds more meaning and, most important, that it strengthens one's intellectual abilities. As a part of this process, students were encouraged to disagree with him, and he rewarded such disagreements when they were based on sound reasoning and appropriate investigation.

Allied to Wolfe's demand that students think for themselves was his insistence that they have courage for their views. He did not encourage dogmatism nor could he abide faintheartedness. If their scholarship were sound, students should have confidence in their conclusions and be willing to defend them against alternative views. For Wolfe, taking a stand on questions was a moral duty inherent in scholarship. He modeled those beliefs in his own behavior as was evidenced in his testimony in the disloyalty hearings. The social and intellectual conditions that led to the hearings were much on Wolfe's mind in the last months of his life. In the last article he wrote, an article published in the month of his death, he discussed the role of education in the creation of the individual. Addressing the role of obedience, Wolfe (1918) wrote:

> Society should now be strong enough to do justice to the individual and not seek to crucify or to dwarf him, hiding behind the palladium of "the king can do no wrong." There is no institution in society worth preserving that cannot withstand all attacks of individual iconoclasts. . . . Now, in truth, obedience is not a virtue any more than eating is a virtue. . . . Too much obedience may ruin character, may dwarf the intellect, may paralyze the will of children and of adults. Unquestioning reverence for authority is necessary on the frontier and in the nursery; but its overcultivation has blinded us to the greatest evils of recent days. It whips into line the doubting Thomases of all political parties. It smothers the indignation of a community when the grossest outrage is committed by its chosen officers. It immolates the individual upon a fetish long since outgrown. It is the cry which the strong have always raised to cow the weak. (pp. 271–272)

Just as he demanded much of his students, Wolfe demanded much of himself. Preparation for his lectures and laboratories involved careful planning and continual refinement. He did not allow his notes to yellow. One of Wolfe's laboratory assistants wrote, "His outlines were made over fresh every year. . . . His laboratory work was changed as well. Students who perfected themselves on the tests in sensation and memory from notes or outlines of a previous class, learned when they reached the laboratory that there was an entirely new set of experiments" (Abbott, 1918, p. 3). Perhaps only teachers can understand the commitment required by such a practice.

Virtually every description of Wolfe as a lecturer by his former students included the word inspiring. His inspiration came from his personal qualities as a lecturer—organization, explanatory skills, sense of humor, optimism, and humility. Partly his inspiration came from his vision for psychology. Again and again he told his students that psychology holds great promise for solving the problems of the world. He believed that some knowledge of psychology would be helpful to all students, regardless of their chosen fields. Wolfe's ability to inspire also came from the breadth of his knowledge. He was extremely well read in a number of diverse fields, and he brought that breadth to bear on his lectures with frequent references from such subjects as art, literature, history, archeology, and biology. His addiction to books was well known; he liked to read them and was constantly buying them. He would bring home a wonderful new set of Shakespeare's plays, only to have his family point out that he already had three others (Benjamin, 1991).

Edgar Hinman (1936), a colleague of Wolfe's, wrote that Wolfe's genius for teaching was partly the result of his passion for human welfare. His lectures gave most of his courses an applied bent, a characteristic that added to their appeal to students. In the lecture and the laboratory there were frequent examples illustrating the utility of the principles or the existence of the phenomena of psychology outside the university. For Wolfe, an appreciation of applicability was important in stimulating lifelong learning.

Wolfe's passion for human welfare embodied his concern for ethics. Indeed, ethical was the companion descriptor to inspiring in the letters written about Wolfe by his former students and colleagues. They described how he made ethics a part of his courses and how he modeled ethical values in his own behavior. Wolfe's papers contain more than 20 lectures associated with ethics. His students learned that ethics imply action—conduct. It is not enough to be right, one has to *do* right. Furthermore, right conduct is constant; it does not "vary with the winds of public opinion" (Wolfe, 1899, p. 466). For Wolfe, right conduct meant making the world a better place. It is not right, for example, to be content with the knowledge that the condition of the working class is better than it had been. He asked his students, "[Is it] not possible to abolish poverty as slavery has been abolished?" (Wolfe, n.d.a, p. 2). He championed the applicability of psychology to solving the problems of the world, and his lifelong commitment to improving educational practices represented his efforts in that regard (Benjamin, 1991).

As Wolfe cared about humanity, he cared deeply for his own students. There is no doubt that most of his energies went toward their benefit. He was a selfless man whose satisfaction was derived from the accomplishments of his students. Students of all intellectual stripes found him to be a willing mentor; he was interested in them whether they were headed for graduate work at Columbia University or for work in Nebraska's kindergartens. Students were frequent dinner guests in the Wolfes' home. Indeed, his daughter Isabel recalled that in her youth there were few dinners that did not involve one or more of her father's students at the table. Wolfe loaned students money, often put them up at his home when they were in need, and worked to find them jobs.

In summary, Wolfe spent his life as a teacher and a very successful one at that. His sense of self was, no doubt, wrapped up in what he was able to accomplish with his students. To have the kind of influence that he enjoyed required that he set aside ambitions for personal accomplishment. It also required a host of personal qualities that define only the very best of educators, as indicated in his obituary in *Science*: "There are few qualities which the teacher should possess which he did not own in exalted measure. Keenness, kindness, unfailing humor and patience and generosity of soul, and the power to inspire, all these were his; and he was loved by those under his influence as few men are loved" (Alexander, 1918b, p. 313).

The American historian Henry Brooks Adams has written that teachers affect eternity, that they can never know where their influence will stop. Such is Wolfe's legacy, continued through generations of his students and their students and their students and beyond. It is an invisible legacy but perhaps no less important than the legacies of his better known contemporaries. Wolfe's immortality resides in the thousands of individuals who bear his imprint, without ever knowing his name.

REFERENCES

Abbott, N. C. (1918, December 8). *Student reminiscences at the Wolfe Memorial Service at the University of Nebraska*. Wolfe Papers, Archives of the History of American Psychology, University of Akron, Akron, OH.

Alexander, H. B. (1918a). *Remarks at the funeral of H. K. Wolfe, August 3, 1918*. Wolfe Papers, Archives of the History of American Psychology, University of Akron, Akron, OH.

Alexander, H. B. (1918b). Harry Kirke Wolfe (1858–1918). *Science, 48*, 312–313.

"All Will Support the War." (1917, April 10). *Nebraska State Journal*, p. 1.

Benjamin, L. T., Jr. (1991). *Harry Kirke Wolfe: Pioneer in psychology*. Lincoln, NE: University of Nebraska Press.

Benjamin, L. T., Jr. (2000). The psychology laboratory at the turn of the 20th century. *American Psychologist, 55*, 318–321.

Bentley, I. M. (1936). Autobiography. In C. Murchison (Ed.), *A history of psychology in autobiography* (Vol. 3, pp. 53–67). Worcester, MA: Clark University Press.

"A Blot Wiped Out." (1905, November 25). *Omaha World Herald*, p. 6.

Cattell, J. M. (1929). Psychology in America. *Science, 70*, 339.

Dr. Wolfe is removed. (1897, April 30). Hesperian [University of Nebraska student newspaper]. p. 7. University Archives, University of Nebraska, Lincoln, NE.

English, H. B., & English, A. C. (1958). *A comprehensive dictionary of psychological and psychoanalytical terms*. New York: McKay.

Fernberger, S. W. (1921). Further statistics of the American Psychological Association. *Psychological Bulletin, 18*, 569–572.

Fernberger, S. W. (1928). Statistical analyses of the members and associates of the American Psychological Association, Inc. *Psychological Review, 35*, 447–465.

Hinman, E. L. (1936). Harry Kirke Wolfe (1858–1918). In D. Malone (Ed.), *Dictionary of American biography* (Vol. 10, pp. 450–451). New York: Scribners.

Miner, B. G. (1904). The changing attitude of American universities toward psychology. *Science, 20*, 299–307.

Nebraska State Council for Defense. (1918, April 19). *Letter to the Nebraska Board of Regents*. Defense Council Records, Nebraska State Historical Society, Lincoln, NE.

Peterson, H. C., & Fite, G. C. (1957). *Opponents of war, 1917–1918*. Madison, WI: University of Wisconsin Press.

"Sendoff for Dr. Wolfe." (1906, February 2). *Missoula Standard*, p. 2.

Wenger, R. E. (1971). The Anti-Saloon League in Nebraska politics, 1898–1910. *Nebraska History, 52*, 267–292.

Wolfe, H. K. (n.d.a). Philosophy and ethics. Wolfe Papers, University Archives, University of Nebraska, Lincoln, NE.

Wolfe, H. K. (n.d.b). The psychology of research. Wolfe Papers, University Archives, University of Nebraska, Lincoln, NE.

Wolfe, H. K. (1886). Untersuchungen über das Tongedächtniss [Studies on the memory for tones]. *Philosophische Studien, 3*, 534–571.

Wolfe, H. K. (1891, May). *Letter to the University of Nebraska Board of Regents*. Board of Regents Papers, University Archives, University of Nebraska, Lincoln, NE.

Wolfe, H. K. (1899). Some questions in professional ethics. *Education, 19*, 455–467.

Wolfe, H. K. (1918). Personality and education. *Mid-West Quarterly, 5*, 259–273.

Chapter 4

James Rowland Angell: Born Administrator

Donald A. Dewsbury
University of Florida, Gainesville

Open any textbook in the history of psychology and you will find a discussion of James Rowland Angell as the premier spokesperson for functionalism, one of the major schools of psychology of the early 20th century. You may also find a brief biography but you will find little or nothing about the kind of man he was. Similarly, the obituaries written by his colleagues in psychology (e.g., Hunter, 1949, 1951; Miles, 1949) portray Angell as a bland and lifeless middle-of-the-road psychologist, leaving Angell, the man, in absentia.

Perhaps the reason for such omissions is that Angell lived nearly 80 years and made most of his contributions to psychology by the age of 45—long enough ago for the details of his work to be forgotten. For the rest of his life he was primarily an administrator. Writings about him as a psychologist reflect this. Accounts of Angell as president of Yale University, however, are rich in their descriptions of his personal characteristics. Although we are primarily interested in Angell's role in psychology, it is to the later years that we must look for an appreciation of the man.

THE LIFE OF ANGELL

James Rowland Angell, born on May 8, 1869, in Burlington, Vermont, was the youngest of James Burrill Angell and Sarah Swope Caswell Angell's three children. The senior Angell, the president of the University of Vermont at the time, assumed the same position at the University of Michigan 2 years later. Sarah was the daughter of Alexis Caswell, president of Brown University. The Angell family traced its roots to Thomas Angell, who came to America with Roger Williams in 1631. With those roots, it is interesting that when he assumed the Yale presidency, Angell was perceived as, and perceived himself as, strictly a Midwesterner.

After attending the public schools of Ann Arbor, Michigan, Angell received a bachelor's degree from the University of Michigan in 1890 and a master's degree the following year. While in school there, he managed to graduate Phi Beta Kappa, play shortstop on the baseball team, win the university and state tennis championships, and play clarinet in the band (Mack, 1931). John Dewey's (chap. 4, *Pioneers II*) textbook and his arrival on the Michigan faculty were influential in Angell's turning to psychology while he was there. Angell spent the next year at Harvard studying with William James, Josiah Royce, and G. H. Palmer and received a second master's degree. With James, Angell did research in conjunction with the American Society for Psychical Research.

In 1892 he went to Leipzig, hoping to study with Wilhelm Wundt (chap. 3, *Pioneers III*), only to find that Wundt's laboratory was full. He moved to Berlin to attend the lectures of Friedrich Paulsen, Wilhelm Dilthey, Hermann Ebbinghaus (chap. 4, *Pioneers III*), and others, and settled at Halle, where he studied philosophy with Hans Vaihinger and psychology with Benno Erdmann. There his doctoral dissertation, on the treatment of freedom in Kant's philosophy, was found acceptable, except for the German writing style, and thus in need of revision. Angell had to decide between completing the doctorate or accepting a position at the University of Minnesota, with the extra benefit of allowing him to marry. To do so would demand his immediate departure. He decided to abandon the doctorate to return to the United States and accept the position at Minnesota. Thus, Angell was a rarity, a prominent psychologist with no earned doctorate degree. He married Marion Isabel Watrous in 1894. They had two children.

After a year in Minnesota, Angell accepted the offer by Dewey, who had moved to the University of Chicago, to run the psychology laboratory there. Although he was initially overworked and made little progress up the academic ladder, competing offers from other universities allowed him to improve his situation at Chicago, and he became the founding chair of the new Psychology Department in 1905. A year later he was elected president of the American Psychological Association (APA).

Angell published a smattering of research papers and had excellent students—including John B. Watson (chap. 12, *Pioneers I*) but he is best known in psychology as the leader of the functionalist school, which opposed the structuralism of Edward Bradford Titchener (chap. 7, *Pioneers I*). Later on, he also became an opponent of behaviorism.

His successful textbook, *Psychology* (Angell, 1908), was heavily influenced by William James (chap. 2, *Pioneers I*). For example, Angell followed James in providing a list of human instincts, which included the instinct of "fear, anger, shyness, curiosity, affection, sexual love, jealousy and envy, rivalry, sociability, sympathy, modesty, . . . play, imitation, constructiveness, secretiveness, and acquisitiveness" (p. 349). He concluded the volume with a chapter on the Jamesian topic of self psychology. The textbook was written within the context of the developing school of functionalism, which, Angell believed, might have more practical significance than the structuralist approach: "It is mental activity, rather than mental structure, which has immediate significance for thought and conduct. . . . Students of philosophy, as well as students of education, may find the book especially useful" (Angell, 1908, p. iii). The book was also clearly influenced by the faculty psychology then prevalent, with chapters on sensation, perception, imagination, memory, emotion judgment, feeling, and volition. Later, Angell's thinking shifted to reflect a lesser influence of James and a greater influence of Dewey. His 1910 *Chapters from Modern Psychology* was based on a series of lectures at Union College and was used as an introductory textbook in various schools and colleges.

Angell, then a budding administrator, became dean of the Senior College at Chicago in 1908 and dean of the faculties in 1911. His service in Chicago was interrupted when he served in Washington, D.C., during World War I, working with the wartime Adjutant General's Committee on Classification of Personnel under the chairmanship of Walter Dill Scott, and later on the Committee on Education and Special Training, under Charles R. Mann. Angell returned to Chicago as the acting president in 1918.

The next year he left Chicago to become chairman of the National Research Council (NRC) in Washington, D.C. There, he made many important contacts that would prove useful later in his career. After a year in that position, he left to become president of the Carnegie Corporation in New York in 1920 and moved to the Yale presidency the following year. His Yale presidency was highly successful. He made major advances in the building program, the academic structure of the university, and its endowment. In 1932, a year after the death of his first wife, Angell married Katharine Cramer Woodman, who became a mainstay of New Haven academic society. Angell retired, as was required at Yale, at the age of 68. He remained active in numerous capacities including service as a trustee of the American Museum of Natural History and as a director for the New York Life Insurance Company and the National Broadcasting Company, where he also served as a counselor. He died on March 4, 1949 in Hamden, Connecticut.

Angell received many honors including election to the National Academy of Sciences (1920), the American Philosophical Society (1924), and the American Academy of Arts and Sciences (1932). Although he lacked an earned doctorate, he received 22 honorary doctorate degrees from such universities as Berlin, Chicago, Harvard, Halle, Michigan, and Yale.

FUNCTIONALISM

Although functionalist thinking is evident in the works of James and G. Stanley Hall (chap. 2, this volume), the origin of that school is generally attributed to Dewey's (1896) "The Reflex-Arc Concept in Psychology." The clearest statement of the functionalist position, however, was in Angell's (1907) APA presidential address, "The Province of Functional Psychology." Angell contrasted the functional approach with the structural psychology of Titchener (1898). Whereas structuralism concerned the structure of consciousness in the adult, human mind, Angell, an evolutionist through and through (e.g., Angell, 1909), placed functionalism in a biological context that allowed it to deal with mental activity within an adaptationist perspective. It is "the psychology of the how and why of consciousness, as distinguished from the psychology of the what of consciousness." (Angell, 1907, p. 85). Angell (1936) characterized functional psychology in terms of three objectives:

> It is concerned first with the identification and description of mental operations, rather than with the mere stuff of mental experience. In the second place, any description of a mental state, if it is to be at all accurate, must take account of the conditions under which it occurs, the circumstances which evoke it, for it largely depends in its precise quality upon these facts, a portion of which are narrowly physical in nature, a portion social. What the conscious state is doing, biologically speaking, contains the clue to what it really is when descriptively approached and analyzed. In the third place, functional psychology is interested in mental activity as part of the larger stream of biological forces which are constantly at work and constitutive of the most absorbing part of our world. (p. 28)

Functionalists were concerned with the role of the mind in mediating between the organism and the environment. They emphasized the importance of analyzing mind–body relationships; this was a "psychophysical psychology" (Angell, 1907, p. 86). This view required reliance on introspection, which Angell embraced: "Introspection in one form or another I held to be indispensable as the method from which inevitably derives our original apprehension of the whole field of study that is the phenomena in question" (Angell, 1936, p. 26).

The functionalist school in psychology bears the mark of Jamesian pragmatism but it matured in the context of a broader pragmatic approach prevalent in a variety of disciplines at the University of Chicago (Rucker, 1969). Whereas structuralists rejected philosophical ties as unscientific, functionalists embraced them (e.g., Angell, 1903a). With such an approach, Angell made psychology more inclusive. It included the study of animal behavior. Angell saw mental continuity among species and "no reason why we should not discover the forerunners of our human minds in a study of the consciousness of animals" (Angell, 1905, p. 458). Individual differences played a much greater role in functionalism than in structuralism. Angell was interested in how behavior develops in the individual organism. He urged the development of a practical psychology that included "pathological psychology" (p. 71). He asserted that "many of the most valuable improvements in the treatment of the insane are based upon psychological principles" (Angell, 1905, p. 456). Angell thus incorporated animal research, developmental studies, and abnormal psychology with psychology's province. This contrasted sharply with the narrower outlook and the lack of concern for utility of the structuralist approach. As consciousness evolved, "it must perforce be by virtue of something which it does that otherwise is not accomplished" (p. 73).

Angell proposed that consciousness was especially important when the organism was dealing with novel situations; he adopted a "conception of mind and body as functional poles in the life of the organism, such that the latter, having as its major task the adjustment of itself to the environment psychical and social in which it found itself, utilized conscious processes at the point where new sensory–motor coordinations were being established, which later, as they became perfected, permitted the mental aspect of the process gradually to diminish until, in the limiting case, consciousness entirely disappeared and the coordination had become completely automatic" (Angell, 1936, p. 32).

With some caution, Angell extended this conception from the lives of individuals to evolutionary changes that suggest Lamarckian inheritance. He wrote "that instinctive and reflex acts, like those exclusively under the control of the autonomic system, may all have originally been acts of the voluntary type which, by some, biological means, got themselves deeply enough established to be handed down by heredity from parent to offspring" (Angell, 1936, p. 24). He saw the process of organic selection, later know as the Baldwin effect, as presenting a compromise between natural selection and the Lamarckian inheritance. He viewed evolution as a progressive process; regarding species differences in behavior and intelligence, he wrote that "there can be no question that these differences in behavior represent historic evolution of the more complex out of the simpler" (Angell, 1922, p. 112).

Angell was devoted to the application of evolutionary principles to animal behavior and to fostering improved methodology in comparative psychology. His views on behavior and evolution have aged well in some respects but poorly in others. He saw Darwin as making three main contributions to psychology: "(1) his doctrine of the evolution of instinct and the part played by intelligence in the process; (2) the evolution of mind from the lowest animal to the highest man; and (3) the expressions of emotion" (Angell, 1909, p. 154). He wrote (1909) of the role of female choice in sexual selection, the continuity of species, the value of studying animals in semi-natural habitats, and the importance of the study of survival value of behavior. Much less acceptable today is his view that "there is fairly definite evidence that extant human races differ appreciably in their native intelligence and those which are living most nearly in the state of nature which we believe to have characterized the early history of our own racial stock are, generally speaking, marked by apparently lower average intelligence and by relatively fewer intellects of high grade" (Angell, 1922, p. 115).

Angell anticipated the later European ethologists in the need for a comprehensive ethogram of an animal's naturally occurring behavior before interpretations of behavioral observations. He wrote that "no observation of animal behavior is likely to be trustworthy, unless based upon a wide and exact knowledge of the animal's usual habits of life" (Angell, 1922, p. 110). "Otherwise, one is exposed to the error of interpreting as a rational process a piece of behavior which may be partly or wholly instinctive, or which may have been acquired by wholly unknown means at some earlier period of the animal's life" (pp. 110–111).

Though often portrayed as a "school" of psychology, functionalism was rather amorphous and difficult to characterize in terms of a few fundamental defining traits such as those that characterize structuralism or behaviorism. Angell recognized this, writing of functionalism as "little more than a point of view, a program, an ambition" (1907, p. 61). Nevertheless, today's psychology resembles the functionalist approach more than any other of its time (see Owens & Wagner, 1992). Like the functionalist approach, today's psychology is broad and inclusive, rooted in biology, and both behavioral and cognitive.

STUDENTS, RESEARCH, AND PUBLICATIONS

Clearly, Angell made great contributions as a spokesperson for functionalism and as a university administrator. He was also a highly successful teacher He used a Socratic approach and reflected that "I really think I had a genuine flair for stimulating teaching" (Angell, 1936, p. 11). He listed, among others, 14 women and 25 men, including 5 APA presidents, who earned doctorates under his supervision. His students' dissertation topics were extraordinarily diverse, including sex differences in mental traits, animal behavior, the psychology of meaning, imagery, volition, hearing, social psychology, testing, memory, space perception, learning, and theory (Hunter, 1951). The lone theoretical dissertation was that of Carl Rahn, which dealt with the place of sensation in theory. Rahn put forth a devastating evaluation of Titchener's structural psychology, maintaining that the theory had to be modified to accommodate criticisms of the doctrine of elements and attributes.

Angell's place in history is not based on his research and theoretical output, however. These are, frankly, rather modest, though a few projects are worthy of some note. Angell's best-known study concerned the speed of reaction when the participants focus attention on a visual or auditory stimuli rather than the motor response required (Angell & Moore, 1896). Wundt believed that the motor set led to faster reaction times than sensory concentration. In Angell's study, three individuals—Angell, Moore, and an assistant—were tested. At the start of testing, the assistant was faster with a sensory set; the other two with motor. The authors interpreted this result as reflecting differential adjustments to different life contingencies in different individuals. With practice, the difference between sensory and motor concentration decreased, with motor being somewhat faster. Angell and Moore took this result to mean that different operations of attention are critical early in testing but that habit is more important later. Wundt had used highly practiced participants and obtained one result; Angell and Moore (along with James Mark Baldwin who found similar results) used participants of different backgrounds and experiences and thus produced results that were more variable, but more meaningful in everyday situations. We see the functionalist tradition focused on individual differences and relationships to real-world problems of adjustment as opposed to the abstract approach of its predecessors.

In a similar vein, Angell and his associates studied some of the factors affecting psychophysiological measures, such as respiration and cardiac function (Angell & McLennan, 1896; Angell & Thompson, 1899). Whereas Wundt had proposed that respiration and pupillary responses showed opposite changes when subjects experience pleasure versus pain, Angell and his associates linked these differences to attention. They suggested that conscious processes function smoothly when adjustment to environmental situations is normal, but become dysfunctional with disturbance and stress.

Angell, who was deaf in one ear as a result of childhood scarlet fever, became interested in monaural localization of sounds (Angell, 1903b; Angell & Fite, 1901). He studied monaural localization in five individuals with similar difficulties and some normal subjects with one ear rendered temporarily nonfunctional. Although the participants had difficulty localizing pure tones, accuracy improved greatly as the stimuli took on greater complexity. Monaural localization improved greatly with practice, so that the monaural deaf participants responded more accurately in proportion to the duration of their deafness.

Two of Angell's other articles merit some mention. The issue of imageless thought was prominent in the psychology of the time stemming from the assertions of Oswald Külpe and the Würzburg school. According to this doctrine, and contrary to Wundt, thought need not have a specific sensation, image, or feeling associated with it. This time, Angell (1911) sided with Wundt and wrote a strong criticism of the imageless thought position. Angell (1913) also wrote in opposition to certain aspects of behaviorist as that approach was being developed by his former student, John B. Watson. In particular, Angell defended the study of conscious process and the use of introspection, noting that we should "refine it, check it, train it, but do not throw away a good tool until you certainly have a better in hand" (1913, pp. 269–270). Angell believed that behavioristic techniques were inadequate to deal with the subtleties of the mind's operation. He wrote, anticipating later criticisms of behaviorism from cognitive psychologists, that

the mind is provided with so many and so flexible shunt systems, it translates from one material into another so quickly, that it promises, for a long time to come, to baffle the skill of the experimental "behaviorist" at many points. It remains for him then to urge the trivial and insignificant character of differences so elusive, and perhaps he is right. But right or wrong, there are at present innumerable instances . . . where objective methods are at present only competent to give rough surface facts. (p. 264)

Angell was specifically concerned with instances in which there were delays between the appearance of the stimulus and the response. He believed that "we have not at present any technique for ascertaining the train of neural units intermediate between a specific sensorial stimulation and a specific delayed response. The gap we must bridge with information gleaned from essentially introspective sources or else leave it open" (1913, p. 266). He predicted that behaviorism will long be with psychology even if it "becomes an esoteric scientific cult" (p. 269) and concluded that we should "forego the excesses of youth" (p. 270).

ADMINISTRATIVE ACCOMPLISHMENTS

Angell was well connected and was able to use his friends and positions to facilitate the programs in which he believed. Haraway (1989) summarized his multiple connections: "Angell paradigmatically represented the elaborate interconnections of university, industry, philanthropy, and science policy in the development of material structures and ideologies of scientific management of society" (p. 67). Some social critics may regard this as dangerous; to those seeking an administrator to develop a university or agency, however, it sounds like music to their ears.

Angell played an important role in National Research Council's planning and raising funds for a new building for the National Academy of Sciences. In his brief, 1-year tenure as president of the Carnegie Corporation, he effected substantive changes (Lagemann, 1989). He modernized the administration of the corporation and concentrated power in the president's office. He opposed government control of research organization and support, favored a wider dissemination of scientific research, and sought a balance of support for different scientific fields. Angell, as might be expected, was especially sympathetic to the social and behavioral sciences. Under his leadership the corporation supported the National Bureau of Economic Research. He left after one year, however; in addition to the attraction of the Yale presidency, Angell found the strained personal relationships at the corporation to render it a difficult place to work and he was happy to leave.

With more than 80 distinguished nominees, the Yale University search that produced only the second president who was not a Yale man was controversial. Competing factions blocked every candidate and new nominations were called for. Finally, Angell emerged as a compromise candidate (Pierson, 1955), and although he had declined several other university presidencies, he accepted this one. He had become a serious Midwesterner with a scientific outlook when he arrived in New Haven and entered an environment of gentlemanly conservatism. There he found a university that was understaffed, with a half-million dollar deficit, an inbred and independent undergraduate faculty, and low morale.

At Yale, Angell's first 10 years were regarded by one author as "the most eventful ten years' empery that any Yale President has ever enjoyed" (Mack, 1931, p. 38). His most obvious accomplishment was in the improvement of the physical nature of the campus. During his tenure, "the entire face of Yale was changed" (Holden, 1968, p. 112). "Gone were the battered classrooms, makeshift offices, and shabby rooming houses which thousands of greying graduates still mistily remembered" (Pierson, 1955, pp. 505–506). In their place were the structures that provide much of the atmosphere of Yale today: the Sterling Chemistry Laboratory, the Sterling Memorial Library, the Sterling Law Buildings, the Payne Whitney Gymnasium, and the Institute of Human Relations, among others.

Angell introduced a system of eight undergraduate colleges, modeled on the British universities, and built quadrangles for each of them. He raised academic standards, limited class size, and increased admissions requirements. "He wished to see a harder working, more intellectual student body" (Holden, 1968, p. 110). "He did not agree that a college should be a glorified country club, open to any sons of the well-to-do who could pass the most infantile tests" (Pierson, 1955, p. 514). This came as a shock to some students and alumni schooled in a more gentlemanly Yale ethic. Angell and his colleagues improved academic programs in the sciences, social sciences, and humanities and developed professional schools as well. He started the School of Nursing, which soon became one of the most respected in the country.

During his tenure, Angell quadrupled Yale's endowment. He was credited with "the first large-scale financial drive launched by any educational institution . . . during this successful $20,000,000 campaign of 1926–27, Angell called for a 'finer, not bigger Yale.' " (Holden, 1968, p. 111). He was able to raise faculty salaries and set up new retirement and group insurance programs for staff. Also improved were the athletic facilities for students.

Of special interest here is Angell's impact on psychology at Yale. During 1928–1929 he separated psychology from the Department of Philosophy. In 1929, Yale hosted the first North American meeting of the International Congress of Psychology, one of the most notable of such meetings. By the 1930s, Yale's had become one of the finest psychology departments in the world, boasting such names as Robert Yerkes (chap. 7, *Pioneers II*), Clark Hull (chap. 14, *Pioneers I*), Arnold Gesell, and a cadre of graduate students who would become leaders in the field. Several, especially Angell and Yerkes, shared a vision of a society improved through management according to principles derived from

improved behavioral sciences. During Angell's presidency important administrative units were developed, particularly the Institute of Psychology in 1924,
which was transformed into the Institute of Human Relations in 1929. Angell
and Yerkes appear to have created the plan for the former jointly before Yerkes
moved to New Haven, as noted in a letter from Yerkes (1922) to Angell:

> Why not a school of psychology at Yale after the manner of the specialized type of
> combined teaching and research institution we have discussed several times. New
> England surely deserves one good center for psychology?

Angell and Yerkes worked on several versions of a plan involving different aspects of psychological research until they finally secured funding from the Laura
Spelman Rockefeller Memorial, whose president was Beardsley Ruml, who had
studied at the University of Chicago when Angell was there, had been associated
with Yerkes and Angell during World War I, and had been Angell's assistant at
the Carnegie Corporation. Anthropologist Clark Wissler and psychologists Raymond Dodge and Roswell Angier were Yerkes's initial associates at the institute. Foundation support brought $2 million for a building, an annual budget of
$150,000, and 21 faculty members. It was also with Angell's support that
Yerkes secured foundation funding for the Yale Laboratories of Primate Biology
in Orange Park, Florida. It became the largest facility for research on chimpan-
zees and other apes. Angell also helped to develop the Child Development
Clinic under Gesell.

ANGELL, THE MAN

It is in Angell's career as an administrator that we catch glimpses of Angell as a
man rather than as a rather disembodied psychologist. Admittedly, the portrait
that emerges is somewhat idealistic. A man as forceful as Angell must have of-
fended some who would present a different picture of him but, although they
may exist, thus far I have been unable to locate such descriptions. An interesting
question is whether the traits that are described were present during the early
part of Angell's career and affected his psychological work or whether they developed only in his later years with administrative experience. Further exploration in archival sources will be required to approach an answer to this question.

Angell was less impressive in appearance than in accomplishment. *Time*
magazine described him as "a chipper, bouncy little man, more distinguished
than handsome ('Apparently Yale doesn't choose its presidents for pulchritude,'
he said)" (Yale-Builder, 1949). One undergraduate called him a "grave-eyed
gentleman" (Mack, 1931, p. 38) and noted that "in dress he is ultra-conservative.
For everyday he likes semi-soft collars, dark suits, dark ties. For more formal
occasions he has an ancient black cutaway" (p. 45).

Descriptions of Angell's general demeanor reveal some complexity, indeed contradiction. His social skills reflected both his buoyancy and shyness. At the same time that he was distinguished and grave eyed, he also was of sunny disposition. "At Chicago, his nickname had been 'Sunny Jim' " (Pierson, 1955, p. 20). He was both shy and at ease in different situations. Angell (1936) himself lamented the lack of a "more aggressive self-confidence" (p. 10). Some quotations help fill out general impressions of Angell:

A man of the widest knowledge, Angell's sympathies and perceptions were wider still. Simple, unassuming, reticent even to the point of shyness, there lurked behind his quizzical grey eyes the quickest of intelligences and a spirit irrepressibly resilient and alive. His was a marvelous buoyancy and good humor. Kindly to everyone, cheerful under crushing burdens, sparkling on the most solemn occasions, he was inevitably the life of any party, and the cynosure in gatherings of statesmen. (Pierson, 1955, p. 510)

His buoyant courage, genial friendliness and expansive gaiety not untouched with satire brought good cheer as well as wisdom to every gathering he entered, whether official or informal. . . . He brought to New Haven and to Yale a wit, an energy, and a keep searching intelligence that profited both town and gown in their association. ("James Rowland Angell," 1949, pp. 5, 6)

Despite his heritage, Angell was perceived as a Midwesterner who lacked in some of the graces possessed by his predecessors, a view that he shared of himself (Angell, 1936).

From the Midwest, perhaps, come his democratic instincts, his modesty, his salty good-humor and impatience with pomp and circumstance. . . . Middlewestern also is his capacity for meeting people on their own ground and putting them immediately at their ease.*

Middlewestern above all is his humor, dry and crackling like a ship's wireless, and yet, withal gusty, like a wind blowing the pages of a book. He has an inexhaustible fund of stories and delights in the exchange of sharp and personal repartee, in which he never takes offense and practically always gets the last word. . . . The most engaging aspect of his humor is that he does not hesitate to apply it to himself. (Mack, 1931, pp. 40–41)

Basically a shy man, Angell nevertheless enjoyed his association with alumni. (Holden, 1968, p. 117)

Like his colleague Yerkes, Angell often held people at arm's length; "his subordinates held him in high admiration. But even his Provosts and Deans, who served with him through good times and bad, never felt personally close" (Pierson, 1955, p. 511). "An indication of the loneliness of his office rather than any want of humanity on his part is the fact that President Angell will next year reach retirement age (68) without having acquired a nickname at Yale. . . . At his Hillhouse Street home he smokes, drinks, and entertains sparingly" ("President at Penult," 1936, p. 43). Nevertheless, this shy man could be the life of the party; "harassed hostesses ... know that in a strained moment with an ill-assorted group it is only necessary to fetch in the President to make the party a howling success" (Mack, 1931, p. 41).

Where Angell shone brighter than in any other venue was on the speaker's platform; Mack (1931) called him "the most fluent of Anglo Saxons" (p. 44). Again, some quotations can provide richness:

> He loves to speak, or at least appears to, and is never so much at home as when discoursing informally at banquets and giving the toast-masters a drubbing on their own ground. With speeches of a more serious nature he is obviously less at ease, particularly with sermons, which he dreads and about which he has a quite misplaced inferiority complex. (Mack, 1931, pp. 44–45)

> Particularly was he felicitous in after-dinner speaking, when there would issue from under his thin, carroty thatch such eloquence, and out of the side of his mouth such humorous commentary, that his hearers sat spellbound. His wit fairly crackled. (Pierson, 1955, pp. 510–511)

> He speaks in paragraphs instead of sentences, and when he is especially excited, as in the first moments of an after-dinner address, he talks out of the side of his mouth. (Mack, 1931, p. 45)

Angell was a business-like and efficient administrator, who preferred to work in policy formulation and leave its execution to subordinates. Furthermore,

> His own temperament and methods of work, he believed, had developed in the direction of persuasion rather than dictation. His teaching had been Socratic rather than didactic. People told him he had a judicial type of mind. In any case he was inclined to see all sides of an issue. Never, if he could help it, would he make a snap judgment, for he found himself temperamentally uneasy unless he could get all the information there was before making a move. (Pierson, 1955, p. 509)

He was also skilled in resolving disputes among faculty members. For example, in 1932, when Yerkes dismissed Otto L. Tinklepaugh from the Yale Laboratories of Primate Biology for alleged "offenses," several powerful faculty members, including John L. Fulton, Chair of the Department of Physiology, came to Tinklepaugh's defense and tried to get him a fellowship in another academic unit at Yale. Yerkes was so outraged at this development that he tendered his resignation as director of the laboratories. Angell acted with skill to effect a compromise acceptable to all.

Angell was a man of strong moral values, who believed in acting on them; he was portrayed as "a highly articulate moral spokesman" ("President at Penult," 1936, p. 43) who possessed "a scrupulous sense of honesty" (Mack, 1931, p. 42). Near the top of his value system were ideals concerning education in general and the university in particular; he was a true academic. Angell was especially vigorous in his defense of academic freedom against all comers, religious, business, and governmental. It is likely, however, that ambitions for education generally were mixed with personal ambition. According to Pierson (1955), "His ideals had been intellectual but never, in his own words, 'purely intellectualistic' " (p. 517). Although he was a strong supporter of athletic programs, "he viewed large gate receipts as making football too commercial" (Holden, 1968, p. 115).

Angell's politics appear to have been pragmatic. Around 1933 he supported Franklin D. Roosevelt's New Deal politics. By 1936, however, he had become far more conservative (Veysey, 1974). This move to the right stemmed from a concern that increased taxation could hurt the university. "Angell identified four forms of taxation which, if long continued, could only have ruinous effects for the country's most venerable educational foundations, hence also for some of its highest values. These were excessive income taxes, inheritance taxes, threatened taxes on philanthropic giving, and the widespread effort to tax the universities' physical properties" (Pierson, 1955, p. 530). As *Time* magazine put it, "who soaks the rich, soaks Yale and him" ("President at Penult," 1936, p. 43).

Accounts of Angell's behavior on the streets of New Haven contradict the impression of a serene and dignified man. Mack (1931) described him as:

The most dangerous man to walk with in the world. The latter title arises from his ineradicable habit of jay-walking across traffic-riddled streets. Stop-lights mean nothing to him . . . With the same reckless assurance and incredible skill, he drives his car. . . . A car goes by so fast that all you can see of its driver is a delighted smile and a dark hat pulled well down over they eyes, you can make on it's the President of your alma mater. (p. 44)

The former Michigan shortstop and band member retained interests in both amateur athletics and music in maturity:

Outside of his office, the President is an ardent golfer. . . . His other avocations include music, the study of social conditions, and Yale athletics. He attends practically all the major athletic events, watches with a discerning eye, and is as well acquainted with the personalities of the various teams as anyone.

Despite his training in a university band [*sic*], he has an excellent ear and can whistle you whole sonatas outright. The story goes that a party of New Havenites were out in a canoe on a lake in the Adirondacks one night, when somebody somewhere out in the darkness began to whistle the last movement of the Cesar Franck symphony. Suddenly another whistle, clearer and truer, broke in from the gloom away down the lake, and while the uncertain gentleman who had started it sat gasping in admiration, the unknown whistler finished the movement without a tremor and paddled away in the shadows. It was President Angell of Yale. (Mack, 1931, p. 46)

CONCLUSION

In this chapter, I have tried to summarize the basic facts of the life of Angell, his work in psychology, his functionalism, and his accomplishments as a university president. In the latter role, Angell had a particularly strong impact on Yale psychology and, because psychology at Yale was so powerful in the 1930s, an influence on psychology throughout the world. Above all, I have tried to flesh out something of the character of this man, a man who appears to be such a disembodied cardboard figure in most textbooks in the history psychology. Regrettably, this portrait is based primarily on the last phase of his life, but it provides some sense of the man, his personality, his values, and his interests.

REFERENCES

Angell, J. R. (1903a). The relations of structural and functional psychology to philosophy. *Philosophical Review, 12*, 243–271.

Angell, J. R. (1903b). A preliminary study of the significance of partial tones in the localization of sound. *Psychological Review, 10*, 1–14.

Angell, J. R. (1905). Recent scientific contributions to social welfare: Psychology. *The Chautauquan, 50*, 453–459.

Angell, J. R. (1907). The province of functional psychology. *Psychological Review, 14*, 61–91.

Angell, J. R. (1908). *Psychology: An introductory study of the structure and function of human consciousness* (4th ed.). New York: Holt.

Angell, J. R. (1909). The influence of Darwin on psychology. *Psychological Review, 16*, 152–169.

Angell, J. R. (1910). *Chapters from modern psychology*. New York: Longmans, Green.

Angell, J. R. (1911). Imageless thought. *Psychological Review, 18*, 295–323.

Angell, J. R. (1913). Behavior as a category of psychology. *Psychological Review, 20*, 255–270.

Angell, J. R. (1922). The evolution of intelligence. In R. S. Lull, H. B. Ferris, G. H. Parker, J. R. Angell, A. G. Keller, & E. G. Conklin (Eds.), *The evolution of man: A series of lectures delivered before the Yale chapter of the Sigma Xi during the academic year 1921–1922* (pp. 103–125). New Haven, CT: Yale University Press.

Angell, J. R. (1936). James Rowland Angell. In C. Murchison (Ed.), *A history of psychology in autobiography* (Vol. 3, pp. 1–38). Worcester, MA: Clark University Press.

Angell, J. R., & Fite, W. (1901). Contributions from the psychological laboratory of the University of Chicago: Further observations on the monaural localization of sound. *Psychological Review, 8*, 449–458.

Angell, J. R., & McLennan, S. F. (1896). Studies from the psychological laboratory of the University of Chicago. III. The organic effects of agreeable and disagreeable stimuli. *Psychological Review, 3*, 371–377.

Angell, J. R., & Moore, A. W. (1896). Studies from the psychological laboratory of the University of Chicago. I. Reaction-time: A study in attention and habit *Psychological Review, 3*, 245–258.

Angell, J. R., & Thompson, H. B. (1899). A study of the relations between certain organic processes and consciousness. *Psychological Review, 6,* 32–69.

Dewey, J. (1896). The reflex-arc concept in psychology. *Psychological Review, 3,* 357–370.

Haraway, D. (1989). *Primate visions: Gender, race, and nature in the world of modern science.* New York: Routledge.

Holden, R. A. (1968). *Profiles and portraits of Yale University presidents.* Freeport, ME: Bond Wheelwright.

Hunter, W. S. (1949). James Rowland Angell, 1869–1949. *American Journal of Psychology, 62,* 439–450.

Hunter, W. S. (1951). James Rowland Angell 1869–1949. *Biographical memoirs of the National Academy of Sciences of the United States of America* (pp. 191–208). Washington, DC: National Academy of Sciences.

James Rowland Angell, fourteenth president of Yale, died at his home, 155 Blake Road, Hamden, Connecticut, on March 4th. (1949, April). *Yale Alumni Magazine,* 4–6.

Lagemann, E. C. (1989). *The politics of knowledge: The Carnegie Corporation, philanthropy, and public policy.* Middletown, CT: Wesleyan University Press.

Mack, M. (1931, November). Portraits from a family album 1. James Rowland Angell. *Yale Literary Magazine,* 38–46.

Miles, W. (1949). James Rowland Angell, 1869–1949, psychologist-educator. *Science, 110,* 1–4.

Morawski, J. G. (1986). Organizing knowledge and behavior at Yale's Institute of Human Relations. *Isis, 77,* 219–242.

Owens, D. A., & Wagner, M. (1992). *Progress in modern psychology: The legacy of American functionalism.* Westport, CT: Praeger.

Pierson, G. W. (1955). *Yale: The University College 1921–1937.* New Haven, CT: Yale University Press.

President at penult. (1936, June 15). *Time, 27,* 41–44.

Rucker, D. (1969). *The Chicago pragmatists.* Minneapolis, MN: University of Minnesota Press.

Titchener, E. B. (1898). Postulates of a structural psychology. *Philosophical Review, 7,* 449–465.

Veysey, L. (1974). Angell, James Rowland (May 8, 1869–Mar. 4, 1949). In J. A. Garraty & E. T. James (Eds.), *Dictionary of American biography suppl. 4. 1946–1950* (pp. 19–23). New York: Scribner's.

Yale-builder. (1949, March 14). *Time, 53,* 51–52.

Yerkes, R. M. (1922, June 11). [Letter to J. R. Angell]. R. M. Yerkes Papers, Yale University Library, New Haven, CT.

Chapter 5

Margaret Floy Washburn: A Quest for the Harmonies in the Context of a Rigorous Scientific Framework

Wayne Viney and Laura Burlingame-Lee
Colorado State University

At the outset of the 21st century there are widespread concerns about the diversity and disunity of psychology. Such concerns have been the subject of extensive discussion in the literature (e.g., see Kimble, 1984, 2000; Staats, 1989; Viney, 1996, 1998; Wertheimer, 1988) and are manifested in the more than 50 divisions of the American Psychological Association and the formation of the American Psychological Society. Contemporary concerns are by no means unique and, in fact, can be seen in the work of some of the early pioneers in psychology. Margaret Floy Washburn was one such pioneer who was visible among other things for her efforts to find the harmonies in some of the early schools of psychology. This chapter seeks to provide an overview of the highlights of Washburn's life and work and to focus on one of her neglected contributions—the attempt to find workable harmonies in the various approaches to the new discipline of psychology.

FIRST YEARS AND EDUCATION

Margaret Floy Washburn, the only child of Elizabeth Floy Davis and Francis Washburn, was born in New York City July 25, 1871. The Washburns lived in financial privilege having inherited property and money from Michael Floy, the maternal grandfather of Elizabeth Floy Davis. Washburn expressed the deepest gratitude for the financial resources that permitted her to be a full-time student without the worry and distraction associated with financial pressures. Furthermore, throughout her professional education and her early career, she enjoyed the encouragement and emotional support of her parents. In her autobiography, Washburn celebrated the advantages of being an only child. Hers was not a noisy and competitive world, but a world marked by undisturbed hours of contemplation and leisure and early feelings of confidence. She noted that her intellectual life began on her fifth birthday: "I remember a few moments when I was walking in the garden; I felt that I had now reached an age of some importance, and the thought was agreeable" (Washburn, 1930, p. 334). She noted that she did not start school until she was 7, but by that time had already learned to read and write. She was nurtured with the best of children's literature and by the age of 12 had already read all of the novels of Dickens and Sir Walter Scott's Waverley novels.

Washburn's first education was in a private school that afforded excellent grounding in French, German, arithmetic, and music. This rich early experience was interrupted with a move to Walden, New York, where Francis Washburn took a position as an Episcopalian parish pastor. The 2 years of residence in Walden were followed by a more lengthy parish appointment in Kingston, New York. At age 12, Washburn entered the Ulster Academy, a public high school in Kingston. She had few positive memories of her high school experiences, which were marked by "terrifying formalities," a strong emphasis on rote memory of topics such as the Constitution of the United States, and extensive examinations in Latin. The pedagogical approach appeared to focus not so much on critical reflection and academic substance, but on preparation for the Regents' examinations. Washburn, however, made the best of a bad situation. She had a good library at home and another at the Ulster Academy and thus filled her spare hours with voracious reading and rereading of the classic works from the pens of such authors as Chaucer, Dante, Dickens, Thackeray, and James Fenimore Cooper. She noted that she read from "a wide range of other literature including *Gulliver's Travels*, Fox's [*sic*] Book of Martyrs, and what [she] could make out of the *Canterbury Tales*" (Washburn, 1930, p. 336).

In 1886 at the age of 15, Washburn entered the preparatory class at Vassar. The curriculum included no majors, but focused instead on a classic liberal arts education. She spoke with fondness of her classes in biology, chemistry, English, and French and her growing attachment to philosophy and poetry. Her commencement oration traced the stoic elements in Matthew Arnold's poetry. She was impressed by a group of young women whose religious radicalism had distressed the college president. These women must have been influential because she pointed out that she also experienced the intellectual freedom and expansion that resulted when she was no longer in the grip of religious orthodoxy.

By her senior year, Washburn was captivated by science and philosophy, and she found these to be combined in a unique way in the new experimental psychology. Her undergraduate course in psychology was taught by the college president, and typical for that day, the focus was on the "Scottish realism" of Thomas Reid. She recalled that

Dr. Taylor (whom, by the way, we regarded with great affection) had no idea of presenting metaphysical systems to us impartially: he wished to preserve our religious convictions by saving us from materialism in the one direction and pantheistic idealism in the other. This vigorous special pleading was more stimulating than the most conscientiously impartial presentation of opposing views could have been. (Washburn, 1930, p. 338)

Following her graduation in 1891, Washburn hoped to study with James McKeen Cattell, who had just arrived at Columbia University following 4 years of work at the University of Pennsylvania, where he had established one of the first psychology laboratories in the United States. Once again, Washburn was to feel the enormous financial and emotional support of her parents, who provided a house for her in New York while she pursued advanced studies. Unfortunately, Columbia University, like so many others, had not yet accepted a woman for graduate studies so Washburn was admitted only as a "hearer." Nevertheless, Cattell was deeply impressed with the knowledge she had acquired in her brief exposure to psychology, and from the beginning she was treated, at least by the psychology faculty, on a completely equal footing with the men. It was clear, however, that Washburn would be hampered in her pursuit of a career because of the restrictive policies of the university regarding women. Accordingly, Cattell encouraged her to apply for admission and for financial support from the Sage School of Philosophy at Cornell University.

Washburn's application was successful and in the fall of 1892 she joined E. B. Titchener (chap. 7, *Pioneers I*), who had just arrived at Cornell following the completion of his doctorate degree with Wilhelm Wundt (chap. 3, *Pioneers III*) at Leipzig. Washburn's experiences with Titchener contrast sharply with those of students who were to follow her. Titchener was a mere 25 years of age; this was his first faculty position and Washburn was his first student. She commented that he didn't quite know what to do with her. He had not yet developed the confidence and the talent for organization for which he was later so well remembered.

Appointments with Titchener to discuss laboratory work were often devoted partially to stories of his graduate experiences. An anecdote illustrates the entirely human and humorous side of their relationship. Washburn recalled that "he once asked me to look over some proof; finding a sentence whose meaning was inverted, I asked, 'Didn't you mean' so and so? 'Of course I did, ass that I am!' was the hearty response, a response that I fancy would have come far less heartily a few years later" (Washburn, 1930, p. 340).

Washburn completed her doctorate degree under Titchener's direction in June 1894. Her dissertation on the influence of visual imagery on space and tactile perception was published in German in Wundt's journal *Philosophische Studien* (Washburn, 1895). Washburn was the first woman to receive a doctorate in psychology in the United States and she expressed strong appreciation for the breadth and quality of her experiences at Cornell. In addition to her work with Titchener, she had a minor in philosophy and ethics. She especially enjoyed her studies in Greek and medieval philosophy and her work on philosophers such as Leibniz (chap. 1, this volume), Hume, and Kant. Her interests in philosophical and ethical issues surfaced in much of her subsequent work in psychology. Indeed, one of her earliest publications was a translation of Wundt's *Ethical Systems* (Wundt, 1897).

EARLY SYSTEMATIC COMMITMENTS AND DOUBTS

Following her completion of the doctorate degree at Cornell, Washburn accepted a position at Wells College as chair of Psychology, Philosophy, Ethics, and Logic. She remained at Wells for 6 years. Though she started her work at Wells with a salary of $300 per year, she had achieved the maximum allowable salary for women, $700, by the end of her sixth year. Despite the demands associated with her new instructional activities, Washburn published several articles during her early years at Wells. This period also witnessed the beginnings of serious critical thought about various schools of psychology and her quest for a rigorous systematic psychology adequate to the plurality of psychological phenomena.

In her early years at Wells College, Washburn accepted the Titchenerian vision of a structural psychology that attempts to discover and classify the irreducible elements of conscious states, but she had nagging doubts about Titchener's introspective methods. Furthermore, questions gradually surfaced about whether there are really irreducible elements of consciousness. In her autobiography she called attention to her inability to "forget James's [chap. 2, *Pioneers I*] conception of consciousness as a stream and the impossibility that it should be at once a stream and a mosaic" (Washburn, 1930, p. 343). Like Titchener and James, Washburn was too much of an empiricist to reject consciousness and the "mental world" as legitimate topical areas. Even if consciousness could not be reduced to static and pure elements, it was for Washburn as real as anything else and a legitimate topic for scientific investigation. Although Washburn accepted consciousness and the mental world, she could not accept Cartesian interactionism. At the same time, however, she was suspicious of radical monistic philosophies with their emphasis on the idea that all things ultimately reduce to one thing. She found a workable middle ground in epiphenomenalism, a mind–body position that enfranchises both the mental and the physical worlds, but assumes that causal forces always reside in the chain of physical and neural events that underlie consciousness. Although she believed that causality resides only in physical events, she insisted that conscious states or processes provide valuable clues regarding the nature of the underlying physical processes. These early ideas about the importance of both the mental and the physical worlds would subsequently undergo elaboration and refinement and serve as part of the foundation for Washburn's mature systematic orientation. In the meantime, she longed for a new academic challenge and made a decision to study for a year at Harvard.

The plans for study at Harvard were interrupted, however, when Washburn received an invitation to return to Cornell as a warden of Sage College at a salary more than double what she was receiving at Wells. The offer at Cornell included the provision that there would be ample time for the pursuit of scholarly research. The new position at Cornell lasted only 2 years, but it was a pivotal period that witnessed several important developments that played major roles in Washburn's later career. For the first time, she taught new courses in animal psychology and in social psychology. Her instructional work in these areas came in parallel with growing doubts about the adequacy of Titchener's structuralism and a new interest in the importance of behavior and underlying motor processes. She also discovered during this period that she did not enjoy the practical tasks of a warden who must deal with the complicated problems and the behavior of others.

It was the turn of the century and American functionalism, influenced by the work of James (chap. 2, *Pioneers I*), John Dewey (chap. 4, *Pioneers II*), and James Rowland Angell (chap. 4, this volume) was attracting widespread attention. Although Washburn has sometimes been recognized for her contributions to American functionalism (Abel, 1927) and although there were parts of this loosely organized school that she accepted and welcomed, she was largely critical. She claimed that through a "congenital disability," she could not read Dewey. "And James, despite the enduring influence of his psychology, as a philosopher inspired [her] with distrust" (Washburn, 1930, p. 345). Her distrust was based on her interpretation of pragmatism as a philosophy that equated the truth of ideas with their capacity to do real work in the world. She argued that "the doctrine that ideas are true in proportion as they 'work' may too readily be used to mean that they are true in proportion as they are comfortable" (p. 345). Such an interpretation of James's pragmatism was common in the early 20th century, although James insisted that it was not an accurate interpretation (see James, 1909, p. 111; Viney, 2001, p. 6). Washburn believed that functionalism was largely descriptive rather than explanatory and that in some of its expressions it appeared to embrace mind–body interactionism, a position Washburn found untenable.

Following her 2 years as warden of Sage College at Cornell, Washburn was eager for a change and happily accepted an offer to move to the University of Cincinnati as an assistant professor. Although she was treated on an equal footing with men at Cincinnati, she was far from her Eastern roots, so in 1903 after only 1 year at Cincinnati, she joyfully accepted a position as associate professor at Vassar College. She would remain at Vassar until her retirement in 1937. The 34 years at Vassar would witness an outpouring of the work and the professional service for which she is so well remembered today.

Washburn's most visible scholarly work as a scientist lay in her pioneering efforts in comparative psychology, her motor theory of consciousness, and the steady stream of laboratory studies published with her students during the Vassar years. Her work in comparative psychology was set forth primarily in her book *The Animal Mind*, first published in 1908. Extensively revised and updated editions of this book appeared in 1917, 1926, and 1936. Washburn's motor theory of consciousness was set forth in numerous journal articles and in her classic book *Movement and Mental Imagery*, published in 1916. Her experimental studies—and her quest for the harmonies in the various schools of psychology—are reported in her many scholarly articles. The materials that follow explore Washburn's contributions in each of these areas.

COMPARATIVE PSYCHOLOGY

In her autobiography, Washburn (1930) referred to her "morbidly intense love of animals" (p. 347). One of her earliest experiments was in collaboration with Madison Bentley on color vision in a brook fish. She noted, "The chub learned with great speed, in spite of lacking a cortex; it discriminated both light and dark red from green" (p. 347). Following the work with Bentley, Washburn engaged in an extensive search of the literature on animal behavior that ultimately culminated in the first edition of *The Animal Mind*. In this book, she revisited the early modern tensions between the mechanistic approach to animals encountered in the works of Descartes and the more celebratory approach encountered in Montaigne's classic work *Apology for Raimond Sebond*. She sensitized her readers to the fact that the modern era (from about 1600) was ushered in on radically different interpretations of animal behavior. This heavily referenced book also reflected her extensive grasp of English, French, and German sources.

The *Animal Mind* afforded an overview of early experimental studies on such topics as: structural and functional dimensions of animal sensory systems, memory, inhibition of instincts, attention, discrimination, and adaptation. Throughout the book, Washburn the philosopher was in constant dialogue with Washburn the experimental psychologist. She discussed limitations and strengths of various methods of studying animals, the grounds for making inferences about animal consciousness, and the advantages and disadvantages of mechanistic approaches that deny animal consciousness altogether versus her approach, which cautiously includes consciousness as a real component of animal life. Washburn quarreled with the extreme position that there is no such thing as animal consciousness or, if there is, that we have no way of gaining access to it. She noted that if that is the case, "we must also admit that human psychology is impossible. Our acquaintance with the mind of animals rests upon the same basis as our acquaintance with the mind of our fellow [human-beings]" (Washburn, 1908, p. 23). She was deeply committed to the belief that inference on the basis of probability is central to all the sciences and that the danger of "a purely physical explanation of animal behavior is that the facts shall be unduly simplified to fit the theory" (p. 18). She also recognized the opposite problem, that facts are distorted by those who attribute too much to animal consciousness. She believed that there is a middle ground that recognizes mental processes as real, but that such recognition can be disciplined by a rigorous methodology that is conservative with respect to the inferences that are drawn.

The *Animal Mind* remains a worthwhile and provocative study today for all who are interested in the evolution of higher cognitive processes. As an example, Washburn led her readers through an elaborate defense of the idea that the development of mental imagery is tied to the gradual emergence of distance receptors. The skin senses are undoubtedly the oldest of the senses, and any stimulus in direct contact with the skin calls for a near instant response because the stimulus may be immediately harmful or beneficial. In either case, delay is a luxury that could prove damaging or even lethal. The evolution of distance receptors, however, provides a margin of safety and a time for evaluation. A dangerous situation is not quite so immediate or imminent and a beneficial situation is not immediately present for mere opportunistic acquisition. Now mental imagery, the primitive cognitive substrate for anticipation, plans, strategies, and foreseeing for the future enters the equation. An immediate motor response is no longer necessary or even desirable, and memory images may now be the key to adaptation and survival. As an aside, Washburn would have found it no accident that most of the metaphors for intelligence are drawn from vision and audition. We "see through," develop "insight," have "real vision," or truly "hear." Although distance receptors may negate the need for an immediate overt motor response, Washburn believed that incipient movement systems nevertheless remain in the animal that is appraising a distant sight, sound, or smell. Thus, the distance receptors, though they provide a basis and necessity for delayed reactions, are no more divorced from the motor system than their more primitive tactile cousins. Motor responses are apt to be overt and immediate where contact receptors are concerned, but in Washburn's view, underlying incipient motor movements are necessary companions in all mental imagery and in all forms of delayed reaction situations.

THE MOTOR THEORY OF CONSCIOUSNESS

In the introduction to *Movement and Mental Imagery*, Washburn (1916) declared that "Movement is the ultimate fact of physical science" (p. xi). Whether the movement be of solar objects, fundamental particles, electrons, or the trajectories of missiles, the goal of science is to capture the direction and velocity of movement in mathematical equations. Psychology, on the other hand, as we encounter it at the individual commonsense level consists of a world of such things as colors, sounds, odors, feelings, and attitudes. Such psychological phenomena appear far removed from the world of everyday physical science, and yet there are clearly identifiable airborne waves or vibrations that result in the smell of kerosene and another set of physical vibrations that make us see red. Neither of these, of course, is experienced as a set of physical vibrations.

Washburn expressed a certain sympathy for those behavioral psychologies that attempt to ape the physical sciences and thus restrict their investigations to the study of movement alone. She found considerable value in such an approach but argued that it would result in an incomplete psychology that ignores what we all encounter in daily life, namely that there is an "inner aspect" of behavior. This inner aspect is, of course, exactly what is investigated by introspection, a method rejected by the behaviorists. Washburn, however, believed that information about the inner aspect of behavior may provide clues about the more available and observable physiological, neurological, and social dimensions of behavior. For example, afterimages or two-point thresholds are assessed only through introspective verbal reports. Such reports, in the case of two-point thresholds, provide clues about the distribution of receptors in a given location. In the case of afterimages, clues are provided about the nature of residual neurological activity following the withdrawal of a strong stimulus. Thus, Washburn believed that the neglect of the mental world, accessed via introspection, could result in the loss of a valuable source of information about the workings of the machinery of the body.

Washburn identified another loss associated with the neglect of conscious processes. She called attention to Locke's distinction between primary qualities and secondary qualities of experience. Primary qualities refer to attributes of matter such as bulk, figure, density, and number, whereas secondary qualities refer to the "sensation qualities" of consciousness such as color, odor, tastes, and tones. The nervous system is so constituted that it cannot respond one to one to the extremely rapid movements of particles or waves, so such movements are translated and experienced in radically different forms such as heat, high pitch or the color green. Heat is not experienced as a machine-gun-like set of vibrations, but is rather experienced as a unique psychological quality. Our psychological worlds are not experienced as mute, colorless, tasteless, odorless vibrations devoid of affect and feeling. Yet, on the physical side such vibrations are the causal stuff behind the world of experience. To neglect the inner aspects of the world of consciousness, according to Washburn, is to miss altogether some important realities. The result is a restrictive and partial psychology that creates an alien universe of discourse far removed from what we all encounter in day-to-day experience.

Movement and Mental Imagery was an attempt at a complete psychology that accords a place for the influence of the physical world, the mediating and causal effects of physiology and neurology, and the world of experience. G. L. Freeman (1948) in his treatise *The Energetics of Human Behavior* pointed out that

"Washburn's *Movement and Mental Imagery* . . . was a classic in a day when American psychology was all but lost in mental statics" (pp. 14–15). We have already noted that Washburn was an epiphenomenalist who regarded the world of experience as real and important. In her view, however, causality always runs from the physical to the mental, never the other way around. Furthermore, she assumed that all psychological phenomena have physical and physiological origins. Washburn's book *Movement and Mental Imagery* was an attempt to describe and explain psychological states and processes in terms of underlying physical movements. She believed it was perfectly admissible in psychology to "push theory ahead of fact" and thereby admitted that her work would contain many purely hypothetical neurological underpinnings for psychological phenomena (Washburn, 1916, p. xiii). Nevertheless, many of the explanations she offered for psychological processes appear to rest on plausible foundations. Some examples of her motor theory will help clarify her position.

Movement may be nowhere more evident as a companion to mental processes than in the arena of attention. Indeed, Washburn (1916) argued that "the essence of attention is movement" (p. 35). Such a claim is immediately evident in the animal world. A predator attending to a potential prey positions and repositions the ears, crouches, strains for a better view, and causes its whole muscular system to be taut with intense activity. Washburn called attention to the idea that some motor activities are phasic and suggested that this may result from the ratio of inhibitory and excitatory processes. If we fix attention on a specific stimulus situation we may notice that figure–ground relations shift back and forth or that we periodically see new relations because of changing ratios of inhibition and excitation. If we fixate on a specific word, we may successively see new meanings or new arrangements of the letters and such successive perceptions may result from incipient inhibitory movements that temporarily block an old way of seeing and thus set the stage for a new organization.

Washburn did not shy away from difficult psychological topics. She understood that critics would challenge her motor theory of consciousness by asking her to explain some of the most difficult and complicated mental processes. The problem of purpose provides a worthwhile illustration. She began by calling attention to the fact that there are obvious differences between ordered or directed thought and random reveries. She cited research demonstrating that simple stimuli such as words may have different aftereffects. A given word may be presented and subjects are then asked to write down all the words they think of following the initial presentation. The dependent measure is the number of times the subject breaks away from the influence of the initial stimulus word. In general, words with greater affective content have stronger aftereffects than more bland words. In other words, the person "stays on track" and continues to respond in a more coherent and more purposive fashion to a stimulus with emotional content.

Washburn argued that there are "problem ideas" that have insistent and perseverative qualities and that these problem ideas are always associated with action or movement systems. A catchy tune is a kind of harmonic idea that re-plays itself over and over in a complicated activity system. Walter S. Hunter (chap. 18, *Pioneers I*), a psychologist whom Washburn sometimes quoted, showed that dogs who observe the baiting of a goal box with meat have a strong tendency to orient toward the goal box. If the dog is restrained, it still orients it-self toward the goal box with what Washburn called "persistent tentative move-ments." Such behavior is "purposive" or goal directed, and if the dog is released it goes immediately to the goal box. If, however, the dog is restrained long enough for it to lose its "postural set" it may, on release, fail to go to the goal box. The dog displays purposive behavior so long as postural set or an "incipient movement system" is intact.

Human problem ideas may be supported by far larger and more complicated persistent tentative movement systems than we encounter in the dog. For exam-ple, a pianist who is thinking about a rehearsal or a practice session may display incipient movements marked by tensions in the fingers, hands, and arms or by actual "fingering" of complex passages. The "mental anticipation" of the re-hearsal may even be regarded as a manifestation of persistent motor inner-vations, some of which are invisible, and some of which are apparent in bodily postures and facial expressions.

For Washburn, purpose cannot be divorced from persistent motor inner-vations that are closely tied to past associations, drives, goals, "activity atti-tudes," and goals. Such motor innervations are sometimes obvious as in the case of a dog oriented toward a goal box and sometimes hidden from view. She was informed by the work of Sir Charles Sherrington who had demonstrated that the simplest of behaviors such as standing at attention is supported by extremely in-tricate and complex networks or systems of very finely tuned reflexes that work in sometimes complementary, sometimes antagonistic, ways to support behav-ior. She argued that all forms of mental imagery are also accompanied by com-plicated muscular innervations. She believed that attitudes persist, even when we are not conscious of them, when their kinesthetic basis persists. In her autobiog-raphy she recalled that "a persistent bodily attitude as the basis of purposive thought and action has strengthened its hold on my mind since its first formula-tion" (Washburn, 1930, p. 348).

Another example of the application of Washburn's motor theory is her at-tempts to explain dissociation. Washburn accepted some of the "facts of mental life" encountered in the works of Sigmund Freud (chap. 4, *Pioneers I*), but she rejected the Freudian explanations of those facts. Freud's explanation of dissoci-ation provides a good example. Freud once recalled an occasion when he was engaged in a conversation on Italian art and was unable to recall the name "Signorelli." He pointed to the fact that the first two syllables "Signor" are Italian for the German word "Herr." Herr is the first syllable in the word Herzegovina, a province that, for Freud, produced disagreeable feelings. Washburn agreed with Freud that an unpleasant emotion may interfere with a normal chain of associative dispositions, but she argued that Freud's actual explanations were "far fetched" and that a simpler explanation was available. As an example, she said:

> I may dream of the illness of a member of my family: at the moment [in the dream] when the illness results in death the person is transformed into a stranger simply because my organic attitude during sleep happens to be too comfortable to supply the strong emotion that would be called for by the death of someone near to me. (Washburn, 1916, p. 229)

One need not invoke the more complicated notion of a "dream censor" that transforms thoughts or prohibits them altogether from occurring.

According to Washburn, dissociation may occur when strong emotion interferes with an associative disposition. She regarded strong emotion as a forceful and extremely intricate movement system. Such a movement system is often initiated by a shock and may interfere with a weaker ongoing movement system. One possible result is a temporary inability to recall or recognize associations that were part of the weaker system. A shock and its accompanying movement system may also result in a shift of attention that varies in duration and that is dissociated from the previous direction of attention. Washburn was convinced that one need not rely on hidden motives and hypothetical unconscious processes of the Freudian variety to explain dissociation. The more parsimonious approach to dissociation is to explore the varieties of antagonisms, accommodations, and interferences of various movement systems and how these systems are influenced by emotions, unexpected events, and conditioning.

EXPERIMENTAL STUDIES

Washburn found that "the results of experimental work, if it is successful at all, bring more lasting satisfaction than the development of theories" (Washburn, 1930, p. 354). She referred to the "small studies" that she performed over a 25-year period with her students at Vassar as one of her greatest sources of satisfaction. These studies, 68 in number, published largely in the *AJP*, covered at least 10 content areas. The majority explored topics in sensation and perception, with feeling and emotion running a close second. There were also significant numbers of studies on learning and memory, methodology, and personality. The range of Washburn's experimental studies can be found in bibliographies of her works. Mull (1927) published a bibliography of Washburn's work from 1894 to 1927, and Kambouropoulou (1940) published a bibliography of her work from 1928 to 1939.

The range of Washburn's experimental work at Vassar is evident in some articles she published with her advanced undergraduates, many of which were on ideas regarded as progressive in her day, including involvement of the United States in the League of Nations, higher rates of taxation for the wealthy, minimum wage laws, employee participation in management, trade unions, and the theory of evolution. As Washburn pointed out, the popular belief in those days was that women were more conservative than men. But Washburn, Kepler, McBroom, Pritchard, and Reimer (1927), using a questionnaire and procedures previously used to study men at Yale and at Dartmouth, showed that the women at Vassar were not more conservative. The scores for Vassar women were generally between those Yale and Dartmouth men.

Washburn conducted a great many experiments on affect and emotion. She was particularly interested in the affective dimensions of colors and articulated sounds and the relationships between emotion and thought. One of her studies (Washburn, Hatt, & Holt, 1923) compared affective sensitivity in students selected for poetic ability with students selected for scientific ability. The results indicated greater affective sensitivity in the poets. In another study, Powelson and Washburn (1913) explored the effect of verbal suggestion on judgments of the affective values of colors. It was found that positive or negative suggestions clearly influenced the affective value of colors for a majority of participants. This kind of study was particularly important in Washburn's day because of the difficulties of separating stated color preferences that might be subject to cultural conditioning from deeper underlying feelings regarding colors. Ellis (1906) provided context and illustrated the problem in an article that explored the history of the color yellow. He argued that in early times, yellow was regarded as a lighthearted and joyous color deeply valued by primitive peoples. Yet in Washburn's day, yellow was almost always rated last in color preference tests. Ellis pointed out that yellow was very prevalent in the typical Roman circus and during the persecution of Christians. As a result, the color yellow was subsequently forbidden in Catholic and Protestant ecclesiastical proceedings. It was also forbidden in priestly garments and was regarded as a symbol of the devil, and of treachery, jealousy, and cowardice. Washburn was fully aware of the difficulty of teasing out cultural influences on color preference tests and demonstrated that even the simplest of suggestions altered preference judgments in her research participants.

Washburn's experimental studies covered both pure and applied problems in psychology, and she employed a great range of methods, including: questionnaires, reaction times, introspection, comparative methods, and controlled observation. Although she attempted to explore problems in a rigorous scientific fashion, she did not permit a narrow approach to methodology to restrict the range of problems she investigated or to interfere with her vision. She argued that her greatest joys came from experimental research, but her record indicates a balance between theoretical and experimental contributions.

THE QUEST FOR THE HARMONIES WITHIN A
CRITICAL AND RIGOROUS FRAMEWORK

Washburn's mature works are filled with references to structuralism, functionalism, behaviorism, and Gestalt psychology. There are also some references to psychoanalysis. The literature in her day was marked by disputes about the appropriate substantive content of psychology as well as about legitimate methodologies. In addition to the many schools of thought, she drew attention to the proliferation of new content areas in psychology. In 1917 she published an article on developments in the discipline over the previous 25 years. She pointed to headings in the *Psychological Index* in 1917 that were not included in the first issue of that reference source. These headings included such topics as advertising, educational psychology, psychoanalysis, psychology of testimony, social psychology, and religion and myths. In addition to these, she referred to the growing literature in abnormal psychology, animal psychology, race psychology, religious psychology, and the psychology of the mentally challenged. Washburn welcomed the proliferation of new content areas, but insisted there were commonalties, if not unities, to be found in this increasingly pluralistic discipline.

As already noted, Washburn believed that any adequate empirical psychology must acknowledge the mental world of the structuralists, but also be enfranchised by functionalism, Gestalt psychology, and psychoanalysis. She quarreled with radical behaviorists who excluded consciousness and experience as legitimate subjects in psychology. Indeed, her presidential address to the APA in 1921 was a defense of introspection and an argument that behaviorists cannot ignore it. Nevertheless, she strongly agreed with the emphasis of behaviorists on movement and peripheral processes. She contended that structuralism and behaviorism have more in common than either system has with functionalism. She believed that her motor theory of consciousness could serve as a basis for the integration of behaviorism and structuralism and, for that matter, as a basis for integrating other systems as well. Although Washburn embraced plurality and diversity, she rejected the idea that disunity is an inevitable consequence of an ever widening field. She believed that psychologists share common scientific values that determine the kinds of questions they raise and the procedures they employ in pursuing answers to those questions. Washburn's was a middle way, informed by and responsive to all things that present themselves as natural parts of experience and behavior. Although her system was dualistic, it was not the substance dualism and interactionism encountered in Descartes. In her view, it was a dualism that was completely compatible with the most rigorous and demanding philosophy of science. It begins where all science begins: with experience.

Washburn believed that science begins with simple description, but that good description must be complemented with explanation. Her criticism of Gestalt psychology was that it took "vocabulary for description and description for explanation" (Washburn, 1930, p. 354). She noted:

> At the 1925 meeting of the Psychological Association I suggested how the nature of the motor response could be used to explain certain phenomena of perception which are fundamental in the Gestalt doctrine, and, in a round-table discussion at the International Congress meeting in 1929, I made a similar suggestion in regard to association. Köhler, in replying, said among other things, "Why should we be expected to explain? Why is it not enough for the present to describe?" or words to that effect. (Washburn, 1930, p. 354)

The obligation of science to explain and the nature of what constitutes an explanation remain as contemporary issues in the philosophy of science. Washburn's position, whether it is ultimately to be judged as an insight or a confusion, was clear; the quest for harmonies is to be found in the complementary functions of description and explanation.

PROFESSIONAL CONTRIBUTIONS AND HONORS

Washburn's professional contributions to psychology were as extensive and impressive as her contributions to the science. In 1921 she served as president of the APA, the second woman to hold that office—the first was Mary Whiton Calkins (chap. 5, *Pioneers I*). In 1931 she was named to the National Academy of Sciences, the second woman to receive that honor—the first was Florence Sabin, an anatomist and physiologist. The appointment to the National Academy is a particularly noteworthy and singular honor extended to very few scholars. The National Academy was founded in 1863 by an act of Congress and signed by Abraham Lincoln to serve as an independent advisory source for the federal government on a great range of technological and scientific issues that are pertinent to national interests. Washburn takes her place among the few early psychologists appointed to the National Academy. Examples of others include James Rowland Angell (chap. 4, this volume), James McKeen Cattell, John Dewey (chap. 4, *Pioneers II*), Edward Lee Thorndike (chap. 10, *Pioneers I*), and James. Washburn was also active in the American Association for the Advancement of the Sciences, serving as vice president of the psychology section of that organization in 1927. She served as chair of the Society of Experimental Psychologists and as president of the New York Branch of the APA, later renamed Eastern Psychological Association. These are but a few examples of the many organizations she served during her illustrious career.

Washburn's work was celebrated in 1927 in a special volume of the *AJP*. The cover page of Volume 39 referred to her as a teacher, editor, author, and scientist. She was recognized for her 25 years as professor of psychology at Vassar and editor of the *AJP* and for 33 years of distinguished service to psychology.

Washburn's editorial work alone was noteworthy. Dallenbach (1939) pointed out that in addition to her work with the *AJP*, she held editorial positions at one time or another with the *Psychological Bulletin* (1909–1915), the *Journal of Animal Behavior* (1911–1917), the *Psychological Review* (1916–1930), and the *Journal of Comparative Psychology* (1921–1935).

In 1927 Washburn was awarded an honorary doctorate by Wittenberg College in connection with an International Symposium on Feeling and Emotion. Washburn was also a key figure in international organizations such as the International Congress of Psychology and the International Committee on Psychology. Scarborough's (1990) authoritative work on Washburn's achievements called attention to her local as well as national and international contributions. Washburn was regarded as the most famous scholar and the best lecturer at Vassar. She was extremely active in college and community life and enjoyed hobbies such as oil painting, dancing, and playing the piano. Scarborough called attention to Washburn's opposition to the introduction of applied courses typically associated with curricula in home economics. This was just one of the ways that Washburn, in the words of Scarborough, was "able to minimize the collegial exclusion that typically worked against women's full participation" (Scarborough, 2000, p. 232).

Washburn concluded her autobiography with the observation that "Scientific psychology . . . seems fuller of promise than ever before" (Washburn, 1930, p. 358). Such an observation in the face of the economic and political woes of the period, nevertheless, proved prophetic. Washburn's spirit of optimism, enthusiasm, and total dedication to the instructional, service, and discovery missions of science remains as a model for our day. She died on October 29, 1939, after more than 2 years of illness that resulted from a cerebral hemorrhage. Her legacy includes more than 200 scholarly publications, the influence of her work on editorial boards and scientific organizations, and the less tangible but equally real influence on generations of students.

REFERENCES

Abel, T. M. (1927). Washburn's motor theory: A contribution to functional psychology. *American Journal of Psychology, 39*, 91–105.

Dallenbach, K. M. (1939). Margaret Floy Washburn. *Science, 90*, 555–557.

Dallenbach, K. M. (1940). Margaret Floy Washburn. *American Journal of Psychology, 53*, 1–5.

Ellis, H. (1906). The psychology of yellow. *Popular Science Monthly, 68*, 456–463.

Freeman, G. L. (1948). *The energetics of human behavior*. Ithaca, NY: Cornell University Press.

James, W. (1909). *The meaning of truth*. Cambridge, MA: Harvard University Press.

Kambouropoulou, P. (1940). A bibliography of the writings of Margaret Floy Washburn: 1928–1939. *American Journal of Psychology, 53*, 19–20.

Kimble, G. A. (1984). Psychology's two cultures. *American Psychologist, 39*, 833–839.

Kimble, G. A. (2000). Behaviorism and unity in psychology. *Current Directions in Psychological Science, 9*, 208–212.

Martin, M. F. (1940). The psychological contributions of Margaret Floy Washburn. *American Journal of Psychology, 53,* 7–18.

Montaigne, M. (1960). Apology for Raimond Sebond (D. F. Frame, Trans.). *The complete essays of Montaigne* (pp. 112–308). Garden City, NJ: Doubleday.

Mull, H. K. (1927). A bibliography of the writings of Margaret Floy Washburn: 1894–1927. *American Journal of Psychology, 39,* 428–436.

Powelson, I., & Washburn, M. F. (1913). The effect of verbal suggestion on judgments of the affective value of colors. *American Journal of Psychology, 24,* 267–269.

Scarborough, E. (1990). Margaret Floy Washburn (1871–1939). In Agnes N. O'Connel & Nancy Felipe Russo (Eds.), *Women in psychology: A bio-bibliographic sourcebook* (pp. 342–349). New York: Greenwood Press.

Scarborough, E. (2000). Margaret Floy Washburn. In A. Kazdin (Ed.), *Encyclopedia of psychology* (Vol. 8, pp. 230–232). Washington, DC: American Psychological Association and Oxford University Press.

Staats, A. W. (1989). Unificationism: Philosophy for the modern disunified science of psychology. *Philosophical Psychology, 2,* 143–164.

Viney, W. (1996). Disunity in psychology and other sciences: The network or the block universe? *Journal of Mind and Behavior, 17,* 31–44.

Viney, W. (1998). A larger canopy for psychology: Unity and disunity as a pedagogical problem. *Psychology Teacher Network, 8.*

Viney, W. (2001). The radical empiricism of William James and philosophy of history. *History of Psychology, 4,* 1–17.

Washburn, M. F. (1895). Ueber den Einfluss von Gesichtsassociatitonen auf die Raumwahrnehmungen der haut. *Philosophische Studien, 11,* 190–225.

Washburn, M. F. (1908). *The animal mind: A textbook of comparative psychology.* New York: Macmillan.

Washburn, M. F. (1916). *Movement and mental imagery.* New York: Houghton Mifflin.

Washburn, M. F. (1917). Some thoughts on the last quarter century in psychology. *Philosophical Review, 26,* 46–55.

Washburn, M. F. (1922). Introspection as an objective method. *Psychological Review, 29,* 89–112.

Washburn, M. F. (1930). Margaret Floy Washburn: Some recollections. In Carl Murchison (Ed.), *A history of psychology in autobiography* (Vol. 2, pp. 333–358). Worcester, MA: Clark University Press.

Washburn, M. F., Hatt, E., & Holt, E. B. (1923). Affective sensitiveness in poets and in scientific students. *American Journal of Psychology, 34,* 105–106.

Washburn, M. F., Kepler, H., McBroom, N., Pritchard W., & Reimer, I. (1927). The Moore tests of radical and conservative temperaments. *American Journal of Psychology, 38,* 449–451.

Wertheimer, M. (1988). Obstacles to the integration of competing theories in psychology. *Philosophical Psychology, 1,* 131–137.

Wundt, W. (1897). Ethical systems (M. F. Washburn, Trans.). New York: Macmillan.

Chapter 6

William McDougall: "A Major Tragedy"?

Nancy K. Innis
University of Western Ontario

"His life is a major tragedy," Robert Yerkes (chap. 7, *Pioneeers II*) is reported to have remarked after reading William McDougall's autobiography (cited in Adams, 1939). "In the strictest sense of tragedy, this is profoundly true. The frustrations of little men with little goals are not the materials of tragedy. McDougall's frustration of his goal—to make a science of psychology—was" (Adams, 1939, p. 8). McDougall referred to himself as a "sane" behaviorist, one for whom "the facts ascertainable from introspective observation, and the objectively observable facts of behavior" were equally "indispensable" (Watson & McDougall, 1929, pp. 53–54). He believed that behavior must be understood "in terms of the end or purpose of activity, rather than in terms only of the antecedent events" (McDougall, 1912, p. 38). This position, eventually labeled hormic psychology, contrasted sharply with the stimulus–response (S–R) psychology of John Watson (chap. 12, *Pioneers I*), whose radical behaviorism left no room for consciousness or mind, for goals or purposes. McDougall (1930) maintained that, as well as seeking understanding of the physiological processes that underlie behavior, psychologists should be concerned with such more difficult problems as "the innate basis of our mental life" (p. 222) and the "relation of mind to body" (p. 223). These issues were irrelevant to most behaviorists and, by the end of the 1920s when McDougall's pessimistic autobiography was written, mechanistic behaviorism, in a variety of forms, was the prevailing view in America. In looking back at his efforts over the previous three decades to convince his colleagues to accept his purposive psychology, McDougall concluded, correctly, that he had failed. Who was this tragic figure?

BACKGROUND

William McDougall was born on June 22, 1871, in Chadderton, Lancashire, England; he died of cancer on November 28, 1938, in Durham, North Carolina. His father, Isaac Shimwell McDougall, was a "dark Highlander," his mother, Rebekah (Smalley) McDougall "of the pure Saxon type." As such he embodied "that blend of the Mediterranean and Nordic races which has produced the English people." However, he believed that his own inability to feel either "typically English or altogether at home in the English social atmosphere" was because he was the first generation of such a crossing. He claimed that he "never fitted neatly into any social group" or "with any party or any system," but rather "stood outside, critical and ill-content, . . . alone in [his] "intellectual interests" (McDougall, 1930, pp. 191–192).

Education

McDougall's father was a chemical manufacturer, and McDougall grew up in comfortable circumstances in the suburbs of Manchester. Like many of the businessmen in the north of England, Isaac McDougall was not part of the Tory establishment, and he opposed sending his sons to their schools. Along with an older brother, McDougall spent a year at a *Real-Gymnasium* in Weimar, Germany, where he learned the language, a skill that would be useful to him in later years. He was a precocious lad, very intelligent, but with "a biting tongue" (McDougall, 1930, p. 194). On returning to England, he entered Owens College, University of Manchester, when he was just 15 years old, graduating with a degree in science (biology and some geology) in 1890. Then, by obtaining a scholarship to St. John's College, he persuaded his father to set aside his prejudices and let him attend Cambridge University. McDougall studied physiology, anatomy, and anthropology in preparation for medicine, a career path chosen after his mother's death from a painful cancer. In 1894, after completing his course of study at Cambridge "with the highest honors obtainable," McDougall received a scholarship to continue his education at St. Thomas's Hospital in London (p. 198). Along with his medical training, McDougall carried out research on muscle physiology in Charles Sherrington's laboratory at St. Thomas's. This research resulted in his first two scientific publications.

From Neurology to Psychology

On receiving his M.B., McDougall was elected a Fellow of St. John's College, Cambridge, an appointment he held from 1898 to 1904. He was now set on a career in research rather than medical practice in neurology. When starting out, McDougall had wanted to study neurology because he believed that in the brain were "locked the secrets of human nature." However, after reading William

James's (chap. 2, *Pioneers I*) *Principles of Psychology* (1890), he realized that these secrets must be approached both "from below upwards by way of physiology and neurology, and from above downwards by way of psychology, philosophy, and the various human sciences" (McDougall, 1930, p. 200). In line with this philosophy, McDougall submitted two very different theses in support of his application for the Cambridge fellowship—one on his research on muscle physiology and the other a philosophical paper on the mind–body problem. McDougall would always be concerned with combining the physiological and the psychological; in his earliest research the emphasis was on the first of these approaches, and in his later research his major focus was on psychology.

Early Career

Soon after receiving his fellowship, McDougall was invited to join anthropologist Alfred Cort Haddon's Cambridge Anthropological Expedition to the Torres Straits. His role was to assist W. H. R. Rivers in measuring the sensory capabilities of the native inhabitants of the islands. Both Haddon and Rivers had been McDougall's teachers when he was an undergraduate, and another member of the group, C. S. Myers, had been a fellow student at Cambridge. After a short stay in the Torres Straits, McDougall moved on to assist Charles Hose with his research on the physical, moral, and intellectual condition of the pagan tribes of headhunters in Borneo (Hose and McDougall, 1912). His experiences on the Cambridge expedition gave McDougall a long-standing interest in individual differences, particularly across different ethnic groups.

Intrigued as he was by anthropological field work, McDougall was becoming more interested in experimental psychology. He spent the year following his return from the South Seas at the University of Göttingen in the laboratory of G. E. Müller (chap. 5, *Pioneers IV*), who was then "the leading exponent of the exact laboratory methods in psychology" (McDougall, 1930, p. 203). Here he developed an interest in studying attention and perceptual phenomena. Accompanying him to Germany was his wife, the former Anne Hickmore, whom he married in late 1899. They would eventually have five children, two daughters and three sons, of all of whom he was "justly . . . proud." Yet in his pessimistic autobiography, McDougall could not help but ask "was it right to bring them into existence?" (p. 223).

ACADEMIC APPOINTMENTS IN ENGLAND

McDougall took up his first university appointment in 1900, a part-time position at University College, London, teaching a course on laboratory methods. Here he joined James Sully, who held the Grote Chair of Mind and Logic from 1892 to 1903. In 1897, Sully had established a small laboratory at University College, the first psychology laboratory in England, and McDougall was able to use it to carry out demonstrations in his course. It was well equipped with apparatus purchased from the University of Freiburg, equipment left behind when Hugo Münsterberg (chap. 7, *Pioneers IV*) moved to Harvard. The London laboratory became the meeting place for informal discussions among psychologists in the region, and it was here, on October 24, 1901, that they established a more formal organization, the British Psychological Society. Sully, McDougall, and Rivers were among the nine founding members (Hearnshaw, 1964). McDougall remained an active member, giving presentations at meetings. He was also a major contributor to the *British Journal of Psychology*, established in 1904 by James Ward and Rivers, and taken over by the Society in 1914.

In 1904, McDougall was appointed to the Wilde Readership in Mental Philosophy at Oxford. This position was also essentially part-time, involving two lectures a week for 21 weeks each year. For many years, he felt like an outsider at Oxford where he had no college affiliation until 1912, when he was elected extraordinary Fellow at Corpus Christi College. The Oxford position did not provide research space; in fact, the sponsor of the readership who did not believe that mental life should be examined experimentally had actively opposed McDougall's appointment. So he continued to teach the laboratory course at University College until 1907, when it was taken over by Charles Spearman (chap. 6, *Pioneers IV*). After he gave up this position, McDougall continued his research on the Oxford campus in three rooms of the physiology laboratory generously provided by Francis Gotch. Over the years he was at Oxford, McDougall had a number of unofficial students, including William Brown, Cyril Burt, J. C. Flugel, May Smith, and Horace English (McDougall, 1930). At University College, he had become acquainted with Francis Galton (chap. 1, *Pioneers I*) and Karl Pearson and their work on mental measurement, and several of these students worked on mental testing with McDougall. McDougall shared Galton's position on the inheritance of intelligence and became "an ardent supporter of eugenics" (Burt, 1955, p. 13).

McDougall's time at Oxford was interrupted by the First World War, most of which he spent as a major in the Royal Army Medical Corps. He was stationed at hospitals at Netley, and later Littlemore, in charge of treating patients suffering from shell shock, a term introduced by his friend Myers to describe the neuroses displayed by men who had been in combat (Hearnshaw, 1964). At Netley, in particular, he encountered "a series of cases of functional disorders which, in respect of variety and severity, was probably unique" (McDougall, 1926, p. xi). Although he had been developing an interest in psychoanalytic theory before the war, McDougall found that "sympathetic rapport with the patient" rather than hypnosis or any other psychoanalytic technique was the most successful method of treatment. He regarded this opportunity to work with patients as "a wonderful experience for a psychologist" (1930, pp. 210–211), and many of the cases he encountered were described in his 1926 *Outline of Abnormal Psychology*. Before the war, McDougall had met Carl Jung (chap. 11, *Pioneers I*), and soon af-ter the hostilities ended he went to Zurich and had his dreams analyzed. He "came away enlightened but not convinced" (p. 211).

EARLY THEORIZING, RESEARCH, WRITING

At the turn of the 20th century, one of the issues that engaged philosophers and psychologists alike was the relationship between mind and body. McDougall's ideas on the psychophysical problem, in which he "foreshadowed the . . . doc-trine of *emergence* of mind from the physical realm" (McDougall, 1930, p. 200), were first published in the journal *Mind* in 1898. Later in a very controversial 1911 book, *Body and Mind: A History and a Defense of Animism*, he expanded on his philosophical position. Animism refers to the view that "those manifesta-tions of life and mind which distinguish the living man from the corpse . . . are due to the operation within him of something which is of a nature different from that of the body, an animating principle generally . . . conceived as an immate-rial and individual being or soul" (McDougall, 1911, p. viii). Because he felt strongly that "mental and vital processes cannot be completely described and ex-plained in terms of mechanism," McDougall was "compelled to believe in the co-operation of some non-mechanical teleological factor, and to adopt the hy-pothesis of the soul" (p. 364). He described a soul not as a substance, but as "a sum of enduring capacities for thoughts, feelings, and efforts of determinate kinds" (p. 365). He saw it as "a being capable of being stimulated to conscious activities through the agency of the body or brain with which it stands in rela-tions of reciprocal influence" (p. 366). Indeed, he suggested that "psycho-physical interaction may be, for all we know, a necessary condition of all con-sciousness" (p. 365).

McDougall realized that in advocating not only a soul, but the interaction of soul and body, he was out of step with current philosophical opinion and ac-knowledged that many would think it "nothing short of a scandal" that an aca-demic would defend the soul. However, he believed that acceptance of any posi-tion should be based on evidence, and he attempted to present a position on the soul that was "in harmony with all the facts established by empirical science" (1911, p. xi).

Psychic Phenomena

Because of his psychophysical position, McDougall also took a stand in advo-cating the empirical investigation, within the university, of two other topics that would continually result in his scientific credibility being called into question. The first of these was support for research on psychic phenomena. McDougall rejected the idea that the capacities of the soul are simply due to brain functioning, primarily because this kind of explanation could not account for the memory, resulting from the intellectual and moral effort of an individual's life, that distinguishes one personal soul from another after death. Although not religious, he was "in sympathy with the religious attitude towards life," suggesting that the belief in life after death "must have . . . a moralizing influence upon our thought and conduct" and that relinquishing it "would be calamitous for our civilization." (1911, xiii). If there is life after death, it should be possible to determine this experimentally, and one form of evidence could come from communication with departed souls. McDougall was an active member of Psychical Societies in both Britain and America, he investigated the genuineness of mediums such as Margery, and he encouraged psychical research in general.

Lamarckian Evolution

A second issue, which McDougall raised but did not deal with in the book, concerned the role of heredity with respect to the soul. He strongly opposed the mechanistic position on evolution being promoted by the neo-Darwinians such as August Weismann, even remarking that it seemed "easier to believe that two souls may somehow co-operate in giving origin to a new one," than that two complex machines should combine to form a new being (McDougall, 1911, p. 377). At the time, when there was little physiological evidence available to support Weismann, perhaps McDougall's statement was not as ludicrous as it seems today. McDougall's position implied the inheritance of knowledge acquired as the result of experience, typically referred to as Lamarckian evolution. For many years after he moved to the United States, he would devote his energies to the experimental examination of this possibility.

Physiological Research and Theory

Although McDougall opposed the idea that all human behavior can be accounted for with mechanistic explanations, he recognized that "the pure psychologist must cease to be content with a one-sided and partial study of mental process and that if he wishe[d] to advance his science, he must descend into the dark places of physiology" (McDougall, 1902, p. 320). A bottom-up physiological approach must go hand-in-hand with top-down psychology. Maintaining his interactionist position, he suggested that "we can only establish or disprove the occurrence of an undetermined activity of the soul by first discovering all other factors, and then showing that there remains, or does not remain, an inexplicable residue" (p. 328). So the earliest years of McDougall's career were devoted primarily to physiological research and theory.

He began by proposing a theory of "neural processes in general" that he believed "was in harmony with all the physiological data" and lent "itself well to the description of the states and processes" involved in consciousness (1902, p.

328). The theory stressed the important role of the synapse in the psychophysical process. McDougall postulated that when neurons are stimulated they produce a fluid that he called neurin, which flows through the neural pathways from the afferent to the efferent neurons. An "increase of the potential of the charge of neurin" (p. 381) leads to a reduction in the threshold of the synapse, making neural conduction more rapid. Thus, sensory-motor neural pathways are established. Although he indicated that one could accept his physiological explanation on its own, McDougall believed that "every psychical state corresponds to the flow of neurin through a certain set of neurones which form a group of conduction-paths . . . [T]he physical processes in direct interaction with the soul, i.e. the psycho-physical processes, are processes that occur in the intercellular substances at the synapses as neurin is discharged through them from afferent to efferent neurones" (p. 332). In response to criticism that he considered neurin a fluid, McDougall reacted that, in the tradition of James, he was taking a pragmatic approach. It was "a good working hypothesis, . . . a useful instrument of description" (p. 350).

From 1900 until his career was interrupted by the war, McDougall published numerous articles presenting accounts of his research findings and theoretical ideas. He recalled that most of these "papers seemed to be still-born," receiving little attention from his colleagues at the time of publication. However, this work obviously had some influence in certain scientific circles, in that it provided the basis for his election as a fellow of the prestigious Royal Society in 1912 (McDougall, 1930, p. 206). Langfeld (1940) provided a good short summary of McDougall's many contributions to psychology as a science during this time.

Attention.   McDougall was concerned with determining the nature of attention, both the state of consciousness and the underlying physiological processes, the factors that result in changes in attention, and how these factors work. In a series of three articles, he dealt with the problem of attention, beginning with the physiological processes. He applied his ideas on the role of neurin discussed previously, developing what became known as the "drainage theory" in the first of these articles (McDougall, 1902). Langfeld (1940) indicated that in this account McDougall displayed two trends that have always characterized his speculation, the one toward explanations in dynamic terms and the other toward physiological principles. The drainage theory maintained that the simultaneous excitation of two nerve paths increases the intimacy of the connection between the paths and facilitates the flow of neurin into the path most strongly activated (1940, p. 109), determining attention. Boring (1929) considered the drainage theory "the only important physiological theory of attention," and although the physiologists rejected it, "for a time it was a useful view. Psychologically attention is drainage, whatever it may be physiologically" (p. 642).

McDougall also made some practical contributions to the study of attention. While he was in Germany, with advice from Müller, he developed the prototype for an apparatus to provide an objective, graphic record of changes in attention. It involved a rotating drum covered with white paper on which eight rows of red dots, each in a different zigzag line, were printed. The subject saw one moving line of dots through a slit in a screen covering the moving paper, and was required to mark each dot in the row with an inked stylo, leaving a permanent record of hits and misses. The apparatus, which became known as the "McDougall dotter," was used extensively, for example in studies by Rivers of changes in attention as the result of fatigue or the influence of drugs (McDougall, 1905).

Visual Perception. When he was in Göttingen, McDougall learned more about Ewald Hering's then popular theory of color vision, first encountered in Rivers's lectures on sensory physiology when he was an undergraduate. His reaction to Hering's theory was typical of his response to all popular theories: He was skeptical. He soon set about devising studies to determine whether his skepticism was justified. Based among other things on observations of afterimages, Hering had postulated three retinal receptors, each sensitive to opposing color pairs: red–green, blue–yellow, and black–white. McDougall (1901) became convinced that a bidirectional reaction in these receptors, depending on the color of the stimulus, could not occur. He favored a theory originally introduced in 1802 by another Englishman, Thomas Young, and modified by the eminent German physiologist, Hermann von Helmholtz (chap. 2, *Pioneers IV*). This trichromatic theory postulated three types of receptors, each activated by one of the primary colors (red, blue, and yellow). McDougall carried out an extensive series of experiments, begun in Germany and continued on his return to England, often under makeshift conditions in a laboratory he set up in his own home, to determine which theory would prevail. His findings supported Young's original position on almost all counts. As physiological techniques advanced, further support for a trichromatic theory of retinal function was obtained. However, McDougall's work is typically not cited in historical accounts of the Hering–Helmholtz debates on color vision, perhaps, as he claimed, because it was largely ignored when it was first published.

McDougall was concerned about the evolution and development of color perception and carried out extensive studies on two of his own children when each was only a few months old to determine whether certain colors were preferred at an earlier age than others. He showed the babies pairs of colored stimuli, such as small balls of wool, and recorded which one was grasped. He found that by the sixth month red, green, and blue were preferred over white and gray, although the three colors were treated equivalently (McDougall, 1908). Given his limited university duties, McDougall spent much of his time at home with his children, and as well as conducting experiments, he made "detailed notes during their earliest years" of many aspects of their behavior and development (1930, p. 208).

THE SCIENCE OF PSYCHOLOGY

From as early as 1905, McDougall was defining psychology as "the positive science of the mind in all its aspects and modes of functioning" or, as he preferred to put it, "the positive science of conduct or behaviour" (McDougall, 1960/1908, p. 13). However, he rejected the increasingly popular idea that for psychology to account scientifically for behavior it must adopt explanations from physics and chemistry: mechanistic explanations. He vehemently opposed mechanism. For McDougall, behavior is the "manifestation of purpose or the striving to achieve an end" (1912, p. 20). Throughout his career, in numerous books and articles, he presented a purposive theory of human behavior, a theory that contrasted sharply with the radical behaviorism of John Watson. In supporting his theoretical position, McDougall accepted a wide range of evidence. Taking the approach he first advanced when he was a medical student, he combined top-down "introspective description" with a bottom-up "comparative and physiological psychology relying largely on objective methods, the observation of the behaviour of men and animals in all varieties under all possible conditions of health and disease" (1960/1908, p. 13).

Social Psychology

McDougall's theoretical ideas were first presented in detail in his 1908 book, *An Introduction to Social Psychology*. Although the title of the book suggests it is a social psychology textbook, "introduction" was the key word. McDougall knew that before we can understand social behavior, we must understand the behavior of the individuals comprising society. So most of the book deals with determining the underlying bases of human conduct, which he identified as instincts. In a later (1920) book, *The Group Mind*, he dealt more specifically with social behavior.

McDougall (1930) indicated that he began to contemplate the importance of instincts when, one day as he was lecturing at Oxford, he heard himself making "the sweeping assertion that the energy displayed in every human activity might in principle be traced back to some inborn disposition or instinct" (p. 208). He soon became convinced of the truth of this principle and determined to present a scientific account of "the innate tendencies to thought and action that constitute the native basis of the mind" (McDougall, 1960/1908, p. 13).

In the first section of the book, McDougall discussed the importance of these innate tendencies, "which are the essential springs or motive powers of all thought and action, whether individual or collective, and are the bases from which the character and will of individuals and of nations are gradually developed" (1960/1908, p. 17). He chose to refer to these tendencies as instincts, a term that later would result in considerable controversy and notoriety for him, particularly during the 1920s after he moved to North America. At a time when instincts were typically defined as chains of reflexes, McDougall used the term to refer to something very different. For him, an instinct is "an inherited or innate psycho-physical disposition which determines its possessor to perceive, and to pay attention to, objects of a certain class, to experience an emotional excitement of a particular quality upon perceiving such an object, and to act in regard to it in a particular manner, or, at least, experience an impulse to such action" (p. 25). There are three components to an instinct: cognition (attention to or perception of objects), emotion, and conation (an impulse to act). In McDougall's conceptualization, both the cognitive and conative aspects of an instinct could be altered by experience; only the emotional core remains constant. Initially, seven principal instincts and their primary emotions were described, including flight (fear), repulsion (disgust), curiosity (wonder), pugnacity (anger), self-abasement and self-assertion (positive and negative self-feeling), and parental (tender emotion). In later editions of the book, McDougall expanded the list of instincts somewhat, but not extensively; however, among the many criticisms of the theory was that it presented an endless litany of instincts.

Although in humans primary emotions are associated with the instincts, they rarely occur in a pure form; rather, they combine to form sentiments, "functional units of mental life . . . comprising all knowledge of and affective tendencies directed upon some object" (1930, p. 217). The most typical sentiments are love and hate; hate, for example, results from the combination of fear and anger toward a particular object. Although similar in some ways to instincts, sentiments are acquired as the result of experience rather than being inborn and are directed to particular objects. In the 14th edition of the book, published in 1919, after various psychoanalytic theories of personality had been introduced, McDougall pointed to the similarity between his idea of a sentiment and the psychoanalysts' concept of "complex" as it had been extended to refer to "structural features of the normal mind." His hope was that the term sentiment would be adopted as a general term for "all those acquired conjunctions of ideas with emotional-conative tendencies or dispositions" acquired in both normal and abnormal "mental development," with "complex" being used to designate only the pathological sentiments (1960/1908, p. ix). However, neither psychologists nor psychoanalysts displayed much interest in the sentiments at all, which for McDougall were as important as the instincts.

For McDougall, the sentiments are basic to the formation of an individual's character or personality. In the 21st edition of the book, McDougall added a chapter on "The Structure of Character." "The stability and integration of character was dependent on the gradual building up of an organized, harmonious, integrated system of sentiments, both concrete and abstract" (Hearnshaw, 1964, p. 191). McDougall believed that his account of character was his "best and most original contribution to psychology" (McDougall, 1960/1908, p. xiii).

Social Psychology was written for a popular audience and was well received, establishing McDougall's reputation as an up-and-coming psychologist in Britain. Twenty-three editions would be published during his lifetime, the last one coming out in 1936. Overall, McDougall's theoretical position remained essentially unchanged, and in revisions of the text he typically added chapters rather than modifying what he had previously written.

Psychology: The Study of Behaviour

The success of his *Social Psychology* resulted in McDougall's being asked to write a text for the Home University Library series. In *Psychology: The Study of Behaviour*, he continued to emphasize that psychology is "the positive science of the behaviour of living things" (1912, p. 19). In this text, he briefly sketched his views on what psychology comprises, its methods, and the research areas that are important for helping us understand human behavior. These research areas include studies of the behavior of animals and children, individual differences, and abnormal and social psychology. These ideas were later expanded in his *Outline of Psychology* and *Outline of Abnormal Psychology*, both published after he came to America.

McDOUGALL IN AMERICA

In 1920, McDougall received an invitation from the Philosophy Department at Harvard University to fill the chair in psychology that had remained vacant since Münsterberg's (chap. 7, *Pioneers IV*) death in 1916. They wanted an eminent psychologist for the post, and McDougall, a member of the Royal Society, was a leading figure in British psychology. His name was well known in America and abroad. A number of factors, both professional and personal, led McDougall to accept the offer. Although he had achieved a certain prominence in England, he did not have an important university position. His appointment as Wilde Reader at Oxford held none of the perquisites of a chair. After the war, his ability to carry out research was curtailed because the rooms he was using in the physiology department were no longer available because of an increase in the number of physiology students. He saw that by remaining at Oxford he might "subside into inactivity." He had been well received on a visit to America in 1913 and felt that Harvard "would be a stimulating adventure" (McDougall, 1930, p. 212). On a more personal note, he was glad to escape the harsh English climate that he believed was responsible for his being totally deaf in his right ear. He also thought that it had contributed to the recent death of his younger daughter, Aline, from typhoid fever. In 1920, McDougall "went to America with good hopes and intentions" (p. 212). This time, however, America was not so welcoming.

Harvard University

At Harvard, McDougall had a substantial teaching load. He taught the introductory course, as well as courses in abnormal and social psychology and the history of psychology. In addition, he was involved in the supervision and examination of graduate students. There were facilities at Harvard for animal research, and soon after he arrived McDougall began an ambitious research project to test the possibility of Lamarckian evolution. However, he did not take over as director of the psychology laboratory, which had been run by E. B. Holt and Herbert Langfeld after Münsterberg's death. McDougall soon began to negotiate with Boring, who was at Clark University, to join the department and take over this position. Boring came to Harvard in the fall of 1922. The correspondence between Boring and McDougall during the 1920s indicates that their personal relationship was cordial, although they disagreed on most philosophical and theoretical issues.

Soon after he took up his Harvard chair, McDougall was invited to give a series of lectures at the Lowell Institute of Boston. He did so in the spring of 1921, and the six lectures on national eugenics were published in the book *Is America Safe for Democracy?* The introduction, which also appeared in *Scribner's Magazine* under the title "The Island of Eugenia," presented a dialogue between a Philanthropist and a Seer. In deciding how a fortune could be used to stem social decay and improve human welfare, the Seer outlines a fantastic scheme for a utopian society, based on eugenic principles, that would produce world leaders (McDougall, 1934). From as far back as his participation in the Torres Strait expedition and his association with Galton in London, McDougall had strong views concerning racial and individual differences. These ideas were received less enthusiastically in North America than in England.

During the nearly two decades following his arrival in America, McDougall gave many public lectures and published several books and numerous articles in popular magazines on other social and political issues, typically addressing controversial topics and "espousing unpopular causes." As a result he "suffered much . . . in the way of loss of reputation, unpopularity, slanderous misrepresentation, and scornful hostility" (McDougall, 1934, p. x). A survey, conducted by Jones (1987), indicated that McDougall's treatment by the popular press (*New York Times*) was consistently harsh and negative. McDougall believed that "the hornets' nest" he stirred up with his Lowell lectures on "the racial question" led to the "hostility of the American press" toward all of his subsequent publications (1930, p. 213).[1]

Reception of McDougall's Purposive Psychology in America

McDougall's ideas on instincts introduced in his *Social Psychology* were well known in America, although he was often misunderstood. The negative reaction

---

[1]Robinson (1943) presents an annotated bibliography of all McDougall's publications.

to his theory was due, in part, to a general opposition to the view that behavior is innately determined. The progressive mood, then prevalent in the United States, was more receptive to the idea that an individual's behavior is shaped by experience, thus permitting anyone to achieve success. The fact that for McDougall only the emotional core of an instinct is not modifiable was typically ignored. Eventually, he would give in and replace the term instinct with *propensity* (McDougall, 1934), which was more representative of what he meant by the construct, but by this time it was too late.

McDougall continued to promote and develop his theoretical ideas and, while he was at Harvard, he published two textbooks, *Outline of Psychology* and *Outline of Abnormal Psychology*. The aim of the latter was to bring "together in one consistent scheme . . . the soundest and most fruitful in contemporary academic psychology and in the teachings of the various schools of abnormal psychology" (McDougall, 1926, p. viii). As the result of his experiences during the war, he was particularly interested in functional disorders, or neuroses, which he saw, in terms of his theory, as "commonly the expression of subconscious purposes" (p. 38). In the book he presented numerous case studies showing that "in the neurotic patient, the various tendencies of character, the sentiments, are not organised as they should be, in one harmonious system. Rather they are more or less divided into conflicting systems" (pp. 54–55).

Outline of Psychology, which he dedicated to the memory of James, was McDougall's most important academic book from this time. In it he expanded on the ideas presented in his other texts published more than a decade earlier. The contrast between McDougall's "sane Behaviorism" and Watsonian Behaviorism became more apparent with the publication of the *Outline*, and it received a hostile reception from American behaviorists. Watson (1923) wrote a sarcastic review of the book, equating McDougall's animistic position with an acceptance of traditional religion and superstition, and bringing up his interest in parapsychology. The two men came face-to-face in a public debate before "a large and distinguished audience" at the Psychology Club in Washington February 5, 1924 (Watson and McDougall, 1929). Watson again attacked McDougall's animism as religious superstition and rejected as nonscientific his endorsement of introspection as a method for psychology.

McDougall, professing that he had no association with conventional religion, countered by asserting that he was "a hard-boiled scientist, as hard-boiled as Dr. Watson himself" (Watson & McDougall, 1929, p. 45). However, McDougall believed that simplistic explanations are not the answer; the problems facing psychologists are "so obscure and difficult" (p. 54) that it is necessary to use all available data, those obtained from both conscious experience and the observation of behavior, if there is to be any hope of understanding human nature. McDougall outlined his disagreement with Watson on the two basic issues that divided them: the nature of behaviorism and the importance of mechanism. He was as caustic as usual in his attack on Watson, implying that the latter's simplified mechanistic behaviorism is "bizarre, paradoxical, preposterous, and outrageous" (p. 41).

Although the Watson–McDougall debate was referred to as "The Battle of Behaviorism," at this point McDougall decided that the term "behaviorism" was so widely used to describe mechanistic accounts that it should no longer be applied to his system. It is interesting to note that when the account of the debate was published 5 years later, by co-authors Watson and MacDougall, the frontispiece misspelled McDougall's name.

Hormic Theory of Action

For McDougall, innate tendencies, or instincts, are basic to the behavior of all animals. If one accepts the fact that human beings evolved from lower animals, it is appropriate to develop a theory of human action that is consistent with accounts of animal behavior. However, rather than suggesting that human behavior is mindless and reflexive, McDougall ascribed purpose to the action of all animals. To emphasize the purposive, goal-directed nature of behavior, he introduced the term "hormic" to describe his theory. The term, from the Greek word meaning "urge to action," was adopted from the work of P. T. Nunn (McDougall, 1923, p. 72) and clearly identified the dynamic properties central to the theory.

In *Outline of Psychology*, McDougall (1923) described many examples of the purposiveness in animal behavior, dealing with situations involving both classical conditioning and trial-and-error learning. He was particularly critical of Thorndike's (chap. 10, *Pioneers I*) law of effect. McDougall could not believe that animals were little automata, whose responses are stamped in by reward; he saw them as acting intelligently with the purpose of reaching a goal, food in Thorndike's puzzle-box studies. To support his arguments against Thorndike's position, McDougall carried out a number of tests, the results of which he believed revealed intelligent responding aimed at achieving a goal. In one situation, the obverse of the puzzle-box procedure, rats were required to open multiple latches to obtain food placed in the box. The fact that the latches were not always lifted in the same order, or with the same movements, indicated to McDougall that Thorndike's mechanistic account was inadequate. Although some of these tests were carried out at Harvard, most were conducted in his home by his youngest son, Kenneth. Incidental observations of the behavior of the rats in his Lamarckian experiment also provided evidence to support McDougall's contention that responding is intelligent and purposive, not automatic and inflexible (McDougall & McDougall, 1927).

Lamarckian evolution, the idea that knowledge obtained as a result of an individual's experience could be passed on to the next generation, was not even considered possible by most scientists. McDougall, however, maintained that until there was objective proof, one way or the other, it could not be rejected outright.

To study the possibility meant a commitment to a long-term research program, examining the behavior of many generations. Albino rats were trained on a discrimination learning procedure in a water maze, in which they were required to swim to a platform to escape from the water. Reaching one of the platforms (S−) resulted in a painful electric shock; reaching the other platform (S+) permitted a painless escape. After they had mastered the task, the rats were bred and their offspring trained on the same task, for many generations. From 1920 to 1926, 13 generations of rats were studied and the data seemed to support the Lamarckian position.

A second phase of the study involving generations 14 to 23 started in 1926 and continued until 1929. These data were even more heartening for McDougall; the offspring of the trained group learned the task much more efficiently than controls whose ancestors had not been trained on the task. McDougall reported his findings at the meeting of the International Congress of Psychology held at Yale University in 1929. His presentation met with a "slashing attack" by James McKeen Cattell, based on what one member of the audience believed was a difference in "fundamental philosophy, rather than the particular 'Lamarckian' experiment under consideration" (Shakow & Rapaport, 1964, pp. 40–41, footnote 13). McDougall moved the apparatus to Duke University when he took a position there in 1927 and continued the experiments with the assistance of J. B. Rhine (chap. 13, *Pioneers II*) until 1933, for a total of 34 generations. Webb (1989) provided an account of these studies, and of the procedural flaws (e.g., control groups that were not from the same litters) that probably produced the observed differences.

Duke University

Duke University in Durham, North Carolina, was established in 1924. William Preston Few, president of Trinity College in Durham, had persuaded the Duke family of American Tobacco Company wealth to endow this new university. Faculty positions included a professor of psychology, and when the man who initially held the post left after a year, Few wrote to McDougall "asking him to suggest possible candidates, either an outstanding mature psychologist or a very promising young one" (Mauskopf & McVaugh, 1980, p. 132). After sending the names of some young men, including Boring, W. S. Hunter (chap. 18, *Pioneers I*), Karl Lashley (chap. 20, *Pioneers I*), and E. C. Tolman (chap. 15, *Pioneers I*), whom he saw as possibilities, McDougall wrote to Few again indicating his own interest in the position. Although advised that McDougall was more of a speculative theorist than an experimenter, and unlikely to build a strong research department at Duke, Few was still eager to hire him. He and McDougall shared an "indomitable opposition to behaviorist psychology and, more generally, to materialistic philosophy" (p. 133)—McDougall was the man for the job. McDougall accepted, and in December 1926 submitted his resignation to Harvard. Again

McDougall had both personal and professional reasons for making a move. The reason he gave Harvard when he resigned was that for health reasons both he and his wife would benefit from the warm and sunny weather in the south. Professionally, however, he had begun to feel (with some justification) that he was not being consulted when decisions concerning the psychologists in the department were being made. He was on leave in Europe when he resigned, and from there he traveled around the world, stopping in Borneo and other points in Asia, and at the University of California, in Berkeley, before going to North Carolina.

McDougall took up his position at Duke in the late summer of 1927. The following year he began to build a psychology department. His first three appointments went to former students or associates at Harvard. Karl Zener, who received his Ph.D. at Harvard, was teaching at Princeton when McDougall offered him a position in 1928. Two years later, they were joined by Helge Lundholm, who had been a Research Fellow at Harvard in the mid-1920s, and in 1931 Donald K. Adams, a Harvard student, just back after two years of postdoctoral study in Berlin was added (Mauskopf & McVaugh, 1980). Berlin, at that time, was the center of the growing Gestalt psychology movement, which McDougall viewed in a very positive light, noting many similarities with his own position (McDougall, 1933). Both McDougall and Kurt Lewin (chap. 7, *Pioneers III*) had developed dynamic theories of motivation, and McDougall was pleased to welcome the Topology Society, established by Lewin after he moved to the United States, when it met at Duke University.

As a firm opponent of mechanism, President Few supported the inheritance research with which Rhine was assisting McDougall. For the same reasons, he supported McDougall's plans, also carried out in collaboration with Rhine who took a position in the Psychology Department in 1931, to establish a field they called parapsychology. McDougall was "philosophically and morally . . . predisposed to accept psychic research; yet his professional training compelled him to adopt a skeptical and critical attitude towards any claim for psychic phenomena, particularly towards any spiritualistic explanation for them" (Mauskopf and McVaugh, 1980, p. 59). Now he was able to fulfill his long-time goal of scientifically examining the viability of various physic phenomena, such as telepathy and clairvoyance, in a university setting. Although in his lifetime McDougall believed that research supported the claims of parapsychology as well the inheritance of acquired characteristics, producing serious problems for the mechanists, he was wrong on both counts.

CONCLUSIONS

In 1964, in his assessment of McDougall's career, Hearnshaw claimed that "were McDougall alive today, he would regard many of his views as being vindicated" (p. 191). Were he alive now he might claim even greater vindication.

His career must be judged, however, not in terms of today's psychology, but on how it was perceived in his lifetime. At the time of his death in 1938, McDougall's goal of a psychology that includes the study of mental life as well as of behavior, a psychology in which purpose is central, a psychology that recognizes the innate propensities underlying all behavior, had not been achieved. The behaviorist Zeitgeist that prevailed in America during the 1920s and 1930s meant that hormic psychology, involving instincts and purpose, concepts that were disparaged by the behaviorists, was not widely accepted. Moreover, although he believed that he was always fair in his assessments, McDougall's caustic criticism of opposing theories did not help him to win others over to his position. His animism and his vehement opposition to mechanism, exemplified in his support of research on Lamarckian evolution and psychic phenomena—areas deemed unscientific by most serious researchers—made his more conventional ideas suspect. Hearnshaw concluded that "there was something fatally wrong [in the way McDougall presented his science], which justified much of the sniping against him. In spite of his prolonged scientific education McDougall was never a scientist at heart. . . . For what McDougall was trying to do was to provide the answers to problems before the factual data needed even for provisional answers were available" (1964, pp. 191–192). McDougall's Duke colleagues, although agreeing that his failure to achieve his goals for psychology was indeed a "major tragedy" (Adams, 1939, p. 8), held out hope for the future. When "satisfactory answers to all the problems with which he wrestled have been finally formulated psychology will have become a science indeed, and the goal of a great mind achieved" (Zener, 1939, p. 192).

REFERENCES

Adams, D. K. (1939). William McDougall. *Psychological Review, 46*, 1–8.

Boring, E. G. (1929). *A history of experimental psychology*. New York: Century.

Burt, C. (1955). The permanent contributions of McDougall to psychology. *British Journal of Educational Psychology, 25*, 10–22.

Hearnshaw, L. S. (1964). *A short history of British psychology, 1840–1940*. London: Methuen.

Hose, C., & McDougall, W. (1912). *The pagan tribes of Borneo*. London: Macmillan.

James, W. (1890). *The principles of psychology*. New York: Holt.

Jones, R. A. (1987). Psychology, history, and the press. The case of William McDougall and the *New York Times*. *American Psychologist, 42*, 931–940.

Langfeld, H. S. (1940). Professor McDougall's contributions to the science of psychology. *British Journal of Psychology, 31*, 107–114.

Mauskopf, S. H., & McVaugh, M. R. (1980). *The elusive science: Origins of experimental psychical research*. Baltimore, MD: The Johns Hopkins University Press.

McDougall, W. (1898). A contribution towards an improvement in psychological method. *Mind, 7*, 15–33, 159–178, 364–387.

McDougall, W. (1901). Some new observations in support of Thomas Young's theory of light and colour vision. *Mind, 10*, 52–97, 210–245, 347–382.

McDougall, W. (1902). The physiological factors of the attention process. I. *Mind, 11*, 316–351.

McDougall, W. (1905). On a new method for the study of concurrent mental operations and of mental fatigue. *British Journal of Psychology, 1*, 435–445.

McDougall, W. (1908). An investigation of the colour sense of two infants. *British Journal of Psychology, 2*, 338–352.

McDougall, W. (1911). *Body and mind: A history and defense of animism*. London: Methuen.

McDougall, W. (1912). *Psychology: The study of behaviour*. New York: Holt.

McDougall, W. (1920). *The group mind*. Cambridge: Cambridge University Press.

McDougall, W. (1923). *An outline of psychology*. London: Methuen.

McDougall, W. (1926). *Outline of abnormal psychology*. New York: Scribner's.

McDougall, W. (1930). William McDougall. In C. Murchison (Ed.), *A history of psychology in autobiography* (pp. 191–223). Worcester, MA: Clark University Press.

McDougall, W. (1933). *The energies of men*. New York: Scribner's.

McDougall, W. (1934). *Religion and the sciences of life*. London: Methuen.

McDougall, W. (1960). *An introduction to social psychology* (23rd ed.). New York: Barnes and Noble. (Original work published 1908)

McDougall, W., & McDougall, K. D. (1927). Notes on instinct and intelligence in rats and cats. *Journal of Comparative Psychology, 7*, 145–175.

Robinson, A. L. (1943). *William McDougall: A bibliography*. Durham, NC: Duke University Press.

Shakow, D., & Rapaport, D. (1964). *The influence of Freud on American psychology*. New York: International Universities Press.

Watson, J. B. (1923). Professor McDougall returns to religion. *The New Republic, 14*, 11–12.

Watson, J. B., & McDougall, W. (1929). *The battle of behaviorism*. New York: Norton.

Webb, W. (1989). William McDougall's Lamarckian experiments. *The Psychological Record, 39*, 159–176.

Zener, K. (1939). William McDougall. *Science, 89*, 191–192.

Chapter 7

June Etta Downey: Pioneer of Personality Measurement

John D. Hogan
St. John's University, NY

Dennis N. Thompson
Georgia State University

June Downey was one of the first psychologists to study personality scientifically. She was also an international expert on handwriting and handedness. In fact, it was her research on handwriting and other motor functions that led to the development of the Downey Individual Will–Temperament Test, a first-generation personality inventory. Downey headed the combined Department of Philosophy and Psychology at the University of Wyoming, the first woman to hold such a position at a state university. From 1923 to 1925 she served on the Council of the American Psychological Association, a rare appointment for a woman at that time. She was also one of the first two women to become a member of the Society of Experimental Psychologists. Although Downey's contributions have become obscure, she was very prominent in her day. Perhaps the most important outcome of her work was to promote a scientific basis for the study of personality and personality testing.

FAMILY BACKGROUND AND EARLY YEARS

June Etta Downey was born on July 13, 1875, in Laramie, Wyoming. She was the oldest daughter and the second of nine children born to Stephen Wheeler Downey and Evangeline Owen Downey. Stephen Downey was a native of Maryland who had practiced law in Washington, D.C. (James & James, 1971). He had also been a colonel in the Union Army, leading the 3rd Maryland Brigade at Harper's Ferry during the Civil War (Busby, 1996). He moved to Wyoming in 1869 and became one of Wyoming's first Territorial Delegates to the United States Congress and a member of the Territorial Legislature (Uhrbrock, 1933). He was the author of the bill that provided for the organization of a university, which was signed by the governor on March 4, 1886. Later, Colonel Downey became known as the "Father of the University" because it was largely through his efforts that the University of Wyoming was founded. He served as president of the University Board of Regents for many years.

Other members of the Downey family were also active and visible. Evangeline Owen Downey, June's mother, had a reputation as a community leader. June's younger brother, Sheridan Downey, served as the U.S. Senator from California from 1938 to 1950 (James & James, 1971). June's uncle, W. O. Owen, was the first known climber to scale Grand Teton Mountain, the most prominent landmark in what is now Grand Teton National Park.

Education

Downey completed her elementary education in public schools in Laramie and continued at the preparatory school of the University of Wyoming. She entered the University of Wyoming and graduated in 1895 with a bachelor's degree in Greek and Latin. She remained in Laramie to teach in a public elementary school for the following year (Faculty of the University of Wyoming, 1934). While at the university she came under the influence of Edwin E. Slosson, a young assistant professor of chemistry. He encouraged her interest in the experimental sciences, including psychology and even aesthetics (James & James, 1971). She later published a book with Slosson, *Plots and Personalities* (1922). It was her interest in aesthetics that led her to the University of Chicago, where she received a master's degree in 1898. Her thesis was titled: "Berkeley's Theory of the Will as Found in His Common Place Book." Serving on her examination committee was the psychologist John Dewey (chap. 4, *Pioneers II*), who later became better known for his writings in philosophy and education (Committee, 1898). While at Chicago, Downey published her first article, "A Musical Experiment," in the *AJP* (1897). The link between psychology and the arts was one of her lifelong interests.

Early Career

After graduation, Downey returned to the University of Wyoming, first as an instructor in English, and in the following year (1899) as an instructor in English and philosophy. She remained on the Wyoming faculty for the rest of her life. In 1901, she attended the summer session at Cornell University, where she studied under Edward B. Titchener (chap. 7, *Pioneers I*), a student of Wundt (chap. 3, *Pioneers III*), and an important leader in early experimental psychology in America. Her strong interest in experimental psychology was evident from that point on, and when she returned to Wyoming she began to teach some psychology courses and to conduct laboratory work.

In 1905, Downey was made a full professor of English and philosophy at the University of Wyoming, but the following year she was granted a sabbatical so she could return to the University of Chicago to work toward a doctoral degree. At Chicago, she was awarded a fellowship in the Department of Psychology to work for her doctorate under the mentorship of James Rowland Angell (chap. 4, this volume). Both John B. Watson (chap. 12, *Pioneers I*), later known for his work in behaviorism, and Angell, who later became the president of Yale, were among the subjects for her dissertation. After her death, Angell described Downey as "an extraordinarily satisfactory student, endowed with an unusually alert and discerning mind and with a maturity of judgment extremely infrequent in students of her age" (Faculty of the University of Wyoming, 1934).

Downey's doctoral research, titled "Control Processes in Modified Handwriting: An Experimental Study," was published in the *Psychological Monographs* (1908). In it, Downey maintained that handwriting provides cues to an individual's temperament and personality. Downey received her doctorate degree in psychology, with honors, in 1908, and she continued to study handwriting throughout her life. From 1910 to 1924, she wrote a series of articles entitled "Graphic Functions" that periodically reviewed handwriting research (e.g., Downey, 1911).

After completion of her doctorate, Downey was named head of the Department of English at the University of Wyoming (Uhrbrock, 1933). In 1915, she was named professor of psychology and philosophy and head of the newly combined Department of Psychology and Philosophy, a position she held until her death. She was the first woman to lead such a department in a state university in the country. Although it is likely that her father's prominence played a role in helping her secure this position, she nonetheless brought strong credentials to her new post (Rossiter, 1982). She was also important to the university in other ways. For example, she acted as principal of the Department of University Extension from 1908 until 1916. During her tenure as chair of the Graduate Committee, the number of graduate students increased from 3 to more than 200.

THE CREATIVE ARTS

Downey was greatly interested in the creative arts. She wrote poems, plays, and stories throughout her life, including a number of popular articles. A volume of her poems, *The Heavenly Dykes*, was published in 1904. She even wrote the music and lyrics to "Alma Mater" for the University of Wyoming. She believed it is possible to learn important things about people by studying their craft. In addition, Downey thought the reaction of people to art says a great deal about them. Her first published article, "A Musical Experiment," examined the reactions of people to various pieces of music. She soon expanded her psychological interests to poetry and prose. In 1912, she published "The Imaginal Reaction to Poetry," one of her most important experiments involving the arts. This study examined the differences in the images people had in response to reading poetry. Downey believed that the variation in such images reveals differences in character. She differentiated two general types of personality from her examination of reactions to poetry. The first was the "diffluente" type, characterized by vague responses that are emotionally laden and full of kinesthetic images. The second was the "plastique" type, characterized by precise responses that are rich in imagery and emphasize spatial relationships. She also explored the relationship between psychology and literature in general (Downey, 1918).

DOWNEY'S CONTRIBUTIONS TO EARLY PERSONALITY TESTING

Perhaps the best known of the early efforts in personality testing was the Army Rating Scale, written by Walter Dill Scott (Committee on the Classification of Personnel in the Army, 1918), designed to test recruits during World War I. The scale called for the ranking of individuals on each of five variables including "leadership" and "personal qualities." The scale met with almost immediate criticism. For instance, it was argued that the Army scales failed to define clearly the traits to be measured. On a trait such as leadership, for example, different raters could have different understandings of the meaning of the term and would therefore be rating different things.

By the early 1920s, research indicated that another approach to assessing personality—that is, basing it on the shape of the head or facial features—was not supported by evidence. Downey (1923) attempted to measure personality traits and other characteristics such as intelligence from facial features. She assembled pictures of psychologists, philosophers, and "good-looking but commonplace pedagogues." She had participants arrange the pictures in order from highest to lowest on a particular characteristic but found poor reliability compared with other more objective assessments. She did, however, report a tendency for participants to rate the pictures of psychologists at the lower end of the curve on several of the characteristics.

Other approaches to personality research in this period were equally nonproductive. Downey (1923) reported on Fernald's Achievement Capacity Test, a test that was constructed to measure "will, persistency, and determination." Downey took a particular interest in the test because it was designed to measure traits similar to those measured with her own instrument. In taking Fernald's test, individuals were instructed to stand with their heels raised one fourth of an inch off the floor. During the test, the participants were monitored and informed if their heels were lowered beneath the height requirement. The score on the test was the duration during which individuals could keep their heels elevated.

In her review of the test, Downey reported that the average score for elevation was about 50 min, with a range from 12 min to more than 2 hr. The rationale was that an individual high on drive or determination would receive a high score on the test. The test did have some adherents, particularly among those who believed it differentiated delinquent youth from those who did not have police records. It was believed that delinquent youths received lower scores. Downey, however, argued that one of the limitations of the test was the difficulty in measuring whether the individual was meeting the required level of heel elevation. Before long, Downey would be equally concerned with problems concerning her own tests, particularly issues of reliable measurement and valid interpretation.

THE DOWNEY WILL–TEMPERAMENT SCALE

Personality measurement was still in its infancy when Downey introduced her Individual Will–Temperament Test. Even 10 years later some writers referred to personality measurement as a new field of inquiry, although by 1929 the field contained more than 100 measures (Bronner, Healy, Lowe, & Shimberg, 1929). The importance of Downey's instrument cannot be overestimated.

Preliminaries

The research that led up to the Will–Temperament Scale dated back to 1908 and consisted of two lines of inquiry. The earlier of the two was an attempt to determine whether "muscle reading" could be developed into a reliable means for the study of personality. This was followed later by research that investigated whether personality could be determined from handwriting.

In the early years of the 20th century, "mind reading" or "muscle reading" was a popular vaudeville stunt. In one example of this, the mind reader would attempt to discover where an object is located by holding the hand of someone who knew where it had been hidden. Questions would be asked and the reader, by noting changes in muscle tension, would locate the object. In other demonstrations, the reader would try to guess the number a person was thinking of, or to identify a target card from a deck.

In her laboratory at the university, Downey attempted to duplicate some of the tricks that were common in vaudeville. In one, she was blindfolded and located a clock that was hidden high on a ledge by holding the wrist of a guide. In her experiment, she followed the guide from place to place and noted change in the tension of the guide's muscles. During her work with muscle reading, she discovered that a reliable way to identify good guides was to have them write something on a piece of paper while they were distracted. Under these conditions, individuals who turned out to be good guides tended to write larger or faster than they normally would. She believed that the distraction caused the "brakes" to be released and therefore individuals would more freely express themselves. Downey termed these individuals "explosive." By her reasoning, they would express emotional states through muscle movement of various kinds.

Initially, Downey explored the possibility of determining personality by some measure of muscle movement. She argued that character is judged from "action." However, she quickly discarded this idea, because she was convinced that muscle reading depends too much on the skill of the operator. She maintained that it is impossible to determine whether a conclusion is due to the skill of the muscle reader or to the subject's actual temperamental makeup.

The next step in Downey's research was to determine whether handwriting analysis could reveal personality differences. Her dissertation had been on handwriting analysis, but by the time her book *Graphology and the Psychology of Handwriting* (1919b) was published, she had become critical of many of the claims of contemporary graphologists. It was commonly believed at the time that small handwriting indicates an interest in detail, and that heavy forceful handwriting indicated a strong will. Similarly, handwriting that slants upward was believed to be a sign of an optimistic temperament, and handwriting that slants downward was a sign of depression. In her book she reported little evidence to support most of these claims. However, she had made her own set of discoveries.

The handwriting exercises she used to identify reliable muscle guides led her to conclude that people who use large handwriting while distracted tend to have different personalities from those who use small handwriting while distracted. This observation led to the development of her first test, which she labeled "motor impulsion." It was designed to differentiate the "explosive" individual from the highly controlled individual.

This preliminary work on personality testing led to the creation of the Downey Individual Will–Temperament Test (Downey, 1919a) and a series of studies culminating in the book, *The Will–Temperament and Its Testing*, which appeared in 1923. By the term "will–temperament" Downey was referring to the amount of energy that individuals have at their disposal, and the manner in which it is expressed. By the time the book was published, the individual version of the test contained 10 subtests. A rationale for the Will–Temperament Test can be gleaned from a review of the subtests.

Structure of the Test

The Will–Temperament Test was divided into three sections, with three to four subtests in each of them. The first section was "Speed and Fluidity of Reaction." One subtest in this section was "Speed of Movement." This subtest was scored by measuring the length of time it takes to write the words: "The United States of America." Downey reasoned that the score on this test gives an indication of the amount of physical work that an individual could "put through in a given time." In her *Graphology and the Psychology of Handwriting* (1919b), she had reported that writing speed was an indicator of general body speed and that writing speed correlates with other measures of psychomotor speed used at the time, such as tests of the rate of tapping.

Another subtest in this section was designed to measure flexibility. Here, individuals taking the test were asked to change or "disguise" their handwriting. Downey argued that adaptable and flexible people would be able to change the appearance of their handwriting, whereas a less flexible individual would have more difficulty. The amount of disguise was scored by comparison with a scale of specimens. A subtest called "Speed of Decision" required individuals taking the test to check from a list of character traits the traits they believed best described them. The score for this subtest was the length of time it took to choose a set of traits and complete the test. Downey argued that the test measured the speed with which individuals make decisions in general, and she reported a wide range of individual differences in the time necessary to complete the test, ranging from 1 min to more than 15 min.

The second section of the Will–Temperament Test was "Tests of Aggressive Traits." By the term "aggressive traits" Downey meant such personality characteristics as forcefulness and decisiveness. It is here that Downey included her test of "motor impulsion" and her concept of the explosive personality. She described this type of personality as follows: "He monopolizes conversation, leads movements of reform, is a convincing speaker, and sells himself well" (Downey, 1923, p. 107). As mentioned earlier, the explosive personality was measured by changes in the size of handwriting when the individual was distracted. Downey argued that distraction served to release an "automatic reaction" in the individual, indicating how forceful the individual could be in daily life.

Several critics noted, however, that the traits she was measuring were not very clearly defined. Descriptions of traits seemed to shift from one place in her writing to another. For example, in addition to maintaining that the explosive personality is a convincing speaker and could lead movements of reform, Downey also offered this description of an explosive personality:

> I may cite in this connection an interesting concrete example of what I mean by explosive expressive tendencies. Recently, after scoring a record for motor impulsion, I remarked that the individual who had just been scored 10 for this trait in a group test should, if as explosive as the sample of writing indicated, give further evidence of it. With this thought in mind I turned over the leaves of the booklet and found three evidences of great impetuosity. Three unsolicited comments on the tests have been entered. On the title page the individual in question had written above the word Test "Acid." After his disguised hand he had penciled "Rah! Rah!" and after his practice on disguises of handwriting "Bunk!" How typical of the uninhibited individual! (Downey, 1923, pp. 107–108)

Downey was particularly impressed by this example and used it in several of her writings.

The third section on the Will–Temperament Test was "Carefulness and Persistence of Reaction." One subtest in this section was a test of "motor inhibition." Downey designed this subtest to measure the ability to keep an impulse under control and to achieve a purpose slowly. She believed that this skill is essential to the careers of surgeons and craftsmen alike. In social life, she saw it as a measure of the ability to refrain from speaking under provocation and to maintain reserve. The test measured how slowly an individual could write the words: "The United States of America." She found wide individual differences in performance on this test, ranging from a few seconds to more than 45 min to complete the task.

Interpretation of Test Performance

The results of the Will–Temperament Test were presented on a graph called the "will profile." As the test became more widely used, she cautioned against the use of a total score, which had become a common practice, and strongly encouraged examiners to look at the intra-individual relationships among the subtest scores. She thought that the components of the test were interrelated and that looking at an individual subtest score or total score did not represent the person as an integrated whole. For example, a will profile showing an emphasis on the "speed" and "fluidity of reaction" subtests characterized a "seat-of-the-pants," "hair-trigger" type of person. A will profile emphasizing "carefulness" and "persistence" scores characterized a deliberate person interested in detail and accuracy. And an emphasis on the aggressive traits is indicative of personal force and initiative. Although she believed that the profile would designate people as primarily one of three personality types, she was open to the possibility that some individuals would exhibit mixed characteristics.

Downey's instrument was one of the first tests intended to evaluate character traits separately from intellectual capacity. But in interpreting a profile, the intelligence level of the individual was often considered. Theoretically, Downey reasoned, two individual will profiles should be interpreted differently if the individuals differ significantly in intelligence. On this point she wrote: "Explosive tendencies which may speed an individual of great ability to success may ruin a less intelligent man. Inhibitions may nullify genius; they may protect a moron" (Downey, 1923, p. 61).

Applications and Evaluations

The Will–Temperament Test generated a flurry of research. A few psychologists thought the test might be particularly useful with people of different races and ethnicities. Because of its emphasis on motor actions, it did not appear to favor any particular group. Research was conducted to determine whether the test had diagnostic value. Some individuals believed that the test successfully differentiated between delinquents and nondelinquents (reported in Reisman, 1976). Other research efforts attempted to establish uses for the test in a variety of public and private settings. For example, the Carnegie Institute of Technology reported that the test had been used in the selection program for insurance salesmen at the Carnegie Bureau of Personnel Research. Their research indicated that the test was useful in predicting the success of salesmen, "whereas tests of general mental ability, aside from assigning a minimum essential, had little predictive value" (Downey, 1922a, p. 162). Another investigation at Carnegie considered the possibility of using the test as a college entrance examination. The evidence indicated that students in different majors had different profiles.

Downey adapted the test to administer to groups, creating the Downey Group Will–Temperament Test (Downey, 1922b). A different group test was also developed by the Carnegie Institute of Technology, and later Downey created a nonverbal version designed for use with school children below the fifth grade (Uhrbrock & Downey, 1929). At one point she even sought to develop a will–temperament test based on speech, but when the reliability of this test proved to be low, she abandoned the effort.

Although highly valuable in its intent and originality, the Downey tests possessed great weaknesses. Downey repeatedly emphasized the importance of the intra-individual relationship among the subtest scores, but did not provide group norms for comparison. A number of researchers conducted evaluations of the test (e.g., Gorham & Brotemarkle, 1929; Herskovits, 1924; Ruch & Del-Mango, 1923). In general, the test had poor reliability, the subtests were very short, and the subtests that supposedly measured similar traits did not correlate highly with each other. Overall, the test possessed poor validity, at least when the results were compared with personality rankings. In fact, 35 pieces of research were consistent in pointing to the questionable validity of the test (Reisman, 1976). In addition, there were complaints that the administration of the test was complicated and the scoring was too subjective. It was concluded that although the Downey tests were among "the most carefully standardized and most highly elaborated" tests yet devised, they were not ready for widespread use in the schools (Reisman, 1976, p. 158).

Downey for her part took the criticism graciously and wrote many articles responding to critics. In these articles she played an active role in helping define how studies on test reliability and validity should be done. There was, however, one line of criticism about which she was particularly sensitive. She consistently maintained that the Will–Temperament Test and its scales were based on a firm research foundation. At one point she wrote:

That the will–temperament tests are in the early pioneer stage I am well aware. Criticism, particularly when backed by experimental material, is warmly welcomed. But I am frequently sensitive to the fact that my critics do not have the background given by my previous studies and that there is little realization that the tests were not selected in a hit or miss fashion, but have developed to a certain extent from the application of a general principle. (Downey, 1922a, p. 168)

All of the weaknesses and criticisms, however, prevented the tests from being generally accepted and respected. Downey was planning to revise the tests at the time of her death.

BRANCHING OUT

As applied psychology continued to grow in the 1920s, many psychologists began to consider themselves "consulting" psychologists. In contemporary terms, they would probably be labeled clinical, school, and industrial–organizational psychologists. Downey joined this applied group, although apparently in name only.

Consultation

In 1925, APA devised a plan to certify "consulting" psychologists in an effort to monitor the quality of the practice of psychologists. This plan was similar to the situation that exists today with state licensing boards. The effort by APA was ultimately a failure. Only two dozen psychologists applied to be certified as consulting psychologists, and the attempt was eventually abandoned. Before it was, however, Downey became a certified consulting psychologist (Hogan & Sexton, 1991).

A Book for Children

Downey tried to reach a student audience with her book The *Kingdom of the Mind* (1927). The book was part of a series of science books published by Macmillan targeted for children and edited by her colleague Slosson. With her pioneering volume, she tried to introduce boys and girls to psychology. The *Kingdom of the Mind* is a delightful book that, in many ways, continues to be enjoyable reading today. She covered most of the areas then current in psychology and did it in a way that would have been of interest to both children and their parents. In the chapter on learning, for example, she not only covered learning curves, offering the reader demonstrations of the point, but she provided a wonderful example of a chart developed by Benjamin Franklin that he used to help himself track and control his bad habits. The book was well reviewed. *The New York Herald Tribune* wrote, "The work is gracefully written and humanly presented so that he who reads can't help wanting to learn" (House, 1928, p. 17). There was, however, at the time some hesitation about taking this still new field of psychology and presenting it to children. For example, a review in the *Wilson Library Bulletin* argued, "One of the dangers involved is that the reader of such a diluted treatment of psychological principles may mistake the froth for the substance and use with harm to oneself or others the semi-psychological or pseudo-psychological information secured" (Good, 1928, p. 127).

THE FINAL YEARS

Despite her visibility, Downey never craved the spotlight. As she grew older, she concentrated on her teaching and left Laramie less often. She was considered a master teacher, with high standards of scholarship. At the same time, she gave student advice gently and filled it with whimsical humor. When a proposal to form Psi Chi, an honor society for psychology, was circulated, she became one of its earliest and strongest supporters. When the organization formally came into existence in 1929, the University of Wyoming was one of fewer than two dozen colleges and universities to attain charter status in the organization. Psi Chi is now the largest psychology society in the world and one of the largest honor societies.

Downey published her last book, *Creative Imagination*, in 1929. In it she attempted to tie together her lifelong interests in psychology and the arts. Here she offered a definition of creativity and began her book by arguing that creative intelligence is the "outstanding mystery of the world." She stated that the imaginative individual is different from the unimaginative individual in the freedom with which materials at one's disposal are used. She went on to argue that the richer and more vivid that material and the more subtle the sense of relationship, the greater is the possibility for creative imagination. Creative intelligence could, she reasoned, be measured in terms of the permutations and combinations in which elements are restored and assigned. As a result, the creative genius is able to create new patterns, new configurations, and new emergents.

Unfortunately, Downey's book was poorly organized and chapters appeared to many to be disjointed and unrelated to each other. Some of the material had been previously published and intended for other purposes. There was little sense that there was a unified logic or theme to the book. It was her most negatively received book. A review from the *Saturday Review* typifies the sentiment: "Miss Downey's book is so loosely constructed, . . . so irritatingly purposeless as to make all her readers, to whatever school of thought they may belong, wish that they had not to undergo the burden of reading it" (*Saturday Review*, 1929, p. 301). Some reviews were derisive. *The Nation* wrote: "It seems doubtful whether a person who pays so much attention to hypnosis and manipulations of the Ouija board, and so little to organization, equilibrium, and awareness is going the right way to work" (Vines, 1929, p. 344).

In the last decade of her life Downey received many forms of recognition, including a 2-year appointment (1923–1925) to the Council of the APA—the equivalent of today's Board of Directors—membership in the Society of Experimental Psychologists (1929), and election as a Fellow of the American Association for the Advancement of Science (1924). These were rare honors for a woman at that time. For example, in the 30 years before Downey was appointed to the Council of the APA, only two other women had been appointed to that position. They were Mary Whiton Calkins (chap. 5, *Pioneers I*) and Margaret Floy Washburn (chap. 5, this volume), each of whom later became president of the APA. After Downey's term on the Council of the APA ended, it was another 9 years before another woman served in that office.

Downey's membership in the Society of Experimental Psychologists was also noteworthy. The society had never been friendly toward women. Its founder, Downey's old Cornell professor, Titchener, had specifically excluded women from the organization and had managed to keep them out until his death, despite the protests of those who had been denied entrance. After Titchener's death in 1927, the society was reorganized. In 1929, Downey was one of the first two women elected to membership, along with Washburn. By that time, however, Downey's trips outside of Wyoming had become rare, and it is doubtful that she ever attended a meeting of the society (Rossiter, 1982).

As a Fellow of the American Association for the Advancement of Science, Downey spoke at the annual meeting of that organization in December 1924, in Washington, D.C. There she presented her observations of the differences between men and women in the dominant use of the right versus left hand ("Science peace role," 1924). She also had the distinction of appearing in the fourth edition of *American Men of Science* (1927) with a star, indicating that she was one of the outstanding scientists included in the volume.

Downey became ill while attending the Third International Congress on Eugenics in New York City. She died 2 months later, on October 11, 1932, of stomach cancer at the home of her sister in Trenton, New Jersey. She was 57 years old.

Several impediments limited Downey's productivity. Her health was not always robust, the university had limited resources, and she carried a heavy teaching load. Despite these encumbrances, Downey made great contributions to the experimental study of personality. She believed strongly in the mind–body connection and identified motor processes as a way to express character traits. In all, she wrote seven books and more than 70 articles. In her later years, her research focused on imagery and handedness.

Although June Downey was not the first to draw attention to personality as an integrated whole, she was the first to devise a test of personality supported by research and theory. Ultimately, research demonstrated that writing specific phrases and scoring them in a variety of ways did not make for a set of reliable measures of personality. Nevertheless, as Uhrbrock (1933) wrote in his obituary of her, nothing can take away from Downey's place in the field of personality measurement or detract from the credit due her for stimulating a vast amount of research on the problems of personality testing.

Downey was buried in Green Hill Cemetery in Laramie, Wyoming, the city of her birth and the place where she chose to spend most of her life. Her family presented her private library to the university shortly after her death. The university held a memorial service for her, and a bronze plaque was unveiled in her honor. In 1999, she was named one of the finalists for the title "Wyoming Citizen of the Century."

REFERENCES

Bronner, A. F., Healy, W., Lowe, G. M., & Shimberg, M. E. (1929). *A manual of individual mental tests and testing.* Boston: Little, Brown.

Busby, M. (1996). Civil War on line. Retrieved 4/21/01 from http://web2.airmail.net~mbusby/nharpers.htm

Cattell, J. M. (Ed.). (1927). *American men of science* (4th ed.). New York: Science Press.

Committee, Examination of June Etta Downey, A.M., Anatomy Building. (1898, March 18). *University Record*, p. 410.

Committee on the Classification of Personnel in the Army. (1918). How the army uses individual differences in experience. *Psychological Bulletin, 15*, 187–206.

Downey, J. E. (1897). A musical experiment. *American Journal of Psychology, 9*, 63–69.

Downey, J. E. (1904). *The heavenly dykes.* Boston: R. G. Badger.

Downey, J. E. (1908). Control processes in modified handwriting: An experimental study. *Psychological Monographs, 9*, 37.

Downey, J. E. (1911). Graphic functions. *Psychological Bulletin, 8*, 311–317.

Downey, J. E. (1912). The imaginal reaction to poetry: The affective and the aesthetic judgment. *The University of Wyoming Department of Psychology Bulletin, 2*, 5–56.

Downey, J. E. (1918). A program for a psychology of literature. *Journal of Applied Psychology, 2*, 366–377.

Downey, J. E. (1919a). The will-profile: A tentative scale for measurement of the volitional pattern. *University of Wyoming Department of Psychology Bulletin, 3*, 8–40.

Downey, J. E. (1919b). *Graphology and the psychology of handwriting.* Baltimore, MD: Warwick and York.

Downey, J. E. (1922a, August 5). Testing the Will–Temperament Tests. *School and Society, 16*, 161–168.

Downey, J. E. (1922b). *Downey Group Will–Temperament Test.* Yonkers, NY: World.

Downey, J. E. (1923). *The will–temperament and its testing.* Yonkers, NY: World.

Downey, J. E. (1927). *The kingdom of the mind.* New York: MacMillan.

Downey, J. E. (1929). *Creative imagination: Studies in the psychology of literature.* New York: Harcourt, Brace.

Faculty of the University of Wyoming. (1934). *In memoriam: June Etta Downey, 1875–1932.*

Good, C. V. (1928, April). [Review of the book *Kingdom of the mind*]. *Wilson Library Bulletin, 24*, 127.

Gorham, D. R., & Brotemarkle, R. A. (1929). Challenging three standardized emotional tests for validity and employability. *Journal of Applied Psychology, 13*, 554–579.

Herskovits, M. J. (1924). A test of the Downey Will–Temperament Test. *Journal of Applied Psychology, 8*, 75–88.

Hogan, J. D., & Sexton, V. S. (1991). Women and the American Psychological Association. *Psychology of Women Quarterly, 15*, 623–634.

House, S. D. (1928, May 6). [Review of the book *Kingdom of the mind*]. *New York Herald Tribune*, p. 17.

James, E. T., & James, J. N. (1971). *Notable American women* (vol. 1). Cambridge, MA: Belknap Press.

Reisman, J. M. (1976). *A history of clinical psychology*. New York: Irvington.

Rossiter, M. W. (1982). *Women scientists in America: Struggles and strategies to 1940*. Baltimore, MD: Johns Hopkins University Press.

Ruch, G. M., & Del-Mango, M. C. (1923). The Downey Will–Temperament Group Test: A further analysis of its reliability and validity. *Journal of Applied Psychology, 7*, 65–76.

Saturday Review. (1929, September 14). [Review of the book *Creative imagination*]. *Saturday Review, 48*, 301.

Science peace role extolled by Hughes. (1924, December 30). *The New York Times*, p. 19.

Slosson, E. E., & Downey, J. E. (1922). *Plots and personalities: A new method of testing and training the creative imagination*. New York: Century.

Uhrbrock, R. S. (1933). June Etta Downey, July 13, 1875–October 11, 1932. *Journal of General Psychology, 9*, 351–364.

Uhrbrock, R. S., & Downey, J. E. (1929). A non-verbal Will–Temperament Test. *Journal of Applied Psychology, 11*, 95–105.

Vines, S. (1929, June 8). [Review of the book *Creative imagination*]. *The Nation and Athenaeum, 45*, 344.

Chapter 8

Kurt Goldstein: Clinician and Philosopher of Human Nature

Wade E. Pickren
American Psychological Association

> *It was this awareness of the metaphysical in life that rendered Goldstein suspect to minor minds who still adhered to atomistic forms of behaviorism and who wondered suspiciously about his many-sided interests, which extended from medical research to psychology and philosophy. What was he really, they asked: a physician, a psychologist, or a philosopher? (Ulich, 1968, p. 15)*

In 1937, a young psychologist named Molly Harrower received a Rockefeller Foundation Fellowship to study with Kurt Goldstein at Montefiore Hospital in New York City. She wanted to engage in psychological research with hospital patients and knew Goldstein's reputation for excellent rapport with patients. Harrower also knew that Goldstein had a long history of collaborating with psychologists and was open to the use of experimental psychology in medical settings. During her fellowship with Goldstein, Harrower met and collaborated with several psychologists who were close to Goldstein, including Joseph Zubin, Bruno Klopfer, Zygmunt Piotrowski, and Martin Scheerer. What Harrower found was that this remarkable neurologist, who had been in the United States for only 2 years, attracted talented people from a wide range of professions into his professional and personal circle (Harrower, 1991). Goldstein's reputation preceded him to this country and expanded once he was here. He was an astute clinician who was also a philosopher of human nature.

BIOGRAPHICAL NOTE

Kurt Goldstein was born in Katowice, Upper Silesia, in 1878. At the time of his birth, Upper Silesia was a part of Germany, but it is now part of Poland. He was the seventh of nine children and grew up in a busy, bustling atmosphere. His father's employees at a lumberyard joined the large family at lunch time. In addition, the house was often full of Goldstein's many cousins, including the future philosopher, Ernst Cassirer. Although Goldstein's father was not well educated, he made sure that all his sons earned advanced degrees. The family was of Jewish descent, but like many Jews of their time and place did not engage in the spiritual practices of Judaism.

While Goldstein was still a child, the family moved to the larger city of Breslau. Not much is known of his childhood, except that his schooling focused on the humanities, Latin, and Greek. He took cello lessons and retained a love for cello music all his life. He was also somewhat bookish as a child, earning the sobriquet, "professor," for his love of reading (Simmel, 1968, p. 3). His early education inspired him to want a professional life centered on literature and philosophy. After his graduation from the local gymnasium, Goldstein stated that he wanted to be a philosopher. His father objected and arranged instead for him to do menial work for a relative.

Goldstein soon tired of such work and entered the University of Breslau where he studied one semester and then transferred to the University of Heidelberg for a period of intense study of literature and philosophy. Goldstein then returned to Breslau, where he earned a medical degree. As he wrote in his autobiography, "Medicine appeared to me best suited to satisfy my deep inclination to deal with human beings and be able to help them" (Goldstein, 1967, p. 147). His training in medicine was supplemented by wide-ranging studies in many other fields, so he was able to incorporate his love of philosophy and the humanities into his training in biology and the natural sciences. The rich vision of human potential that he found in philosophy informed his life work in medicine.

Goldstein was attracted to the study of disorders of the nervous system, an area that seemed to be particularly in need of further research. Because it was suspected that brain pathology underlies mental and nervous disorders, neurophysiology and neuroanatomy were the fields of research that attracted him. He sought out individuals who were doing interesting work in these areas and found that he both enjoyed laboratory research and was proficient at it (Goldstein, 1959). Among those with whom he studied was the psychiatrist Carl Wernicke (1848–1904), best known for his seminal work describing types of aphasia and postulating a localized brain center for speech comprehension (Wernicke, 1874/1977). Goldstein acknowledged Wernicke's influence in shaping his own interest in aphasia, which remained an important research focus for the rest of his career. What Goldstein did not take from Wernicke was the latter's atomistic, associationist explanation of how the brain works. An important lesson Goldstein learned from Wernicke was the use of psychological research methods. According to Goldstein, Wernicke's appreciation of the importance of psychology for understanding psychiatric disorders was well ahead of its time (Goldstein, 1967). Perhaps this is what inspired Goldstein to work closely with experimental and clinical psychologists for his entire professional career. Kurt received his MD under Wernicke's supervision in 1903 with a dissertation on the organization of the posterior column pathways of the spinal cord. Even at this early stage, Goldstein showed signs of being a prolific publisher: four other papers in the same year as his dissertation. By the end of his long career, he had more than 300 publications.

THE CULTURAL CONTEXT
OF GOLDSTEIN'S SCIENCE

Goldstein's science is an example of the richness possible in the clinical view of human nature. There is a long tradition in Western philosophy of insightful writing about human nature that is based on clinical work (Porter, 1997). Goldstein is best understood as an inheritor of that tradition. The Germany he was reared in was marked by debates about the nature of human nature, especially in relation to the newly unified German state (Harrington, 1996). The mechanistic explanations of nature, including human nature, generated by the work of such scientists as Hermann von Helmholtz and Emil DuBois-Reymond seemed to remove any need for or possibility of spiritual truths. The success of the mechanistic scientific worldview accompanied the rapid industrialization of Germany, and for many Germans these two developments evoked paradoxical responses. On the one hand, science and industrialization were evidence of German leadership in the rise of modernity. After unification in 1871 they helped make Germany a respectable modern nation-state. On the other hand, by the last third of the 19th century, the same developments left many Germans with a sense of human life as no more than mechanical and devoid of the richness of meaning that was part of the German philosophical heritage.

By the time that Goldstein was working on his medical degree at Breslau, calls for wholeness in personal and national life were common, especially among German youth and, increasingly, among academic scientists. These calls took various forms, but a common thread running through them was the need to resist the machine mentality and its fractionation of knowledge. The work of Johann Wolfgang von Goethe (1749–1832) was recalled as an exemplar for German science. Goethe sought to demonstrate unity and continuity in his science. He was not opposed to analysis, the breaking down of knowledge into constituent parts; rather, he insisted that analysis must be accompanied by synthesis. Above all, he argued that nature must be understood in its wholeness, both qualitatively and quantitatively. Those who aligned themselves with this movement sought to find through their science alternatives for the atomistic, reductionistic, and materialistic explanations that, they claimed, had failed to capture the richness of life.

It was in this context that Goldstein was educated and began his career. He added his voice to the debates as he sought ways to merge the truths he found in philosophy and literature with the insights gained from the clinic. For him, the humanities offered a guide to interpreting the data discovered with natural science methodologies. Goethe remained a lifelong inspiration, as evidenced by the portrait of Goethe that hung above Goldstein's desk throughout his career. He used the methods of the clinical sciences: trial and error, repeated assessment, intuitive deduction, and innovation in the face of insufficient knowledge, all informed by an understanding of human nature gained from the humanities. Philosophy and the clinic were merged in his work to such a degree that it is hard to disentangle one from the other. The acrimony fueled by some scientists' claim that all techniques need validation before use and some clinicians' insistence on using whatever it takes to help a patient in need was obviated in the work of Goldstein. A philosopher and clinician, or better, a clinician-philosopher, Goldstein exemplified the best of what science and practice can be when both are undergirded by a deep philosophical understanding of human nature.

EARLY CAREER AND LEARNING
FROM BRAIN-INJURED SOLDIERS

In 1904, Goldstein became an assistant to the comparative neuroanatomist, Ludwig Edinger (1855–1918) at the Neurological Institute in Frankfurt am Main. According to Goldstein, Edinger had a major influence on his development as a scientist and clinician (Goldstein, 1967). Under Edinger's tutelage, Goldstein made important contributions to our understanding of the limbic system and anencephaly (Teuber, 1966). Goldstein then spent a year each in Freiburg and Berlin before taking a position in 1906 at the Psychiatric Clinic of the University of Königsberg.

Over the next 8 years he focused on research and treatment of psychiatric disorders. His publications from this period were diverse, with papers on sensory and motor disturbances, hallucinations, memory deficits, bipolar disorder, and schizophrenia, among others. Although his research was interesting, Goldstein found the neglect of treatment of the patients deeply disturbing. This was the era of therapeutic nihilism, when accurate diagnosis was all that many psychiatrists hoped for (Harrington, 1996). Goldstein found this unacceptable and determined to find effective treatments for at least some of his patients.

Goldstein also had extensive contacts with psychologists during this period, primarily those from the Würzburg school of Oswald Külpe (1862–1915). Külpe and his students sought to explicate the higher mental processes. Among their findings was that thought can always be traced to particular sensations or feelings or even some residue of these; that is, thought was irreducible to specific contents. Külpe and his students linked their work to the newly emerging Gestalt approach and to the phenomenology of such thinkers as Edmund Husserl, Külpe's student, and Narziss Ach (1871–1946), who was the psychologist with whom Goldstein had the closest contact during his years at Köningsberg. Ach's work on concept formation influenced Goldstein's thinking and research. Perhaps due in part to his interaction with the Würzburgers, Goldstein developed a close affinity for both Gestalt psychology and the phenomenological tradition in philosophy.

In 1914, Goldstein moved to Frankfurt to become Edinger's first assistant in the Neurological Institute. Although Edinger had hoped that Goldstein would return to laboratory work, the clinical demands generated by the First World War led Goldstein to focus on treatment of brain-injured patients. Military casualties were the patients of the institute. Goldstein and his staff offered diagnostic, treatment, and rehabilitation services for these patients.

Like his mentor, Wernicke, before him, Goldstein valued the role of psychologists in assessment and research. Not long after moving to Frankfurt, he recruited psychologist Adhémar Gelb (1887–1936) as a collaborator. Gelb had been a student of Carl Stumpf's (chap. 4, *Pioneers IV*) in Berlin and was one of the first to identify with the new Gestalt psychology (Ash, 1995). Late in 1914, Goldstein set up a clinic for brain-injured soldiers in a house outside Frankfurt. Gelb was brought in to head the psychology department. From the beginning, the clinic focused on diagnosis and assessment of the extent of disability and the determination of rehabilitative possibilities.

The clinic became institutionalized in 1916 as the Institute for Research into the Consequences of Brain Injuries, an offshoot of Edinger's Neurological Institute. Goldstein was the head of the institute until 1930 and maintained a close association with it even after he moved to Berlin in 1930. The Institute included a medical ward, physiological and psychological laboratories, and facilities for occupational therapy. What is perhaps most remarkable about the institute in hindsight is the degree of therapeutic optimism it embodied in an era when most neurologists believed little could be done for brain-injured individuals (Goldstein, 1959).

Goldstein and Gelb and, later, other collaborators, developed an extensive research and treatment program. The strict localization of brain function exemplified by Wernicke and other late-19th-century researchers was challenged by their work (Ash, 1995). Goldstein and his collaborators showed that brain-injured patients could recover some functions over time, thus indicating that brain plasticity is greater than Wernicke and others had argued. This research led Goldstein to develop his mature theories about the organism, to be discussed later.

The 19 years that Gelb and Goldstein worked together in the institute were remarkably productive. The two of them published or edited at least 16 major papers on visual perception, perceptual disturbances, tonus and cerebellar function, and visual agnosia, among others. They had many collaborators and colleagues during this time, including: Frieda Reichman (later Fromm-Reichman after she married Erich Fromm), known for her work with psychotic patients, as exemplified in the popular book, *I Never Promised You a Rose Garden* (Green, 1964); Fritz Perls, founder of Gestalt Therapy; psychologist Egon Weigl; psychologist-phenomenologist Aron Gurwitsch; and theologian Paul Tillich, to name just a few. Goldstein also interacted frequently during this period with the Gestalt psychologists, Max Wertheimer (chap. 13, *Pioneers I*) and Wolgang Köhler (chap. 17, *Pioneers I*). Goldstein was named one of the original coeditors of the Gestalt journal, *Psychologische Forschung* (*Psychological Research*), and remained a coeditor through the first 17 volumes.

As an indication of his diverse interests, Goldstein was also one of the founders of the International Society for Psychotherapy in 1927. He rejected much, but not all, of what he read in Freud, but was very concerned about the treatment of patients. In fact, he continued to see patients in a private psychotherapy practice almost until his death. Goldstein incorporated his insights from working with brain-injured patients into his larger theory about the necessity of considering the person in the total context of the person's life. In this way, Goldstein the neurologist and psychotherapist was one with Goldstein the philosopher.

Berlin and World War II

In 1930, a hospital in Berlin offered Goldstein the chairmanship of its neurology department, which was to be housed in a new wing constructed according to Goldstein's wishes. He was able, finally, to have adequate space and equipment to implement fully his research agenda and pursue his theoretical work. To entice Goldstein to accept the appointment, he was also offered a teaching position in neurology and psychiatry at the University of Berlin (Goldstein, 1967). Here, Goldstein was in a position to contribute more fully to the development of a holistic approach to medicine. In this last era before he had to leave Germany, Goldstein elaborated an approach to the practice of medicine that focused on the whole person and that person's responses to the environment. In part, Goldstein's work fit within the nascent movement toward a psychosomatic medicine, but more accurately, his work in this era is best seen as an elaboration of a new, organismic view of knowledge (Harrington, 1996).

Goldstein was not able to accomplish all he had planned in Berlin. What should have been the crowning glory of an already distinguished career was cut short by the advent of the National Socialists. On April 1, 1933, Goldstein was dragged from his examination room by SS troopers. His arrest was part of a general roundup of professionals across Germany who were Jews or Marxists or foreigners. A colleague had anonymously denounced Goldstein as a Jew and a socialist; both charges were, of course, true. He was a member of the Democratic Socialist Party and the Association of Socialist Physicians. Goldstein was held in an SS prison for a week, during which he was repeatedly beaten with a sand-filled rubber hose. A psychiatrist colleague, Eva Rothmann, asked Hermann Göring's brother, the psychiatrist Matthias Göring, to intervene. Göring did and Goldstein was released after he signed an agreement that he would leave Germany. Goldstein went briefly to Switzerland, then to Amsterdam. The Rockefeller Foundation supported him while he was in Amsterdam and then helped bring him to the United States in 1935. During the year in Amsterdam, he dictated the first draft of what proved to be his major book, *Der Aufbau des Organismus*, over a few weeks. The book was a statement of his holistic approach to understanding life and addressed clinical, theoretical, and methodological issues. It was published in Holland in 1934 and in the United States in 1939 under the title, *The Organism: A Holistic Approach to Biology Derived from Pathological Data in Man* (1939/1995). It reflected Goldstein's years of integrating clinical work with theoretical understanding.

"THE ORGANISM IN ITS TOTALITY"

The experiences of Goldstein at the Institute for Research into the Consequences of Brain Injuries in Frankfurt led him to develop an alternative approach to understanding brain function in both its normal and its pathological manifestations. The clinical results indicated a need, Goldstein wrote, "for a new approach to study the functioning of the brain, the so-called holistic approach, which assumes that every phenomenon—normal as well as pathological—is an activity of the whole organism, in a particular organization of the organism" (Goldstein, 1959, p. 7). Goldstein developed this approach into his central insight: The behavior of organisms is best understood as a series of adaptations toward the highest possible level of self-actualization (Pickren, 2000).

Goldstein used the work at the institute as a clinical foundation for a philosophy of life, which bore some affinity with work in psychology, philosophy, and theology. He felt close ties with the emergent Gestalt theories but did not identify himself as a Gestaltist. His cousin, the philosopher Cassirer, cited Goldstein's work in support of his theory of symbolic thought. Phenomenological philosophers, such as Aron Gurwitsch, also found support in Goldstein's clinical-theoretical writings. Late in his career, the theologian Paul Tillich, a close friend and colleague, cited Goldstein as an influence on the development of his work on the possibility of personal transformation through confrontation of that which provokes the deepest existential anxiety (Tillich, 1959).

The Case of "Sch"

The case of "Sch" (Schneider) served as the departure point for Goldstein and exemplifies his preference for an exhaustive analysis of a single case. Schneider was wounded in 1915 at the age of 23. One of the wounds penetrated into the occipital lobes. After the exterior wounds healed, Goldstein and Adhemar Gelb extensively studied Schneider with the psychological laboratory techniques Gelb developed for the case study. Extensive psychological testing did not reveal any obvious sensory deficits. The two investigators determined, however, to look beyond the immediate test results to an examination of his total behavior. They discovered that he was in fact psychologically blind, but had adapted and compensated for his deficits. For example, he could not read because he could not recognize words directly. However, he could "read" by tracing the words with small head and hand movements. When Goldstein and Gelb prevented him from moving his head and hands, he could not read at all, because all he saw were marks on paper. Schneider was totally unaware of his adaptive strategy and thought he read in the usual way. He had adapted strategies to compensate for his "figural blindness" so that he could fill in the gaps of a landscape or infer the difference between men and vehicles (Harrington, 1996).

Goldstein and Gelb interpreted the case of "Sch" as an indication that the classical models of specific cerebral localization developed by Wernicke, Paul Broca, and others in the 19th century are inadequate. Those models were developed on the psychological laws of association, according to which basic brain functions are joined together to produce more complex functions according to laws of contiguity, similarity, and so forth (Young, 1970). So, a behavior like reading is the summation of stimulation of discrete parts of the brain, each with its own function, and alexia (inability to read) is due to damage to one or more of those parts. Wernicke developed this associationist approach into a reflex model of brain functioning, in which various brain centers communicate via associative fibers according to associative laws. Sensory stimulation is processed at the back of the brain and reflexively communicated to the motor centers at the front of the brain. Brain pathology, such as aphasia, is a result of a breakdown in one or more specific brain centers and could be understood in isolation, that is, in the laboratory. As noted earlier, the understanding of man and society in mechanical terms reflected and shaped these models of brain function.

Goldstein and Gelb rejected the reflex models of Wernicke and other 19th-century neurologists. Schneider's problems simply did not match associative-reflexive theories of function or dysfunction. Schneider had lost the ability to see the Gestalt of the world. When restrained from movement, he could not organize the lines or marks on a page or the dark spaces on the ground under trees into any meaningful configuration. Nineteenth-century localizationist models argued that brain functions had to be understood as functioning in isolation. Goldstein argued that it was the research methodologies and epistemological models of the 19th-century neurologists that led them to that conclusion. Functions elicited in laboratories where the participant, human or nonhuman, is isolated from its natural context, provide incomplete pictures of the total capacities of the participant. An organism studied in the context of the total environment will display tendencies to adapt toward the highest possible level of functioning.

Basic Principles of the Human Condition

In his research with "Sch" and others, Goldstein saw deeper principles about the human condition. For example, clinical results led Goldstein to characterize behavior as abstract or concrete. The "abstract attitude" or categorical thinking is what allows human beings to move beyond the merely actual to the symbolic, to what is possible; it is what allows us to grasp what is essential about a concept and apply that concept to new situations. Concrete thinking, on the other hand, is directed at what is, at what currently exists, and excludes the ability to imagine alternatives or sort individual items into conceptual groups. Gelb's and Goldstein's tests for abstract and concrete behavior—for example, the Gelb–Goldstein Color Sorting Test in which the subject has to sort skeins of colored wool into superordinate color categories—supported their theory (Goldstein & Scheerer, 1941). According to Goldstein, when brain-damaged patients realize their inability to perform at the usual or normal level, a deep sense of failure results, which Goldstein (1959) called the "catastrophic condition." The patient experiences a severe anxiety brought on by the deeper realization that self-realization at former levels will now be impossible. The movement to functioning at the concrete level allows the person to stabilize by producing a new set of possibilities for self-actualization. In this view, movement to concrete functioning is adaptive and reflects the necessity for taking a holistic perspective that takes the total environment into account. In Goldstein's words, "It is of the utmost importance that one evaluate any aspect of the human organism in relation to the condition of the organism in its totality. On this understanding is based what I have called self-realization. The trend toward self-realization is not merely a stimulus but a driving force that puts the organism into action. What one usually calls the influence of the environment is the coming to terms between the organism and the world in 'adequacy' " (Goldstein, 1967, pp. 150–151).

The therapeutic and rehabilitative work at the institute was designed to help brain-injured patients live in an ordered world that would not constantly provoke the catastrophic reaction, but the price for this stability was an acceptance of limitations. Goldstein applied this understanding to normal functioning as well. As he wrote, "Becoming healthy demands a transformation of the individual's personality which enables him to bear restrictions" (Goldstein, 1959, p. 10). Because human beings are not perfect, there are limitations. We must have the courage to bear those limitations and the anxiety they bring if we are to find ways to actualize ourselves. Goldstein stated it this way: "Courage, in its final analysis, is nothing but an affirmative answer to the shocks of our existence, which must be borne for the actualization of one's own nature" (Goldstein,

1957, p. 68). The assessment of restrictions and of anxiety and of the organism's responses can only be accurate if the total context is considered.

LOST AND FOUND DREAMS IN AMERICA

When Goldstein arrived in New York in 1935, he was in the odd position of being a world-renowned scientist without a job and with few financial resources. His English was not good when he arrived and although it improved, he was never fully comfortable in English (Simmel, 1968). Nevertheless, Goldstein began a private practice, seeing patients in the afternoon. He also secured an appointment as a clinical professor of neurology at Columbia University. He had an office and a well-equipped laboratory at Columbia's affiliate, Montefiore Hospital. He worked at the hospital every day from 9 a.m. to 2 p.m. with twice-weekly visits to the New York Psychiatric Institute. Between January 1936 and June 1941, the Rockefeller Foundation provided him with $9,800 in research support, almost all of which was used to pay for research assistants.

During his first 5 years in New York, Goldstein was highly productive. Two Columbia students completed their doctoral dissertations under his supervision, Marjorie Bolles (d. 1962) in 1937 and Aaron Nadel (1911–1992) in 1938. From 1936 to 1937, Nadel was his first paid assistant. In 1937, Goldstein was able to hire another German émigré psychologist, Martin Scheerer (1900–1961) as his assistant. Scheerer had earned his doctorate degree at Hamburg in 1930 under William Stern (chap. 6, *Pioneers II*). After fleeing Nazi Germany, Scheerer taught briefly at the University of Louisville. The collaboration he began in 1937 with Goldstein proved fruitful for both of them. Perhaps their most salient joint publication was the 1941 monograph, "Abstract and Concrete Behavior: An Experimental Study with Special Tests."

It was during this period that Molly Harrower worked with Goldstein. She and Scheerer assisted Goldstein with the translation of *Der Aufbau des Organismus*. Harrower had sought out Goldstein because of his reputation with patients and his insistence that a psychological understanding of neurological patients is necessary for therapeutic success. Although work with Goldstein was meant to prepare her for work with the neurosurgeon Wilder Penfield (1891–1976), Harrower made the most of her time with Goldstein. From data drawn from Goldstein's clinical cases, she published on the perceptual differences between normal and brain-injured patients, assisted Goldstein in the assessment of alexia and aphasia on New York's Welfare Island, and learned about the Rorschach Projective Technique from Bruno Klopfer (1900–1971) during his weekly visits to Goldstein's laboratory (Harrower, 1991).

Goldstein's research in this period was rich and diverse. He collaborated with Klopfer and Zygmunt Piotrowski (1904–1985), both expert in the research use of the then-new Rorschach technique, to corroborate the neurological findings with Rorschach results from the same patients. With the help of Carney Landis (1897–1962), chief psychologist at the Psychiatric Institute, Goldstein developed an extensive program of research on the degree of mental deterioration of schizophrenics and their prognosis at Montefiore Hospital and the Psychiatric Institute. Electroencephalographic studies, research on reflexive behavior, studies of speech disturbances, and a large-scale comparative study of pathological changes in personality were all part of Goldstein's professional work during this time. With his wife, psychiatrist Eva Rothmann (d. 1960), he studied an idiot savant, a retarded young man with a perfect calendar memory. Goldstein also continued his pioneering film studies in this period. He brought extensive footage of clinical cases with him from Germany and added to it from cases studied in his laboratory at Montefiore. His intent was to make the films available for teaching and demonstration purposes. In addition to all his research, he also taught a course in advanced abnormal psychology for Columbia undergraduates.

In the 1938–1939 academic year, Goldstein was the William James (chap. 2, *Pioneers I*) Lecturer at Harvard University. His friend, psychologist Karl Lashley (1890–1958, chap. 20, *Pioneers I*), who had visited Goldstein in Frankfurt in the early 1920s and who became one of his close friends in the United States, arranged for the lectureship. The lectures were published in 1940 as *Human Nature in the Light of Psychopathology*. Although the book did not receive the same critical acclaim as *The Organism*, it did help keep Goldstein's name in public circulation. Despite his research success in New York, he needed more stable employment, so in 1940, he accepted a position as a clinical professor of neurology at Tufts University Medical School, working mostly in the school's Boston Dispensary (Simmel, 1968). The Rockefeller Foundation supported him there from 1940 to 1945.

According to some who knew the Goldsteins in Boston, it was a happy period for them. Their home became a center of intellectual life in Boston, filled with students, professors, and German émigré scientists (Teuber, 1966). For example, his relationship with personality psychologist Gordon Allport dates from this period. It was also a productive time for Goldstein. He found a group of young psychologists, including Eugenia Hanfmann (1905–1983) and Marianne Simmel, who were interested in his work. At nearby Worcester State Hospital, he found the research group led by psychologist David Shakow (1901–1981) highly stimulating and a welcome place to share his ideas and rich experience. While at Tufts, Goldstein summarized the results of his long involvement with brain-injured patients in *Aftereffects of Brain Injury in War* (1942). He then began to work on his major statement on aphasia, *Language and Language Disturbances: Aphasic Symptom Complexes and Their Significance for Medicine and Theory of Language*, published in 1948.

Eva Rothmann, Goldstein's wife, suffered from periods of severe depression. Partly because of her illness and partly for financial reasons, the Goldsteins returned to New York City in 1945. Goldstein resumed the private practice of neurology and psychotherapy. To make financial ends meet, he also taught at several colleges and universities, including the New School for Social Research, Columbia University, and the City College of New York. Then, in the 1950s, he began commuting to Brandeis University to teach in the graduate program in psychology headed by Abraham Maslow (1908–1970). In New York, as in Boston, his home was a center of intellectual richness. Goldstein's circle of friends included Karen Horney (chap. 10, *Pioneers IV*), his cousin Ernst Cassirer, Rollo May, Aron Gurwitsch, Albert Einstein, Niels Bohr, and Gardner Murphy, to name just a few. It was in New York that Abraham Maslow, then at Brooklyn College, met Goldstein. He was immensely impressed with Goldstein's insight and human kindness. Maslow found Goldstein's concept of self-actualization or self-realization intriguing and borrowed it as he developed his own theories of human motivation (e.g., Maslow, 1943).

After the publication of *Language and Language Disturbances*, Goldstein began to write on a broader array of topics. For example, he warned against the use of lobotomies 1 year after Egas Moniz (1874–1955) won the Nobel Prize in medicine for his role in developing the lobotomy procedure. He also wrote on health, stress, the nature of anxiety, and psychotherapy, among other topics. His writing was infused with the richly philosophical insights gained from a long and productive career, and his publications gained for him a wider audience among both the lay public and the professionals.

In 1958, on his 80th birthday, friends gathered to celebrate his contributions to science and philosophy. Three journals devoted commemorative numbers to Goldstein: the *American Journal of Psychoanalysis* (vol. 19), the *Journal of Psychotherapy* (vol. 13), and the *Journal of Individual Psychology* (vol. 15). Goldstein, at the end of his career was celebrated as much more than a devoted scientist. Scientists, therapists, artists, and poets all found inspiration in his work. During the 1960s, the interpretation of his ideas by such "Third Wave" psychologists as Abraham Maslow, Carl Rogers (chap. 15, *Pioneers III*), and Rollo May was incorporated into the counterculture movement in the United States.

In 1960, Eva Rothmann committed suicide. The loss of his wife, his junior by more than 20 years, devastated Goldstein. He felt his otherness, his foreignness even more deeply than before. In the last 5 years of his life, he did have the happiness of having one of his daughters and her family near him. He also retained a circle of friends and admirers who were sources of emotional and intellectual support. Goldstein fell ill while on summer vacation with friends in Vermont in 1965. He returned to New York, where he suffered a stroke that left him paralyzed and unable to speak. He died 3 weeks later.

Goldstein found ways to infuse his clinical insights into topics and concerns that reach beyond the clinic into how humans live their lives. In the richest tradition of clinical medicine and psychology, he drew from his work with those who had suffered loss to write about the richness that is possible in human life. His clinical work and his philosophy continue to serve as an inspiration to those who believe that life is more than the sum of physical and chemical processes.

REFERENCES

Ash, M. (1995). *Gestalt psychology in German culture, 1890–1967: Holism and the quest for objectivity.* New York: Cambridge University Press.

Goldstein, K. (1940). *Human nature in the light of psychopathology.* Cambridge, MA: Harvard University Press.

Goldstein, K. (1942). *Aftereffects of brain injury in war.* New York: Grune & Stratton.

Goldstein, K. (1948). *Language and language disturbances: Aphasic symptom complexes and their significance for medicine and theory of language.* New York: Grune & Stratton.

Goldstein, K. (1957). The structure of anxiety. In J. H. Masserman & J. L. Moreno (Eds.), *Progress in psychotherapy* (pp. 61–70). New York: Grune & Stratton.

Goldstein, K. (1959). Notes on the development of my concepts. *Journal of Individual Psychology, 15,* 5–14.

Goldstein, K. (1967). Kurt Goldstein. In E. G. Boring & G. Lindzey (Eds.), *A history of psychology in autobiography* (vol. 5, pp. 145–166). New York: Appleton-Century-Crofts.

Goldstein, K. (1995). *The organism: A holistic approach to biology derived from pathological data in man.* New York: Zone Books. (Original work published 1939)

Goldstein, K., & Scheerer, M. (1941). Abstract and concrete behavior: An experimental study with special tests. *Psychological Monographs, 53,* 1–151.

Green, H. (1964). *I never promised you a rose garden.* New York: Holt.

Harrington, A. (1996). *Reenchanted science: Holism in German culture from Wilhelm II to Hitler.* Princeton, NJ: Princeton University Press.

Harrower, M. (1991). Inkblots and poems. In C. E. Walker (Ed.), *The history of clinical psychology in autobiography* (pp. 125–169). Pacific Grove, CA: Brooks/Cole.

Maslow, A. (1943). A theory of human motivation. *Psychological Review, 50,* 370–396.

Pickren, W. E. (2000). Kurt Goldstein. In A. E. Kazdin (Ed.), *Encyclopedia of Psychology* (vol. 3, pp. 506–507). Washington, DC: American Psychological Association and New York: Oxford University Press.

Porter, R. (1997). *The greatest benefit to mankind: A medical history of humanity.* New York: Norton.

Simmel, M. L. (1968). Kurt Goldstein, 1878–1965. In M. L. Simmel (Ed.), *The reach of mind: Essays in honor of Kurt Goldstein* (pp. 3–11). New York: Springer.

Teuber, H. L. (1966). Kurt Goldstein's role in the development of neuropsychology. *Neuropsychologia, 4,* 299–310.

Tillich, P. (1959). The significance of Kurt Goldstein for philosophy of religion. *Journal of Individual Psychology, 15,* 20–23.

Ulich, R. (1968). Kurt Goldstein. In M. L. Simmel (Ed.), *The reach of mind: Essays in honor of Kurt Goldstein* (pp. 13–15). New York: Springer.

Wernicke, C. (1977). The aphasic symptom complex. In G. H. Eggert (Trans.), *Wernicke's works on aphasia: A sourcebook and review.* The Hague, The Netherlands: Mouton. (Original work published 1874)

Young, R. M. (1970). *Mind, brain, and adaptation in the 19th century: Cerebral localization and its biological context from Gall to Ferrier.* Oxford: Clarendon Press.

Chapter 9

Walter Van Dyke Bingham: Portrait of an Industrial Psychologist

Ludy T. Benjamin Jr.
Texas A&M University

David B. Baker
University of Akron

When Walter Van Dyke Bingham was elected secretary-treasurer of the American Psychological Association (APA) in 1910, the APA membership numbered 222, most of whom were employed in college and university settings. Forty years later, APA's membership was 7,273, "of whom a majority were practitioners in industries, business offices, railways, hospitals, schools, clinics, welfare agencies, employment services, and government bureaus" (Bingham, 1952, p. 1). Bingham not only witnessed this transformation of psychology from academe to the "real world," he was a leading figure in that disciplinary change. Indeed, for much of his life he was the principal advocate for applied psychology, particularly in merging the science of psychology with business. Psychologist historian E. G. Boring has called Bingham the "dean of industrial psychologists," a label he richly deserves (Ferguson, 1963a, p. 13). At the time of his death most industrial psychologists in America had some direct personal link to the influence of Bingham. The importance of his work, especially at the Carnegie Institute of Technology, is evident in Leonard Ferguson's history of industrial psychology, which focused heavily on Bingham and his legacy.

STUDIES IN PSYCHOLOGY

Bingham's list of educational mentors in psychology reads like a who's who of the discipline. He began college with plans to be a teacher in mathematics and physics. At Beloit College in Wisconsin he came under the influence of Guy Allen Tawney, who had earned his doctorate in psychology with Wilhelm Wundt (chap. 3, *Pioneers III*) at the University of Leipzig in 1897. After completing his degree at Beloit, Bingham taught in secondary schools for 4 years and then entered the philosophy and psychology program at the University of Chicago in 1905. There he worked with James Rowland Angell (chap. 4, this volume) in the very year of Angell's presidency of the APA, and in the experimental laboratory with John B. Watson (chap. 2, *Pioneers I*).

In the middle of his doctoral studies, Bingham went to Europe in the summer of 1907 where he visited Kurt Koffka, Wolfgang Köhler (chap. 17, *Pioneers I*), Carl Stumpf (chap. 4, *Pioneers IV*), Erich von Hornbostel, Charles Spearman (chap. 6, *Pioneers IV*), Cyril Burt, and Charles S. Myers. Because of his minor in philosophy he decided to spend a year at Harvard University, where he studied with Josiah Royce, William James (chap. 2, *Pioneers I*), George Santayana, and Hugo Münsterberg (chap. 7, *Pioneers IV*). He returned to Chicago, completing his dissertation with Angell in 1908. He spent the next 2 years at Columbia University as a research assistant to E. L. Thorndike (chap. 10, *Pioneers I*).

Surely, exposure to such talent should signal a career of great accomplishments, and in Bingham's case it did. But Bingham's contacts with his teachers were not accidental. He had a genuine hunger for knowledge; he sought to develop himself broadly and in the company of the acknowledged leaders of his day. He enjoyed not only a strong intellectual curiosity (evidenced in his childhood when he and several friends conducted experiments to test their hypotheses about what psychologists today call the moon illusion; see Bingham, 1953) but an open-mindedness that perhaps was key to his vision for applied psychology and his unwillingness to be bound by the artificial barriers separating academic psychology and the world of application.

Bingham left Columbia in the fall of 1910 to accept the chair in psychology at Dartmouth College. Initially given a 5-year appointment, he was granted a permanent professorship in 1914 (Bingham, 1952). He was generally satisfied with his Dartmouth position, but a chance encounter was about to change his life and psychology forever.

CARNEGIE INSTITUTE OF TECHNOLOGY

Career paths are rarely, if ever, linear. Job changes are not always predictable, and serendipity affects careers in ways that cannot be anticipated. In 1914, the APA held its 23rd annual meeting on the campus of the University of Pennsylvania at the end of December during the holiday break for the university. At the meeting, Bingham delivered a talk on "norms of college freshmen" based on a study of 200 Dartmouth students (Bingham, 1915a). After the session Bingham was approached by a man who handed him his business card. It read "A. A.

Hamerschlag, Carnegie Institute of Technology" (CIT). Hamerschlag indicated that his school was a new technical university in Pittsburgh, then only 10 years old, and asked, "What are you doing this weekend after the meetings? Won't you come look us over, and then tell us what in your opinion psychology could do for such a technical institution?" (Bingham, 1952, p. 11).

Bingham did visit Carnegie Tech—as it was more commonly known—on New Year's Day in 1915. Afterward he sent President Hamerschlag a report on what he saw as the potential for psychology's contributions to the programs at CIT as well as his recommendation for a psychologist, Guy M. Whipple, who could meet CIT's needs. Hamerschlag interviewed Whipple but then offered the job to Bingham. Bingham began his tenure at CIT in September, 1915 as director of the Division of Applied Psychology, a psychology program unlike any other in the country (Bingham, 1952; Ferguson, 1963a).

CIT had been founded and endowed by Andrew Carnegie, who wanted a university that blended instruction in the arts and sciences with an emphasis on practical training for jobs, a university that would offer affordable education and training for America's poorer classes. In 1915, when Bingham visited, CIT consisted of four colleges: an engineering college, a vocational college for women, an industrial arts college, and a fine arts college that included programs of architecture and interior design. The faculty included many people from the industrial trades, and all of the colleges offered courses and other instructional experiences related to specific vocations.

Bingham's report to Hamerschlag had emphasized ways psychology could serve a practical function in (a) helping students identify their talents and matching those talents to the jobs for which they were best suited, and (b) teaching students to use psychology to be able to understand human actions and to be able to influence those actions. The first of those goals was a blending of the growing popularity of vocational guidance, stimulated by the work of Frank Parsons (1909) and the founding of the National Vocational Guidance Association in 1913, and the mental tests developed by psychologists. The second goal drew on the work of psychologists Walter Dill Scott, Münsterberg, Harry Hollingworth (chap. 9, *Pioneers II*) and others in the use of psychology in advertising and sales.

America was undergoing considerable social, political, and economic changes in the early part of the 20th century related to urbanization, industrialization, and increased immigration. Hundreds of new occupations were evolving that meant increased vocational choices. More jobs, especially factory jobs, meant more specialization in work. The new mantra for American business was efficiency, which meant more effective advertising, more scientific management, better trained workers, improved employee selection procedures, and improved worker productivity and quality of worker output. Business looked to science for answers for its problems, and psychologists were quick to volunteer. In a best-selling book, *Psychology and Industrial Efficiency* (1913), Münsterberg promoted psychology as the science of human efficiency. He argued that efficiency starts with a good match between worker and job. And psychologists, armed with a multitude of mental tests, seemed well suited to that task. Perhaps President Hamerschlag had read Münsterberg's book, because he invited him to Pittsburgh in 1914 to speak on his work and to consult about the possibility of establishing similar psychological work at CIT (Münsterberg, 1915). There is no evidence that Münsterberg recommended contact with Bingham, but it seems likely that his message at CIT reinforced Hamerschlag's plans for psychology.

When Hamerschlag heard Bingham speak at the 1915 APA meeting, Bingham had published a total of 18 journal articles, beginning with his dissertation on audition. Other than 2 articles on educational psychology, there was nothing in Bingham's record that would suggest that he would be well suited to the kind of applied work that Hamerschlag envisioned at CIT. Perhaps the study on student norms that Hamerschlag heard at the APA meeting convinced him that Bingham could conduct the kinds of research needed to assist students in their vocational preparation. Certainly Bingham's consulting report identified clear goals that were consistent with CIT's mission as well as the vocational guidance and business emphases of the time. Whatever the reasons for hiring Bingham, it was a decision that Hamerschlag would consider one of his best.

THE DIVISION OF APPLIED PSYCHOLOGY

The applied research that Hamerschlag had hoped for began almost immediately. When the division opened in September 1915, Bingham had a staff of four. Two were existing faculty, both with master's degrees in psychology and education, one jointly appointed in the women's college and the other in the industrial arts college. Bingham added two new faculty: James Burt Miner, who had earned his doctorate at Columbia University with James McKeen Cattell and Thorndike and was a faculty member at the University of Minnesota; and Louis L. Thurstone (chap. 6, *Pioneers III*), who had spent a summer working for Thomas Edison in his Menlo Park laboratory and had yet to complete his dissertation research in Angell's laboratory at the University of Chicago (Ferguson, 1963b).

Miner began work on the measurement of nonintellectual traits in students and developed those measures into an interest test for students. That test would form the basis of later work by Edward K. Strong Jr. that led to the *Strong Vocational Interest Blank* (Strong, 1943). Thurstone began experiments on human learning, working with students learning linotype operations in the printing department at CIT. All of the staff, including Bingham, were involved in the development and standardization of group tests, for example, the measurement of spatial abilities that seemed important to a number of occupations such as architecture, costume design, sheet-metal work, and pattern making (Bingham, 1952).

Bingham began a mental testing program of all incoming CIT students, including tests of intelligence, language ability, memory, reasoning, manual dexterity, and spatial abilities. This program was housed in what was called the "Bureau of Mental Tests" and was largely coordinated by Bingham. His hope was that these data would eventually prove useful in identifying traits and abilities that correlate with success in college, and more specifically with success in various CIT programs and in subsequent jobs.

A program of teacher training, coordinated by the Division of Applied Psychology, was also established in each of CIT's four colleges. Courses on educational psychology, applied psychology, and vocational guidance were the principal offerings, tailored individually to meet the needs of the different colleges. Miner and Thurstone taught most of those courses. This instruction had been a priority for both Bingham and Hamerschlag; that is, they wanted the science of psychology to be brought to bear on the training of teachers of art, of domestic arts, of engineering, and of manual arts.

BUREAU OF SALESMANSHIP RESEARCH

Bingham's interest in applied psychology and his willingness to break down the barriers that separate the academy and the world of business are clear in the establishment of the Bureau of Salesmanship Research. Several weeks after arriving at CIT, Hamerschlag introduced Bingham to Edward A. Woods, who was manager of the Pittsburgh office of The Equitable Life Assurance Society of the United States. Woods lamented the absence of courses on salesmanship at colleges and disparaged those typically offered by various individuals of questionable expertise. He and Bingham agreed that what was needed was a research base on such topics as consumer behavior, sales strategies, and the selection and training of salespeople.

Bingham presented a plan to Woods that called for a 5-year research program to be funded by the business community. He envisioned the support of 30 businesses contributing $500 each per year for a total of $75,000. The bureau would establish an advisory board from among those businesses that could suggest research questions to be investigated. As the knowledge in the area grew, CIT would offer that information to the cooperating business members. The genesis of this model of cooperation between university and business was not original with Bingham. CIT had already used it in at least one other program (Ferguson, 1963c). For American psychology in 1915, however, the plan was probably unique, and for CIT it was on a scale the university had never before envisaged.

Woods began accumulating the business partners by recruiting two friends: H. J. Heinz of the Heinz Company and Norval Hawkins, general sales manager of the Ford Motor Company. They agreed to underwrite the costs for the entire program if support from other businesses was not forthcoming. By the summer of 1916 there were 18 business partners, including the Aluminum Company of America, Carnegie Steel, B. F. Goodrich, John Hancock Mutual Life Insurance, Eli Lilly, Metropolitan Life Insurance, Pittsburgh Steel, Prudential Insurance Company, and Westinghouse Electric. By March 1917, the number of partners had reached 30 (Bingham, 1917).

The financial support of these businesses allowed the hiring of additional staff for the bureau rather than adding its responsibilities to the existing staff of the division. To launch the bureau, Bingham hired Walter Dill Scott, the psychologist who was arguably the best known in America for his work on the psychology of business. Scott had received his doctorate with Wundt in 1900 and was on the faculty of Northwestern University. At the time of his hiring as director of the bureau, Scott was the author of four books on the psychology of business: three on advertising and persuasion and one on efficiency (Scott, 1903, 1908, 1911a, 1911b). In addition to hiring Scott, five fellows and research assistants were added to the bureau's staff, including Edward S. Robinson, who later would become professor of psychology at Yale University, and Dwight L. Hoopingarner, whose expertise on labor relations would make him a member of President Franklin D. Roosevelt's four administrations (Ferguson, 1963d).

In the brochure announcing the establishment of the bureau, four aims were listed in support of improving selection and training of sales personnel and improving sales techniques:

(a) Collecting and systematizing information regarding methods now used by successful selling organizations in the employment, development, and supervision of salesman; (b) Analyzing the traits that are found to be characteristic of highly successful salesmen . . . in contrast to . . . unsuccessful salesmen; (c) Carrying forward actual experiments in the selection and training of salesmen; (d) Making available the results of these researches by personal conferences with the executives of the different Co-operating Members. (*Preliminary Announcement*, 1916, p. 6)

The bureau made rapid progress on that agenda, developing forms and tests that were accumulated in a privately published booklet of 36 pages, *Aids in the Selection of Salesmen* (Scott, 1916), that was distributed to the cooperating businesses. The booklet included a "Personal History Record" to be filled out by the salesperson; an "Interviewer's Scale" in which the interviewer rated the candidate on such traits as convincingness, industry, value to the firm, and appearance; a "Range of Interest" form developed by Robinson that assessed the candidate's knowledge of such diverse subjects as Chopin, crank shafts, Rodin, silos, mimeographs, mayonnaise, Bismarck, colanders, and Rhode Island Reds; a paper-and-pencil adult intelligence test; and other tests and forms, all copyrighted by the bureau. The businesses were asked to administer the tests and complete the forms on their salespersons, and to return that information to CIT along with information on the relative sales success of the individuals.

Analyses of these data were intended to discover valid predictors of sales success (Bingham, 1952).

PSYCHOLOGICAL EXAMINING AND SELECTING DURING THE WAR

When the United States declared war on Germany in 1917, psychologists, under the leadership of APA President Robert Yerkes (chap. 7, *Pioneers II*), were quick to volunteer for service. They found themselves occupied principally on two tasks: the assessment of intelligence of recruits and selection testing for various military assignments. Bingham was part of a committee of seven psychologists, chaired by Yerkes, charged with the development of a group intelligence test for military personnel. The committee also included Henry Herbert Goddard, who had rendered the first translation of the Binet (chap. 5, *Pioneers III*) Scale in America, and Lewis Terman (chap. 8, *Pioneers III*) who had recently published his version of the Binet Scale, known as the Stanford–Binet. The meetings began in Vineland, New Jersey, in May 1917. Preliminary testing began the next month, and by September actual testing began using an instrument that would become known as the Army Alpha. In the next year, more than 1.7 million military recruits would be assessed by that test (Yerkes, 1921).

While the Army Alpha was being developed, Bingham took on another assignment, the Committee on the Classification of Personnel in the Army. Scott served as director of the committee and Bingham as executive secretary. This committee was formed chiefly through the efforts of Scott, who had argued that one of the most important tasks for the war was officer selection and assignment. He convinced the secretary of war of this need and was authorized to develop and implement a testing program. The committee began by modifying the selection tests for salespersons that had been developed by Scott, Bingham, and others at CIT. By the end of the war, this committee had developed selection tests for more than 80 military jobs and had tested more than 3.5 million military personnel. The success of this program earned Scott the Distinguished Service Medal; he was the only psychologist to be so honored for service during World War I (von Mayrhauser, 1989). Virtually all of the staff of the Bureau of Salesmanship Research had worked in the Army selection program. It is not surprising that they were especially well suited to such work. Indeed, Bingham (1952) considered his years at CIT "to have been a rehearsal for the enormous task of military classification and assignment" (p. 15).

When the war was over, applied psychology had earned a new respectability. Not only were the military and the public aware of the contributions of psychological science, but many academic psychologists had their occupational horizons expanded. There was a perception among the public and among psychologists that psychology had contributed substantially to the success of the war effort. That perception (perhaps not deserved; see Samelson, 1977) led to significantly expanded opportunities for applied psychology after the war.

THE RISE AND FALL OF THE DIVISION
OF APPLIED PSYCHOLOGY

Miner served as acting director of the division in Bingham's absence, and Whipple, who had worked with Bingham in developing the Army Alpha, was hired to direct the bureau while Scott continued his war work. Bingham was approached in 1917 by Edgar Kaufmann, owner of Pittsburgh's largest department store, who proposed the establishment of a research program dedicated to the personnel problems (selection, training, supervision) of the retail industry. Kaufmann had enlisted the support of six other stores who promised to provide $32,000 per annum for 5 years in support of such research. Thus was born the Research Bureau for Retail Training, which was headed initially by Miner, and then by W. W. Charters in 1918. It "prepared employment tests, training manuals, merchandise manuals, and specific procedures for correcting defects of sales personality and of supervision" (Bingham, 1952, pp. 15–16).

Bingham returned to CIT full time in 1918, taking the reins back from Miner (Scott would remain in war work for another year and would return to CIT for only a few months before leaving to found The Scott Company, a consulting firm). The division underwent considerable growth shortly after the war, partly because of the reputations of Bingham and Scott, but also because of the new confidence in psychology as an applied science. By 1920 the expanded Division included a Department of Psychology, a Department of Vocational Education, a Department of Educational Research, a School of Life Insurance Salesmanship, and a Department of Personnel Administration. The last of those contained the Research Bureau for Retail Training and the Bureau of Personnel Research (the new name for the Bureau of Salesmanship Research). The division's staff numbered 25 in 1923, not including research fellows, and included as new faculty, Edward K. Strong Jr., Clarence Yoakum, and Marion Bills. A few of the faculty members and most of the research assistants and secretarial staff were supported on funds from sources other than the university.

By almost any measure, Bingham's division was impressive. He had accumulated an excellent faculty, even though some of them stayed for only a few years. The success of the early applied programs had spawned others, some of which brought considerable funding to the division. Between 1916 and 1921, the division received more than $235,000 from local and national businesses for support of its research and training efforts. Bingham had established good relations between the university and a number of local businesses. The published output of the division was considerable and dominated the literature in industrial psychology from 1916 through 1924. About 65 graduate students were trained (mostly as research fellows, meaning that they took much of their course work elsewhere) and several of them would become important contributors to applied psychology, for example, Bruce Moore (who got his doctorate with Bingham in 1921 at CIT and was the first president of APA's Division of Industrial Psychology), Bearsdley Ruml, Arthur Kornhauser, and Richard Uhrbrock. In short, Bingham had created a research institute, largely funded by grants from business and industry. It was the first institute of its kind in psychology and a model for others to follow, including the many university-based research institutes in existence today.

The Division of Applied Psychology had appeared very suddenly on the campus of CIT in 1915. It was to disappear just as quickly. In the summer of 1922, Hamerschlag was replaced as president of CIT. By the summer of 1924 the Division—by then renamed the Division of Cooperative Research—had essentially disappeared. The reasons for its demise are not clear. Certainly, Hamerschlag and Bingham enjoyed a good working relationship. Bingham's division was a source of great pride for Hamerschlag, and he had supported it strongly throughout Bingham's tenure, both by words and by funds. Given the nature of academic politics there seems no doubt that Bingham's success and his favored relationship with Hamerschlag (whether real or perceived) could have created jealousy among other colleagues at CIT. Some critics voiced concerns about the amount of graduate training going on in the division in what was largely an undergraduate institution. There were complaints about competition with the University of Pittsburgh and a belief that some division programs seemed better suited to that university.

In his autobiography, Bingham (1952, p. 17) referred to the end of the division as "the dispersal," referring to the widespread departure of the division's faculty and its programs to other universities. He offered no real criticisms of CIT administrators, nor can such criticism be found in his personal papers that are housed in the archives of Carnegie-Mellon University. Hilgard (1987, p. 709), in his history of American psychology, called it a "dismemberment," and Prien (1991, p. 44) labeled it "the October massacre." Prien's account is the most dramatic. It claims that one of the first actions of the new CIT president was to call Bingham into his office and say "Dr. Bingham, you and your associates are no longer associated with Carnegie Institute of Technology" (p. 45). It is possible that such an account is accurate, but it could not be corroborated by documents in the Carnegie-Mellon University Archives.

The most comprehensive account of the demise of the division is provided by Keith, Roberts, Harris, and Baker (2000), who suggested that there were many reasons for its closure, some of which have already been discussed, but that perhaps the most important was that a change in educational strategy championed by the university's board of trustees called for a greater emphasis on research within the engineering programs. Although psychology's research had received much attention nationally, probably it was not the kind of research the board and new administration wanted to see as the flagship program of the university. In short, there were those who wanted CIT to be recognized as an engineering school, and psychology's prominence was interfering with that vision.

It is difficult to imagine a university's killing its goose that laid the golden eggs but CIT did just that, and it would be decades before the university regained any prominence in psychology. In the year of his program's demise, Bingham (1923) referred to his CIT experience as "an adventure in higher education" (p. 141). It was a short-lived adventure, but one that was demonstrably important in spreading the word and the methods of the new psychology. Bingham (1952) wrote:

> It was not easy to say goodbye to so many superb collaborators, but I knew that each, transplanted to favorable soil, would in due course help to multiply the number of practicing psychologists and add steadily to our store of psychotechnical knowledge. (p. 18)

AMBASSADOR FOR APPLIED PSYCHOLOGY

Bingham's psychology collaborators did indeed find favorable soil. Thurstone went to the University of Chicago, Strong to Stanford University, Miner to the University of Kentucky, Scott to Northwestern University (as president), and Yoakum to the University of Michigan. In leaving Carnegie Tech in 1924 at the age of 43, Bingham would never again hold an academic post. Instead, in 1924 he became director of the Personnel Research Federation (PRF) in New York City, an organization that he had helped found in 1921. The purpose of the organization was to coordinate the activities of multiple business, government, and disciplinary entities "to find solutions of those crucial problems which center about personnel in industry, . . . particularly the economic, social and generally humanistic aspects of the case" (Gilmer, 1962, p. 59). The PRF published a journal beginning in 1922, which Bingham had also helped to found, entitled the *Journal of Personnel Research* (the name changed to *The Personnel Journal* in 1927). Bingham became the editor of that journal in 1923, a job that he held through 1933.

As director of the PRF, Bingham was responsible for coordinating research projects that sought to answer the questions generated by management in business and industry. In his early years at PRF, he spent much of his time in the field, interviewing workers and management personnel in a variety of work settings. He also consulted with government agencies and a variety of academic disciplines. Ultimately, his job was to bring the science of psychology to bear on personnel questions. Bingham (1952) described his work in the 1920s and 1930s as follows:

One of my principal functions from 1924 to 1940 seems to have been that of emissary of psychology to the heathen—the heathen being experts in the various aspects of human behavior who claimed little familiarity with the science of psychology. Among them could be found outstanding economists, engineers, business executives, and social work administrators, as well as employment managers, occupational counselors, labor leaders, safety specialists, college registrars, and university presidents. . . . A complementary function was to tell my own profession what I saw beyond our borders. (pp. 18–19)

In 1924 there may have been no one in America better suited to that task than Bingham. He was well trained as an experimental psychologist and extremely well connected within the psychological community, both in the United States and abroad. He had an incredible entrepreneurial spirit that he had demonstrated so well at CIT that served him well in his assignment at PRF. He was a good judge of talent, and as the efficiency experts demanded, he was able to match people and jobs as he had shown in his hiring of staff at CIT. He was also respectful of persons of varying educational and experiential backgrounds, and he believed that such individuals had something important to offer to the field of psychology. That respect for the ideas and talents of others was key in his success as an applied psychologist.

Bingham published three books as part of his emissary role that dealt with personnel issues: *Procedures in Employment Psychology* (Bingham & Freyd, 1926); *How to Interview* (Bingham & Moore, 1931), which went through three editions in Bingham's lifetime; and *Aptitudes and Aptitude Testing* (1937). Vocational counseling was an especially strong focus of the first and third books. All were written as textbooks but were also directed toward individuals in management positions. They reflected the changes in the 1920s that embodied a more compassionate view of labor, consistent with Bingham's values, and in contrast to the harsher programs of "scientific management" espoused by Frederick Winslow Taylor (1911) and his followers, that were generally resented by workers. In Bingham's time, industrial psychology was typically viewed by labor as a tool of management. Bingham's writings, and later those of Ross Stagner (1956), would change that perception.

Bingham's 1937 book on aptitude testing is arguably his most important published work. His work on a revision of that book was terminated by his death. There had been earlier publications on aptitudes as well as collections of aptitude tests. But Bingham's book was unique in its time for its combination of theory, method, and scope of interpretation. It was a book written for three audiences: guidance counselor, manager/employer, and worker. Its appendix included recommendations of tests in categories such as manual, mechanical, scientific, and clerical aptitudes; intelligence; sensory abilities; and interests. Furthermore, it included the complete Minnesota Occupational Rating Scales that allowed users of the book to see the way various abilities correlated with more than 400 occupations. The book was written to promote the value of standardized aptitude testing, using a small set of tests, ones that Bingham considered valid (in some cases with little scientific evidence) in a time when invalid aptitude assessment procedures were both popular and rampant, for example, the characterological system of Katherine Blackford (Blackford & Newcomb, 1914) that appealed to American businesses in the 1920s and 1930s. In addition to helping estimate the probability of success a person would enjoy in a particular occupation, Bingham's (1937) book was intended

> to discover unused talents; to suggest possible alternative fields; to bring to attention endowments which might well be capitalized, and disabilities which should be recognized and removed or compensated for; and in general to provide the inquirer, whether youthful or mature, with food for objective thinking about himself and his future relations to the world of work. (p. 14)

During his emissary period Bingham wrote occasionally for the popular press, such as *The New York Times*, and in management, occupational, and vocational guidance magazines to promote the importance of industrial psychology. He also organized a set of 30 radio lectures that aired Saturday evenings in 1931–1932 on a nationally broadcast program entitled *Psychology Today*. Lecturers were a who's who in psychology including such prominent psychologists as James Rowland Angell, Edward L. Thorndike, John B. Watson, Robert Woodworth, Carl Seashore, Leta Hollingworth (chap. 16, *Pioneers I*), Arnold Gesell, Florence Goodenough, and Gardner Murphy. Listeners could get brochures in advance of the lectures that included tests for them to complete after the lectures. The final lecture in the series was Bingham's "Making Work Worthwhile" (see Bingham, 1932).

During the 1930s, Bingham was also involved in organizational work that promoted the practice of psychology. As noted earlier, World War I provided an important impetus to the growth of applied psychology. Academic psychology continued to expand as well, but when the Great Depression struck America in the 1930s, jobs in universities became scarce—a situation exacerbated by attempts to find university jobs for many European émigrés fleeing from the Nazis' rise to power. Thus, psychologists looked outside of the universities to expand job opportunities.

In 1938, the American Association of Applied Psychology (AAAP) was founded as the first truly national organization for professional psychologists in the United States. Because the APA was viewed as reluctant to promote the profession of psychology, the AAAP was organized principally to meet the needs of psychologists who earned their income through consulting and application of psychology outside of universities. Originally AAAP was organized in four "sections," with Section D entitled "Industrial and Business Psychology" (Benjamin, 1997a). The initial president of that section was Harold Burtt, who had been an undergraduate at Dartmouth when Bingham was there and who had been encouraged by Bingham to pursue a career in applied psychology. Burtt had been one of the principal organizers for Section D. Bingham became president of the section for the next year (1939) and later was elected president of AAAP (1942), the only industrial psychologist to have that honor during the short 8-year history of the organization, evidence of his standing among applied psychologists. In 1945, AAAP ceased to exist. It officially merged with APA and the now five AAAP sections (clinical, consulting, industrial, educational, and military) became charter divisions of APA (see Benjamin, 1997b).

PSYCHOLOGY GOES TO WAR AGAIN

In his autobiography, Bingham wrote that like many Americans of his generation he felt certain he would never see a world war again. That changed in 1939 when the Nazis invaded Poland, an event that stimulated Bingham and other psychologists who were veterans of World War I to renew their military contacts. In April 1940, the adjutant general, Emory Adams, asked the National Research Council to create a committee of psychologists to advise him on classification of military personnel. Seven psychologists, including Thurstone, were appointed to the committee; Bingham asked to serve as chair (Bingham, 1952).

> For seven years we met when summoned, to consider questions related to the work of the Personnel Research and Procedures Branch of The Adjutant General's Office, which was responsible for developing aids in classifying officers and men with respect to their abilities and skills, educational background, civilian and military experience, intellectual capacity, personal qualifications, special aptitudes, and indicated best Army usefulness. (p. 22)

The committee consulted on many tasks, including the Army General Classification Test, procedures for selecting officers, interview procedures, aptitude testing, and officer efficiency reports.

In August, 1940, Bingham was appointed chief psychologist in the Adjutant General's Office in the War Department, a job he held until June 1947. In the First World War he had risen to the rank of lieutenant colonel, but he decided he could be more effective during the Second World War as a civilian (Burtt, 1952). His duties were "to supervise a very small staff, civilian and military, and to speak for The Adjutant General when psychologists and pseudopsychologists descended on him with fluent proposals and offers of service, some of which were of great help" (Bingham, 1952, p. 23).

Unlike the First World War where psychologists were regarded with suspicion by military officers, Bingham found in 1940 that there was considerable acceptance of the validity of psychology, particularly in personnel issues, and it was personnel work that chiefly occupied Bingham during his tenure as chief psychologist. But he also aided psychology and the military in other ways, for example, in using clinical psychologists to train officers in counseling soldiers leaving the military, an action that did not become much of an issue until 1943. Throughout his years as chief psychologist, Bingham continued to promote the value of industrial psychology through speeches and publications.

CONCLUSION

After he resigned his position as chief psychologist in 1947 at the age of 66, Bingham continued as a consultant to the Army General Staff and to the secretary of defense until the time of his death in 1952 (Burtt, 1952). He was survived by his wife, Millicent Todd Bingham, the first woman to receive a doctorate in geology and geography at Harvard University. Their's was a marriage of shared intellect and love, and she was an adviser on much of his work. After Bingham's death, his wife endowed a lectureship in her husband's name as well as a chair in psychology at Carnegie-Mellon University.

In February 1915, a few weeks after accepting the job at CIT, Bingham (1915b) wrote to Münsterberg expressing genuine humility about his selection. He wondered why Hamerschlag should have preferred him "over Whipple or David Spence Hill, or many others who have accomplished so much more than I have." Münsterberg (1915) replied, "I am delighted to hear about your Pittsburgh plans. You are certainly the right man for the place, and I consider the place a most important one. . . . Your possibilities there are unlimited."

Bingham was the right man for the job, the right person in the right place at the right time. Although his career in psychology lasted more than 40 years, the 9 years he spent at CIT were the years of greatest impact and influence, and probably of greatest personal satisfaction and enjoyment. Bingham was more administrator and entrepreneur than he was researcher. He saw opportunities for psychology's interface with business and he was quick to seize them. He had a talent for working with the business community, to learn its needs, and to provide solutions for those needs. Although he initiated numerous projects at CIT, he was typically involved only in their formation. Once initiated, he would hire someone to assume the responsibilities, while he sought out the next opportunity.

Bingham's Division of Applied Psychology was a business. He produced products, mostly in the form of psychological tests, interview forms, aptitude tests, and other instruments that were used in selection. His research training in psychology provided him with the background for construction of those products. And he possessed the marketing skills to understand the generalized utility of his products, with appropriate modifications, to many other business needs, and even to the needs of the United States Army. Much of the division's work was funded not by the university, but by the consumers of Bingham's personnel services. The services to businesses by the division's faculty and staff were considerable, especially in bringing order to the personnel process:

> They standardized forms, tests, rating scales, and interest batteries; and they adapted all of these to an acknowledged measure of comparison for quantitative and qualitative value. . . . Furthermore, they showed companies how to record and route their information, coordinate their activities, and analyze their internal operations. (Kraus, 1986, p. 88)

Whereas Scott played an important role in personnel research and development, his tenure in the field was short-lived. Bingham, however, devoted his career to proselytizing for the value of psychology in personnel work and working to improve selection procedures with more valid tests that could be administered more easily and at lower costs. In her book on the history of personnel research, Kraus (1986) credited Bingham with the greatest influence on personnel work in the 20th century, concluding that his work influenced "1) future corporate funding of university applied research; 2) the field of industrial selection and testing; and 3) decision-making within the American corporation" (p. i). Kraus labeled Bingham "the first academic entrepreneur" (p. ii) whose melding of the academy and industry allowed him to "structure a working relationship, balancing human potential, applied learning and the profit motivated demands of the modern corporation" (p. i).

Bingham's lifework was in the service of personnel psychology and, more broadly, industrial psychology. His work at CIT, his service on the Committee on Classification of Personnel in the Army, his directorship of the Personnel Research Federation, his editorship of *The Personnel Journal*, his job as chief psychologist with the Adjutant General's Office during the Second World War, his lifelong behavior of preaching the value of applied psychology to the business community and to psychologists and students of psychology, and the demonstrated legacy of his work on contemporary psychology and industry more than justify his designation as the dean of American industrial psychologists. Münsterberg (1913) stated that the foremost concern in efficiency is matching the worker's abilities to the requirements of the job. In Bingham's case, he and industrial psychology proved to be a very good match.

REFERENCES

Benjamin, Jr., L. T. (1997a). Organized industrial psychology before Division 14: The ACP and the AAAP (1930–1945). *Journal of Applied Psychology, 82,* 459–466.

Benjamin, Jr., L. T. (1997b). The origin of psychological species: History of the beginnings of American Psychological Association divisions. *American Psychologist, 52,* 725–732.

Bingham, M. T. (1953). Beyond psychology. In J. H. Baker & C. W. Buchheister (Eds.), *Homo sapiens auduboniensis: A tribute to Walter Van Dyke Bingham* (pp. 5–29). New York: The National Audubon Society.

Bingham, W. V. D. (1915a). Some norms of college freshmen [Abstract]. *Psychological Bulletin, 12,* 68.

Bingham, W. V. D. (1915b). Letter to Hugo Münsterberg, February 13, 1915. Boston: Boston Public Library, Münsterberg Papers.

Bingham, W. V. D. (1917). *Applied psychology at the Carnegie Institute of Technology: Abstract of the Second Annual Report of the Division of Applied Psychology* [Brochure]. Pittsburgh, PA: Carnegie-Mellon University Archives, Bingham Papers.

Bingham, W. V. D. (1923, February). Psychology applied. *Scientific Monthly, 16,* 141–159.

Bingham, W. V. D. (Ed.). (1932). *Psychology today: Lectures and study manual.* Chicago: University of Chicago Press.

Bingham, W. V. D. (1937). *Aptitudes and aptitude testing.* New York: Harper.

Bingham, W. V. D. (1952). Walter Van Dyke Bingham. In E. G. Boring, H. S. Langfeld, H. Werner, & R. M. Yerkes (Eds.), *A history of psychology in autobiography* (Vol. 4, pp. 1–26). Worcester, MA: Clark University Press.

Bingham, W. V. D., & Freyd, M. (1926). *Procedures in employment psychology.* Chicago: Shaw.

Bingham, W. V. D., & Moore, B. V. (1931). *How to interview.* New York: Harper.

Blackford, K., & Newcomb, A. (1914). *The job, the man, the boss.* New York: Doubleday, Page.

Burtt, H. E. (1952). Walter V. Bingham: 1880–1952. *Psychological Review, 59,* 403–404.

Ferguson, L. W. (1963a). Walter Van Dyke Bingham: Dean of industrial psychologists. In *The heritage of industrial psychology* (pp. 13–23). Pittsburgh, PA: Carnegie-Mellon Archives, The Ferguson Papers.

Ferguson, L. W. (1963b). Division of Applied Psychology, Carnegie Institute of Technology. In *The heritage of industrial psychology* (pp. 25–34). Pittsburgh, PA: Carnegie-Mellon Archives, The Ferguson Papers.

Ferguson, L. W. (1963c). Edward A. Woods: Scientific salesmanship. In *The heritage of industrial psychology* (pp. 37–49). Pittsburgh, PA: Carnegie-Mellon Archives, The Ferguson Papers.

Ferguson, L. W. (1963d). First students and their careers: Bureau of Salesmanship Research. In *The heritage of industrial psychology* (pp. 69–88). Pittsburgh, PA: Carnegie-Mellon Archives, The Ferguson Papers.

Gilmer, B. von H. (Ed.). (1962). *Walter Van Dyke Bingham, memorial program.* Pittsburgh, PA: Carnegie Institute of Technology.

Hilgard, E. R. (1987). *Psychology in America: A historical survey.* Orlando, FL: Harcourt, Brace, Jovanovich.

Keith, K. W., Roberts, M. K., Harris, C. L., & Baker, D. B. (2000). *Carnegie Tech: The early history of American applied psychology.* Unpublished manuscript.

Kraus, M. P. (1986). *Personnel research, history and policy issues: Walter Van Dyke Bingham and the Bureau of Personnel Research.* New York: Garland Publishing.

Münsterberg, H. (1913). *Psychology and industrial efficiency.* Boston: Houghton Mifflin.

Münsterberg, H. (1915). Letter to Walter Van Dyke Bingham, February 17, 1915. Pittsburgh, PA: Carnegie-Mellon University Archives, Bingham Papers.

Parsons, F. (1909). *Choosing a vocation.* Boston: Houghton Mifflin.

Preliminary Announcement of the Bureau of Salesmanship Research [Brochure]. (1916). Pittsburgh, PA: Carnegie-Mellon University Archives, Bingham Papers.

Prien, E. P. (1991). The Division of Applied Psychology at Carnegie Institute of Technology. *The Industrial-Organizational Psychologist, 29*(2), 41–45.

Samelson, F. (1977). World War I intelligence testing and the development of psychology. *Journal of the History of the Behavioral Sciences, 13,* 274–282.

Scott, W. D. (1903). *The theory of advertising.* Boston: Small, Maynard, & Co.

Scott, W. D. (1908). *The psychology of advertising.* Boston: Small, Maynard, & Co.

Scott, W. D. (1911a). *Influencing men in business.* New York: Ronald Press.

Scott, W. D. (1911b). *Increasing human efficiency in business.* New York: Macmillan.

Scott, W. D. (1916). *Aids in the selection of salesmen* [Booklet]. Pittsburgh, PA: Carnegie-Mellon University Archives, Bingham Papers.

Stagner, R. (1956). *The psychology of industrial conflict.* New York: Wiley.

Strong, E. K., Jr. (1943). *Vocational interests of men and women.* Palo Alto, CA: Stanford University Press.

Taylor, F. W. (1911). *The principles of scientific management.* New York: Harper & Brothers.

von Mayrhauser, R. T. (1989). Making intelligence functional: Walter Dill Scott and applied psychological testing in World War I. *Journal of the History of the Behavioral Sciences, 25,* 60–72.

Yerkes, R. M. (1921). (Ed.). Psychological examining in the United States Army. *Memoirs of the National Academy of Sciences* (Vol. 15). Washington, DC: Government Printing Office.

Chapter 10

Albert Michotte: A Psychologist for All Sites and Seasons

Eileen A. Gavin
College of St. Catherine

As you look through the contents of this book, you may ask, "Who on earth was Albert Michotte?" And as you begin to read about this celebrated Belgian psychologist, you may wonder what a privileged white man from a bygone century could possibly contribute to psychology in this new century, when so much has changed and so much more change is inevitable. You may find some answers to these questions as you become familiar with Michotte's work and with what his peers and contemporary psychologists have said about him. In a review of the English translation of Michotte's magnum opus, *The Perception of Causality* (1946/1963), for example, a peer from beyond Belgium's borders said, "There are few psychologists with the originality of mind, the ingenuity in experimental design and techniques, the psychological insight and the expertise in argument" who can rival Albert Michotte (Vernon, 1964, p. 75). Knowledgeable contemporary psychologists also admire Michotte's experimental-phenomenological research and remark on its pertinence to current issues in the psychology of perception, developmental psychology, and social psychology (Thinès, Costall, & Butterworth, 1991). It would not surprise me if, after you scrutinize Michotte's life and work, some of you, like me, will put him on your short list of great contributors to psychology. In any case, I hope that what you learn about the life and work of Albert Michotte will enrich your lives and careers.

Like you, I never met Michotte. Probably, however, I have more regrets than you, for I could have met him toward the end of his career but failed to take advantage of the opportunity. The closest that I came to meeting him was 8 years after Michotte's death, when I visited the University of Louvain in Belgium, site of his creative life and work. While spending part of a sabbatical leave there, I had access to Michotte's unpublished research reports, mostly on perception, a process that he regarded as the first phase of action. During that period, I also met and conferred with several of Michotte's former colleagues and students, who remembered him as brilliant, original, and kind.

Many years before I traveled to Louvain, while I was an undergraduate student at the College of St. Catherine, I became acquainted with two college teachers who had studied with Michotte. They introduced me to Michotte's contributions to psychology and told me about his profound influence on their lives. Later, when I went to Louvain, I found myself longing for just one meeting with Michotte himself. Throughout my stay in Louvain, I reflected on what E. G. Boring, an eminent historian of psychology, might have said about the Ortgeist, the spirit of the place. Indeed, the very walls in which I studied Michotte's documents and met some of his former colleagues and students seemed to speak eloquently of him. I felt that I was getting to know him much better than before my Louvain visit, even in his absence.

Now an opportunity has arisen to share with you some of the best that this highly original, accomplished, and warmhearted man contributed to psychology. This opportunity led me to reflect on what Michotte might say to you who belong to a new generation if he were resurrected. I decided to let you meet Michotte through the medium of a quasi last lecture, in which he presents the highlights of his life and work. The sources for this fancied last lecture were Michotte's research reports, his own words, the recollections of his colleagues and friends, and comments on Michotte's work by his colleagues. Afterward, a postscript will return us to the present time. In the final section, I will comment on Michotte's words and works and on his legacy for contemporary and future psychology.

MICHOTTE'S LAST LECTURE

Years ago, someone asked me to contribute the story of my life to a collection of autobiographies reporting the contributions and styles of life of eminent psychologists. At first I thought of declining the invitation. In so many ways my happy academic and private life seemed quite ordinary. It "proceeded so simply, so regularly, and indeed so logically that it seemed to promise little of interest to anyone outside my immediate environment" (Michotte, 1952, p. 213). My life would never make sensational headlines. For instance, I was fortunate from the beginning of my career in research and teaching because I chose to marry Lucie Mulle. "Our home which six children came to brighten has never ceased to be a perfectly happy one" (p. 215). My wife's consistent "understanding of my scientific activity . . . has always endeavored to relieve me of other cares" (p. 215).

The "amiable insistence of a few of my colleagues" (p. 213) made me reconsider my initial intent to decline the invitation to present my account. Today you can find my *petite histoire*, as the French would call it, in sources that trace the evolution of ideas in my life and summarize my major academic projects and scientific contributions (Michotte, 1952, 1954/1991). In this last lecture I will present some highlights of my private life, the educational path that prepared me for my career, my outlook on psychology and psychological issues, my major lines of research, and my words to you who are just starting out.

Personal and Educational Background

I was the second and last child born in 1881 into a well-to-do and intellectual family in Brussels, a family that placed high value on the fine arts and the sciences. All my ancestors that I knew about were sincere and devoted Catholics. Intellectually and religiously, I have followed in my ancestors' footsteps in these matters throughout my own life. Because of my socioeconomic background excellent educational opportunities were part of my upbringing. While still in my midteens, I entered the University of Louvain, where I studied philosophy and science for the next 8 years. There I experienced the beneficent influence of two great scholars. The first, Professor Desiré Mercier, a Roman Catholic cleric, headed Louvain's Institut Supérieur de Philosophie. That incomparable man later became a cardinal, an honor that made him a prince in the Roman Catholic Church. As cardinal, he joined the select company of about 150 clerics worldwide who are eligible for succession to the papacy. "His influence was determinative in my intellectual and 'human' development" (Michotte, 1954/1991, p. 214). Mercier encouraged me to follow my research bent, which consisted in a passion to seek the precise knowledge that experiments can reveal. The future cardinal strongly advocated scientific psychology and supported experimentation on issues that could clarify human action. Because Mercier believed in my ability to contribute to psychology if I chose to follow my natural talent for and interest in laboratory research, I decided to specialize in psychology. I regarded Mercier as a very enlightened philosopher. He not only recognized the importance of psychology as a science, but he also knew that psychology's parent disciplines of philosophy and biology provide sound moorings for students of human and animal activity.

The second major influence on my professional development was Professor Arthur van Gehuchten, an outstanding Louvain neurologist. I did my earliest scientific research under his direction. My work with Van Gehuchten—on the histology of the nerve cell—impressed on me the indispensable role the body plays in bringing about action. To avert unproductive psychologizing, the structures and functions of the body must not be ignored. Because of the influence of Van Gehuchten and Mercier, I became steeped early in life in psychology's connections with its "parents," that is, with biology and philosophy.

My study of philosophy and biology in relation to psychology reinforced my conviction that this newly developing field of study proposed altogether too many theories based on too few facts. My philosophical studies, in particular, made me wary of invoking metaphysical principles as evidence for psychological laws (Michotte, 1936, p. 208). I determined to avoid that error by providing scientific evidence that other scientists could check, evidence that casts light on issues such as adaptive action, which greatly interested me.

Study at Sites Beyond Louvain

Just as many other psychologists-in-the-making before me had done, I decided to study at Wilhelm Wundt's (chap. 3, *Pioneers III*) laboratory at the University of Leipzig. I spent two semesters there, familiarizing myself with Wundt's scientific psychology. Although I appreciated what I learned at Leipzig, I found the approach inadequate. For instance, I disagreed with Wundt's insistence on shearing meaning from psychology. I have always recognized the importance of "meanings that certain actions or objects could have for a person or animal" (Michotte, 1954/1991, p. 34). It seemed obvious to me "that a thorough study of behaviour must take into account the way in which people and animals 'understand' the situation in which they are placed and the actions of other people and animals, as well as those they perform themselves" (p. 34).

I have also steadily regarded as important the presentation of scientific evidence that aims to clarify the processes that contribute to adaptive action. It is essential, I believe, to include the meaning or significance that a situation has for participants in research. Moreover, from very early in my career I have acknowledged "the directing and motivating roles of needs and dispositions, as well as the characteristic attitudes of the active individual" (Michotte, 1954/1991, p. 46). Many important aspects of psychological activity, such as affective states, wishes, choices, and beliefs, have essential characteristics that may initially elude the observer (Michotte, 1936, p. 211). I believe that disregarding such elusive phenomena is ill advised. At the same time, however, identifying appropriate ways to investigate complex psychological phenomena scientifically poses a great challenge.

I have long believed that, to clarify adaptive action, the situation of the behaving individual must be defined and specified (Michotte, 1936, p. 220). Although this may be hard to accomplish, it must be done because "situation" and "response" are necessary and interlocking prime components of adaptive action. Provision of a definite, well-defined experimental situation can greatly benefit the scientific quest. Identification of a relation that unites situation and response sometimes provides a window through which one may better see and understand the actions of an individual human being or animal (p. 220), which is the goal of psychological investigation. Through my efforts to clarify individuals' responses, I have also become convinced "that social psychology is of fundamental importance in the study of behavior, because ... behavior is primarily determined by the human environment" (Michotte, 1954/1991, p. 29). Social psychology, when properly formulated, should greatly advance knowledge of adaptive action. Throughout most of my career, though, social psychology was not really well developed. It lacked the precise scientific techniques that could make it a worthy scientific partner for the study of adaptive action. Late in my career, however, I began to realize that improved techniques for exploring social phenomena were on the horizon. Their availability should benefit those of you who are interested in adaptive action but are just beginning your work in psychology.

Physiological phenomena such as glandular, cardiovascular, and muscular responses are easier to assess than phenomena that show marked social components. This is because scientific observers can reliably describe situations and responses in studies involving physiological phenomena (Michotte, 1936, p. 220). Some investigations of psychological phenomena—such as memory—also meet the canons of science when they specify precise stimulus conditions (such as the amount of material to be recalled and the time since learning it) and responses that can be denoted exactly (such as the accuracy and speed of the response). Because various observers reliably report data in such cases, objective science can easily assimilate the findings (p. 225).

In many psychological domains, however, the essential character of a response must be defined by modifying the situation in ways that alter the individual's attitude toward a task. In those cases, different people will regard the meaning and significance of the task differently. I am convinced that no apparatus can measure changes of that kind (Michotte, 1936, p. 226). Investigations that assess adaptive action by limiting themselves to objective features of situations and overt glandular or muscular responses that are similar for different people may fail to clarify complex behavioral phenomena. Nevertheless, important questions about human activity must not be avoided simply because they are difficult. For example, in an everyday situation that may evoke almsgiving, the retinal imprint of a beggar will be similar for most people. Muscular responses, too, may be similar from person to person. However, the meaning of the situation may differ greatly for different individuals (Michotte, 1936, p. 221). Some people will pity the beggar; others will not. Within a scientific framework, one can address such problems that bear on human action by finding ways to quantify the values that differ from one person to another (p. 226). For example, the investigators might look for factors that determine human personality, some of which may be basic to an individual's psychologically significant behavior (p. 228). Analogously, physical scientists have done research that pertains to hypothesized but unseen variables, such as force and gravity (p. 228). Two of my brightest former students, J. Nuttin and A. Godin, have tackled equally difficult issues in psychology, issues that bear on personality and religious outlook. They have been concerned with aspects of the structure of personality that are not directly observable. Their work provides leads that some of you may choose to follow (Godin, 1981/1985; Nuttin, 1953/1962).

Influence of Oswald Külpe and Alfred Binet

During the year I studied psychology in Leipzig, I got a big lift that affected my future investigations by attending a professional meeting at which I met Oswald Külpe. That same year I read research reports by Alfred Binet (chap. 5, *Pioneers III*). Both Külpe and Binet impressed me greatly. I found that their investigating the behavioral impact of complex psychological processes in well-defined situations made sense to me. Therefore I decided to enter the University of Würzburg, where Külpe was teaching at the time. The breadth and brilliance of Külpe's work and my contacts with him contributed much to my professional development. In fact, "it is to Külpe that I owe my real maturation as a psychologist" (Michotte, 1954/1991, p. 214).

Early Years on the Faculty at Louvain

After I finished my studies under Külpe's direction in Würzburg, I returned to the University of Louvain where I launched my teaching and research career as a faculty member in the Institute of Philosophy—the university had no psychology department at that time. My research on voluntary choice (Michotte & Prüm, 1910) and logical memory (Michotte & Portych, 1912; Michotte & Ransy, 1912) belong to this time and exemplify Külpe's influence on me. I regard my study of voluntary choice as my most important early work because it demonstrated that situations alone, however well defined, will not fully account for the responses that individuals make to them.

To cast light on the role of individuals in responding to well-defined situations that do not evoke automatic or reflex responses, my colleague Prüm and I (Gavin, 1972a; Michotte & Prüm, 1910) set out to study voluntary choices and their immediate antecedents. Research participants received successive stimulus sets, each of which consisted of two numbers that were either three or four digits in length, for example, 383 and 529, and required to select and then apply some self-chosen arithmetic operation (such as addition or subtraction). After they finished that task, the participants reported on their experiences. The principal findings in this research were that participants attributed the choice of specific arithmetic operations to themselves, not to situational constraints or conditions, and that they were acutely conscious of selecting the operation. Furthermore, they reported that they could have done otherwise: They insisted they could have selected another arithmetic operation, but they chose this one instead. Thus, consciousness of self—that is, consciousness of their own agency in making choices—clearly marked the participants' reports in choosing one arithmetic operation rather than another. Consciousness of self as agent, therefore, was an immediate, unambiguous datum (Gavin, 1972a). Designation of self as agent does not negate the important roles of bodily structures and situational factors. It simply shows that research participants are clearly conscious of their personal role in tipping the balance by selecting one option rather than another. This is voluntary choice, evidenced in an experimental setting. It is miles away from the philosophy of indeterminism, the doctrine that human actions come out of the blue or happen by accident. Instead, personal choice is self-determined; situational factors and organismic factors contribute but they do not have the last word in determining a person's choices.

A second set of early investigations, in the tradition of Külpe, looked at logical memory (Gavin, 1975; Michotte & Portych, 1912; Michotte & Ransy, 1912). In one study of logical memory, research participants studied a succession of word-pairs linked by obvious relationships, such as belonging, whole-part, similarity, opposition, and causality. For example, the word-pair "nose-face" depicts a belonging relationship. In the experimental condition of this study, research participants were instructed to look for some relationship, such as whole-part or similarity, that seemed to unite the word-pairs. Participants in a control condition did not look for those relationships. Five minutes later, the participants in both groups—in an application of the classical paired-associates technique for measuring recall—saw one member of each stimulus pair and tried to recall the second. Afterward, they reported on their experiences during the preparatory and recall periods (Michotte & Ransy, 1912).

These investigations showed that logical memory, which the experimental condition encouraged, was far superior to memory that did not evoke looking for relationships between members of the word-pairs. Requesting participants to find a relationship between members of the word-pair evidently facilitated rearousal of the missing word. Again and again, participants reported that the word they awaited in the recall test was not just any word. Even in its absence, a word that was just right was somehow in their minds. This evidence and a host of related findings point up the integrative role of thought in memory. Related items to be memorized "become embedded in a complex relational whole (a Gestalt!) so that the reactivation of one aspect leads to the reproduction of others or allows an intentional search for them" (Michotte, 1954/1991, p. 31).

Related and, at times, paradoxical questions remain to be answered. Why, for instance, did research participants who tried especially hard to recall a missing word find that their very efforts interfered with recall? Such research-worthy questions continued to beckon following this line of investigation, but the search for answers was interrupted by World War I.

Professional Activity During World War I

Early in World War I, Louvain came under fire and was burned. In 1914, I moved with my family to Utrecht and remained in Holland for 4 years, where I taught university students who, as members of the Belgian army, had been interned there. I also did research on the measurement of acoustical energy and on other scientific projects at the laboratory of my friend, Professor Zwaardemaker (Michotte, 1954/1991, p. 32).

Throughout this period, my views on psychology matured. For example, I lost confidence in the scientific value of introspective reports, partly because of compelling critiques by Titchener (chap. 7, *Pioneers I*) and by proponents of the behavioristic movement. I also began to realize that contradictory introspective reports sometimes occurred in experiments that qualified people conducted under similar circumstances. The low reliability of introspective reports convinced me to stop using them in my research. On the other hand, I continued to include in my reports the information that I consider essential for all psychological research: the participants' understanding of the situation in which they found themselves (Michotte, 1954/1991, p. 33).

During World War I, I also became "convinced that psychology [is] not a science of mental life but rather a science of behavior or action" (Michotte, 1954/1991, p. 34). That conviction, which helped support my research on motor behavior for years thereafter, resembled the outlook of early behaviorists. However, my insistence on including information that reflects research participants' understanding of experimental situations was clearly at odds with behavioristic doctrine. Except for research on simple reflexes that do not depend on it, I think that investigations of psychological questions ordinarily require inclusion of meaning. In my view, an object tends to influence other-than-reflexive behavior only insofar as it has meaning for the individual.

Some Postwar Highlights

After World War I, I returned to Louvain and resumed my research and teaching at the university. Many of the problems I worked on during that period were similar to those of behavioristic investigators who studied motor reactions. Until 1923, I taught university students and conducted research in scientific psychology in the university's Institute of Philosophy. Even though it had no formal psychological institute, the University of Louvain had become known as a center for psychological studies. When the university's psychology institute was finally founded in 1923, it was called the "School of Pedagogy and Psychology Applied to Education" (Misiak & Staudt, 1954, p. 58). Its aim was "instruction and research in both psychology and education" (p. 58). Later, the institute became very sensitive to applying psychological findings to additional areas such as industrial and vocational psychology. Throughout my career, I have always been open to applying psychology appropriately to related fields. My own exacting research in no way negates what I regard as valuable: that is, using psychological findings wherever they are appropriate. That outlook fits well with what contemporary psychologists call "giving psychology away."

In the same year that the psychology institute at Louvain became a formal reality, I had my first opportunity to become acquainted with Gestalt psychology. During the 1923 International Congress of Psychology meeting, held at Oxford University, I met two leaders of Gestalt psychology, Wolfgang Köhler (chap. 17, *Pioneers I*) and Kurt Koffka. It was heartening for me to discover that some of our research findings, arrived at independently, were similar and complementary. Nevertheless, as with my behavioristic colleagues, I did not always agree with the Gestaltists on theoretical matters. For instance, I did not accept the construct of isomorphism—the hypothetical identity of psychological and brain processes—which is very important to Gestalists. This theoretical difference, however, did not keep me from appreciating my Gestalt colleagues greatly.

Throughout my research career I have placed high value on my associations with colleagues and graduate students. The cross-fertilization of ideas that results from interaction and collaboration with senior and junior colleagues has greatly enhanced my life and work. At times these interactions have helped me sort out my ideas. Moreover, associations with professional associates from far and wide has led to heartwarming friendships. From time to time colleagues who have become friends have invited me to teach in various Western European countries and in the United States. I especially enjoyed serving as visiting professor at Stanford University during the summer of 1929 (Michotte, 1954/1991, p. 47). In all my years at the University of Louvain, I never had what you would call a "research assistant." My graduate students, many of whom have gone on to become university professors themselves, were more like apprentices in the workshops of old, who learned from an experienced person how to be artisans and craftsmen, while I, in turn, learned from them.

Research That Paralleled the Behaviorist and Gestalt Movements

Much of the experimentation that my colleagues and I did during the 1920s and 1930s paralleled the investigations of behavioristic psychologists. In the late 1920s, for example, Van der Veldt (Michotte, 1954/1991, p. 35) and I studied motor training in relation to adaptive behavior. A discovery that I had made earlier triggered our investigations. I had found that speed in performing a chain of movements that involved reaching for a succession of targets arranged irregularly on a surface and separated by a rather long distance from one another "was practically the same whether the subject had performed this activity a great many times or for the first time, as long as sufficient time was given for an examination of the targets in advance" (p. 35). This finding raised a serious question regarding "the exact role of motor training as such" (p. 35).

Seeking an answer to this question, we went on to study training in relation to movements that occur after a research participant is told to pick up something lying on a table. We used photographic records as an objective way to study variations in the form and timing of the trajectories described by the research participants' reachings. We soon found that training resulted in profound changes in these movements. This research objectively confirmed what had been known for some time: that exercise results in "unitary, global motor reactions . . . that are triggered all at once." Additional experimentation complemented and extended this finding by showing that the forms of trajectories become stereotyped in the course of training. Sometimes the forms of these trajectories remained constant "even when the subject was required to perform the task in another plane or on a different scale . . . the forms often showed the Gestalt property of transposition. . . . This result prompted the conclusion that motor practice leads to the development of motor forms that are global and autonomous and possess similar properties to perceptual forms" (Michotte, 1954/1991, p. 35). We had demonstrated experimentally the importance of Gestalt principles in motor activity. The observations made in this experimentation were new because Gestalt psychologists, at that time, had only dealt with problems in the sensory domain (p. 35).

A series of related studies that belong to this same period demonstrated the importance of Gestalt-like structural organizations in other contexts. For example, we demonstrated that rhythm is a temporal form, analogous to spatial form. Accuracy of motor performance, we discovered, is as much a function of rhythm as it is of speed. (Michotte, 1954/1991, p. 37). Additional studies from this period dealt with improvement of accuracy for rapid movements, morphological characteristics of automatic motor reactions in everyday life, movement acceleration, and the transfer of motor training (p. 37).

Changes in Research Beginning About 1940

My research undertakings have always been based on the conviction that people strive to make sense of their experience by adapting to situations in terms of what they mean to them. Because perception, which is the first phase of action, is crucial to adaptation, my research during this period aimed to cast light on what characterizes the first phase of action. My research, from about 1940 until the end of my research career, tackled a number of pertinent perceptual problems, such as phenomenal causality, permanence, and apparent reality (Michotte, 1954/1991, p. 39). In my best-known research—on phenomenal causality—which I describe here, I used illusions.

My strategy in using illusions may at first seem puzzling. Perhaps you think of illusions as merely props for parlor games and remote from adaptation to everyday life. In fact, however, the illusions that we incorporated into our research yield information about the perceptual cues that prompt adaptive action. Clarifying the structure of situations that evoke perception is important because people use perceptual information whenever they assess a situation, whether in the laboratory or in everyday life.

Our research demonstrated that the phenomenological reports of our observers changed as we tinkered with situational factors such as the velocity of apparent objects and their spatial and temporal relationships to other objects. For example, very specific and narrowly limited spatial–temporal conditions in our visual displays resulted in research participants' reporting an impression of causality: One object in a visual display seemed to bring about or cause a change in another object. Our demonstrations of impressions of causality made me wonder whether analogous impressions of causality that also depend on precise features of situations enable individuals to adapt to real-life situations.

I hope that my clarifying the conditions needed for perceived causality in relation to adaptation will convince you that our research on phenomenal causality is not an ivory tower game but is an undertaking that may well have significance for everyday life. If you accept that point, you may want to know how we did our research, what our chief findings were, and what we concluded. To that end, I will guide you through one of our major programs of research, which yielded evidence for two chief causal impressions: of *launching* and of *entraining*.

Picture a research participant seated in front of a large screen that has a narrow, clearly visible horizontal slit in it. Behind the screen, and outside the observer's view, is a motorized color-wheel apparatus—the kind you may have seen in classroom demonstrations—equipped with a large circular rotating disc that displays concentric circles and spirals. When the color wheel is turned on, the disc revolves, presenting a changing visual display but, at any moment, an observer sees only the portions of the display that are shown through the slit in the screen. What the person actually sees at any moment, of course, is simply a sector of the moving disc. The disc apparatus and the technique that we used in some of our best-researched studies of causal impressions are further described in easily accessible sources (Gavin, 1972b, p. 307; Michotte, 1946/1963, pp. 27–34).

The simple visual displays we used in our experiments enabled us easily to make systematic modifications in the spatiotemporal conditions presented to our observers. Whenever timing and velocity of patterns on the disc fall within certain limits, the research participants report seeing objects that look like rectangles in relation to each other. The observers' specific phenomenological reports depend on the portion of the disc that comes into view and the velocity at which the disc is turning. These reports under varied conditions constitute the major data of our research. By subjecting participants to systematically varied conditions, we discovered the exact conditions that prompt the two main impressions of causality that our experimental demonstrations produced: launching and entraining.

For example, under specific spatiotemporal conditions, research participants consistently reported that the first of the two "rectangles" they observed through the slit in the screen appeared to launch or set off the action of the second rectangle. Altered spatiotemporal conditions in the visual displays led observers to report instead that the first rectangle seemed to take the second one along with it, like a train's engine conveying an attached car behind it. We called this second causal impression entraining. The conditions under which the causal impressions launching and entraining occurred had to be precise. If we altered the situation even slightly, impressions of causality did not occur at all. We surmised that people probably use information from their experience in an analogous manner, enabling them to adapt to situations they meet in everyday life.

Conclusions Prompted by Our Research
on Phenomenal Causality

As we gradually amassed experimental data, consisting of phenomenological reports of impressions of causality, such as launching and entraining, my theory of "ampliation of the movement" emerged (Michotte, 1946/1963, pp. 217–230). The research participant who experiences the causal impression of launching notes that a motion that previously characterized an active primary object resembling a rectangle is now carried over to or extended to a second, previously passive rectangle. This perceived extension of movement from an active object to a previously passive object marks the essence of ampliation. In ampliation, the observer directly perceives that one object produces movement in another. This impression is unleashed by stimuli that show very specific spatiotemporal characteristics. Timing, position, and velocity must be exactly right for causal impressions to occur. The observers' impressions of causality, which express ampliation of movement, thus, arise not from intuitive appreciation of something that often occurs in the natural world or from past experience, but from the very structure of the stimulus situation that comes into view. Repeated, amply documented reports of the psychological experience of "phenomenal causality" strongly confirm my theory of ampliation of the movement. Whenever a visual display manifests certain exact spatiotemporal characteristics, observers predictably report a displacement of the moved object by the blow it receives (Michotte, 1954/1991, p. 4l). The phenomenal impressions of causality convey the intrinsic meaning of the situation to the observer (p. 41).

I want to make one further comment about our work on the psychology of causal impressions. Our data show that the eminent 18th-century Scottish philosopher David Hume was mistaken about the psychology of perceptual experience. Hume's classic thesis "denied the possibility of perceiving the production of one event by another" (Michotte, 1954/1991, p. 41). Our findings on phenomenal causality contradict Hume's speculations about the psychology of causal experience. I want to make very clear, though, that because my research is based solely on phenomenological evidence, I am not addressing the broader philosophical issue that goes beyond our data, that is, the epistemological status of causality (p. 41). That philosophical issue certainly merits extended treatment but not in the present context. The facts that I present are limited to the psychology of perceptual experience. They do not apply directly to such philosophical concerns that govern a theory of knowledge or the rules that pertain to the concept of causality.

An Unexpected Lead Opened by Research
on Phenomenal Causality

In addition to prompting theoretical conclusions about ampliation of the movement and about Hume's speculations concerning causal experience, our research on phenomenal causality also generated an intriguing, unexpected lead that future investigators may choose to follow up. Paying attention to unanticipated findings sometimes results in important outcomes. For example, our findings on phenomenal causality occasionally evoked incidental observations that superficially seemed alien to our major purpose. At times, for instance, in our studies of impressions of causality, participants spontaneously compared what they saw through the slit in the experimental screen with something they had experienced in real-life situations involving human or animal actions. Sometimes particular kinetic patterns suggested "emotional states, attitudes, tendencies attributed to the objects" (Michotte, 1950/1991, p. 105). An observer whose eyes met a stimulus that displayed a particular set of spatiotemporal conditions through the slit in the screen occasionally volunteered statements such as the following: "It is like a cat coming up to a mouse and suddenly springing on it and carrying it off" (p. 105). Another participant also said of the rectangles that appeared on the screen: "It is as though B was afraid when A approached, and ran off" (p. 105). People who are interested in body language seem to be addressing similar issues. In everyday life specific kinetic structures (such as facial expressions, movements, and gestures) frequently lead people to draw conclusions about another individual's present state. The unanticipated verbal reports that our research garnered also raise questions about conditions that underlie emotion. Therefore, these incidental observations could serve as a basis for additional experimental research into emotion in real-life situations. In everyday life, it is evident that people read facial expressions, bodily movements, and gestures with amazing accuracy. Responses to kinetic relationships that we documented through research and participants' spontaneous responses to visual displays that show particular space–time relations are clearly akin to what occurs in analogous situations in everyday life. The unexpected reports that turned up in our research may fit with related topics in the psychology of emotion and in social psychology. In a single lifetime, one psychologist cannot investigate all the phenomena that merit study. Perhaps some of the unexpected leads that our perceptual work uncovered, such as phenomenological reports pertinent to emotion, may entice someone to follow them up some day.

My Final Words to You

My research was never a "mere 'hunt for facts' . . . for this would have been a rather sterile enterprise" (Michotte, 1954/1991, p. 46). Rather, "the experiments I have performed, as well as my efforts at deriving conclusions, have always been dominated by the concern to contribute to the study of one or another of the large questions that has continued to preoccupy me. If my work has been productive it is precisely for this reason, for I have thought again and again about the questions that intrigue me" (p. 46). I can certainly say that throughout my career I have consistently followed the lead of my interests and my special talent for experimental research.

I hope that you, too, will develop your own special gifts and interests. Following curiosity about questions that intrigue you is an excellent guide. Seeking a broad and liberal academic background that includes philosophy and the biological sciences will be a great asset. Keeping up with what is going on in psychology, but retaining your own counsel, will help you focus on central issues. I think you will also discover, as I have, that friends you meet along the way will enhance your enjoyment and insight. I have always been grateful to mentors who helped me as well as for the support and encouragement of students, colleagues, and friends from all over the world.

POSTSCRIPT

A number of psychologists who knew Michotte and have found a place on my short list of heroes in the field greatly appreciated him. Among these are Wolfgang Köhler (chap. 17, *Pioneers I*) and James Gibson (chap. 17, *Pioneers II*). They have praised Michotte for his creative experimentation, his insights, and his values. Arguably, the highest compliment ever accorded to Michotte came from renowned American perceptual psychologist James Gibson. He remarked in his autobiography that although his sociocultural background differed strikingly from that of Michotte, and although his (Gibson's) behavioristic orientation was in some respects very different from Michotte's phenomenological approach, on the most important thing they agreed: "We got the same results. This is what counts. It makes one believe in the possibility of getting at the truth" (Gibson, 1967/1991, pp. ix–x).

Michotte would be the last to say that the questions that interested him, for example, those related to adaptation to everyday life, have been laid to rest, so that there is no more work for others to do. In his autobiography, he said that toward the end of his life, "after many long years, long-standing problems have suddenly appeared in a quite different light" (Michotte, 1954/1991, p. 46). If this is so, truth may be better approached when regarded as a verb than as a noun. Viewed in those terms, Michotte's work is far from finished. Fortunately, an edited work by Michotte's last research associate, Georges Thinès; by an English psychologist, Alan Costall; and by a Scottish psychologist, George Butterworth, now provides easy access to translations into English of many of Michotte's papers, along with thoughtful commentaries that underline Michotte's significance for contemporary psychology (Thinès, Costall, & Butterworth, 1991). Today, therefore, there is no good excuse for not getting to know the contributions and legacy of Michotte. It seems a pity that for reasons too numerous to consider at this time, Michotte's contributions have often been overlooked on the American side of the Atlantic. Perhaps some of you who choose to study him further will come to agree with me that he ranks as one of psychology's "men for all seasons." Nevertheless, whether you choose to study Michotte's work further or not, I hope this essay dealing with his career and legacy may encourage you to reflect on his timeless values: a balanced life, friendship, academic breadth, truth seeking, and openness to pertinent insights and facts, wherever they might lead.

REFERENCES

Gavin, E. A. (1972a). The case for self-determination. In J. D. Bastable (Ed.), *Philosophical Studies* (Vol. 21, pp. 40–56). Dublin, Ireland: The National University of Ireland.

Gavin, E. A. (1972b). The causal issue in empirical psychology from Hume to the present, with emphasis upon the work of Michotte. *Journal of the History of the Behavioral Sciences, 8*(3), 302–320.

Gavin, E. A. (1975). Albert Michotte and memory. In J. D. Bastable (Ed.), *Philosophical Studies* (Vol. 24, pp. 196–205). Dublin, Ireland: The National University of Ireland.

Gibson, J. J. (1991). Preface. In G. Thinès, A. Costall, & G. Butterworth (Eds.), *Michotte's experimental phenomenology of perception* (pp. ix–x). Hillsdale, NJ: Lawrence Erlbaum Associates, Inc. (Reprinted from autobiography in E. G. Boring & G. Lindzey [Eds.], *A history of psychology in autobiography* [Vol. V, pp. 142–143]. New York: Appleton-Century-Crofts.)

Godin, A. (1985). *The psychological dynamics of religious experience: It doesn't fall down from heaven* (M. Turton, Trans.). New York: Basic Books. (Original work published 1981)

Michotte, A. (1936). Psychologie et philosophie. [Psychology and philosophy]. *Revue Néoscolastique de Philosophie, 39*, 208–228.

Michotte, A. (1952). Albert Michotte van den Berck (J. G. Beebe-Center, Trans.). In E. G. Boring, H. S. Langfeld, H. Werner, & R. M. Yerkes (Eds.), *A history of psychology in autobiography* (Vol. 4, pp. 213–236). Worcester, MA: Clark University Press.

Michotte, A. (1963). *The perception of causality* (T. R. Miles and E. Miles, Trans.). New York: Basic Books. (Original work published 1946)

Michotte, A. (1991). The emotions regarded as functional connections. In G. Thinès, A. Costall, & G. Butterworth (Eds.), *Michotte's experimental phenomenology of perception* (pp. 103–116). Hillsdale, NJ: Lawrence Erlbaum Associates, Inc. (Reprinted from M. L. Reymert, Ed., 1950, *Feelings and emotions: The Mooseheart Symposium* [pp. 114–125]. New York: McGraw-Hill.)

Michotte, A. (1991). Autobiography of Professor A. Michotte van den Berck (A. Costall, Trans.). In G. Thinès, A. Costall, & G. Butterworth (Eds.), *Michotte's experimental phenomenology of perception* (pp. 24–49). Hillsdale, NJ: Lawrence Erlbaum Associates, Inc. (Reprinted and adapted from *Psychologica Belgica*, 1954, 1, 190–217).

Michotte, A., & Portych, T. (1912). Deuxième étude sur la mémoire logique. La reproduction apres des intervalles temporels de différentes longueurs. [Second study of logical memory: Reproduction after temporal delays of different lengths]. *Études de Psychologie (Louvain), 1*, 237–364.

Michotte, A., & Prüm, E. (1910). L'étude experimentale sur le choix volontaire e ses antécedents immédiats. [Experimental study of voluntary choice and its immediate antecedents]. *Archives de Psychologie, 10*, 113–320.

Michotte, A., & Ransy, C. (1912). Contribution à l'étude de la mémoire logique. [Contribution to the study of logical memory]. *Études de Psychologie (Louvain), 1*, 1–96.

Misiak, H., & Staudt, V. (1954). Albert Edouard Michotte. In H. Misiak & V. Staudt (Eds.), *Catholics in psychology: A historical survey* (pp. 98–110). New York: McGraw-Hill.

Nuttin, J. (1962). *Psychoanalysis and personality: A dynamic theory of normal personality* (G. Lane, Trans.). New York: Mentor Books. (Original work published 1953).

Thinès, G., Costall, A., & Butterworth, G. (Eds.). (1991). *Michotte's experimental phenomenology of perception.* Hillsdale, NJ: Lawrence Erlbaum Associates, Inc.

Vernon, M. D. (1964). [Review of *The perception of causality*]. *British Journal of Social and Clinical Psychology, 3,* 74–75.

Chapter 11

Wolfgang Metzger: Perspectives on His Life and Work

Herbert Götzl (Translated by Heiko Hecht)
Psychologisches Institut der Ruhr-Universität Bochum

Wolfgang Metzger was the most significant representative of the second generation of German Gestalt theorists who were active before and after the Second World War. He was recognized as the leading Gestalt theorist in Germany until his death in 1979.

THE FOUNDING OF GESTALT PSYCHOLOGY

The founder of the Gestalt approach, Max Wertheimer (chap. 13, *Pioneers I*), was born in Prague on April 15, 1880. He launched the School of Gestalt Psychology in Frankfurt in 1912, but later on Gestalt theory moved to Berlin and was sometimes called the Berlin School. Wertheimer's theory had the ambitious aim of revolutionizing the traditional European science of the psyche, an attempt that was (often sarcastically) rejected by the main proponents of more traditional psychology. The Gestalt revolt was a version of the Platonic motto, "The whole is more than the mere sum of its parts". But Gestalt psychology goes further, maintaining that the whole is neither equal to nor more than, but fundamentally *different* from the sum of its parts. To understand this motto, we must look into the attitudes and perspectives of the psychologists who were members of the Berlin School, because those intangibles were crucial to their attempt to renew psychological science.

In 1770, Immanuel Kant proclaimed that the soul acquires knowledge about the world around it by synthesizing the chaotic impressions it receives via the sensory organs. The soul uses innate categories of judgment to bring order to immediate experience of the world. In his *Physiological Optics* Hermann von Helmholtz (chap. 2, *Pioneers IV*) agreed with Kant's basic notion that sensory perception comes about as an assimilation of a chaotic input and attempted to improve on it. Helmholtz argued that the sensory core of experience is an orderly whole, albeit a mosaic, consisting of many atom-like sensations. Compared with reality, however, this mosaic is imperfect and can only serve as a basis for drawing conclusions about that reality. Unconsciously, the perceiving individual uses the capacity of judgment—an act of reason guided by accumulated world knowledge— to generate a complex percept out of the sensory mosaic.

Wundt (chap. 3, *Pioneers III*), a student of Helmholtz, called attention to a serious problem—he called it the "chaos problem"—that arises in this theory. As the British empiricists had pointed out, every element of sensation in Helmholtz's mosaic is associated with a host of other images and feelings that have been experienced during the lifetime of the individual. If all of these associations entered consciousness together with the initial sensation, the result would be a veritable battlefield of sensory and associated elements. The postulated assimilative thought processes that ensue could never result in the unity of sensory experience.

Because human beings clearly possess such unity of experience, one must assume the existence of a mechanism that guarantees it, a mechanism that guides and directs perceiving, thinking, and feeling. Following Leibniz (chap. 1, this volume) Wundt called this mechanism *apperception*. Apperception assures that, of all the activated sensory and cognitive elements, only those that are necessary for the satisfaction of current needs for action enter the individual's awareness. Thus, the notion of apperception applies to the functioning of the psyche's assimilative and apperceptive processes that are based on the mosaic of sensory and associative elements.

The founders of Gestalt psychology, however, rejected all of this. They believed that it is bad philosophy and argued that psychological processes are of a completely different nature. To appreciate the Gestalt position, it is necessary to understand its basic tenets:

1. The neural correlate of the world of objects is a brain field.
2. The field forces at work in this neural system drive the pattern of activation there toward the best organization possible. This is the principle of Prägnanz, also known as the tendency to achieve a "good Gestalt".
3. The structure of phenomenal experience is functionally isomorphic with the pattern of its neural correlates.
4. It is therefore possible to investigate the functional and dynamic processes of the brain by studying the phenomenal experiences that correspond to these neural correlates.

The systematic study of phenomenal objects requires a comparison of their metric relations with those of the corresponding physical stimulus objects. These four precepts suggest that traditional psychology, which refers only to an interaction of associative and voluntary action tendencies, is utterly inadequate to explain perceptual, cognitive, and behavioral functioning.

THE LIFE OF METZGER

Wolfgang Metzger was born in Heidelberg, Germany, on July 22, 1899. His father, a strict Prussian educator, taught at the local gymnasium—a high school for the gifted. When Metzger himself became a teacher, he did not adopt his father's tyrannical posture but he did inherit one trait from him. He scrutinized every written text for logic, style, and grammar. Woe to the assistant who failed to use proper punctuation or who employed a foreign word where a German expression would have sufficed. Metzger even corrected the marginal comments that his assistants made when grading papers, often to the students' delight.

As soon as he graduated from the gymnasium, Metzger was drafted into the military and ordered to the front lines during World War I in France. Here unhappy fate caught up with him. When his platoon was retreating under fierce attack, the commanding officer shouted, "Metzger, secure the machine gun!" Metzger intended to follow that order but, before he could secure the gun, the soldier who operated it was struck by a hand grenade that had been hurled at him. Metzger was also hit by the grenade and the left part of his face, particularly his eye and ear, was severely wounded. He was then taken prisoner by the French army. Although a French military surgeon worked hard to save his injured eye, it eventually had to be removed. This, coupled with the memory of the horrible pain he suffered, was a traumatic experience that troubled Metzger for the rest of his life.

When he returned from prison camp, Metzger left for Munich, where he enrolled in the university as a student in German Studies. After four semesters, he moved to Berlin to write his dissertation under a professor named Heusler. On arrival in Berlin, however, Metzger found that Heusler had taken a position in Basel. Saddened by this news, Metzger became a free-floating student. One day, out of curiosity, he found himself in a seminar on introductory psychology, taught by two professors. One of them, Wolfgang Köhler (chap. 17, *Pioneers I*), was a tall man of aristocratic bearing who resembled a military officer in his rigorous argumentation. The other was quite the opposite, a man with alert, kind eyes, but inexhaustible in his arguments that took the position of a devil's advocate who challenges whatever seems most evident. This second professor was Wertheimer.

During the seminar, these two professors introduced the problems of perceptual constancy and contrast in a manner that immediately captivated Metzger.

Although the topic was very different from anything in his intended field—German literature—the approach was from a perspective that he had vaguely and vainly hoped to find there. This new perspective entailed an unusual way of dealing with one's personal prejudices. It required responsible consideration, not only of everything that speaks for one's own thesis, but also of everything that might contradict it. Conducted in this way the Köhler–Wertheimer discussions were methodical and almost devoid of emotion. Both men impressed Metzger so strongly that he decided to dedicate his further efforts to the study of psychology under these two professors. In his new field of study, Metzger exhibited such energy and ability that, in the spring of 1926, he was promoted to the position of "extraordinary assistant." In the fall of that same year, he presented his dissertation on a topic of motion perception. The following semester he went to America, to work on psycho-acoustics at the University of Iowa. On his return to Berlin, Metzger started to work on his habilitation thesis.

Throughout this period, Metzger, in a somewhat surprising way, took time to share the scientific advances in his field with office and factory workers. He helped educate them by regular contributions to the monthly publication *Sozialistische Monatshefte*. Between 1924 and 1936 Metzger wrote about advances in psychology in a language that was readily comprehensible. In particular, he communicated about the "New Psychology" that was practiced at the Berlin institute. This New Psychology was intended to provide a basis for the explanation of everyday behavior and experience. Metzger's work was held in such high regard by the institute that he was assigned as a substitute for Köhler in teaching experimental methods. Metzger also taught English language psychology classes for foreign students as well as night classes in an adult education program.

In 1929, Wertheimer left Berlin and was appointed professor at the University of Frankfurt to replace Friedrich Schumann. Two years later, Metzger learned that Wertheimer had a vacancy at the assistant level. Köhler wanted to fill it with his own doctoral student, Karl Duncker (chap. 10, *Pioneers III*), but Metzger desperately wanted to join Wertheimer and he persuaded Duncker to trade places with him. As a result, Metzger ended up in Frankfurt and Duncker gladly moved to Berlin. This liberation from Köhler's influence was important because Metzger felt that Köhler had no respect for him. At one point, Köhler had even subjected Metzger to a humiliating examination on the book *Physische Gestalten*, exposing Metzger's weaknesses regarding the mathematical content of the book.

In contrast, Metzger shared with Wertheimer an orientation that stood in sharp contrast to Köhler's temperament. With the move to Frankfurt, Metzger realized his first major goal in life, a respectable appointment under his preferred mentor. The Frankfurt years turned out to be fateful ones for Metzger. As soon as he had settled in, Wertheimer made it clear that working on Metzger's habilitation thesis under him would be possible only if he finished quickly, because Wertheimer feared that the Nazis would soon win the national elections—

and with the Nazis in power, he (Wertheimer) would have to leave the country. Metzger, together with his wife, worked frantically to meet this challenge. He produced the text that she, while caring for their small child and expecting a second, typed into a final draft. Wertheimer allegedly phoned Metzger everyday, asking for a progress report.

While this was going on, Mrs. Metzger was developing a negative and angry image of Wertheimer. Apparently, on the occasion of a dinner party at his home, Wertheimer had insisted that Mrs. Metzger play a Mozart piece on the piano in front of all the guests. Although mortified, she complied with his request and despite her anxiety was able to get through the piece. However, from this moment on she harbored a secret grudge against Wertheimer despite her usual respectful behavior. Eventually, however, Metzger's ambition—and that of his wife, too—prevailed. The typewritten manuscript was presented to and was accepted by the faculty at the University of Frankfurt for Metzger's habilitation.

Just before Hitler's rise to power Wertheimer left Germany, and the dark years of Metzger's life ensued. Bereft of his protector, Metzger was left to his own devices to reach his ambitious goal of a professorship. He was unable to assume Wertheimer's now vacant position, because the philosophical faculty had reclaimed it from the natural science faculty, where it had been moved at Wertheimer's request. To whom should Metzger turn in his distress? In the eyes of the Nazis, Metzger was a friend of the Jews and asking help from Köhler, who suspected Metzger of having Nazi sympathies, seemed unwise. Finally he turned to Albert Michotte (chap. 10, this volume) in Belgium and sent him everything he had ever written, including formal publications as well as rough manuscripts. But his efforts were all in vain.

Short of renouncing his academic ambitions, Metzger was left with two choices: He must either follow Wertheimer into exile or come to terms with the new regime. For whatever reason, Metzger ended up collaborating with the Nazis. He joined Hitler's police (SA) in the hope that this would make him eligible for upcoming vacant professorships. At this point in his career, Metzger had high hopes of acquiring Gelb's professorship at Halle because Gelb, a Jew, had been forced out of his position. And, indeed, Metzger was appointed substitute lecturer in Halle. To increase his chances of receiving tenure in this position, Metzger and his wife felt it advisable for Metzger to reinforce his ties with the Nazi regime. He joined the fascist party and began to pose as a "brown shirt educator" in a subsection of the SA and published pro-Nazi views on adolescence and primary education.

These developments plagued Metzger with the guilt of having betrayed his teacher and pursued a position that would rightfully be Gelb's. And to what avail? Initially, Metzger felt devastated but his wife helped him regain composure. She convinced him that their reputation was already destroyed and that they might as well go through with it. After all, the bills had to be paid. "You may as well throw yourself headlong into the enemy's arms," she said. In doing so, Metzger (1942) created a political cocktail containing some fundamental Gestalt tenets and a dose of Christian humanitarian beliefs mixed with a measure of cynicism, and fine-tuned by a Buddhist variety of Daoism. The resulting concoction was a blend of theory and ideology that made the Nazis happy.

Indeed, the concoction turned out to be a success. In 1942, Metzger received a full professorship in psychology at the University of Münster. He remained in that position until the allies' bombs put an end to the Nazi regime. Metzger then moved to the countryside, where he made a living as a farm hand during the week and, drawing on his Christian leanings, as an adjunct minister on Sundays. In 1945, the American psychologist and allied officer H. L. Ansbacher, who was given the task of resurrecting the remains of German academic psychology after the war, found Metzger in that situation.

Metzger must have made quite an impression on Ansbacher, for he was soon reinstated with all rights in his old position at Münster. However, Metzger was hesitant about rebuilding the psychological institute and his first major decision in this regard turned out to be a mistake. Rather than joining the science faculty, he had his chair integrated into the philosophical faculty. With his choice of departmental affiliation, Metzger had destroyed his chances of conducting experimental research because there were no funds for such research. He received the money to stock the library but lacked the funds to equip a laboratory and to pay a laboratory technician. Metzger's requests in this matter caused lengthy and frustrating quarrels with the university administration. When asked about his choice, he remarked, perhaps cynically, that a good experimenter can get by with a broomstick and a few pieces of cardboard. The researchers who worked in Metzger's institute had to be resourceful enough to procure the materials needed for experimentation on their own. Consequently, no significant experimental work in perceptual psychology was performed at the institute for a long period. Only shortly before his retirement did Metzger resume experimentation with the same enthusiasm he had shown before and during the war.

What had happened to Metzger? The collaboration with the enemy crushed his spirit, and irrationally, he saw the tragic death of one of his children, who was struck by a car while crossing a road, as punishment for his sins. As penance Metzger declined to conduct further experiments on perception or to elaborate Gestalt theory. Instead, he concentrated on preventing the kinds of atrocities that he had seen committed by the Nazis from ever occurring again. He initiated a postgraduate curriculum for teachers with the goal of instilling in pedagogues the foundations for independent thinking, and teaching them to support the principles that have been recognized as right while strongly opposing everything that is incompatible with respect for human rights.

It was Metzger's foremost wish to establish such courses for government employees and parents as well as teachers. He wanted to retrain the obedient German bureaucrats to see the betterment of humanity as their first and foremost duty, while giving the enforcement of rules and regulations a secondary priority.

Inspired by the reeducation program devised by Kurt Lewin (chap. 7, *Pioneers III*), Metzger wanted to teach parents how to use their authority over their children wisely and kindly. But this educational ambition was frustrated by administrative resistance. Metzger's efforts were not only curtailed by his administrators but also were not appreciated by his former advisor, Köhler. When Köhler came to Münster to receive an honorary doctoral degree, he scolded his former assistant for having discontinued his experimental work. Metzger tried to redeem himself by explaining how he had focused all his energy on a reeducation program. Köhler, however, did not acknowledge these efforts and expressed contempt for Metzger's educational ambitions.

After his 65th birthday, Metzger held on to his professorship for 2 more years, during which he concentrated on pointing out Wertheimer's contributions to the field of psychology. It was Metzger's foremost endeavor to keep the memory of his beloved teacher alive. His students were not only quizzed about Wertheimer's scientific contributions, they also had to know the details of his curriculum vitae. In 1968, Metzger withdrew from the university to his home in Bebenhausen, where he occasionally received visits from his former students. He traveled to such remote places as Cambodia and China to spread his message to "reject prejudice and to live tolerance." Metzger died in his sleep on December 20, 1979.

METZGER, THE EXPERIMENTER

According to Stadler and Crabus's (1986) account, Metzger produced 354 papers and books. Among these were seven experimental studies, two of which were published in several parts. What establishes Metzger's pioneering role in psychology? Primary is his contribution to two fundamental areas of perceptual psychology. In the first series of studies, he showed that local luminance differences perceived as jumps in brightness within the visual field are both necessary and sufficient for the perceptual segregation of figure and ground. Metzger thus defined the minimal conditions for perceiving the world as a manifold of objects that are spatially related to one another (Jung, 1971; Marr, 1982; Strasburger, Scheidler, & Rentschler, 1988).

In the second series of studies, Metzger explored the minimal conditions of depth perception. For this purpose he created a so-called Ganzfeld, a uniformly lit white wall whose surface structure is as fine grained as possible. If the illumination of the Ganzfeld drops below a certain threshold, the observer loses the feeling of sitting in front of an illuminated wall (Gibson, 1950) and has the experience of floating in a fog or haze, a sensation that can be quite unpleasant (Heron, 1957). What are the reasons for such an experience? Under conditions of critically diminished illumination it is impossible for individuals to detect any irregularities in the surface structure of the wall in front of them. There is nothing to differentiate figure from ground and the observer loses the sense of being located in a space that is perceptually organized in depth. The room illumination and the surface brightness of the wall itself cannot be separated perceptually. The same holds true for a world in which all objects have the same color regardless whether the illuminant is a homogeneous white light or a light of a different color, provided that the whole scene is uniformly illuminated, i.e. without any shadows.

Besides this pioneering work, Metzger contributed to an already established field by following Wertheimer in studies of the principles of perceptual organization for moving objects. For this purpose, Metzger presented moving rod-like vertical objects produced by casting shadows of real rods onto a screen visible within a rectangular window that gave free view only of the midsections of the projected rods—the tops and bottoms of the objects were covered. The rods could be arranged in numerous ways on a rotating platform. Metzger found that the projections of these rods organized themselves perceptually according to Gestalt laws equivalent to those already postulated by Wertheimer for stationary patterns.

Why did Metzger choose this particular experimental set-up? His intention was to demonstrate that perceptual organization within the visual field can not be explained with empiricist principles. His reasoning was as follows. Without motion the projected rods appear as a two-dimensional surface covered with a host of lines filling the entire window. As soon as the platform starts to rotate, the three-dimensional layout of the rods is perceived just as they are positioned in reality. Observers recognize the uniform circular motion around a common center although the actual projection consists of nothing more than a two-dimensional array of shadows moving back and forth at different velocities. The primary factors of depth perception, as required by the empiricist position, could not alone have contributed to the correct construction of the three-dimensional structure by the visual system (Johansson, 1978; Wallach & O'Connell, 1953).

What is the importance of this demonstration? Whereas in the two-dimensional view the perceptual events look complex and confusing, in the three-dimensional view they appear quite simple and in accord with what is really happening. That point warrants this conclusion: Under the conditions employed in this demonstration, the visual field takes on the perceptual organization that is biologically useful because the stimulus objects are perceived accurately. This conclusion specifies that perceptual organization is more than just an aesthetic caprice of nature. It also provides a selective advantage—as that idea appears in evolutionary theory—and is the basis for adaptive behavior.

Guided by those results, Metzger (1975) posed the question: How does the visual field come to be organized according to the principle of "good Gestalt", if only a small part of the stimulus pattern can be looked at through a spy tube with one eye only, thus creating a situation of uncertainty for the subject? Such a situation gives rise to the suspicion, paraphrased as follows: "There is probably something which might pose a risk to my well-being." Such a suspicion in turn demands the processing of the incoming information with respect to a processing regime, paraphrased as follows: "First make clear what the threatening events might be which are made possible in each case by the stimulus information under the given situational conditions—and then, from all these possible events, focus on the one which can be realized optimally in the neuronal medium—and make the result of this modeling process appear in the corresponding phenomenal medium." Accordingly, what becomes evident to the subject here and now, i.e. the actual environment in his perception, bears—in a most plausible way—all the signs of imminent danger. Thus, the occurrences as perceived may not correctly map out what is happening in the physical environment. However, despite this mismatch, such occurrences are of an adaptive nature insofar as they alert subjects to potential dangers.

Metzger also sponsored additional experiments, including one by Calvarezo (1934) exploring the stereoscopic effects of changes in perceived size, studies by Turhan (1937) and Lauenstein (1938) that examined the stereoscopic effects of brightness distributions, a study by Zöller (1969) on color constancy, and three experiments that established the superiority of process theories of perception over alternative theories, such as association theory, the perspective theory of optical illusions, and the decision theory that came out of the information-theoretic approach. In this work, Metzger stressed the point that the exact same retinal excitation may lead to very different perceptions, depending on the actual conditions. Metzger also supported three investigations of the relationship between phenomenal distance and the underlying physiological distance (Jacobs, 1933; Madlung, 1934; Schnehage, 1939). Several of these investigations had been begun under Wertheimer, but Metzger helped to carry them to completion.

METZGER, THE TAXONOMIST
AND THEORIST

Metzger published a total of twelve books, the first of which appeared in 1936. Entitled, *Laws of Vision* (*Gesetze des Sehens*), this first book contains one dozen chapters directed to a broad audience. *Laws of Vision* describes almost all phenomena of visual perception that have been known at the time. It is well organized and written in a style that is straightforward and entertaining to the reader. With its impressive wealth of examples and illustrations, it invites readers to form their own opinions about the issues raised by the author. Metzger does not present the reader with simple solutions, however. Rather, he supplies them with information that would enable future researchers to understand the neural basis of perception (Spillman, 1999). Through this work, Metzger won many friends for Gestalt psychology, most notably in Italy, Japan, and the United States (Gibson, 1950; Hochberg, 1964).

Metzger's second book covered the world of radio broadcasting. The third, *Psychologie* (1941/1975) was his main theoretical work. It was reprinted in much augmented form, in five additional editions. The book was Metzger's attempt to lay the epistemological and philosophical foundations of a science of psychology. It was clear to him that all of the established theoretical positions of his day—associationism, empiricism, vitalism, and every extant mechanistic position—were inadequate. The Gestalt concept alone, he argued, is adequate for explicating psychological phenomena, and Metzger defended its tenets against all other positions.

After a brief overview of the history of psychology, Metzger took up what he called the first problem in the field, the concept of reality. He described how different psychological experiences constitute different varieties of reality (cf. Popper & Eccles, 1977). Then he turned to the problems of traits, relatedness of experiences, frames of reference, and centration or organization around a focal point or center (Zentrierung). In connection with these topics Metzger explored the old and fascinating question, originally posed by Heraclitus, of why the perceived world is not a disorderly conglomeration but rather is an orderly whole. Metzger's answer, taken from Wertheimer, is in terms of self-organizing systems. In phenomenological terms, the organizational principles are Wertheimer's "Gestalt laws."

This conceptual approach led critics to say that Gestalt psychology denies the role of the individual in the processes of perceiving, thinking, feeling, and acting, but Metzger argued against such criticism in the following way: Living is problem solving, and problems are incomplete Gestalten whose lack of completion causes the individual to manage problem situations by inventing appropriate mental or behavioral strategies and by restructuring problem situations in ways that fulfill the requirements of the current concern. In such situations the living being—endowed with the capacity of reasonable understanding and prepared to make rational judgments—is confronted with the necessity of making a decision for solving a problem in either a competitive or cooperative way. In the competitive mode, the self-organizing processes of restructuring problems will be suppressed, whereas in the cooperative mode, they will be enhanced. The cooperative mode is in operation whenever the individual's behavior is focused on the whole rather than on individual aspects of the problem. In more general terms, life's problems require a holistic attitude.

METZGER, THE EDUCATOR

On a very different subject, Metzger published three books on parenting, one on toilet training, one on tantrums, and one on mood and achievement. These volumes, which addressed the needs of parents, were followed by three more that conveyed Metzger's ideas on education, namely *Creative Freedom, Psychology for Educators*, and *Psychology and Education in the Face of Theories of Learning, Clinical Psychology, Gestalt Theory, and Behavioral Theory*. His last books were *Political Education from the Psychologist's View, What Is Education—What Could It Be?*, and *From Prejudice to Tolerance*. In his works on education, Metzger held that human beings strive naturally toward realizing their innate social and intellectual potentials. They organize their lives within a social context (cf. Perls, Hefferline, & Goodman, 1962) as long as this development is not misguided by unhealthy rules or unnatural forces. What are such misguiding influences? Metzger argued that they are nothing less than yielding to temptation, the product of the indeterminacy of human will that can lead either to community-oriented or to egocentric organization of the self. Community-oriented self-creation recognizes the needs of the social group and uses personal strengths to further those goals—even to the extent of individual self-sacrifice. Two particularly human traits help in this social function: the need to explore and to understand the logic of things on the one hand, and the need to trust authority and to follow charismatic leaders on the other.

In egocentric orientation, other individuals are treated as adversaries and ego development is established by displacing competitors and by defining societal work as power over others. Metzger (1942) criticized this behavior as an expression of Western thinking and denounced all democracies that promote it. To prevent such misguided developments the educator should be concerned with three tasks.

First, one should understand the motivating tendencies that drive a person who is in the process of growing up. These tendencies should be recognized with compassion and channeled with support and guidance (cf. Bettelheim, 1967).

Second, children should not be protected from multiple demands as long as they remain socially adequate (cf. Ainsworth, Bell, & Stayton, 1971).

Third, children should learn that their own interests and those of the group can both be served at the same time. This requires the educator to provide the feeling that the child is an equal and valuable member of the group.

For Metzger these rules derive from the nature of human coexistence, which has its unequivocal logic. This logic is tantamount to the thesis that objectivity and sense of community are inextricably linked.

It was Metzger's expressed interest to subject his pedagogical convictions to empirical and experimental test. At his urging two experiments were performed for this purpose. The first showed that human performance in a state of object centeredness is superior to that obtained in states of ego centeredness. The second experiment had to be cut short, but it showed that children who are raised according to the principles of community-oriented objectivity are more cooperative than children who were socialized according to the principle of egocentric competition.

During the last phase of his sociopolitical endeavors Metzger softened his opposition to democratic principles. He recognized the value of questioning authority and ideology to the point that he suggested the motto: Educate children to help them become independent thinkers, to give them the courage and skill to defend their own opinions, and to help them stand up against authority. To achieve these goals, children should be trained in critical judgment and empathy together with a thorough education in national and world history. It should be of foremost importance to learn from history, to critically reflect one's own thoughts and egocentric tendencies (cf. Adorno, 1977) in favor of an objective attitude.

METZGER, THE NAZI

Metzger was among a group of scientists who collaborated with the Nazis not only in recognizing the new social and national order they tried to realize but also in promoting the presumed scientific legitimacy of their regime. Why was Metzger willing to do so? During the Nazi regime, he believed that the social-nationalist order proposed and implemented by the Nazis was the social order best able to reconcile social and national interests. Unlike democratic societies, he described Nazism as capable of forming a society that would be an optimal societal. Metzger even argued that Nazism is a system that, when applied to society at large, is consistent with the principles of Gestalt psychology. Metzger, an ultrafundamentalist Christian, went along with the Nazi policy of segregating and destroying Jews. How much his pro-Nazi writings were generated in efforts to placate his wife or to promote and maintain his prominent academic position may never be known. Although after the Nazi period he denounced the Nazi ideology and its atrocities, his earlier active efforts to promote Nazism make him remain a highly controversial figure in contemporary American and especially German psychology.

METZGER, THE HUMAN BEING AND TEACHER

After all of this the reader may wonder what Metzger was like in his everyday dealings with other people, especially in his role as teacher. Had one encountered Metzger during the 1950s, one would have met a man of rather distinct appearance. Clad in black, wearing a dark beret, and of rather stubby figure, he came across as a caricature of the absent-minded professor. He was slightly hunched forward, looking down and whistling a quiet tune. Passers-by might well have feared to collide with this strange man. Once addressed or greeted, however, Metzger's changed his demeanor instantaneously. Straightening up, he would seek eye contact, smile, and offer a friendly greeting that came across as warm and personal, instilling immediate trust. It is thus not surprising that a loyal group of fans among his students always gathered around him. The moment he entered the lecture hall students applauded until he had installed himself behind the lectern and silenced the hall with a hand gesture.

Male and female students both loved Metzger and they did so for the same reason. Metzger listened to each individual's concerns and helped whenever he could. He wrote letters of recommendation and provided funds. In short, he cared for his students like a father and many of them had a portrait of Metzger on their desks or somewhere in their living quarters. They worshipped Metzger as a mentor and were saddened by his retirement from the university.

Metzger took his teaching responsibilities very seriously. Over the course of five semesters he covered the psychological knowledge of his time in two lecture series. The first dealt with general cognitive psychology, public and private consciousness, perception, productive thinking—he translated Wertheimer's book on the subject into German—motivation and volition, and the self. The second series covered personality; intellectual, social, and motivational dispositions; and development of the psyche, which he treated in terms of general principles and stages of development. Metzger's closing lecture was on facial and bodily expression, accompanied by a particularly popular laboratory exercise. During summer terms Metzger also gave lectures on the significance of psychology for life. The largest lecture hall of the university could not fit all students who wanted to attend his class.

Metzger was famous, but also feared, for his hands-on course on experimental methods spanning three semesters. The first semester included lectures and demonstrations, and the second and third semesters required students to design and perform an experiment every 2 weeks, conducting interviews and gathering introspective data from human research participants. The experiments had to be written up according to Köhler's guidelines for psychological publications, keeping in mind what Metzger himself had told them about conducting good experiments in psychology (Metzger, 1952). When giving exams, Metzger was very patient, but he had the intimidating habit of asking theoretical and practical questions that had not been covered in his lectures.

Some of Metzger's students began to deviate from his teachings while he was professor emeritus at the University of Münster. To his chagrin, one student turned to behaviorism and another to behavior therapy. Metzger was deeply shocked by such defections and expelled both students from the circle of his disciples. He left Münster embittered and hoping that Gestalt psychology was not dead but just in a temporary slumber, soon to be recognized as psychological truth.

ACKNOWLEDGMENTS

The author would like to express his thanks to Gregory A. Kimble and Michael Wertheimer for their editorial assistance; to Abigail Carpio, Christel Zepter, Walter Ehrenstein, Steve Lehar, and John S. Werner for their special help; to Mimsey Stromeyer and Lothar Spillmann for critical comments and encouragement; and last but not least to Heiko Hecht for his work as translator.

REFERENCES

Adorno, T. W. (1977). Erziehung nach Auschwitz [Education after Auschwitz]. In R. Tiedemann (Hrsg.), *Theodor W. Adorno. Gesammelte Schriften [Collected works]*, Vol 10.2, *Kulturkritik und Gesellschaft [Cultural criticism and society]* (Vol. 10.2, pp. 674–690). Frankfurt, Germany: Suhrkamp.

Ainsworth, M. D. S., Bell, S. M. V., & Stayton, D. J. (1971). Individual differences in strange-situation behaviour of one-year-olds. In H. R. Schaffer (Ed.), *The origins of human social relations* (pp. 17–52). New York: Academic.

Bettelheim, B. (1967). *Love is not enough. The treatment of emotionally disturbed children.* New York: Free Press.

Calvarezo, C. (1934). Über den Einfluß von Größenänderungen auf die anschauliche Tiefe [On the influence of size on perceived depth]. *Pychologische Forschung, 19*, 311–365.

Gibson, J. J. (1950). *The perception of the visual world.* Boston: Houghton Mifflin.

Heron, W. (1957). *Scientific American, 196*, 52–56.

Hochberg, J. (1964). *Perception.* Englewood Cliffs, NJ: Prentice Hall.

Jacobs, M. H. (1933). Über den Einfluß des phänomenalen Abstandes auf die Unterschiedsschwelle für Helligkeiten [On the influence of phenomenal distance on the differential threshold for brightness]. *Psychologische Forschung, 18*, 98–142.

Johansson, G. (1978). Visual event perception. In R. Held, H. W. Leibowitz, & H.-L. Teuber (Eds.), *Handbook of sensory physiology, VIII Perception* (pp. 675–711). Heidelberg and New York: Springer.

Jung, R. (1971). Kontrastsehen, Konturbetonung und Künstlerzeichnung [Perception of contrast, emphasis on contour, and artistic drawing]. *Studium Generale, 24*, 1536–1565.

Köhler, W. (1920). *Die physischen Gestalten in Ruhe und im stationären Zustand [The physical Gestalten at rest and in a stationary state].* Braunschweig, Germany: Vieweg.

Lauenstein, L. (1938). Über räumliche Wirkungen von Licht und Schatten [On spatial effects of light and shadow]. *Psychologische Forschung, 22*, 267–319.

Madlung, K. (1934). Über anschauliche und funktionelle Nachbarschaft von Tasteindrücken [On apparent functional proximity of touch sensations]. *Psychologische Forschung, 19*, 193–236.

Marr, D. (1982). *Vision.* San Francisco: Freeman.

Metzger, W. (1926). Über Vorstufen der Verschmelzung von Figurenreihen, die vor dem ruhenden Auge vorüberziehen [On rudiments of the disintegration of figures passing before the resting eye]. *Psychologische Forschung, 8*, 114–221.

Metzger, W. (1930a). Optische Untersuchungen am Ganzfeld. II. Mitteilung: Zur Phänomenologie des homogenen Ganzfelds [Optical investigations of the Ganzfeld II. Report of the phenomenology of the homogeneous Ganzfeld]. *Psychologische Forschung, 8*, 6–29.

Metzger, W. (1930b). Optische Untersuchungen am Ganzfeld. III. Mitteilung: Die Schwelle für plötzliche Helligkeitsänderungen [Optical investigations of the Ganzfeld, III. Report on the threshold for sudden changes in brightness]. *Psychologische Forschung, 8*, 30–54.

Metzger, W. (1935). Tiefenerscheinungen in optischen Bewegungsfeldern [Appearances of depth in optical movement fields]. *Psychologische Forschung, 20*, 195–260.

Metzger, W. (1940a). Zur anschaulichen Repräsentation von Rotationsvorgängen und ihrer Deutung durch Gestaltkreislehre und Gestaltpsychologie [On the apparent representation of rotation events and their significance in the description of the Gestalt circle and Gestalt psychology]. *Zeitschrift für Sinnesphysiologie, 68*, 261–279.

Metzger, W. (1940b). Zur Theorie der Rotationserlebnisse [On the theory of rotation experiences]. *Zeitschrift für Sinnesphysiologie, 69*, 94–96.

Metzger, W. (1942). Der Auftrag der Psychologie in der Auseinandersetzung mit dem Geist des Westens. Volk im Werden [The task of psychology in the confrontation with the western spirits: Becoming a nation]. *Zeitschrift für Erneuerung der Wissenschaften, 10*, 133–144.

Metzger, W. (1952). Das Experiment in der Psychologie [The experiment in psychology]. *Studium Generale, 5*, 142–163.

Metzger, W. (1949; 1962). *Schöpferische Freiheit [Creative freedom]*. Frankfurt, Germany: Waldemar Kramer.

Metzger, W. (1961). Ergänzende Beobachtungen über Gestaltfaktoren für Bewegungsverläufe [Additional observations on Gestalt-factors for the organization of motion-patterns]. *Psychologische Beiträge, 6,* 607–619.

Metzger, W. (1975). *Gesetze des Sehens [Laws of vision]*. Frankfurt, Germany: Waldemar Kramer. (Original work published 1935)

Metzger, W. (1975). *Psychologie*. Darmstadt, Germany: Dietrich Steinkopff. (Original work published 1941)

Perls, F. S., Hefferline, R. F., & Goodman, P. (1962). *Gestalt therapy: Excitement and growth in the human personality*. New York: Julian.

Popper, K. R., & Eccles, J. C. (1977). *The self and its brain*. New York: Springer.

Schnehage, H. J. (1939). Versuche über taktile Scheinbewegung bei Variation phänomenaler Bedingungen [Experiments on tactile apparent movement with variations in phenomenal conditions]. *Archiv für die gesamte Psychologie, 104*, 175–228.

Spillmann, L. (1999). From elements to perception: Local and global processing in visual neurons. *Perception, 28*, 1461–1492.

Stadler, M., & Crabus, H. (1986). Wolfgang Metzger, Leben und Wirkung [Wolfgang Metzger's life and work]. In M. Stadler (Hrsg.), *Gestalt-Psychologie: Ausgewählte Werke aus den Jahren 1950–1982 [Gestalt psychology: Selected works from the years 1950–1982]* (pp. 540–558). Frankfurt, Germany: Waldemar Kramer.

Strasburger, H., Scheidler, W., & Rentschler, I. (1988). Amplitude and phase characteristics of the steady-state visual evoked potential. *Applied Optics, 27*, 1069–1088.

Turhan, M. (1937). Über räumliche Wirkungen von Helligkeitsgefällen [On the spatial effects of brightness reductions]. *Psychologische Forschung, 21,* 1–49.

Wallach, H., & O'Connell, D. N. (1953). The kinetic depth effect. *Journal of Experimental Psychology, 45*, 205–217.

Chapter 12

Nancy Bayley: Pioneer in the Measurement of Growth and Psychological Development

Judy F. Rosenblith
Wheaton College

Nancy Bayley was born in Oregon in September 1899, into a family of pioneers. Perhaps this heralded her own pioneering spirit. Nancy's paternal grandparents had shipped around Cape Horn to Victoria, British Columbia, where her grandfather was a member of the colonial government. Her maternal grandparents—Dutch immigrants who had settled in the eastern United States in the 1600s—came to Oregon by covered wagon. An aunt who was on that trek had become a physician after being widowed and delivered Nancy and her four siblings (perhaps a forerunner of Bayley's pioneering in another field).

Bayley went to the University of Washington, intending to become an English teacher. An introductory course with E. B. Guthrie (chap. 10, *Pioneers II*) stimulated her interest in psychology, however, and both her bachelor's and master's degrees were in psychology. For her master's thesis publication, Bayley studied motor behavior in preschool children. Even at this early age, she had set out on the course she was to follow all of her life.

Bayley received her doctorate at the University of Iowa in 1928. For her thesis she studied fear in human beings, using a psychogalvanic technique she had learned as a research assistant at the University of Washington and a psychogalvanometer borrowed from Carl Seashore, who was both dean of the Graduate School and professor of philosophy and psychology. Bayley was a teaching fellow at Iowa from 1922 to 1924, and a graduate assistant from 1924 to 1926. As a graduate student, she developed performance tests for preschoolers and published her master's thesis (Bayley, 1926), which was the first of her almost 200 articles, chapters and books.

Bayley was an instructor at the University of Wyoming from 1926 to 1928. Then, she went to the University of California, Berkeley, at the invitation of Harold Jones, to be a research associate at the Institute of Child Welfare (now the Institute of Child Development) and lecturer in psychology. Many women today (and some in Bayley's time) would be disturbed at not having a professorial appointment, but the lecturer arrangement may actually have suited her better because of the freedom it gave her. At Berkeley, Bayley initiated the Berkeley Growth Study, which has been very productive and is now world famous. It was also there that she met her husband of many years, John R. Reid, who was studying for his doctorate in philosophy. They were married on April 27, 1929.

PHYSICAL GROWTH

Physical growth is of interest to the medical profession as an indicator of health, and during the 1920s and 1930s interest in physical growth was high, but there were no good standards to measure it against. Doctors needed better measures than their own experience by which to judge patients' development. Bayley (1936) provided such a measure. A number of long-term growth studies began during that period, of which the Fels study, based in Ohio, and Bayley's Berkeley Growth Study, were the most comprehensive. They were not limited to physical growth but looked at behavior as well.

Bayley's early growth studies focused on body size and the changes in the proportion of height accounted for by different parts of the body. Anyone who has taken a course in child development will remember the pictures (sometimes caricatures) showing how much the head, trunk, and legs contribute to total height at different ages. Bayley and Davis published data on 153 measures of size—nine different measures obtained at 17 times during the first 36 months[1] (Bayley & Davis, 1935). Body length and head circumference were the two measures that were most closely correlated across that span of time.

To obtain the data that were needed to calculate correlations[2] between earlier physical characteristics and later outcomes, it was necessary to study large sam-

---

[1]In those days analyzing data was handicapped not only because there were no computers but also because there was so little financial aid. The only support one was apt to have for recording and analyzing data was from interested students or from students with a National Youth Administration (NYA) job. The NYA was a government agency set up during the Great Depression to help students gain an education by paying them up to 50 cents an hour for work in laboratories and libraries and around the grounds of colleges and universities.

[2]The concept of correlation appears frequently in this chapter. The statistical measure of correlation (r) is an index of the degree of relationship between two variables. In this chapter, this measure (r) is used most often to indicate the degree of relationship between measures of development obtained at different ages. It also is a measure of the reliability of tests (the extent to which scores obtained on two administrations of the test are similar) and the validity of tests (the extent to which test scores are related to later outcomes). The values of r range from +1.0, through 0, down to –1.0. Positive correlations occur when high measures go with high measures on the two correlated variables. Negative correlations mean that high numbers on one measure go with low numbers on the other.

ples of children and, where possible, to study them over time—that is, to have the data from longitudinal studies. Bayley published the first of such correlations between children's sizes as infants and their sizes as adults in 1940 (Bayley, 1940b).

In 1946, using data from the Berkeley Growth Study, Bayley published separate tables for boys and girls that predicted adult height from current height, skeletal age obtained from x-rays, and the rate at which the child was growing. For girls from 7 to 12 years of age, it was possible to predict adult height to within 1 in. using current height and a single x-ray. The same degree of accuracy was possible for boys in the age range from 7 to 14 years. These tables were revised when newer standards were developed for evaluating the x-rays (Bayley & Pinneau, 1952), a technological advance that allowed Bayley (1956a) to make the first effort to produce standards for height that took account of rate of growth.

Predictions of adult height do more than just satisfy parental curiosity. They enable physicians to determine which short children will grow to normal height and, therefore, do not need growth-hormone therapy, and which will grow up to be very short if they do not receive the hormones. Tanner (1978) pointed to another use of such predictions: They made it possible for the ballet schools to reject students who are apt to "waste" their training by growing up to be too large to be ballet dancers.

Bayley (1943) also studied the rate at which the skeleton matured in boys and girls and related it to their mature body build. For boys she found that early maturing was related to becoming tall and broad hipped, whereas late maturing was related to being slender hipped and long legged. She found that early-maturing girls were large in adolescence but small as adults and that late-maturing girls were the opposite.

In a different area of research, Bayley was a pioneer in the study of androgyny (Bayley, 1951b). She had three raters rate nude photographs of the backs of adolescents of 17 and 18 years of age on femininity and masculinity and compared these ratings with scores on the Kuder Masculinity–Feminity Scale for the same adolescents obtained 6 months earlier. It is interesting that the boys with the most masculine body builds were the most feminine on the Kuder scale. Boys who were intermediate, asexual, or bisexual in masculine physical characteristics were significantly more masculine. Girls did not differ in femininity according to body build.

MOTOR DEVELOPMENT

In 1935 Bayley published the results of a longitudinal study of motor abilities in 61 infants who were tested repeatedly during their first 3 years. Her California Infant Scale of Motor Development (Bayley, 1936) included some items that measured mental development, primarily items that involved eye–hand coordination and prehension (the ability to grasp an object).

Development with Age

Bayley found that motor abilities develop rapidly during the first 21 months but that cognitive abilities develop rapidly a bit later—in fact during the third year. At 15 months, motor and mental scores correlated only slightly. Actually, the age at which the child first walked was as closely related to both the motor and mental abilities scores at 3 years as the entire battery of tests given at 1 year. Although early walking is related to 3-year motor and mental scores, the correlations ($r = .40–.60$) are not high enough to predict what an individual child will do even at 3 years, much less later on. More generally, don't think that early-kicking babies will be good at soccer, that early punchers will be fighters, or that early-anything will predict adult or even teenage sports or cognitive abilities.

Environmental Correlates of Development

In 1937, Bayley and Jones published a study examining environmental correlates of motor and mental development in the first 6 years of life. They found that infant mental scores were related to parental education but motor scores were not. Other social factors such as social class and income tended to be slightly negatively correlated with motor scores during the first year. In 1939, Bayley reviewed the existing studies of motor and mental development from 2 to 12 years and noted that the various studies tended "to agree in reporting age changes in the abilities measured, . . . in positive correlations between scores on different tests, . . . in absence of correlation with socioeconomic factors; and in improvement with practice on certain skills" (Bayley, 1939, p. 37). This was largely during a period of economic depression when children were not always well nourished and were not surrounded by stimulating objects, and when toddlers had few toys. Altogether, childrearing and children's environments were very different from what they are today. It is not clear that these findings would be the same today.

Bodily Correlates of Development

In 1940 Bayley published a monograph, *Studies in the Development of Young Children*. In the chapter on "Gaining Control Over the Body," she pointed out that the usual childhood illnesses did not affect motor abilities, nor did skeletal maturity. Overall, rapid early growth in coordination seemed to result from increasing maturity of the nervous system, from changes in body proportions that make more efficient functioning mechanically possible, and in increased strength of the muscles.

Bayley (1951a) noted in a chapter on "Development and Maturation" that the dimensions and hardness of bones, the size of muscles, and vestibular sensitivity (for maintenance of balance) play a large role in the development of motor functions. Motor function in turn affects all the other behavior of the young infant.

She noted that there is a positive relationship between sitting erect and mental achievement, and suggested that this could be due to the achievement of a stable sitting posture that permits the perceptual and manipulatory behavior that is scored in the mental tests. The manipulatory skills requiring coordination of small muscle groups and the sensory discriminations that depend on the tactile and muscle senses are somewhat more related to intelligence scores than other aspects of the newborn examination. Skill in athletic events that require strength showed sex differences after 12 or 13 years, and within each sex the degree of physiological and anatomical maturity was related to skill.

It is important to remember that changes over historical time may affect these types of data. In today's world, sex differences in strength may be smaller because girls are much more active than in the generation studied by Bayley. For example, women athletes today break records made by men in previous generations. This would not, however, necessarily change Bayley's point about the relationship of maturity to age.

MENTAL DEVELOPMENT

Bayley's name is known in modern psychology largely because of her infant tests. Although these tests had both motor and mental scales, more attention today is paid to the mental scales. For her master's thesis, Bayley (1926) developed quickly administered performance tests that were correlated with mental age (MA) and the IQ as measured by the Stanford–Binet test of intelligence. In her thesis, she noted that a child's performance in placing forms in a form board is related to both physical and intellectual development.

In 1933, Bayley raised questions that she spent the rest of her life trying to answer. These are still valid questions today.

> What infant behaviors may we call "mental"? . . . To what extent are these later achievements dependent on the earlier? . . . How do individual growth rates compare with the norm for a group of infants? To what extent are these rates affected by environmental conditions? (Bayley, 1933, p. 7)

Relationships to Age

Developmental psychology has focused less on the questions raised here than on questions of prediction. The data show that scores on mental scales obtained before 3 months are not related to those at 9 months, and scores from 10 months through 12 months are not related to those at 3 years. Partly on this basis, Bayley concluded that there might not be a single intelligence "which can be tapped and evaluated at any convenient stage in a child's development. . . . [T]here may be multiple factors, different ones entering into the score at different age levels" (Bayley, 1933, p. 49).

In a later discussion of the same issue, Bayley once again concluded "that there is a pervasive change in mental organization during the early preschool period, . . . most rapid between one and two years of age" (Bayley, 1940a, p. 43). Still later (1955), she suggested, from data obtained in the Berkeley Growth Study, that those functions measured in the first 2 years of life could be characterized as measuring "sensori-motor alertness," those measured at 2 to 4 years as measuring "persistence," and those measured at 4 years and over as measuring the "manipulation of symbols." Inasmuch as the manipulation of symbols is a major component of grade school performance, it is not surprising that tests given at 4 years did enable at least a rough prediction of performance in grade school later on.

Test-Score Variability.   As Bayley's Berkeley Growth Study sample grew older, and after she had analyzed more data, she was able to write "Consistency and Variability in the Growth of Intelligence From Birth to Eighteen Years" (Bayley, 1949). Her consideration of age changes in the variability of intelligence test scores made that study unique. The scores for any baby vary from one testing to the next. The amount of variability increases rapidly from 1 to 6 months, then drops sharply from 6 to 12 months, and then increases again until 36 months. Data from other tests that extended the age range produced the same results. There is less variability at 1 year than before or after and, following age 1, variability increases, but then decreases until 6 years. From 6 until 11 or 12 years variability increases, after which it drops again. These data mean that relationships among measures of intelligence will be higher if they come from ages where variability is high. For example, in one study (Rosenblith, 1992, p. 131) later measures were not related to assessments at age 4, when variability was low (Rosenblith, 1979), but they were related to assessments at age 7, when variability was higher and the challenges of school were being faced.

Such observations led Bayley (1949) to derive an "intelligence lability" score for each child. She found that these scores showed wide individual differences and changed from age to age. Boys and girls did not differ in lability scores and although one fourth of her group changed IQ by 10 or more points in a single year and by 17 or more points over a 3-year period, lability scores were not affected by level of intelligence.

Validity of Individual Test Items.   Bayley (1940b) had found that her Mental Scale was a poor predictor of later IQ, and that led her to wonder whether at least some items from the First-Year Scale might discriminate between the brightest and the dullest youngsters in her sample. There were 30 items had been passed at least 2 months earlier by the brightest 16- to 17-year-olds than by the dullest, but even they did not differentiate between the two groups during the first year. She concluded that "it is possible, of course, that tests might be devised for use in infancy that would predict later intelligence. But the present efforts have been fruitless" (p. 43).

Environmental Variables

Because there was contradictory evidence in existing studies as to whether social class variables affect mental development, Bayley and Jones (1937) looked at a number of such variables, including the average education of the parents, income, and play-school attendance (literally "play school" as opposed to today's "preschools," which have a higher cognitive component and a lower motor component). They found that play school had a small positive effect on intelligence in the third year.

The variable most closely related to mental development was average parental education; family income was least closely related. Mental development at 2 years of age was most highly related to the mother's education ($r = .50$), but it was not related to that of the father until 5 years. As this last-mentioned result indicates, some correlations increase with age.

The Nature–Nurture Issue

Bayley and Jones noted that their data could not decide the relative roles of environmental and genetic factors in determining mental scores. To quote them:

> The increasing correspondence between mental scores and environmental variables is not necessarily attributable to the influence of the environment; it may be that . . . inherited parent–child resemblances become evident only after a certain stage in the process of maturation has been reached. . . . [T]he probability is that . . . the growth of children involves both an increasing assimilation of environmental pressures and an increasing manifestation of complex hereditary potentialities. (Bayley & Jones, 1937, p. 339)

As Bayley concluded later,

> Attempts to isolate factors influencing rates of mental growth . . . point repeatedly to the great complexity of these factors, and at the same time to minimize the influences of environmental factors on intelligence *under relatively normal conditions* [italics added]. (1940b, pp. 77–78)

Much later Bayley (1958) wrote an article, "Value and Limitations of Infant Testing," which brought this message home to parents and professionals who are interested in finding out from some test in infancy how bright their child will be in later life. She noted that such outcomes are determined by a complex interaction between heredity and environment—which includes prenatal environment as well as style of parenting and the nature of the school and of the community—and that this interaction takes place over a long period of time. As a result of this complexity, and as Bayley's data show, such predictions have little probability of hitting the mark exactly.

THE NIMH PERIOD

Nancy Bayley had two careers. After her long career at Berkeley (1928–1954), and after initiating and conducting the Berkeley Growth Study, she moved to Washington, D.C., to head the section on child development of the National Institute of Mental Health (NIMH), a part of the National Institutes of Health complex. The 1950s were a crucial time in the history of developmental psychology because of two quite separate happenings: The first was the beginning of the National Collaborative Perinatal Project (NCPP); the second was the introduction of computerized data analysis.

The NCPP

The NCPP followed the prenatal and postnatal development of 50,000 children in several parts of the country. The Bayley Scales of Mental and Motor Development were selected to examine development at 8 months of age. Before the start of this study, Bayley supervised the revision and standardization of her scales in the most comprehensive test standardization ever done to that time. More than 1,400 infants ranging from 1 to 15 months of age were tested. This sample came from different locales and represented the population of the country quite well.

Despite the 30 years between them, certain findings on this more representative sample were the same as those obtained in the Berkeley Growth Study. There were no differences related to sex, birth order, or education of parents on either scale. Moreover, the growth curves of performance were similar—with one exception: The period of very rapid growth occurred some 2 months earlier in the newer sample, perhaps because of the more stimulating environment provided at the later time. There were no differences on the motor scale by geographic region or ethnic origin, although African-Americans were superior. The quesion of genetic differences accounting for African-American superiority had been raised earlier (Geber, 1958; Geber & Dean, 1957) and disputed (Warren, 1972; Werner, 1972). Subsequent data showed that there were differences between various African-American groups and that those differences were related to childrearing customs (Super, 1976). Some customs associated with rapid motor development (e.g., massage) are more frequently found in African-American groups.

Questions of Reliability.   In 1966, Werner and Bayley went on to ask important questions about the reliability of examiners and test–retest reliability. Would an individual observing the examination of an infant assign the same score as the person actually administering the test? Would babies receive the same scores if they were tested twice at different times? The answer to both questions at 8 months of age was "yes." There was 89% agreement between observers and examiners and 75% agreement between tests separated by a week. The lower agreement for the tests given a week apart might reflect advances in the babies' skills or differences in attention, sleepiness, hunger, and the like.

Item Reliability.   Werner and Bayley (1966) also tested the reliability of separate items on the Mental and Motor Scales. Item reliability is important in cases where a specific item is found to be related to mental retardation because, if that item is unreliable, labeling a baby as having mental retardation could do much harm. As it turned out, the items that differentiated between babies without mental retardation and those suspected of having mental retardation were usually those for which both interscorer agreement and test–retest reliability were high.

With this point made, Bayley began to train people from the various sites to administer the Bayley Scales. One or more examiners from each site came to Washington to be trained until there was almost no disagreement between any two examiners. In turn, they could go back to their home sites and train new examiners as needed.

The Computer Difference

Bayley's move to NIMH also led to an entirely new phase in her work. The advent of computers and federal research money meant that data in the files that could never have been analyzed by hand could now be entered into computers and the relations between different measures examined.

In 1958, Schaefer and Bell developed a Parental Attitude Research Instrument (PARI) based on data from the Berkeley Growth Study. In 1959, Schaefer, Bell, and Bayley announced the "Development of a Maternal Behavior Research Instrument." With these instruments and Schaefer's (1959) "Circumplex Model for Maternal Behavior" available, Schaefer and Bayley undertook an analysis of the relationships between maternal childrearing behavior and mental development. Because previous studies had emphasized motor behavior and looked at maternal behavior only over very short time spans, this was another of Bayley's pioneering efforts.

Rigorous methods were used to make sure that the ratings of both childrearing and the behavior of the children were reliable. Then the relations of maternal behavior to child behavior and intelligence were determined (Bayley & Schaefer, 1964; Schaefer & Bayley, 1963). The most important dimensions of parental behavior discovered in this study were love—hostility and autonomy—control. Among their findings were that these two dimensions of maternal behavior affect the development of boys and girls very differently, and that mothers behaved differently toward boys and girls. There were also differences that depended on the age of the child.

Boys' intelligence is strongly related to the love–hostility dimension of maternal behavior. Hostile mothers have sons who score high in intelligence in the first year or so, but have low IQs from 4 through 18 years. The highly intelligent boys, in addition to having loving mothers, were characteristically happy, inactive, and slow babies, who grew into friendly, intellectually alert boys and well-adjusted extroverts as adolescents. The girls who had loving, controlling mothers were happy, responsive babies, who earned high mental scores. However, after 3 years the girls' intelligence scores show little relation to either maternal or child behavior variables, with the exception of being negatively correlated with maternal intrusiveness. The girls' childhood IQs are correlated primarily with education of the parents and estimates of the mother's IQ (Bayley & Schaefer, 1964, p. 71).

Bayley (1964) also looked at the question of whether mother–child relationships are consistent over time. The mothers' expressions of affection, emotional involvement, irritability, and ignoring were most consistent ($r > .50$ for both sexes). Mothers were slightly less consistent with girls than boys—and when they were consistent, it was on different dimensions. For girls, mothers were most consistent on autonomy, emotional involvement, fostering dependency, and achievement demands. For boys, they were most consistent on positive evaluation, egalitarian treatment, and using fear to control.

Independent of mothers' behavior, ratings of children's activity level and extroversion were most consistent over time. Girls who were high on either were more aggressive and less positively task oriented throughout childhood and adolescence. The same relationship held for boys, but only until early adolescence—perhaps age 13. One of Schaefer and Bayley's studies (1963) called attention to the fact that efforts to facilitate positive parent–child relationships are more likely to succeed than efforts to correct negative behavior, a finding confirmed in later decades.

These studies offered no evidence that social patterns are fixed in infancy. Rather they suggested that enduring behavioral traits are developed during adolescence and that social and emotional behavior show marked and rapid changes during that period. Boys are more influenced by the mother's behaviors than are girls. The authors recommended that all future studies of parental behaviors and their relation to that of offspring be examined for each sex separately and concluded that

the child's social, emotional, and task-oriented behaviors are, to some extent, a reaction to the parental behaviors he has received throughout the period of childhood. . . . [T]he consistency of a dimension of activity–passivity, and its relative independence of parent–child relationships, also supports hypotheses that the human is not completely plastic, but responds to his environment *in accordance with his innate tendencies* [italics added]. (Schaefer & Bayley, 1963, p. 96)

Origins of Maternal Behaviors

Using the Berkeley Growth Study data and computer capabilities, Bayley and Schaefer (Bayley & Schaefer, 1960; Schaefer & Bayley, 1963) also looked into the question of what determined the mothers' maternal behavior. They found that differences between mothers of different socioeconomic status were small. Higher status mothers had a slight tendency to be warmer and more understanding and accepting, whereas lower status mothers tended to be more controlling, irritable, and punitive. On the dimension of autonomy versus control, boys of higher status mothers were granted more autonomy (were less closely supervised) and girls of lower status mothers received less supervision. However, the degree to which mothers showed hostility to their children was associated with poor relationships with their husbands, environmental stresses, and emotional maladjustment—conditions often associated with lower status.

RESEARCH PHILOSOPHY

In her mature years, Bayley published three articles that should be required reading for serious students of development. One entitled "Implicit and Explicit Values in Science as Related to Human Growth and Development" contained a clear statement of her philosophy of research. In it she stated that despite the joys of discovery for its own sake, the "ultimate values lie in the application of scientific knowledge in the interests of human welfare and happiness" (Bayley, 1956b, p. 121). For true understanding of any aspect of psychological development she felt that one had to know about its earliest appearance, its course of development, and its relationship to the development of other processes. Bayley had the patience to do this in her own work. However, longitudinal studies like Bayley's raise severe problems of data management, which fortunately have been lessened in the computer age. Indeed, Bayley herself, after becoming involved in the computer analysis of data that had been catching dust on her shelves, would plead in talks at professional meetings that researchers not throw away their longitudinal data—they might be useful at a later time.

In a 1965 article Bayley discussed the criticisms of longitudinal studies, but also pointed to questions that could only be answered by longitudinal research. A major problem is that one can never be sure how differences in conditions at the time of rearing—diet, feeding patterns, prosperity, depression, childrearing advice, changes of school, whether both parents work—affect results. Would the findings be the same in a similar sample studied 20 years later or in a sample from another culture?

BAYLEY AS A PERSON

In an article mentioned earlier, Bayley (1956b) discussed the importance of studying children in their natural environments and the importance of being concerned with the welfare of research participants. The fact that she was able to keep her participants involved throughout their lives and even to involve members of the next generation is a testimony to the effectiveness of her concern.

It is interesting to contrast her ability to maintain contact with her participants with the fact that she did not encourage intimacy with colleagues. Several people who were close to her maintain that, even though they were in what could have been called her inner circle, they did not feel they truly knew her in a personal way. Some of them noted that she was a superb listener who did not intrude her own life into that of her participants or colleagues. Perhaps these are both part of the same picture—Bayley was a private and reserved person but also a responsible citizen of the community.

Bayley was extremely generous in sharing her data with others. It is quite possible that she was a secondary author on several of the articles because she provided the data on which they were based. She was always concerned with the importance of informing colleagues and lay persons of research findings. Thus, she not only wrote many research articles and reviews of research, but in 1931, she and Jones made movies depicting the development of locomotion from 6 to 15 months, using pictures of the same infants over time. They also made a movie in 1935 of their procedures as applied to one infant beginning at age 1 month and extending to age 12 months.

An example of Bayley's commitment to communicating knowledge is that in 1952 she gave talks to eight professional groups with highly varied backgrounds and two talks to totally nonprofessional groups. Although she was reserved, she gave many interviews to lay journalists, wrote for the popular press, and appeared on radio shows. She frequently held appointments at other universities, especially Stanford, often in both psychology and medicine. Her concern with the growth of all aspects of the child (physical and behavioral) was relevant to the medical profession. She was a consultant and frequent lecturer to various medical groups, and she held positions in medical schools (e.g., in the Department of Anatomy at Stanford). Bayley also published with pediatricians, endocrinologists, anatomists, and mathematicians, in addition to people from various subdisciplines of psychology. One could wonder whether she was especially attracted to medical subjects because her husband taught medical ethics. Equally, one could wonder whether her concern with the ethical treatment of her participants influenced his views of medical ethics.

TESTIMONIES TO BAYLEY'S STATURE

Bayley became prominent early in her career. By the late 1930s she was already being cited for her contributions by national organizations. She was listed in the fifth edition of *American Men of Science* (now *American Men and Women of Science*). James Tanner, one of the world's foremost authorities on human growth, acknowledged the importance of Bayley's work and wrote "Dr. Nancy Bayley, a psychologist by profession, whose papers on physical growth in the period 1930–1960 rank with those of the American 'immortals' " (Tanner, 1981).

In the *Handbook of Research Methods in Child Development* (Mussen & Baldwin, 1960) Bayley was cited seven times in five chapters by five different authors. On the 60th anniversary of her first publication, the fourth volume of *Advances in Infancy Research* was dedicated to Bayley, and it was noted that she had been a pacesetter all of her professional life (Lipsitt & Rovee-Collier, 1986).

In 1966, Bayley was the first woman to be awarded the APA Distinguished Scientific Contribution Award. She was president of the APA Division of Developmental Psychology in 1953–1954 and of the Division of Adult Development and Aging in 1957–1958. She received the G. Stanley Hall Award for outstanding contributions to knowledge in the field of developmental psychology in 1971. She also served as president of the Western Psychological Association in the mid-1950s. Bayley was a founding member of the Society for Research in Child Development, was its president in 1961–1963, and received its Scientific Contribution Award in 1983. In addition to such recognition of her scientific work, Bayley was a diplomate in clinical psychology and served as an examiner for the American Board of Professional Examiners in Professional Psychology. In the latter part of her life she practiced as a clinical psychologist.

Finally, the citation that accompanied her receiving of the Distinguished Scientific Contribution Award from APA catches the spirit of Bayley's contributions to developmental psychology.

> For the enterprise, pertinacity, and insight with which she has studied human growth over long segments of the life cycle. With consummate skill in the use of available but imperfect instruments and with respect and sensitiveness for her subjects, she has rigorously recorded their physical, emotional, and social development from birth to middle life. Her studies have enriched psychology with enduring contributions to the measurement and meaning of intelligence, and she traced important strands in the skein of factors involved in child development. Her participation in a number of major programs of developmental research is a paradigm of the conjoint efforts which are essential in a field whose problems span the generations.

ACKNOWLEDGMENT

The author wishes to thank Dr. Dorothy Eichorn of the University of California, Berkeley, for her contributions to this chapter. Dr. Eichorn, who was one of Nancy Bayley's colleagues and knew her personally, spent a considerable amount of time on the telephone discussing Bayley with the author. If her situation had permitted she would have been a co-author of this chapter.

REFERENCES

Bayley, N. (1926). Performance tests for three, four, and five year old children. *Journal of Genetic Psychology, 33*, 435–454.

Bayley, N. (1933). Mental growth during the first three years: A developmental study of sixty-one children by repeated tests. *Genetic Psychology Monographs, 14*, 1–92.

Bayley, N. (1935). The development of motor abilities during the first three years: A study of sixty-one infants tested repeatedly. *Monographs of the Society for Research in Child Development, 1*, 26–61.

Bayley, N. (1936). *The California Infant Scale of Motor Development.* Berkeley, CA: University of California Press.

Bayley, N. (1939). Mental and motor development from two to twelve years. *Review of Educational Research, 9*, 19–37.

Bayley, N. (1940a). Mental growth in young children. In G. M. Whipple (Ed.), *Intelligence: Its nature and nurture: Yearbook of the National Society for the Study of Education* (Vol. 39, part II, pp. 11–47).

Bayley, N. (1940b). *Studies in the development of young children.* Berkeley, CA: University of California Press.

Bayley, N. (1943). Size and body build of adolescents in relation to the rate of skeletal maturing. *Child Development, 14*, 51–89.

Bayley, N. (1946). Tables for predicting adult height from skeletal age and present height. *Journal of Pediatrics, 28*, 49–64.

Bayley, N. (1949). Consistency and variability in the growth of intelligence from birth to eighteen years. *Journal of Genetic Psychology, 75*, 165–196.

Bayley, N. (1951a). Development and maturation. In H. Helson (Ed.), *Theoretical foundations of psychology* (pp. 145–199). New York: Van Nostrand.

Bayley, N. (1951b). Some psychological correlates of somatic androgyny. *Child Development, 22*, 47–60.

Bayley, N. (1955). On the growth of intelligence. *American Psychologist, 10*, 805–818.

Bayley, N. (1956a). Growth curves of height and weight by age for boys and for girls, scaled according to physical maturity. *Journal of Pediatrics, 48*, 187–194.

Bayley, N. (1956b). Implicit and explicit values in science as related to human growth and development. *Merrill-Palmer Quarterly, 2*, 121–126.

Bayley, N. (1958). Value and limitations of infant testing. *Children, 5*, 129–133.

Bayley, N. (1964). Consistency of maternal and child behaviors in the Berkeley Growth Study. *Vita Humana, 7*, 73–95.

Bayley, N. (1965). Research in child development: A longitudinal perspective. *Merrill-Palmer Quarterly, 11*, 1883–208.

Bayley, N., & Davis, F. C. (1935). Growth changes in bodily size and proportions during the first three years: A developmental study of sixty-one children by repeated measurements. *Biometrica, 27*, 26–87.

Bayley, N., & Jones, H. E. (1937). Environmental correlates of mental and motor development: A cumulative study from infancy to six years. *Child Development, 8*, 329–341.

Bayley, N., & Pinneau, S. R. (1952). Tables for predicting adult height from skeletal age: Revised for use with the Greulich–Pyle hand standards. *Journal of Pediatrics, 40*, 423–444.

Bayley, N., & Schaefer, E. S. (1960). Maternal behavior and personality development: Data from the Berkeley Growth Study. In C. Shagass & B. Pasamanick (Eds.), *Child Development Research Reports of the American Psychiatric Association* (Vol. 13, pp. 155–173).

Geber, M. (1958). The psycho-motor development of African children in the first year, and the influence of maternal behavior. *Journal of Social Psychology, 47,* 185–195.

Geber, M., & Dean, R. F. A. (1957). Gesell tests on African children. *Pediatrics, 20,* 1055–1065.

Lipsitt, L. P., & Rovee-Collier, C. (1986). *Advances in infancy research.* Norwood, NJ: Ablex.

Mussen, P. H. & Baldwin, A. L. (Eds.) (1960). *Handbook of research methods in child development.* New York: Wiley.

Rosenblith, J. F. (1979). The Graham/Rosenblith examination for newborns: Prognostic values and procedural issues. In J. Osofsky (Ed.), *Handbook of infant development.* New York: Wiley.

Rosenblith, J. F. (1992). *In the beginning: Development from conception to age two.* Newbury Park, CA: Sage.

Schaefer, E. S. (1959). A circumplex model for maternal behavior. *Journal of Abnormal and Social Psychology, 59,* 226–235.

Schaefer, E. S., & Bayley, N. (1963). Maternal behavior, child behavior and their intercorrelations from infancy through adolescence. *Monographs of the Society for Research in Child Development, 28,* (3, Serial No. 87).

Schaefer, E. S., & Bell, R. Q. (1958). Development of a parental attitude research instrument. *Child Development, 29,* 339–361.

Schaefer, E. S., Bell, R. Q., & Bayley, N. (1959). Development of a maternal behavior research instrument. *Journal of Genetic Psychology, 95,* 83–104.

Super, C. M. (1976). Environmental effects on motor development. *Developmental Medicine and Child Neurology, 18,* 561–567.

Tanner, J. M. (1978). *Foetus into man.* Cambridge, MA: Harvard University Press.

Tanner, J. M. (1981). *A history of the study of human growth.* Cambridge, England: Cambridge University Press.

Warren, N. (1972). African infant precocity. *Psychological Bulletin, 78,* 353–367.

Werner, E. E. (1972). Infants around the world: Cross-cultural studies of psychomotor development from birth to two years. *Journal of Cross Cultural Studies, 3,* 111–134.

Werner, E. E., & Bayley, N. (1966). The reliability of Bayley's revised scale of mental and motor development during the first year of life. *Child Development, 36,* 39–50.

Egon Brunswik: 1903-1955

Chapter 13

Egon Brunswik:
Student of Achievement

Elke Kurz-Milcke and Nancy K. Innis

Egon Brunswik is not a familiar figure in the history of American psychology. Nevertheless, his contributions were such that a small group of researchers thought it fitting to establish the Brunswik Society, which meets annually to promote the approach to psychological research that Brunswik introduced. The impact of Brunswik's work on present-day research is found mainly in the application of his ideas to the study of judgment and decision making; Hammond and Stewart (2001) provide a comprehensive treatment of several aspects of his psychology by a variety of contributors. However, Brunswik's idea that the environment to which an organism must adjust presents itself as "semierratic" (Brunswik, 1955, p. 193), that is, as partly unpredictable by the organism, had a subtle, if typically unacknowledged, influence on American experimental psychology.

Most of Brunswik's own research was concerned with perception, in particular with perceptual constancy or *thing constancy*. The latter term is a direct translation of the German term *Dingkonstanz*. Brunswik's native language was German, but as a scientist he was bilingual. Practically all of his publications before 1937, with one notable exception (see later section, "The Organism and the Causal Texture of the Environment"), were in German, but after that year nearly all were written in English. Brunswik started out in Vienna, but in 1937 moved to the United States. Thus, he is among the many intellectuals who emigrated from Germany and Austria after Hitler's rise to power (Fleming & Bailyn, 1969). Ash (2001) has analyzed Brunswik's career path in the context of these other émigrés. Brunswik's case can be understood best in terms of both a "push factor" and a "pull factor." The push was the political and economic situation in

Austria that had become increasingly uncertain, especially for intellectuals, after the Austrofaschists took power in 1934. The situation became even worse after Austria was annexed to Nazi Germany in 1938, by which time Brunswik was already in the United States.

The strong pull was Edward C. Tolman (chap. 15, *Pioneers I*) at the University of California, Berkeley. Brunswik first met Tolman in 1933, when Tolman was in Vienna on a sabbatical leave. Although Brunswik worked on perception in humans and Tolman studied learning in rats, the two men found that they shared "a common point of view as to the general nature of psychology" (Tolman & Brunswik, 1935, p. 43). Tolman was eager to have Brunswik join him at Berkeley where he believed that together they could "build up an experimental and theoretical movement of great importance and of some renown" (Tolman to Deutsch, December 2, 1937; see Ash, 2001).

Brunswik accepted a permanent position at Berkeley in 1938, and in 1943 became an American citizen. Thus, the late 1930s and the early 1940s were a time of major transition for Brunswik. His move from Austria to the United States gave a new institutional and intellectual context to his work, and to his research on perceptual constancy phenomena in particular. (Perceptual constancy refers to a broad class of phenomena in which the percept remains relatively unchanged despite major changes in the physical stimulus. For example, the apparent size of a person approaching you doesn't increase substantially even though the retinal image of the person grows larger, and a gray object remains perceptually gray whether viewed indoors at low illumination or in bright sunlight.) The studies Brunswik published during this time are interesting in that they show his ideas, so to speak, on the move. However, before examining his work in this transitional period in detail, we consider Brunswik's early years in Vienna.

BACKGROUND AND EDUCATION

Egon Brunswik was born in Budapest, Hungary, on March 18, 1903. His mother, Helene, née Wiser, was Austrian and his father, Julius Brunswik, who worked as an engineer for the Austro-Hungarian government, was a Hungarian from the minor nobility. Brunswik's full last name was von Brunswik de Korompa (E. C. Tolman to R. M. Elliott, March 10, 1936; see Ash, 2001, for biographical details). Although his native language was German, Brunswik also learned Hungarian as a child. When he was 8 years old, Brunswik was sent to the noted *Theresianum*, a gymnasium (high school) in Vienna, where, along with the usual classical and mathematical curriculum, he was exposed to the history of the Austro-Hungarian Empire in both German and Hungarian—a biographical detail that led Tolman later to suggest that perhaps the discrepancies Brunswik observed between these two accounts "gave him his initial insight into the merely probabilistic character of one's knowledge of one's environment" (Tolman, 1956, p. 315).

The effects of World War I briefly interrupted Brunswik's education when, in 1918, he and his sister spent a few months in Sweden to regain their health, which had been threatened because of malnutrition during the war. After completing his studies at the gymnasium in 1921, Brunswik spent 2 years studying engineering before turning to psychology. In 1927, he graduated with a joint degree as a teacher of mathematics and physics and a doctorate in psychology, a customary pattern in Vienna in those days. His dissertation, supervised by Karl Bühler (1879–1963), was interdisciplinary, as can readily be seen from its title *Strukturmonismus und Physik* (*Structural Monism and Physics*). It contained a critical appraisal of the philosophical aspects of modern physics that had found application in the field of Gestalt psychology.

As well as Bühler, the philosopher Moritz Schlick (1882–1936) was on Brunswik's doctoral advisory committee. Schlick is known for having brought together a group of intellectuals who formed the *Wiener Kreis* (Vienna Circle). Members of the Vienna Circle promoted logical positivism, a philosophical program that sought to liberate science from metaphysics and thus help science to ask better questions, questions that could be answered on the basis of empirical observations. Brunswik was not really a member of the Vienna Circle and was not a logical positivist. However, there were points of contact between him and those who were a part of this philosophical movement. One of their issues, in particular, concerned Brunswik. This was the idea that science is, in some sense, unified in a very principled way that goes beyond a loosely linked group of separate sciences. For Brunswik, this raised the question of where psychology stands as a science—an issue that kept resurfacing in Brunswik's publications. It had already concerned his teacher Bühler (see Bühler, 1927) and was an issue that Brunswik considered inseparable from his research activity. The issue found its most comprehensive treatment in Brunswik's proposal for "The Conceptual Framework of Psychology," published in 1952 in the *International Encyclopedia of Unified Science*. Here, Brunswik cautioned the discipline not to sacrifice psychology's distinctive needs, especially in terms of experimental methodology, on the altar of ideals hastily adopted from physics and the natural sciences. With his early training in engineering and physics, Brunswik had first-hand experience with these other sciences and knew what to expect of them.

EARLY CAREER AT THE UNIVERSITY OF VIENNA

After receiving his doctorate, Brunswik became "first assistant" to Bühler, who with his wife, Charlotte Bühler (1893–1974), headed the Vienna Psychological Institute (see Bühler, 1972). Brunswik took charge of the experimental work and taught a methodology course, for which he wrote a handbook, *Experimentelle Psychologie in Demonstrationen* (*Experimental Psychology in Demonstrations*), that presented a wide range of topics for experimental study. Brunswik spent

1931–1932 in Turkey as a visiting lecturer at the Gazi Institute, a college of education in Ankara, where he set up the country's first laboratory of psychology (see Benetka, 1995, for a detailed account of Brunswik's early career). He returned to Vienna and in 1934 was appointed *Privatdozent* at the Psychological Institute. The institute was a vibrant center of psychological research attracting students and visitors, many of whom came from the United States, including Tolman. Soon after they met, Tolman and Brunswik realized their theoretical positions had a lot in common. They spent many hours in lively discussion in Vienna coffeehouses (Tolman, 1952) and began collaborating on an article, "The Organism and the Causal Texture of the Environment" (Tolman & Brunswik, 1935), that addressed these similarities. Brunswik developed his theoretical position as a result of his research on visual perception; Tolman developed his theory, *purposive behaviorism*, as a result of his research with rats in mazes.

Brunswik's Gegenstands Psychology

Brunswik's theoretical position was initially presented in a book, *Wahrnehmung und Gegenstandswelt–Grundlegung einer Psychologie vom Gegenstand her* (*Perception and the World of Objects: The Foundations of a Psychology in Terms of Objects*), published in 1934. In the foreword Brunswik (1934, p. VIII) thanked Bühler for fostering his interest in perceptual constancy research, for instilling in him a "biological orientation," and for the support that had allowed him to develop his research program. In this way, Bühler's influence on Brunswik "was profound and lasting" (Leary, 1987, p. 118). On a general level, Brunswik shared his teacher's aim to determine a general and unifying basis for scientific psychology. On a more specific level, Brunswik's constancy research was inspired by his teacher's theoretical position, which was embodied in the *duplicity principle*. This principle stated that perceptual constancy is based on a "twofold (at least) stimulus basis" (Brunswik, 1937, p. 230). Thus, perception of a particular "object" such as size or brightness entails context—in these examples, distance or illumination. But, most important, these "varying circumstances" (Brunswik, 1937, p. 240) cannot be eliminated, not even for psychological experimentation. Although the book was not translated into English, Tolman wrote a long and very complimentary review, drawing the attention of American psychologists to what he referred to as "an extremely important theoretical doctrine" (Tolman, 1935, p. 608).

Bühler's, and later Brunswik's, emphasis on "context" in perception is also reminiscent of the Bühler's intellectual heritage, which stems in part from Oswald Külpe and the Würzburg School. Researchers from this tradition emphasized the importance of context—for instance, by acknowledging the crucial role of the instructions given to participants in experimental research. By their instructions researchers could induce differing attitudes (Einstellungen), or tasks, in participants. The careful consideration of the induced "attitude" under which participants made their perceptual judgments was invariably a feature of Brunswik's perception research, and one of the ways, besides the duplicity principle, in which "context" mattered in his theorizing and experimentation.

For Brunswik the study of perceptual constancy meant the study of *perceptual achievement*. In the first English exposition of his Viennese research program to the American reader, Brunswik defined "thing constancy" as "*good correspondence* [italics added] between intuitive judgment and measurement of the characteristics of the environmental bodies, regardless of the varying circumstances under which the intuitive judgments occur" (Brunswik, 1937, p. 240). For instance, one of the first research projects at the Vienna Psychological Institute carried out under Brunswik's supervision investigated albedo perception (i.e., brightness constancy) from a developmental perspective. To be able to compare attained constancy and to determine developmental trends, Brunswik developed a measure of perceptual constancy. This measure combined the following values in a single index: (a) a surface's apparent brightness, (b) its "physiological color" (luminance), and (c) its albedo (reflectance). Using this index, Brunswik and his coworkers found an increase of brightness constancy, with age showing a peak around the age of 15, a subsequent slight decrease, and then a plateau for young adults. Brunswik used this measure, which became known as the *constancy ratio* or as the *Brunswik ratio*, in a parallel fashion with other constancy phenomena. For example, in the case of size perception, it combined the values of apparent size, retinal-image size, and objectively measured size. Brunswik carefully explored the computational properties of this index which became his measure of "achievement" for all the various kinds of perception he investigated during his time at the Bühlers' Institute in Vienna.

In his research on constancy phenomena, Brunswik found that perceptual constancy is approximate. Theoretically, he conceptualized perception as being based on a *compromise* between "poles," in the case of brightness constancy, for example, between albedo and luminance. These kinds of compromises were referred to as *in-between objects* (*Zwischengegenstände*; Brunswik, 1937, p. 249). These "objects" were original with Brunswik and embodied an explanatory principle, namely, that the study of perception mandates a distinction between "pure objects" and "attained objects." Perception *intends* pure objects such as, for instance, brightness or physical size. Perception *attains* objects that are intermediary between pure objects, in the case of size constancy, for example, between objectively measured size and projective (retinal) size. However, Brunswik also espoused another way of thinking about constancy phenomena, namely, a kind of unconscious inference, where explanation was sought in terms of a cue-based principle. As Gigerenzer and Murray (1987, p. 66) have pointed out, Brunswik did not distinguish between these two principles in his writing. Moreover, Gigerenzer and Murray showed that the two principles are not only conceptually different but can lead to contradictory predictions. But Brunswik never confronted the two principles in this way.

Soon after Brunswik came to the University of California the notion of in-between objects fell into oblivion and the cue-based principle gained prominence in his thinking. As discussed later, the flip side of this development was Brunswik's proposal in 1940 to use correlational statistics to measure "perceptual achievement." Thus, this cue-based approach presented a major continuity in his work as it developed over time, first in Vienna and subsequently in Berkeley; it was also crucial in the collaboration between Brunswik and Tolman (Tolman & Brunswik, 1935). When these two men met in Vienna in 1933, each of them had just recently finished a book-length account of his respective theoretical position. Consider first a brief outline of Tolman's position before examining their collaborative work. Given Brunswik's appreciation for a "biological orientation" and his emphasis on "achievement," it is not surprising that the two of them had something to share over coffee in Vienna.

Tolman's Purposive Behaviorism

Tolman's theoretical position, "purposive behaviorism," was presented in *Purposive Behavior in Animals and Men* (1932). Tolman believed that "mental processes are most usefully to be conceived as dynamic aspects, or determinants, of behavior. They are functional variables which intermediate in the causal equation between environmental stimuli and initiating physiological states, . . . on the one side, and final overt behavior, on the other" (Tolman, 1932, p. 2). Most important of these intervening variables were the "immanent determinants," purposes (demands) and cognitions. The purposive nature of behavior was defined by its persistence until a goal is achieved. Cognitions are expectations about the relationship between environmental support stimuli, referred to as signs, and the goals, or significates, indicated by them. Thus, cues in the animal's environment provide information about expected goals and the means of achieving them. Implicit in this notion was the idea of "selectivity as regards stimuli, and as regards the responses to be made to such stimuli" (Tolman & Krechevsky, 1933, p. 60). One of Tolman's students, Isadore Krechevsky (later David Krech, chap. 18, *Pioneers III*), introduced the term *hypotheses* to refer to the relatively specific set of expectations the animal selectively samples as it attempts to achieve a goal (see Innis, 1997).

The Organism and the Causal Texture of the Environment

In their joint publication, Tolman and Brunswik (1935) outlined the similarities in their theoretical positions. In both theories, distant objects (to be perceived or got at) are "achieved" through a process involving local representation or signs. These signs may be stimulus cues for the intended object, or they may provide means for attaining a goal. However, these causal connections between cues and object, or means and goal, usually do not involve simple one-to-one relations;

they are equivocal. As a result, the organism develops *hypotheses* "as to what the given means-object will 'most probably' lead to in the way of goals" or by what means "the given cues have with 'most probability' been caused" (p. 75). "Hypotheses" was Tolman's term; Brunswik did not adopt this terminology for his subsequent work.

Successful achievement in perception then depends on a probability relation, that is, on whether the cues (signs) are reliable, ambiguous, nonsignificant, or actually misleading. Similarly, means-objects relative to goals in learning may be good, ambivalent, indifferent, or bad. As a result of the collaboration each man extended his own position. For Tolman, this involved a tendency to pay more attention to the multiplicity of causal factors in behavior. Brunswik was stimulated to extend his approach beyond perception to problems of learning.

GOING WEST

Tolman was impressed with Brunswik and wanted to continue their collaboration. In 1935–1936, a fellowship from the Rockefeller Foundation allowed Brunswik to spend a year in Tolman's laboratory. The Berkeley psychology department was "very keen about trying to keep him" (Tolman to Elliott, February 10, 1936), and he received an appointment as assistant professor in the fall of 1937. However it seems that, despite Brunswik's fine credentials and performance, the administration was hesitant about giving him a permanent appointment. Eventually, Tolman put pressure on the administration, declaring that if Brunswik could not remain at Berkeley he (Tolman) would "honestly regret, deep down, [his] previous decision to remain at California rather than to accept a call from elsewhere" (Tolman to Deutsch, December 2, 1937). A few years earlier Tolman had chosen to remain at Berkeley rather than accept the offer of an appointment at Harvard. In 1938, Brunswik was appointed associate professor in the Psychology Department at Berkeley. That year he married Else Frenkel (1908–1958), who had obtained her doctorate with Charlotte Bühler in 1930 and then remained at the Vienna Institute as an assistant. Because she was Jewish, Frenkel had been forced to flee from Austria; they were married when she arrived in New York. Frenkel-Brunswik, who obtained an appointment as a research psychologist at Berkeley's Institute of Child Welfare, made many significant contributions to psychology, including an analysis of the authoritarian personality (see Heiman & Grant, 1974).

Probability as a Determiner of Rat Behavior

When he took up his Rockefeller Fellowship at Berkeley, Brunswik (1939) began to directly apply his views on the probabilistic nature of environmental events to animal learning. He believed that the typical maze-learning experiment, in which a rat is faced with a choice between absolutes—food always available on one arm and not on the other—does not reflect what happens in the real world. So he carried out an extensive study in which the conditions of reward on the arms differed in probability. The different probability conditions were carefully chosen to permit a number of comparisons. Five groups of rats (48 animals in each) were studied on an elevated T-maze where one side of the maze was more profitable than the other. The probabilities of obtaining food on the two arms for the five groups were: 100:0, 50:0, 100:50, 75:25, and 67:33. Throughout the study, a correction procedure was used; if an animal ran to an arm without food it found a door at the end of the arm locked and it was free to retrace its path and go to the other arm. The results showed that the rats in all but one condition learned to choose the more profitable side.

Brunswik computed critical ratios for a number of comparisons. The 67:33 condition was the only experimental group that did not discriminate between reward probabilities, continuing to respond at a level not significantly different from chance throughout the study. Performance in the other conditions differed significantly from chance and differed from the 67:33 group. Rats in the 100:0 group received an additional series of 6 days on which reward conditions were reversed daily. The animals rapidly learned the successive reversals, in fact anticipating them as the reversals continued. Finally, in an additional "danger" experiment, shocks were given, with probability conditions of 75:25 and 100:50, when a locked door (no food) was encountered, for three training and three reversal sessions. Learning was rapid and increased with "an increase of the probability ratio of punishment" (Brunswik, 1939, p. 185); thus, shock probability outweighed reward probability in determining performance. In other words, the animals' "emphasis" was on avoiding punishment rather than on reaching food quickly.

The results of the study were clear-cut: Animals can learn about the relative probability of reward in a choice situation and "discriminations increase with increasing differences in probabilities even when their ratio is held constant," the latter being the case for conditions 100:50 and 67:33 (Brunswik, 1939, p. 182). Where the difference between probabilities was held constant (conditions 50:0, 75:25, and 100:50), there was also some evidence of an "influence . . . due to the varying ratio of probabilities" (p. 183) with more choices of the less profitable side as the ratio decreased. This was also evident in the punishment conditions. This was one of the first (if not the first) studies of probability learning in animals. However, Brunswik's contribution to the field of probability learning is generally not recognized by animal learning researchers or historians of psychology.

Thing Constancy as Measured by Correlation Coefficients

At Berkeley, Brunswik soon returned to research on human perception. Another significant article from his transition period in the late 1930s and early 1940s was published in 1940 under the title "Thing Constancy as Measured by Correlation Coefficients."

"Thing constancy" was a European phenomenon: Europeans created constancy phenomena in their laboratories, considered them important, and theorized about them. So when Brunswik, in 1937, first published an article in English on his Viennese research program, he had to introduce this class of phenomena to an audience in the United States that was not familiar with it, or even interested in it. In such a situation an example can be helpful; here is the one that he gave: "An approaching visitor will not grow from a tiny finger-like dwarf up to an immense giant, but will, within certain limits, quite fairly retain a constant apparent size" (Brunswik, 1937, p. 228). This example used a familiar situation, a person approaching, to criticize the theory that the perception of the approaching person would grow from dwarf to giant as the size of the retinal image increases. This example, in fact, resembles a thought experiment (Gooding, 1992). Typically, thought experiments rely on familiar situations, in this case a person approaching, and imply a course of action or development, here that the approaching visitor would grow from dwarf to giant, only to rule out that same course of action or development. With this thought-experiment-like demonstration of perceptual constancy, Brunswik was in good company. Hermann von Helmholtz (chap. 2, *Pioneers IV*), a pioneer of constancy research, had illustrated brightness constancy in a similar way (as translated in Hurvich & Jameson, 1966, p. 121): "A grey sheet of paper exposed to sunlight may look brighter than a white sheet in the shade; and yet the former looks grey and the latter white, simply because we know very well that if the white paper were in the sunlight, it would be much brighter than the grey paper which happens to be there at the time."

These examples were demonstrations of perceptual constancy that appealed to the everyday experience of the reader. Brunswik, however, wanted to measure the degree of constancy achieved. This goal required methodological sophistication, a means Brunswik pursued ceaselessly. In Vienna he had used the constancy ratio to represent the degree of perceptual achievement. The novelty of the 1940 research was that he proposed to measure perceptual constancy using correlation coefficients. Consider the details of his experimental demonstration, of which a recent replication may be found in Kurz and Hertwig (2001).

The eight research participants in Brunswik's (1940) experiment observed a setup of wooden cubes of various sizes at various distances. Their task was to compare each of 15 test cubes, arranged in five rows of 3 cubes each at distances of 2, 4, 6, 8, and 10 m from the observer, with cubes in a comparison series that were at a distance of 12 m. The test cubes had either 50, 55, 60, 65, or 70 mm edge length; the comparison series comprised 13 cubes ranging from 30 to 90 mm. Participants were required to name the cube in the comparison series that corresponded in actual size to a specified test cube. In subsequent analysis their estimates were combined to yield an average estimate for each test cube.

Brunswik also computed "projective" or retinal size for each test cube. Projective size depends simultaneously on the size of the cube and its distance from the observer; it was computed with respect to a standard distance, in this case the distance of the comparison series at 12 m. For example, to correspond in projective (not actual) size, a cube at a 12-m distance would have to have an edge length of 84 mm to correspond with a cube of 70 mm at 10 m. This result is determined by a simple computation that is related to the way the visual angle, α, is computed, namely as tan α = edge length/distance. Projecting computationally, so to speak, each cube onto the distance of the comparison series, Brunswik determined projective retinal size for each test cube.

Thus, Brunswik reported three values for each of the 15 test cubes: (1) actual size represented by the cube's edge length, (2) projective retinal size determined geometrically, and (3) average estimated size as determined from the participants' judgments of equality. Brunswik correlated the values of (1) and (2), of (2) and (3), and of (1) and (3); the corresponding values of the correlation coefficients were: .10, .26, and .97. Obviously, the value for the correlation between actual size (1) and estimated size (3) was very high, or in other words, a high level of constancy was achieved. That the other two correlations were comparatively low was exactly to Brunswik's taste. Brunswik was an "achievement fanatic" when it came to perception; for him the study of perception meant the study of perceptual achievement and not perceptual illusions. Size constancy, as demonstrated in this experiment, comprised two related aspects of achievement: (a) the high value of the correlation between actual and estimated size and (b) the fact that this value was high in combination with the low correlation between projective size and estimated size. This achievement means that, to perceive size accurately, the individual must infer distance from available distance cues and is capable of doing so. What an achievement!

It may seem that Brunswik's experimental demonstration was not particularly sophisticated. However, this demonstration came at the end of many years of experimentation on perceptual constancy phenomena in Vienna. The simplicity of this study (compared with studies that were conducted under his aegis in Vienna) may therefore also be seen as just the flip side of the highly developed skill that Brunswik had with experimentation in this area. He knew what he wanted to demonstrate, namely achievement, and how it could be measured by correlation coefficients, and he knew how best to achieve this end, that is, in the simplest and most effective manner. One may also add "most elegant" to the list if one considers the way he presented the experimental setup and data in a single display (see Table 1 in Brunswik, 1940, republished as Fig. 16 in Brunswik, 1956).

A feature of Brunswik's psychological demonstration that may seem especially unsophisticated at first sight was the way he averaged the individual estimates, treating the aggregate as if it were "the result of one single experiment with one observer only" (1940, p. 71). What was at stake, however, was the liberation of a measure, the correlation coefficient, that had emerged from the study of individual differences, especially from Francis Galton's (chap. 1, *Pioneers 1*) anthropometric studies; in Brunswik's words: "At no stage of our considerations will the matter of individual or of time differences be considered nor will the correlation technique be applied to these latter" (p. 71). Brunswik's aim was to show how this measure is useful in measuring something of a very different kind, namely the degree of perceptual constancy. It seems that in this act of liberation, Brunswik could not allow for the slightest hint of the statistic's origins. For Brunswik, this liberation was completed in his 1940 article, and the usefulness of correlation statistics in the measurement of constancy phenomena was firmly established as fact.

Not so, however, for his colleagues. Psychologists at the time remained mostly unreceptive to Brunswik's ideas. His unconventional use of statistics and the role of uncertainty in his American research program, known as *probabilistic functionalism*, marked him an outsider. For Brunswik, the most important source of uncertainty was located in the relationship between organism and environment. His contemporaries found this place for uncertainty difficult to locate, as is especially apparent from some of the reactions of prominent psychologist, among them Ernest R. Hilgard, David Krech, and Leo Postman, to Brunswik's program (their commentaries were published along with Brunswik's own account in the *Psychological Review* in 1955).

Gigerenzer (1987) has argued that the resistance to Brunswik's work at the time was due to the division of psychology into two more or less unrelated disciplines: experimental and correlational psychology. The president of the American Psychological Association, Lee Cronbach, described *The Two Disciplines of Scientific Psychology* in his address at the Association's Sixty-Fifth Annual Convention in 1957 in the following terms:

> In contrast to the Tight Little Island of the experimental discipline, correlational psychology is a sort of Holy Roman Empire whose citizens identify mainly with their principalities. The discipline, the common service in which the principalities are united, is the study of correlation presented by Nature. While the experimenter is interested only in the variation he himself creates, the correlator finds his interest in the already existing variation between individuals, social groups, and species. (1957, p. 671)

The trouble was that in the United States Brunswik became a "correlator" among "experimenters." His program "integrated the study of perception, *the* topic of experimental psychology, with the methods of the second discipline, correlational psychology" (Gigerenzer, 1987, p. 50). The consequence was that his program, which was too sophisticated to be rejected offhand, met with incomprehension and dismissal.

THEORETICAL PSYCHOLOGY

Charlotte Bühler (1965, p. 190) once described Brunswik as her husband's "main student" in his special area of *theoretical psychology*. Against Brunswik's minutely detailed research and graphical displays stood a passion to find and present the "larger picture." This picture he pursued in a unique mixture of historical and philosophical analysis with an emphasis on psychological, especially experimental, methodology. While in Vienna working under Bühler, Brunswik presented his first comprehensive program, his *Gegenstands* psychology. This program was presented as constituting an innovative impulse to "classical psychophysics," which "fell short of the specifically psychological problems of perception," studying perception under the most favorable conditions (Brunswik, 1934, p. 9, our translation). For many years Brunswik couched his program in terms of an extension of classical psychophysics. In his 1934 book, *Wahrnehmung und Gegenstandswelt* [*Perception and the World of Objects*], this extension was carried so far as to include research on "intentional systems with multiple 'poles.' " For example, in one experiment two groups of coins of different value were used. Comparisons were possible with respect to the combined monetary value of each group, to the number of coins in each group, or the total area covered. Whichever of these "poles" was *intended*, judgment attained an in-between object, or, in other words, was "displaced" by the other two "poles."

Extending psychophysics remained the programmatic goal in the studies Brunswik published shortly after his arrival in the United States. Brunswik saw "Probability as a Determiner of Rat Behavior" as a "contribution to what might be called a 'psycho-physics of probability' " (1939, p. 194). The kind of psychophysics Brunswik envisioned was capable of capturing important aspects of "the natural environment of a living being," in which "cues, means, or pathways to a goal are usually neither absolutely reliable nor absolutely wrong" (p. 175). Similarly, in "Thing Constancy as Measured by Correlation Coefficients," Brunswik sought to "establish a multidimensional psychophysics which will include the distal environment within its scope" (1940, p. 78). His programmatic aim was to reconstruct psychophysics in terms of the distal (physical) environment. Later, Brunswik (e.g., 1956) used the term "ecology" to capture a similar idea.

This programmatic goal was mirrored by his rethinking of experimental methodology. In fact, Brunswik came to propose a radically different type of experimentation—representative design. Pointing to problems with the standard design in which experimenters hold all but one variable constant, Brunswik (1944, 1947) suggested a method that exposed a small number of participats to multiple environmental conditions. The key feature here, then, was that stimulus situations, not participants, should be sampled. He regarded the strategy of extending the case of one independent variable to the simultaneous variation of several independent variables as a step in the right direction. But it remained inherently unsatisfactory because the systematic variation of factor levels still meant that such research remained "confined to self-created ivory-tower ecology" (Brunswik, 1956, p. 110). As Brunswik said himself, representative design is "a formidable task in practice" (p. viii), and most psychologists rejected it outright. They rejected it not only because of its difficulty but because it violated the traditional research practices that had become well established in America.

Ironically, analysis of variance was, at this time, just becoming firmly institutionalized in the United States (Rucci & Tweney, 1980). Again, Brunswik was out of step with contemporary psychology.

THE LENS ANALOGY AND MODEL

Most often, Brunswik's name is mentioned in the same breath as the "lens model." This model has gained prominence in psychological research on judgment and decision making, where it captures the statistical features of the interaction between ecology and cognitive processes (detailed accounts can be found in Cooksey, 1996; Doherty & Kurz, 1996). Brunswik had introduced the underlying lens analogy in his 1934 book. There the analogy was used as a graphical analog to the duplicity principle, formulated by Karl Bühler, which guided Brunswik's early constancy research. Subsequently, this analogy helped Brunswik communicate his approach to perception, more precisely to perceptual achievement alias perceptual constancy, to an English-speaking audience (see Brunswik, 1937, p. 231). Only in the 1950s did the lens analogy inspire the formulation of a "generalized lens model" (Brunswik, 1952, p. 678). Then, the model embodied the principle of "vicarious functioning," the "defining criterion of the subject matter of psychology" (p. 675).

In Brunswik's writings the lens analogy appeared as a graphical representation and as a verbal description. Both aspects evolved over the decades (see Kurz & Tweney, 1997). In *Wahrnehmung und Gegestandswelt* (Brunswik, 1934, p. 97), the lens analogy was introduced by a graphical representation depicting, in a schematized way, a "collecting lens" (Sammellinse). This "schema of synthesis," as Brunswik called the depiction of "rays" emanating from a point P, and being bent by a "lens" to meet in a common point P', corresponded to Bühler's duplicity principle in that the "schema" incorporated multiple (at least twofold) mediation (a) by a "central ray," the "immediate stimulus p," and (b) by "marginal rays," the "additional mediating data" (weitere Vermittlungsdaten). Some of the English terminology attached to Brunswik's early Viennese version of the lens analogy was introduced by Brunswik when, in 1937, he presented the English version of his "Gegenstands psychology." In this article, the lens analogy was presented in words only. Moreover, the analogy of the lens to a perceptual system that functioned in a way to allow for the achievement of perceptual constancy was presented in the more literal sense where it referred to the *visual* system's functioning: The "central ray" stands for the "direct retinal projection of the physical bodies in question" which "are, *per se*, unable to represent in a satisfactorily unambiguous manner their size, forms, colors (reflectivity) etc."; the "marginal rays" represent "cues for circumstances," indicating distance, illumination, and so forth. In this particular case of the analogy, the lens represented "the eye together with the optical sector of the nervous system"

(Brunswik, 1937, p. 231). The lens of the eye, however, he emphasized, was "but a part of this bringing together of differently spread-out and randomly diverging effects of the situation which is to be mastered in regard to its behaviorally important physical traits" (p. 232).

Brunswik's research on constancy was not restricted to visual perception; in fact, as indicated earlier, it was not even restricted to the classical domain of perception, but rather extended to include perception of such abstract categories as the value of an assembly of coins or even the intelligence of a person. The pattern of "central" and "marginal rays" was less amenable to these extended constancy problems, because "direct" stimulation of the perceptual system is not easily discernible. Such were the limitations of the early rendition of the lens analogy. However, for Brunswik the lens analogy was embedded in a broader theoretical proposal that was aimed at establishing a psychology that, in studying "organismic achievement," would focus as much (or even more) on the environment than on the organism (Brunswik, 1943, p. 255). This general agenda was the force behind the occasional reappearance of the analogy in his subsequent English writings, before it eventually assumed a central role in the presentation of his ideas in and after 1952.

In 1941, Brunswik gave an address in a Symposium on Psychology and Scientific Method at the Sixth International Congress for the Unity of Science. In this address, later published in the *Psychological Review*, the lens analogy made a brief appearance, and then only in words, when Brunswik argued for a common core of a number of approaches in psychology, among them approaches by Tolman, C. L. Hull (chap. 14, *Pioneers I*) and F. Heider (chap. 12, *Pioneers IV*). Brunswik saw communality in the shared general interest in "behavioral achievement" and the related concept of "vicarious functioning," for instance, of cues or habits. In his attempt to bring out a common core, the lens analogy provided the concept of achievement with an icon. However, in the verbal rendition it assumed in 1943, it must have appeared less of an icon and more of a far-fetched analogy by a perceptual psychologist to his audience.

In subsequent years the lens analogy did not appear prominently in Brunswik's writing. There is, however, a notable exception: a minutely detailed "schema" of size constancy that appeared as Fig. 10 in a booklet published in 1947 in the University of California Syllabus Series. This text was republished in 1956 as part 1 of Brunswik's well-known *Perception and the Representative Design of Psychological Experiments*. In part 2 of this book, which was written in the 1950s, Brunswik (1956, p. 141) referred to the "schema" of size constancy as "the lens-like model in figure 10." Originally, in 1947, the figure had not been described in those terms. Chances are that in 1947 Brunswik did not even conceive of this figure in terms of a "lens." (Figure 10 was probably constructed as an extension of a figure that Brunswik had introduced in 1940 to illustrate the application of correlational statistics to constancy research; see Brunswik, 1940,

p. 72, Table 2; redrawn in Brunswik, 1956, p. 69, Fig. 17.) Further support for this interpretation can be drawn from the fact that Brunswik, in preparing for the text's republication (see Brunswik, 1956, preface), inserted a passage to the original text of part 1 where "Figure 10" is mentioned in close proximity to Bühler's duplicity principle (Brunswik, 1956, p. 23). In this inserted passage Brunswik (1956, p. 23) alluded to "naturally grown and artificial lenses" as manifesting the principle of a stabilization mechanism and then referred the reader to his study of 1952 in which he spelled out the lens model. Thus, it seems possible, even likely, that aspects of what later would constitute the lens model were developed independently of the lens analogy and were only subsequently assimilated to this analogy. We consider next two such lens model "ingredients," namely, ecological validity and cue hierarchy, before turning to Brunswik's introduction of the lens model in 1952.

As mentioned before, the initial years in the United States were a transition period for Brunswik. The experimental studies he carried out in those years were attempts to extend the scope of psychophysics and to lead psychophysics in a more biological direction. In the 1940s this general aim gave way to the formulation of *probabilistic functionalism*, a program aimed at an "ecological psychology" (Brunswik, 1943, p. 271). Brunswik viewed Tolman's purposive behaviorism as a related but distinct approach toward the same general aim. A core concept in Brunswik's ecological psychology was ecological validity, and it, too, was not achieved in one step but in iterations. In 1944, Brunswik spoke of "the 'ecological' correlation" (p. 46) when he referred to the correlation between the objectively measured sizes of objects and their retinal or projective size. This was new terminology and conceptually one step beyond referring to this correlation merely by the mathematical designation r (as in Brunswik, 1940). By 1947, Brunswik referred to this correlation, and in general to a correlation relating one feature of the environment with another, as "ecological validity" (p. 37). However, the net was cast wider than correlational statistics.

The "methodological counterpart of probabilistic functionalism" was, in Brunswik's words, "the necessity of representative design of experiments" (1949–1950, p. 61). Brunswik found the traditional experimental design of controlled manipulation of one or a few independent variables too narrow a conception for psychology. A functional psychology that is concerned with achievement has to take strides to secure "ecological generality" of results in a very fundamental way (Brunswik, 1956, p. 38). Against isolation and controlled manipulation of variables, he set a "laissez-faire policy for the ecology" (Brunswik, 1955, p. 198). Such a policy would include the sampling of situations with the aim of capturing representative variation and covariation of variables. Brunswik found correlational statistics especially amenable to an experimental policy of noninterference with the ecology and the measurement of the limited validity of perceptual cues. But again, Brunswik conceived of ecological validity in broader terms, namely, as "the trustworthiness, or statistical validity, of cue-to-object relationships" (1949–1950, p. 60), which, as he later put it, "may in first approximation be expressed by a correlation coefficient" (Brunswik, 1955, p. 198).

Cues pointing to the same "object," for instance, depth cues such as binocular disparity, interception, linear perspective, or space filling, could vary in ecological validity and thus hierarchies of such cues according to their validity could be formed. This ordering according to ecological validity, which also found its way into the graphical representation (ordering them top down from highest to lowest, for instance in Fig. 10 of Brunswik, 1947/1956), was very different from the earlier distinction between "central" and "marginal rays" that had dominated Brunswik's early lens analogy (see previous quotes from Brunswik, 1937). With this change in the interpretation of cues, Brunswik had untied his account of perceptual constancy from its roots in Bühler's duplicity principle and the corresponding lens analogy. In fact, he had pointed to an alternative interpretation of the usefulness of cues all along, namely, their characterization by adjectives such as misleading, nonsignificant, or reliable that Tolman and Brunswik had presented in their joint article of 1935. However, and by contrast to this earlier way of differentiating between cues, the cues were ordered along one dimension from most valid to less valid, also numerically. This ordering of cues was described as a hierarchy. As metaphors, "hierarchy" and "arch" dominated his "schema" of size constancy of 1947. The latter was drawn as a semicircle connecting variables, especially the distal variable of measured physical size with judged size.

When the lens reappeared as a graphical representation in 1952 it had a new look about it (see Brunswik, 1952, p. 678, Fig. 1). It combined the earlier lens analogy with a hierarchical ordering of cues, specifically, a column of cues labeled "vicarious mediation (family-hierarchy of cues, habits)," which represented the lens. Similarly, the metaphor of the arch entered as "functional arc," again connecting variables. Brunswik inserted a number of further considerations into the graph, such as "stray causes" pointing as arrows to and from the lens, and a " 'feedback' loop" (p. 678). These additions, as well as the designation of the rays on both sides of the lens as "process detail," indicated a new influence on Brunswik's work, and more generally on psychology as a discipline, which was cybernetics (pp. 743–750).

Once again, in 1952, the lens analogy was brought in to signify a unifying basis for psychology. And, again, the lens analogy provided an icon for the advocated functional approach and the concepts of achievement and vicarious functioning, in particular. As with the first rendition of the analogy in graphical form, the lens model embodied a principle, only this time it was not Bühler's "duplicity principle" but rather the "principle of vicarious functioning" (Brunswik, 1952, p. 679; Gigerenzer & Kurz, 2001).

One is left to speculate why Brunswik chose to label his new rendering of the analogy a model. However, one can get some indication from the way he approached a unifying basis of science and, particularly, of psychology. Not by chance was his 1952 article published in the *International Encyclopedia of Unified Science*. As mentioned at the beginning of this chapter, he shared the logical positivists' concern with the unity of science but approached the issue very much in the way that Bühler, who was not a logical positivist, had advocated (see Kamp, 1984). Bühler had proposed a framework for psychology, advocating a strategy according to which its "guiding principles" (Leitsätze) had to be of a double nature: (a) extracted from the knowledge available in a domain and (b) the product of the direct study of phenomena. Brunswik took both parts very seriously, and the analysis of the available knowledge as it affects theoretical positions in psychology was always a major concern for him. Thus, one could argue that vicarious functioning became *his* guiding principle, and consequently, the lens analogy became a model to be applied to particular areas within psychology.

Indeed, in 1955 Brunswik presented a graphical representation subtitled: "The lens model as *applied* [italics added] to perceptual constancy" (adapted from Brunswik, 1952, p. 206). Figure 13.1 reproduces Brunswik's "application." It truly was an icon, and it functioned as model in other areas of psychology, most prominently in research on judgment and decision making (see Hammond & Stewart, 2001; Kurz-Milcke & Martignon, 2002). This lens model was no

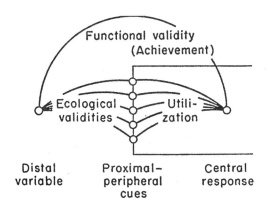

FIG. 13.1.   An icon: The lens model as applied to perceptual constancy. For example, the distal variable in this model might be physical size. In that case, the proximal peripheral cues would be retinal size and distance cues (retinal disparity, linear perspective, etc.). Each proximal–peripheral cue has a particular limited ecological validity or trustworthiness, which can be represented by a correlation between the values of that cue and the distal variable. Correspondingly, cue utilization can be indicated by the correlations between values of the proximal–peripheral cues and the central response. The degree of perceptual constancy achieved is functional validity—a measure that relates the values of the distal variable and the central response (from Brunswik, 1955, p. 206).

longer only informed by a lens analogy but also by other metaphors, such as hierarchy and arch; it was a mixed metaphor and has been ever since.

CONCLUSION

Brunswik died by his own hand on July 7, 1955, in Berkeley, California. Tolman wrote a brief, traditional obituary for *Science* magazine and a longer "eulogy" in the *American Journal of Psychology* (Tolman, 1955, 1956, reprinted in Hammond, 1966). The latter was really a means of once again drawing the discipline's attention to the creative, if somewhat unorthodox, views of a brilliant man. This chapter has emphasized the period just after Brunswik arrived in the United States, a period of transition. In a way, the development of the lens analogy into the lens model brackets this transition period: Still in Vienna, Brunswik designed a geometrical lens analogy (using only straight lines); at the end of the transition stood an icon, called the lens model (dominated by curved lines). Leary (1987) concluded his assessment of Brunswik's legacy for psychology by pointing out that "his system represented many of the major trends that have emerged more clearly into view in the years since [his] death. Brunswik foresaw and advocated the emergence of probabilism, psychological ecology, perception, and cognition as key areas of psychological interest" (p. 137).

ACKNOWLEDGMENT

Some sections of this chapter are based on presentations by the second author at the International Congress of Psychology, Stockholm, Sweden, and the meeting of the International Society for Comparative Psychology, Warsaw, Poland, July 2000.

REFERENCES

Ash, M. (2001). Egon Brunswik vor und nach der Emigration—Wissenschaftshistorische Aspekte [Egon Brunswik before and after emigration: History of science aspects]. In K. R. Hammond & T. R. Stewart (Eds.), *The essential Brunswik: Beginnings, explications, applications* (pp. 453–464). New York: Oxford University Press.

Benetka, G. (1995). *Psychologie in Wien: Sozial- und Theoriegeschichte des Wiener Psychologischen Instituts, 1922–1938* [*Psychology in Vienna: Social and theoretical history of the Vienna Psychological Institute, 1922–1938*]. Vienna: Wiener Universitätsverlag.

Brunswik, E. (1927). *Strukturmonismus und Physik* [Structural monism and physics]. Unpublished doctoral dissertation, University of Vienna.

Brunswik, E. (1934). *Wahrnehmung und Gegenstandswelt—Grundlegung einer Psychologie vom Gegenstand her* [Perception and the world of objects: The foundations of psychology in terms of objects]. Leipzig and Vienna: Deuticke.

Brunswik, E. (1935). *Experimentelle Psychologie in Demonstrationen* [Experimental psychology in demonstrations]. Vienna: Springer.

Brunswik, E. (1937). Psychology as a science of objective relations. *Philosophy of Science, 4,* 227–260.

Brunswik, E. (1939). Probability as determiner of rat behavior. *Journal of Experimental Psychology, 25,* 175–197.

Brunswik, E. (1940). Thing constancy as measured by correlation coefficients. *Psychological Review, 47,* 69–78.

Brunswik, E. (1943). Organismic achievement and environmental probability. *Psychological Review, 50,* 255–272.

Brunswik, E. (1944). Distal focussing of perception: Size-constancy in a representative sample of situations. *Psychological Monographs, 56,* 1–49.

Brunswik, E. (1947). *Systematic and representative design of psychological experiments: With results in physical and social perception.* Berkeley: University of California Press. (Republished as part 1 in Brunswik, 1956)

Brunswik, E. (1949–1950). Discussion: Remarks on functionalism in perception. *Journal of Personality, 18,* 56–65.

Brunswik, E. (1952). The conceptual framework of psychology. In O. Neurath, R. Carnap, & C. Morris (Eds.), *International encyclopedia of Unified Science* (Vol. 1, No. 10, pp. 655–750). Chicago: University of Chicago Press.

Brunswik, E. (1955). Representative design and probabilistic theory in a functional psychology. *Psychological Review, 62,* 193–217.

Brunswik, E. (1956). *Perception and the representative design of psychological experiments.* Berkeley: University of California Press.

Bühler, C. (1965). Die Wiener Psychologische Schule in der Emigration [The Vienna psychological school in emigration]. *Psychologische Rundschau, 16,* 187–196.

Bühler, C. (1972). Charlotte Bühler. In J. Pongratz, W. Traxel, & E. G. Wehner (Eds.), *Psychologie in Selbstdarstellungen* (pp. 9–42). Bern, Switzerland: Huber.

Bühler, K. (1927). *Die Krise der Psychologie* [The crisis of psychology]. Jena, Germany: Fischer.

Cooksey, R. W. (1996). The methodology of social judgment theory. *Thinking and Reasoning, 2,* 141–173.

Cronbach, L. J. (1957). The two disciplines of scientific psychology. *American Psychologist, 12,* 671–684.

Doherty, M. E., & Kurz, E. M. (1996). Social judgment theory. *Thinking and Reasoning, 2,* 109–140.

Fleming, D., & Bailyn, B. (Eds.) (1969). *The intellectual migration; Europe and America, 1930–1960.* Cambridge, MA: Belknap.

Gigerenzer, G. (1987). Survival of the fittest probabilist: Brunswik, Thurstone, and the two disciplines of psychology. In L. Krüger, G. Gigerenzer, & M. S. Morgan (Eds.), *The probabilistic revolution* (Vol. 2, pp. 49–72). Cambridge, MA: MIT Press.

Gigerenzer, G., & Kurz, E. M. (2001). Vicarious functioning reconsidered: A fast and frugal lens model. In K. R. Hammond & T. R. Stewart, (Eds.), *The essential Brunswik: Beginnings, explications, applications* (pp. 342–347). New York: Oxford University Press.

Gigerenzer, G., & Murray, D. (1987). *Cognition as intuitive statistics.* Hillsdale, NJ: Lawrence Erlbaum Associates, Inc.

Gooding, D. (1992). The procedural turn; or, how do thought experiments work? In R. N. Giere (Ed.), *Cognitive models of science* (Minnesota Studies in the Philosophy of Science, Vol. 15, pp. 45–76). Minneapolis: University of Minnesota Press.

Hammond, K. R. (1966). *The psychology of Egon Brunswik.* New York: Holt, Rinehart & Winston.

Hammond, K. R., & Stewart, T. R. (Eds.). (2001). *The essential Brunswik: Beginnings, explications, applications.* New York: Oxford University Press.

Heiman, N., & Grant, J. (Eds.). (1974). *Else Frenkel-Brunswik: Selected papers.* New York: International University Press.

Hurvich, L. M., & Jameson, D. (1966). *The perception of brightness and darkness.* Boston: Allyn & Bacon.

Innis, N. K. (1997). A purposive behaviorist: Edward C. Tolman. In W. G. Bringmann, H. E. Leuck, R. Miller, & C. E. Early (Eds.), *A pictorial history of psychology* (pp. 214–220). Carol Stream, IL: Quintessence.

Kamp, R. (1984). Axiomatische Leitfäden statt dogmatischer Gängelbänder: Karl Bühlers Beitrag zur Wissenschaftstheorie der Einzelwissenschaften [Axiomatic guiding principles instead of dogmatic leading-strings: Karl Bühler's contribution to the epistemology of the individual sciences]. In A. Eschbach (Ed.), *Bühler Studien* (pp. 40–97). Frankfurt, Germany: Suhrkamp.

Kurz, E. M., & Hertwig, R. (2001). To know an experimenter. In K. R. Hammond & T. R. Stewart (Eds.), *The essential Brunswik: Beginnings, explications, applications* (pp. 180–191). New York: Oxford University Press.

Kurz, E. M., & Tweney, R. D. (1997). The heretical psychology of Egon Brunswik. In W. G. Bringmann, H. E. Lueck, R. Miller, & C. E. Early (Eds.), *A pictorial history of psychology* (pp. 221–232). Carol Stream, IL: Quintessence.

Kurz-Milcke, E., & Martignon, L. (2002). Modeling practices and tradition. In L. Magnani & N. Nersessian (Eds.), *Model-based reasoning: Scientific discovery, technological innovation, values* (pp. 127–146). New York: Kluwer Academic/Plenum.

Leary, D. E. (1987). From act psychology to probabilistic functionalism: The place of Egon Brunswik in the history of psychology. In M. G. Ash & W. R. Woodward (Eds.), *Psychology in twentieth century thought* (pp. 115–142). New York: Cambridge University Press.

Rucci, A., & Tweney, R. D. (1980). Analysis of variance and the "second discipline" of scientific psychology: An historical account. *Psychological Bulletin, 87,* 166–184.

Tolman, E. C. (1932). *Purposive behavior in animals and men.* New York: Century.

Tolman, E. C. (1935). [Review of the book *Wahrnehmung und Gegenstandswelt—Grundlegung einer Psychologie vom Gegenstand her*]. *Psychological Bulletin, 32,* 608–613.

Tolman, E. C. (1952). Edward Chace Tolman. In E. G. Boring, H. S. Langfeld, H. Werner, & R. M. Yerkes (Eds.), *A history of psychology in autobiography* (Vol. 4, pp. 323–339). Worcester, MA: Clark University Press.

Tolman, E. C. (1955). Egon Brunswik, psychologist and philosopher of science. *Science, 122,* 910.

Tolman, E. C. (1956). Egon Brunswik: 1903–1955. *American Journal of Psychology, 69,* 315–342.

Tolman, E. C., & Brunswik, E. (1935). The organism and the causal texture of the environment. *Psychological Review, 42,* 43–77.

Tolman, E. C., & Krechevsky, I. (1933). Means-end-readiness and hypothesis. A contribution to the comparative psychology of learning. *Psychological Review, 40,* 60–70.

Chapter 14

Leona Tyler:
Pioneer of Possibilities

Ruth E. Fassinger
University of Maryland at College Park

> *[Understanding comes from] looking out through a clean, clear window*
> *with no obstacles between you and what you are doing. . . . You look out*
> *through your own persona, not into it.*
> —Leona Tyler (in Gilmore, 1977, p. 458)

Leona Tyler was born in the first decade of the 20th century and died in its last decade. Her first published article in psychology appeared on the eve of World War II and the last was a chapter published in the mid-1990s, 2 years after her death. Tyler was a key participant in the development of both the science and the profession of psychology during the second half of the century, serving a crucial role as a synthesizer and interpreter of psychological research for audiences with applied concerns. She was a pioneer in the field of individual differences, did significant work in the measurement of interest, and developed her own "possibility theory" to explain how individuality is expressed through personal choices. She was highly instrumental in the development and definition of the field of counseling psychology and left her enduring mark on countless numbers of applied psychologists in their practice of counseling and psychotherapy.

CHILDHOOD AND EARLY EDUCATION

I grew up believing that life has a purpose, that it is required that one cultivate and use his or her talents to help others, that integrity is far more important than popularity or personal happiness.—Leona Tyler (in Gilmore, 1977, p. 452)

Leona Elizabeth Tyler was born May 10, 1906, on a small farm in Chetek, Wisconsin, the first child of Leon M. and Bessie J. Carver Tyler, poor but dignified people who proudly traced their ancestry on both sides back to the American Revolution. Leon was a farmer and bookkeeper who dabbled in real estate and the renovation of houses; Bessie was a housewife and former country school teacher. Three younger brothers followed Leona, and Tyler later described herself as a serene, contented, affable child in a close-knit family.

Tyler's family held strong fundamentalist Protestant religious convictions, and Tyler's mother was particularly strict. Although Bessie Tyler treated her children equally in her expectations of achievement, she imposed greater restrictions on her daughter's behavior based on biblical injunctions regarding women. Tyler later noted that the "general religious attitude and high moral principles instilled in me at that time have persisted long after their dogmatic foundation disintegrated" (in Gilmore, 1977, p. 452). She described painful conflicts with her fundamentalist mother as she grew into adulthood and chose paths that challenged that dogma.

When she was 6, Tyler's family moved to the Mesabi Iron Range in northern Minnesota and Tyler spent her school years in the small mining towns of Hibbing and Virginia in this beautiful, wild country populated mostly by Scandinavian, Italian, Yugoslavian, and Cornish immigrants. Tyler (in Gilmore, 1977, p. 452) described the area as backwoods and primitive in many ways, but also as "an extraordinarily cosmopolitan setting" because of tax revenues from the booming mining industry that brought a great deal of cultural enrichment to these communities—large schools with excellent teachers, libraries, and frequent traveling cultural events. Tyler also was taught by her mother at an early age to play the piano, instilling a passion for music that would last Tyler's entire life.

Already reading before she entered school, the precocious Tyler completed the first six grades in only 3 years. The age gap between Tyler and her schoolmates, exacerbated by the religious constraints on her activities (dancing, for example, was strictly forbidden), made social life exceedingly difficult for Tyler. She spent much time alone, immersed in music and literature, and developing a reserve that would characterize her throughout her life. Tyler described herself in adolescence as neither popular nor conspicuous. She participated in no extracurricular activities, was socially introverted and awkward, and felt quite set apart from her peers: "There are very few people in the world like me; . . . it's like being a different species. . . . I like other people and get along with them well . . . but when I find someone of my own species that is a real special occasion" (in Gilmore, 1977, p. 452). Tyler slowly came to identify difference that separated her from other students as that of being an intellectual, as the aesthetic values she was adopting through her dedication to music and books began to replace her family's constrictive religiosity and moral values.

Although neither of Tyler's parents had been educated beyond high school, they respected and nurtured intelligence; books and magazines were read and discussed regularly in the household. Leon and Bessie Tyler valued education highly, and despite the lack of a strong intellectual tradition in the extended family (most of the women having been schoolteachers and most of the men farmers or small business proprietors waiting to strike it rich), they expected that all of their children would attend college.

Tyler graduated from high school at 15, planning to follow in the footsteps of her mother and aunts and become a schoolteacher—one of the few occupations thought suitable for women in the early 1900s. An assistant principal in her high school, recognizing Tyler's exceptional abilities, warned her not to go to a teachers' college (the most common educational route for women at the time), but to a university instead. However, her family's meager financial circumstances dictated that Tyler complete college as cheaply as possible, so she attended the newly organized Virginia Junior College in her hometown for 2 years. After that, she transferred to the University of Minnesota, where she had to work part time to meet her educational expenses.

Tyler wanted to major in chemistry, having experienced overpowering awe when she first discovered the universal order embodied in the periodic table of elements and the structure of organic compounds, presaging her lifelong appreciation of orderly and systematic ways of dealing with knowledge. Having emphasized literature in high school, however, she lacked the necessary prerequisites for a chemistry major and could not afford the extra year to catch up. Moreover, she was expected to graduate quickly and help put her brothers through college. So, Tyler majored in English, in part because she had a notion of becoming a writer some day and in part because this major allowed her to read the many books she had been wanting to read. But she also took advanced math courses, in case the opportunity ever arose for her to pursue a career in science.

Tyler described her undergraduate years as ones of "omniverous reading" in which she completed her assignments as quickly as possible so that she could spend all of her spare time in the beautifully furnished Upson Library at the university, which she described as "my real spiritual home" where "I could continue my relationship with books of my own choosing" (in Gilmore, 1977, p. 452). Tyler claimed no mentors or role models during this time, but rather felt that her education had come from books, not teachers. It is interesting that for someone who was later to become a president of APA, Tyler initially rejected psychology because the one course she took in junior college was "poorly taught and seemed very dull" (p. 452). Tyler graduated from Minnesota in 1925 at the age of 19, the first person in her family to obtain a college degree.

TEACHING CAREER AND DOCTORAL EDUCATION

It is obvious that no one begins life as a psychologist. For me this identity was not achieved until more than thirty years of my life had passed. The fact that during my youth and early adulthood I had no thought of professional psychology as a ca-

reer undoubtedly influenced the shape that career took after it was initiated.—
Leona Tyler (1978b, p. 289)

Bachelor's degree and teaching certificate in hand, Tyler spent the first 13 years
of her career as a junior high school teacher in Mt. Iron, Minnesota, and
Muskegon Heights, Michigan, putting her education to the practical use of providing income to her family and consonant with the expectations of women in
her day. Tyler viewed teaching junior high subjects as a step up from the country schools in which her mother and aunts had taught, and the roots of her entry
into psychology can be traced to these early career experiences. Tyler enjoyed
teaching (mathematics as well as English), but found the maintenance of classroom discipline both stressful and distasteful: "I was not the sort of person who
'commands respect,' . . . a person whom it is natural for others to obey without
question" (in Gilmore, 1977, p. 453). Stimulated by the need to anticipate and prevent trouble in maintaining classroom order, Tyler increasingly found herself interested in understanding and predicting human behavior. She also experienced
great curiosity and pleasure in reading student essays written for her English
classes—essays in which she glimpsed their individual struggles and aspirations
as they dealt with self-discovery and decisions in their lives. These experiences
formed the foundation of Tyler's later psychological research in interest and
choice. They also help account for the concern with helping young people that
would continue throughout her career.

The final root of Tyler's interest in psychology was in her activities outside
the classroom and her growing sense of self. During this time, Tyler's self-
confidence and self-assurance increased, and she became more socially at ease.
These changes permitted Tyler to become involved in community social and political activities for the first time, and she experienced the first of a number of
close friendships with men that she would enjoy throughout her life. Tyler was
passionate about experiencing, discussing, and sharing music, and was making
many musical discoveries at the time that were very significant to her. Forced by
lack of income to return to her family home every summer, Tyler took advantage of the time to read and play the piano without interruption.

Unfortunately, at this time, however, Tyler found herself arguing increasingly
with her mother about drinking, smoking, and bobbed hair, and she began to reject the strict conservatism of her family with even greater determination than
she had before. Describing this as a "time of liberation and transformation," Tyler commented: "Slowly I found myself abandoning the dogmatic religion, the
self-righteous intolerance, and the conservative ideology I had grown up with
and becoming a vowed liberal, an internationalist, a supporter of unpopular
causes" (Tyler, 1988, p. 48). The chief of these unpopular causes was the peace
movement, an involvement that would continue throughout her life and lead her
directly into psychology. Wanting to understand why rational human beings engage repeatedly in the irrational activity of waging war, Tyler decided in 1936 to

pursue a master's degree in psychology. Again, because of financial constraints and family obligations, she planned to live at home in St. Paul, where her family had relocated, and to work toward her degree during several summers at the University of Minnesota.

As it turned out, this decision, though based solely on financial considerations, was fortunate for Tyler. The "attitude of tolerant skepticism" that Tyler found in Minnesota's famed "dust bowl empiricism" (in Gilmore, 1977, p. 456), as well as the applied and counseling emphases in psychology at the university, created the perfect atmosphere for Tyler to apply her penchant for mathematical rigor to the understanding of human concerns. In the summer of 1937, she took a course from one of psychology's most prominent figures in individual differences, Donald G. Paterson, who, recognizing Tyler's prodigious talent, requested an interview with her to discuss her plans. This interview, commented Tyler, "changed the whole pattern of my life; . . . the direction of my intellectual efforts for the rest of my life was set then" (Tyler, 1988, p. 49). Paterson arranged a graduate assistantship for Tyler so that she could afford to attend graduate school full time, and worked out a plan for a master's thesis on the interests of high school girls that Tyler could undertake during her last year of teaching, bridging her dozen years of working with adolescents and the research in interests that she would come to do. She later commented, "At the end of this one interview, I was no longer a struggling junior high school teacher but a prospective psychologist" and then confessed with characteristic modesty, "I was pleased but incredulous. I could not possibly be as able as he seemed to think I was, but I would do everything in my power not to disappoint him" (p. 49).

Thus, from 1938 to 1940, Tyler spent 2 years of "sheer delight" obtaining her doctorate in psychology, with a minor in statistics, at Minnesota, where "to spend the best hours of the day reading and studying . . . was almost too good to be true" (Tyler, 1988, p. 49). Minnesota's leadership in individual differences, psychometrics (particularly interest measurement), and developmental and vocational psychology created a fertile ground for Tyler's blossoming focus on the three areas in which she would make significant contributions throughout her career: individual differences, interest measurement and research, and counseling.

In addition to the mentoring Tyler received from Paterson, she was strongly influenced by Florence Goodenough, the prominent developmental psychologist (whose textbook Tyler later would revise), and by Richard Elliott, who became Tyler's lifelong friend and the editor of her early books. Tyler was so stimulated and happy at Minnesota that she might have lingered, except that ever-escalating conflicts with her mother—who viewed psychology with skepticism and believed that her daughter's pursuit of it marked failings in her own mothering—spurred Tyler to finish her dissertation in 1940 (with her doctorate conferred in 1941) and leave the family home as quickly as she could.

In those days it was still possible to read all of psychology's great books and keep up with all current work reported in the journals in the field, and Tyler, voracious reader that she was, came close to achieving this objective. She enjoyed gleaning ideas from diverse sources and combining them in unique ways, a strength that characterized her work throughout her career, making her a superb integrator and translator of psychological research. For her doctoral dissertation, she developed an interest test for high school girls, laying the foundation for work she would continue through five decades of her career as a psychologist, and for her first book on individual differences (Tyler, 1947, revised in 1956 and 1965).

By this time, the influence of William James (chap. 2, *Pioneers I*) was making itself felt in Tyler's thinking, and she was particularly struck by several lines in James's *Principles*: "The mind is at every stage a theatre of simultaneous possibilities" but "with most objects of desire, physical nature restricts our choice to but one of many represented goods. . . . [One must review the list of possibilities] carefully and pick out the one on which to stake his salvation. . . . I am often confronted by the necessity of standing by one of my empirical selves and relinquishing the rest" (James, 1890, pp. 288–289, 309–310). As we shall see, these lines found their way into Tyler's own theorizing about possibility and choice: the "possibility theory" that she would develop more fully in the next stage of her career.

THE UNIVERSITY OF OREGON

The value of such diversified experience [at Oregon] is that it requires one constantly to reevaluate one's ideas and concepts and to combine them in new ways.—Leona Tyler (1978b, p. 294)

When, in 1940, Tyler accepted a position in the psychology department at the University of Oregon in Eugene—as the fourth member and the only woman on the faculty—she found a home where she would remain for the rest of her life. Paterson again had intervened on Tyler's behalf, urging her to take the position as lecturer in the department and head of the Personnel Research Bureau. Tyler noted, "I was asked if I would like to go to Oregon, was recommended, and was accepted for the position before I had even filled out an application blank. It seems that the 'old boy' network occasionally let an 'old girl' through" (Tyler, 1988, p. 50).

Once again, Tyler seemed to fit perfectly in her new environment. She fell in love with the wild natural beauty of Oregon—the Pacific Ocean, the mountains, the deep green valley between. Moreover, the small department fostered the expression of Tyler's broad range of interests. Well accepted by both the basic and applied psychologists in the department, she was promoted through the ranks, becoming full professor in 1955.

Tyler was a gifted teacher and taught many courses over the years. In addition to testing, individual differences, and counseling that were her own specialty areas (she taught the first clinical and counseling methods courses ever offered in the department), she also taught most of the rest of the psychology curriculum: general, experimental, abnormal, child, adolescent, educational, and social psychology. During the shortages of faculty in World War II, she even taught mathematics. She was a very popular mentor for graduate students who sought her out, not only because of her knowledge of statistics and methodology, but also because she was unfailingly kind, helpful, and generous (stories of her sharing books from her personal library with students abound; see Delworth, 2000; Gilmore, 1977).

Tall and dignified, Tyler was firm and disciplined, and she commanded great respect from students, to whom she was able to express warm sympathy without fostering dependency. She also possessed a rather droll sense of humor that was surprising in one characterized by such reserve and propriety (Norman Sundberg, April 20, 2001, personal communication). During her years as a faculty member, she advised more master's and doctoral students than any other faculty member, including many students outside her own department.

Concerned as always with the needs of young people, Tyler founded a counseling service for students at the university; she continued counseling work for one fourth to one third of her time throughout her career. Warm, wise, pragmatic, and open in her counseling style, Tyler valued highly the opportunity to integrate counseling with her research and teaching. These components formed a mutually enriching system of professional activities that allowed her to produce a body of writing that is rigorous in its careful presentation of comprehensive and accurate science, and relevant to a wide range of practical concerns.

Tyler remained a committed pacifist, and during World War II she extended her counseling work to include weekly visits to conscientious objectors in the reforestation camp at Elkton in the Coast Range. After the war, she obtained Veteran's Administration funding to expand the university counseling service to meet the needs of returning veterans and to establish it as a permanent center in the university. Tyler also was a founder of the rehabilitation and counseling psychology programs at Oregon and became a force to be reckoned with in university affairs. Seen as "neither soft soap nor bludgeon in her approach," Tyler was organized, decisive, and rational in her task focus, but also direct, honest, and fair in her relationships with others, so she was sought out often for her trustworthiness, mettle, and "warm intelligence" (Sundberg & Littman, 1994, p. 212).

Tyler's years at Oregon highlighted her enormous capacity to create and maintain friendships, including friendships with male colleagues Robert Campbell, Richard Littman, and Robert Leeper. She credited Leeper with moving her away from the strict behaviorism she had learned at Minnesota to the cognitive approach that dominated her later theoretical work. In particular, Norman Sundberg, who arrived at Oregon in 1952—his decision strongly affected by having encountered Tyler's friendliness and forthrightness when she interviewed him— became a dear friend, frequent coinvestigator and coauthor, and champion of her ideas and work. Tyler and several colleagues and their families bought land and built houses together on the same street—which came to be called "Psychopath" because so many psychologists lived there. Tyler was considered the favorite "grand aunt" of the children in the neighborhood, who visited her with such frequency (occasionally crawling through the dog door) that Tyler took to tying green or red ribbons on her door to signal when a visit was welcome or when she did not wish to be disturbed. Tyler's sharp wit and ironic humor permeated her relationships. Ever dedicated to her family, Tyler financially supported a young nephew during his "hippie phase" by quietly leaving cash for him in a volume of Adam Smith's *Wealth of Nations* (Deborah L. Tyler, July 11, 2001, personal communication). Tyler, who took her friendships seriously and entertained frequently, enjoyed good food and sherry. She was an excellent cook but seldom retained recipes because she liked trying something new. She remained an insatiable reader, averaging a novel a week (Jane Austen was her favorite author), and engaged in several other hobbies as well—in her official portrait at the University of Oregon she is wearing a dress that she knitted herself. She also continued in her dedication to pacifism, once using her own income to bring a promising young researcher from India to Oregon so that what it cost her would not go into taxes supporting the war in Vietnam (Norman Sundberg, April 20, 2001, personal communication).

Tyler declared her years at Oregon to be the happiest in her life: "For a confirmed aesthete and nature lover, the sheer physical beauty of the surroundings was a constant inspiration. I was surrounded by people I like and who liked me—faculty members, graduate students, students in my classes. I was free to do the things I most wanted to do—initiate a research program, organize a part-time counseling service, write a new textbook on individual differences. . . . I considered myself a great success" (Tyler, 1988, p. 50).

The book to which Tyler refers is her 1947 book, *The Psychology of Human Differences* (revised in 1956 and 1965) which became one of the major textbooks in the field. Like all the works that Tyler generated throughout her highly productive career, this book was created during 2 disciplined hours of writing at the beginning of every morning—written out by hand on yellow legal paper and later typed with very few changes. Tyler felt strongly that textbook writing is an important adjunct to empirical research. It keeps one open to important developments both in and outside the field, and thus prevents one from becoming too narrowly focused and specialized. It forces the organization, synthesis, and interpretation of large and disparate bodies of knowledge in order to make sense of them—for oneself as well as others. Because Tyler was such an outstanding integrator of science and practice, her textbooks are impeccably informed syntheses of diverse strands of knowledge. She was a "skilled and graceful writer" who strove for clarity of thought and possessed a gift for organizing large, complex ideas in deceptively simple (never simplistic) ways, rendering her books "models of lucidity, aptness, economy, mastery of material, and judiciousness of evaluations and conclusions" (Sundberg & Littman, 1994, p. 212).

What are the ideas in these books? Tyler's work over her years at Oregon gradually progressed from an early focus on measured interests at a given point as a key component of individual differences to a later focus on changes in interests over time and the cognitive structures underlying choice behavior. Tyler had noticed in her early longitudinal studies of children that dislikes and avoidances were more important than likes in determining interests. She also had noted gender differences in children's early lives that she suspected had an impact on interest development. She had begun reading Jean Piaget (chap. 9, *Pioneers III*) and Erik Erikson (whose influence in American psychology was not yet strong), and she became intrigued by the concept of qualitatively distinct cognitive developmental stages. This conception led to a shift in her focus from measurable traits, such as specific interests, to cognitive structures controlling choices.

In 1951–1952, Tyler spent a sabbatical year in London studying at Maudsley Hospital with Hans Eysenck (chap. 20, *Pioneers IV*) doing research on children's interests. As often occurs in foreign travel, a new world opened up for Tyler during this visit, and she reveled in London's rich cultural offerings. At a production of Jean Paul Sartre's play, *The Flies*, Tyler encountered existentialism for the first time, a very powerful experience for her. She soon became familiar with all of the major existential writers, drawn especially to the work of Karl Jaspers. Existential philosophy solidified her notions about the supreme importance of choices made by individuals, and she integrated these ideas into her growing focus on the cognitive organization of choice behavior. Increasingly dissatisfied with the limitations of psychometric practices of the time, Tyler also began to reconceptualize the measurement of choices and the cognitive structures that underlie them. She later noted that London was a turning point for her. She had begun to receive widespread recognition for her work and ideas, and when she returned to Oregon, her sense of self was transformed: "Just when I was transformed in my own eyes from an ordinary to an influential psychologist I cannot remember precisely, but the transformation did take place"; she then adds with characteristic modesty, "It did not change the core of my personality. I have never really felt like an important person, a leader in my field" (Tyler, 1988, p. 51).

During her year in London, Tyler began work on her second textbook, *The Work of the Counselor*, published in 1953 (with later editions in 1961 and 1965). An immediate success, it was the most widely used text in counseling for several decades, and it was read by thousands of counselors and psychologists in America, Europe, and Asia. Based on extensive research, Tyler's book represented a "unique blending of the concepts of Carl Rogers [chap. 15, *Pioneers III*], individual differences and psychometrics, psychoanalytic theory, behaviorism, developmental stage theory, and existentialism" (Zilber & Osipow, 1982, p. 337). Tyler viewed the purpose of counseling as encouraging natural lifelong development, "to facilitate wise choices of the sort on which the person's later development depends" (Tyler, 1965b, p. 13). According to Tyler (expressing ideas that hark back to James's *Principles of Psychology*), development consists of transforming a wide range of possibilities into more limited actualities. This process occurs unidirectionally over time, so some possibilities must be discarded, and individuals actively select, consciously or unconsciously, which potentialities will be actualized. The basic organizational structures for guiding and making choices develop—that is, become increasingly qualitatively complex—as a person matures. The job of the counselor is to help people examine their potentialities and make appropriate choices, and one of the things Tyler appreciated most about her own counseling work was watching clients choose paths that were different from hers, thereby allowing a brief glimpse of the road not taken (Delworth, 2000).

Thus, *The Work of the Counselor* presented Tyler's embryonic articulation of a theory of personality and life-span development centered on individual possibilities and choices, a theory that would be elaborated and sharpened in her later works. In addition, Tyler's assumption that the purpose of counseling is to help facilitate natural developmental processes explains her strong conviction about keeping the mission of counseling psychology distinct from that of clinical psychology and firmly rooted in normal development, including vocational decisions and choices. She would continue to advocate this position in one form or another until her death (e.g., Tyler, 1958, 1960, 1972, 1980, 1992). Her lucid image of counseling psychology as a distinct psychological specialty had profound impact on the definition, scope, and direction of this field as it emerged in the second half of the 20th century.

During this time, Tyler reconciled herself to remaining single. She always had expected to marry and have children, but several very special male friends (who she felt were of the "same species" as she) had been unavailable as romantic partners, and the idea of dating strangers as a means of searching for the right person felt dishonest and repugnant to her. She also noted that it had been exceedingly difficult for women to combine home and professional roles at that time: "I would have had to marry a man who would take care of my family, encourage my work, and overlook my lack of social skills" (Tyler, in Gilmore, 1977, p. 453). Tyler later acknowledged that remaining single had freed her from family responsibilities that surely would have interfered with her professional activities and allowed her to concentrate on her work as a psychologist with unusual clarity and focus: "Being on my own has contributed to my success, although it is not the life I would have chosen. 'She travels fastest who travels alone,' to adapt a famous quotation" (Tyler, 1988, p. 52). Freedom from obligations to a partner or children also permitted Tyler to maintain close bonds with her friends and extended family.

During the mid- to late-1950s, Tyler rose to positions of professional leadership in psychology. She served as president of the Oregon Psychological Association in 1956–1957 and then as president of the Western Psychological Association in 1957–1958 while she completed a year as a visiting professor at the University of California, Berkeley. Her presidential address, "Toward a Workable Psychology of Individuality" (Tyler, 1959), is particularly important because in it Tyler presents a clear articulation of ideas she had been developing for more than a decade on patterns of choice and possibility theory, with the concept of multiple possibilities as the cornerstone of her theorizing about individuality. She proposed that individuality is a product of *choice* and *organization*—that it stems from differences in the choices that different people make from among many alternatives, as well as the cognitive structures they use to organize their experiences. To better assess these choices and their underlying cognitive structures, Tyler developed the "Choice Pattern Technique," still used in various forms by career counselors. The Choice Pattern Technique is a card-sort method in which people express their preferences for occupations and free-time activities, and articulate the reasons behind those choices, thus revealing the cognitions guiding individual choice. Tyler's pioneering contributions in interest development, psychometrics, and counseling were at the leading edge of the then-evolving specialty of counseling psychology, and her ideas were exerting powerful influence on the direction the field would take; this impact was crystallized further when she served as president of APA's Division 17 (Counseling Psychology) in 1959–1960.

During this time, Tyler immersed herself further in developmental theory to collaborate with her old mentor Goodenough on the 1959 revision of Goodenough's *Developmental Psychology* text, incorporating the work of Piaget and Erikson before they had become widely influential in the United States (Zilber & Osipow, 1982). In 1962, Tyler published *Clinical Psychology* with her friend and colleague Sundberg. This text, which saw two revisions (1973 and 1983 with Julian Taplin), was the most widely used in the field at that time. Like Tyler's book on counseling, it influenced the clinical practice of generations of psychologists.

Tyler spent 1962–1963 in Amsterdam using her Choice Pattern Technique to study the interests, values, and time perspectives of Dutch and American male and female adolescents. Interested in testing the assumption that environment affects cognitive orientation and therefore choice, Tyler was one of a handful of midcentury psychologists concerned with cross-cultural issues. In 1963, by then considered a leading scholar in psychometrics, Tyler published *Tests and Measurements* (with later editions in 1971 and 1979). In 1964, she received the University of Minnesota's Distinguished Achievement Award.

During the last 6 years of her career at Oregon, 1965–1971, Tyler served as dean of the Graduate School, one of the very first female graduate deans in American universities. Never having sought leadership and never really seeing herself as a leader, Tyler felt that her rise to such positions simply came from her inclination to notice that something needed to be done and then taking the responsibility to do it. Tyler found the role of dean difficult to get used to because she always had assumed that such positions are unsuitable for women. She observed, "Had the opportunity come ten years later, after the resurgence of militant feminism, perhaps my struggle with myself would have been easier" (Tyler, 1988, p. 52). During her years as a university administrator, Tyler continued to write, producing new editions of previous books as well as editing *Intelligence: Some Recurring Issues* (Tyler, 1969). She also maintained her deep involvement in professional affairs, serving on the APA Board of Directors in 1966–1968 and then again in 1970–1974. In 1971, Tyler retired (at the then-mandatory age of 65) from the University of Oregon as professor and dean emerita, and received the Strong Gold Medal for Interest Measurement that same year.

LATER CAREER ACHIEVEMENTS

Had anyone predicted at the beginning of my career that I would one day be President of the American Psychological Association, I would have viewed such a prediction as sheer fantasy.—Leona Tyler (1978b, p. 300)

Formal retirement did not hamper Tyler's work in the least, and she remained intellectually and professionally active in her career for the next 20 years. An experienced freighter traveler, Tyler visited Australia, Europe, and Asia (where she met and interviewed Indira Gandhi), continued and extended her cross-cultural studies of adolescent interests and values, and wrote increasingly on broad professional and philosophical issues facing psychology in general and counseling psychology in particular. Tyler's own comment about retirement was that, because she saw herself as a writer, "retirement did not constitute a new situation for me as it does for many academicians. I went right on writing" (Tyler, 1988, p. 53).

In 1972, Tyler was elected the 81st president (only the fourth woman) of the APA, a very challenging job during some of APA's most turbulent years. As she had many years before, Tyler again used a presidential address as an opportunity for a wonderfully cogent presentation of her ideas, this time to introduce a vision of psychology healed of the ever-widening rift between its scientific and professional arms. Entitled "Design for a Hopeful Psychology" (Tyler, 1973), Tyler's address is surprisingly contemporary and relevant to the issues facing psychology today. She challenged psychology's deterministic obsession with attempting to predict and control behavior, and advocated the incorporation of free will and individual choice into conceptualizations of human behavior. She proposed that the purpose of assessment is better served by aiming toward self-understanding and self-knowledge, rather than toward selection or diagnosis. Tyler also criticized psychology's model of research, recommending the abandonment of methods borrowed from physics and biology and the creation of new methods more suitable for "sciences in which the scientist, subject, and consumer all belong to the same species" (Tyler, 1973, p. 1024). She also implored psychologists to make their research more useful to participants and their communities. Finally, Tyler applauded the articulation of ethical codes to guide research and practice. It is interesting that in 1990, toward the end of her life, Tyler commented on re-reading this address that the future of psychology looked even less promising to her than it had previously, with little or no progress made in solving the problems she had delineated two decades earlier (Sundberg, 1993).

In 1974, Tyler published *Individual Differences: Abilities and Motivational Directions*, and in 1978, she published *Individuality: Human Possibilities and Personal Choice in the Psychological Development of Men and Women*, which contains the clearest articulation of what Tyler by then had termed "possibility theory," her principal theoretical contribution to psychology. According to Tyler, individual lives consist of a series of turning points in which many choices are available. Because time and physical and environmental circumstances dictate limits, personal development depends on selecting and actualizing the most viable possibilities from the vast array within reach. Choices made reveal values, they represent what individuals find desirable, and they are rooted in cognitive structures that organize the process of choosing. When one of many possible selves is chosen for actualization, other selves are repressed.

In this final elucidation of her possibility theory, Tyler's progression as a thinker is illuminated clearly. Always flexible in her conceptualizations, Tyler had moved from the narrow perspective of individual differences to broader concerns regarding individuality, from a merely psychometric approach to a systems-ecological view of real-world choices, and from a limited consideration of concrete vocational interests to an expansive reflection on various selves that a person might actualize (Sundberg, 1993; Sundberg & Littman, 1994). Becoming more contextually oriented over time, Tyler applauded the emergence of the field of social ecology, which she thought showed promise in explicating the interaction between person and environment (Delworth, 2000). In her growing emphasis on context, Tyler anticipated some of the most important advances in contemporary psychology.

In her 1983 book, *Thinking Creatively: A New Approach to Psychology and Individual Lives*, Tyler further elaborated possibility theory as a way to examine the scientific enterprise of psychology. She emphasized the idea that before an event occurs it is one of many possibilities that may not be seen unless searched out, and that conscious choice transforms multiple possibilities into deliberate action. Linking this concept to scientific inquiry, Tyler argued that discipline-based conformity and commonalities in the professional training of psychologists cause them to distort or limit their perceptions of methodological choices available to them, and that psychological science would be better served if different research paradigms could coexist and inform one another.

Tyler's work garnered her many honors toward the end of her life—awards and honorary degrees from several universities, the American Board of Professional Psychology's award for Outstanding Contribution to Professional Psychology (1984), and APA's prestigious Gold Medal Award for Life-Time Contribution in the Public Interest (1990). Tyler remained very active in local, state, and national boards and committees, including Amnesty International, Common Cause, and other peace organizations.

Shortly after retiring, Tyler had moved to a small cottage at Heceta Beach on the Oregon coast, where her vintage Corona electric typewriter sat beside shelves full of the Harvard classics, and her baby grand piano faced the window so that she could gaze out to sea while she played (Arnold, 1980). Although she regularly attended a Christian church, Tyler experienced God through music (Deborah L. Tyler, July 11, 2001, personal communication) and remained a dedicated pianist and faithful patron of the annual Bach festival and other local musical events. With her beloved golden retriever Sheila, Tyler walked 2–4 miles on the beach every day, glimpsing dunes deer, sea lions, California gray whales, and other wildlife of the Oregon coast (Arnold, 1980). Eventually, deteriorating health forced Tyler's move to a retirement facility in Eugene, where, at almost 87 years old, she died of congestive heart failure on April 29, 1993. Vital and alert to the end, Tyler prohibited life-prolonging measures and spent her last days with a few close family members gathered at her side (Sundberg & Littman, 1994; Deborah L. Tyler, July 11, 2001, personal communication).

TYLER IN CONTEXT

> Throughout my entire life, being female has never made me feel inferior. I accepted many aspects of prevailing sex roles without thinking much about them, and I have probably been discriminated against on occasion, but I never had to struggle with such discrimination, and I never saw it as a tremendous obstacle.—Leona Tyler (1978b, p. 289)

Tyler came of age professionally between the two great women's movements of the 20th century, and thus was not the feminist activist she otherwise might have been (Delworth, 2000), especially given her interests in the effects of gender on development. Tyler's mother had believed firmly that the Nineteenth Amendment solved the problem of discrimination against women permanently and completely. This assumption seems to have been internalized by Tyler herself, who once commented, "My assumption that intelligent people no longer considered women inferior persisted. I never had occasion to question it" (Tyler, 1988, p. 50). Although she is one of the few women in psychology to claim no experiences of discrimination (Stevens & Garner, 1982), even the idealistic, optimistic Tyler realized in retrospect that progress in her career probably had been slower than it should have been because of sexism, and she acknowledged the importance of the women's movement in creating more favorable circumstances for women generally.

Almost certainly, Tyler's reserve, modesty, and reticence about pushing herself into the limelight, as well as her insistence on devoting significant amounts of her time to textbook writing, counseling, mentoring, music, community and professional service, teaching, and university administration—in short, the multipotentialities in her possibility theory as embodied in her own life (Zilber & Osipow, 1982)—prevented her from attaining the reputation as a theorist that she otherwise might have enjoyed. It is apparent, however, that acceptance by powerful male mentors and colleagues was instrumental in Tyler's entry into "the inner sancta of psychology's establishment" (Stevens & Gardner, 1982, p. 113), and she is one of the few women in the history of psychology who experienced such uniformly supportive relationships with men. Perhaps Tyler's freedom from domestic and childrearing responsibilities, her singular focus on her career, her obvious intellectual and scientific prowess, her personal dignity and no-nonsense style, and historical shifts in the acceptance of professional women all combined to secure her place among men who accepted her as a true peer.

Tyler received many of the most prestigious honors bestowed in the fields of psychology and counseling. The most coveted awards in the Oregon Counseling Association and in the counseling psychology division of APA are named for her. She served in editorial roles in several of the preeminent journals in psychology and counseling, and her publications numbered nearly 100 at her death. During her distinguished career, Tyler made pioneering contributions to understanding the development of interests in children and adolescents. She is credited with deepening and expanding psychology's conception of the nature and complexity of individual differences. Her theoretical contributions reveal the astute original thinker that she was, and her now-classic texts display the brilliant translation and synthesis of scientific knowledge that were her hallmark strengths. Tyler was a visionary leader who left her indelible imprint on entire fields of psychology and counseling, and she was a generous human being who shaped the lives of many thousands of individuals through her counseling, teaching, and writing. Committed equally to empiricism and humanism, Tyler was a lifelong learner who will remain a model of rigorous thinking, breadth of view, and flexibility in ideas and actions. Perhaps her greatest legacy is her enduring "concern for allowing and encouraging people to find themselves, to learn, and especially to clarify and choose their potentialities in an often chaotic world" (Anonymous, 1991).

REFERENCES

Anonymous. (1991). Leona E. Tyler: Citation for the Gold Medal Award for Life-Time Contribution in the Public Interest. *American Psychologist, 46,* 330–332.

Arnold, D. (1980, June 17). On the inside looking out. *Register Guard.*

Delworth, U. (2000). Leona Tyler: Explorer and map maker. *The Counseling Psychologist, 28,* 425–433.

Gilmore, S. K. (1977). Mountain iron woman: A case of androgyny. *Personnel and Guidance Journal, 55,* 451–459.

Goodenough, F. L., & Tyler, L. E. (1959). *Developmental psychology* (3rd ed.). New York: Appleton-Century-Crofts.

James, W. (1890). *The principles of psychology.* New York: Holt

Stevens, G., & Garner, S. (1982). From possibilities to actualities: Leona Elizabeth Tyler, 1906– . In G. Stevens & S. Gardner (Eds.), *The women of psychology, Volume II: Expansion and refinement* (pp. 112–119). Cambridge, MA: Schenkman.

Sundberg, N. D. (1993). In memory of Leona E. Tyler (1906–1993). *Oregon Counseling Journal, 15,* 30–31.

Sundberg, N. D., & Littman, R. A. (1994). Leona Elizabeth Tyler (1906–1993). *American Psychologist, 49,* 211–212.

Sundberg, N. D., Taplin, J. R., & Tyler, L. E. (1983). *Introduction to clinical psychology: Perspectives, issues, and contributions to human service* (3rd ed.). Englwood Cliffs, NJ: Prentice-Hall.

Sundberg, N. D., & Tyler, L. E. (1962). *Clinical psychology: An introduction to research and practice.* New York: Appleton-Century-Crofts.

Sundberg, N. D., Tyler, L. E., & Taplin, J. R. (1973). *Clinical psychology: Expanding horizons* (2nd ed.). Englewood Cliffs, NJ: Prentice-Hall.

Tyler, L. E. (1947). *The psychology of human differences.* New York: Appleton-Century-Crofts.

Tyler, L. E. (1953). *The work of the counselor.* New York: Appleton-Century-Crofts.

Tyler, L. E. (1956). *The psychology of human differences* (2nd ed.). New York: Appleton-Century-Crofts.

Tyler, L. E. (1958). Theoretical principles underlying the counseling process. *Journal of Counseling Psychology, 5,* 3–10.

Tyler, L. E. (1959). Toward a workable psychology of individuality. *American Psychologist, 14,* 75–81.

Tyler, L. E. (1960). Minimum change therapy. *Personnel & Guidance Journal, 38,* 475–479.

Tyler, L. E. (1961). *The work of the counselor* (2nd ed.). Englewood Cliffs, NJ: Prentice-Hall.

Tyler, L. E. (1963). *Tests and measurements.* Englewood Cliffs, NJ: Prentice-Hall.

Tyler, L. E. (1965a). *The psychology of human differences* (3rd ed.). Englewood Cliffs, NJ: Prentice-Hall.

Tyler, L. E. (1965b). *The work of the counselor* (3rd ed.). Englewood Cliffs, NJ: Prentice-Hall.

Tyler, L. E. (1969). *Intelligence: Some recurring issues: An enduring problem in psychology.* New York: Van Nostrand Reinhold.

Tyler, L. E. (1971). *Tests and measurements* (2nd ed.). Englewood Cliffs, NJ: Prentice-Hall.

Tyler, L. E. (1972). Reflections on counseling psychology. *The Counseling Psychologist, 3,* 6–11.

Tyler, L. E. (1973). Design for a hopeful psychology. *American Psychologist, 28,* 1021–1029.

Tyler, L. E. (1974). *Individual differences: Abilities and motivational directions.* New York: Appleton-Century-Crofts.

Tyler, L. E. (1978a). *Individuality: Human possibilities and personal choice in the psychological development of men and women.* San Francisco: Jossey-Bass.

Tyler, L. E. (1978b). My life as a psychologist. In T. S. Krawiec (Ed.), *The psychologists: Autobiographies of distinguished living psychologists* (Vol. 3, pp. 289–301). Brandon, VT: Clinical Psychology.

Tyler, L. E. (1979). *Tests and measurements* (3rd ed.). Englewood Cliffs, NJ: Prentice-Hall.

Tyler, L. E. (1980). The next twenty years. *The Counseling Psychologist, 8,* 19–21.

Tyler, L. E. (1983). *Thinking creatively: A new approach to psychology and individual lives.* San Francisco: Jossey-Bass.

Tyler, L. E. (1988). Leona E. Tyler. In A. N. O'Connell & N. F. Russo (Eds.), *Models of achievement: Reflections of eminent women in psychology* (Vol. 2, pp. 44–55). Hillsdale, NJ: Lawrence Erlbaum Associates, Inc.

Tyler, L. E. (1992). Counseling psychology: Why? *Professional Psychology: Research & Practice, 23*, 342–344.

Zilber, S. M., & Osipow, S. H. (1982). Leona E. Tyler (1906–). In A. N. O'Connell & N. F. Russo (Eds.), *Women in psychology: A bio-bibliographic sourcebook* (pp. 335–341). Westport, CT: Greenwood.

Chapter 15

Solomon Asch:
Scientist and Humanist

Clark McCauley and Paul Rozin
Solomon Asch Center for Study of Ethnopolitical Conflict
University of Pennsylvania

Perhaps the easiest way to introduce Solomon Asch is to say that he had a dedication to psychology as a natural science and a talent for arresting experiments, joined with the cultural knowledge and sensitivity of William James (chap. 2, *Pioneers I*). James was long gone by the time Asch came into psychology, and the complex humanity of Jamesian psychology was largely forgotten. Asch lived and worked in a mid-20th-century psychology dominated by behaviorist paradigms that were a reaction against the speculative excesses of psychoanalysis and Titchener's (chap. 7, *Pioneers I*) structuralism. For Asch, the behaviorists and the Freudians were alike in their reductionism. Asch aimed instead to represent the scope and depth of Homo sapiens in a Gestalt psychology that focused on context and relationships.

CONTEXT: JAMES, THE MODEL
OF HUMANIST PSYCHOLOGY

For many years James was professor of philosophy at Harvard at a time when psychology was a subdiscipline of philosophy. It was not until the 1880s, when G. Stanley Hall (chap. 2, this volume) at Johns Hopkins University and James McKeen Cattell at the University of Pennsylvania became professors of psychology, that psychology departments were organized and psychologists began moving out of philosophy. This exodus is generally celebrated by psychologists as a transition from speculation to science. But James's *Principles of Psychology*

(1890/1950) is worth reading today, not for the research referred to but for the cultural and humanistic concerns that directed the psychological questions James raised and the answers he attempted.

The humanities survey the peaks of human creativity and achievement, and James made psychology come alive to the human conditions and capacities represented at these peaks. Experimental psychology starts at the bottom—with issues simple enough to be brought into the laboratory—and tends therefore to produce a psychology that human beings share with other animals. Humanistic psychology starts at the top—with issues raised by creativity and genius—and reveals human beings in their uniqueness and complexity. The humanists note, for instance, that religion has been an important part of the human experience for many centuries, and James in *Varieties of Religious Experience* (1902) laid out a road that can still bring psychologists to unsettled lands. When psychology moved out of philosophy, most psychologists left behind the humanist education that could leaven empiricist paradigms. Asch brought a humanist perspective back to psychology.

ASCH'S EARLY EXPERIENCE IN PSYCHOLOGY

Solomon Asch was born in Poland in 1907, and emigrated to the United States as a teenager. He attended the City College of New York, where he majored in both literature and science. He received a bachelor's degree in 1928 at the age of 21. Asch heard about psychology toward the end of his undergraduate career and developed an impression of this new field by reading James and philosophers such as Santayana and Royce (Ceraso, Rock, & Gruber, 1990, pp. 4–5). As a graduate student in psychology at Columbia University, he took an interest in anthropology and attended seminars with Ruth Benedict and Franz Boas. In 1930, Asch married Florence Miller and took his bride with him on a summer fellowship to study Hopi children and their culture. In those studies he noticed that Hopi children sent to the blackboard to do a math problem would not turn from the board until all the children at the board had completed the problem, suggesting the powerful effects that culture has on human behavior.

Although such experiences laid the foundation of Asch's humanist interests, these were not obvious in his master's and doctoral research at Columbia. Robert S. Woodworth supervised and provided the data for Asch's master's degree, awarded in 1929 for a statistical analysis of test scores of 200 children. H. E. Garrett supervised his doctoral research and, in the custom of the day, gave Asch his thesis problem. Garrett wanted Asch "to find out whether all learning curves had the same form" (Ceraso et al., 1990, p. 6). Thus, Asch's graduate studies, with the exception of his study of Hopi children, provided little scope for his humanist interests and little basis for his work in social psychology.

After obtaining his doctorate in 1932, Asch became a faculty member at Brooklyn College. Soon after taking up this position, he met Max Wertheimer (chap. 13, *Pioneers I*), then at the New School for Social Research, the Gestalt psychologist who became the major intellectual influence in his life. When Wertheimer died in 1943, Asch replaced him as chair of psychology at the New School. Like Wertheimer, Asch became a moderate, someone who offered an alternative to behaviorism's highly analytic but impoverished accounts of the human condition. Dismayed at the attempts of the behaviorists to capture the complexity of human beings with a few elementary principles, Asch turned to Gestalt psychology with its focus on emergent properties and relations as a more promising starting point. He believed that the Gestalt principles of perception could support a psychology of whole persons in their social context.

Asch moved to Swarthmore College in 1947 and spent 20 productive years there. His time at Swarthmore was special because, uniquely in the history of the discipline, a small college became the intellectual center of a major movement in psychology. Wolfgang Kohler (chap. 17, *Pioneers I*) and Hans Wallach were at Swarthmore, and Asch was in contact with two of the brightest stars of Gestalt psychology. It was in this environment that Asch completed his classic studies of social psychology to be described later.

In his last years at Swarthmore, in his later years as director of the Center for Cognitive Psychology at Rutgers University (1966–1972), and in his final appointment as professor at the University of Pennsylvania (1972–1979), Asch turned his attention away from social psychology to study, among other topics, the psychology of metaphor and the nature of association (Asch, 1958, 1968). In this work, in typical Aschian form, he showed the poverty and inadequacy of existing formulations and proposed deeper accounts and more promising lines of investigation. His contention that learning of associations reflects something more than temporal and spatial contiguity, and depends on the nature of the material and the relations among the elements, served as the inspiration for his undergraduate student, Robert Rescorla, who became the leading scholar of association learning of a later generation (Rescorla, 1990).

ASCH'S FIRST PRINCIPLES

Asch aimed always for a psychology that brings scientific method to the understanding of human behavior without losing its complexity. In his uniquely thoughtful textbook, *Social Psychology* (1952), he reacted against behaviorism and argued for the primacy of the social world in human psychology:

> We conclude that to discover the full potentialities of men we must observe them in the social medium, that the basic problems of psychology require the extension of observation into the region of social processes. (p. 34)

> Most social acts have to be understood in their setting, and lose meaning if isolated. No error in thinking about social facts is more serious than the failure to see their place and function. (p. 61)

It will be the contention of this work that the decisive psychological fact about society is the capacity of individuals to comprehend and to respond to each other's experiences and actions. This fact, which permits individuals to become mutually related, becomes the ground of every social process and of the most crucial changes occurring in persons. (p. 127)

The essential problem of social psychology [is] how individuals create the reality of groups and how the latter control their further actions. (p. 256)

Asch also argued for research methods that are appropriate to the complexity of the social world. While respecting traditional experimental methods, he was careful to warn against losing the phenomenon of interest in a desire for rigor. Experiments, which hold everything constant but one or a few factors, are necessarily decontextualizing. The art of experimentation has to do with knowing how much context one can strip away from a phenomenon and still find out something useful. Only experiments thus informed are useful (Asch, 1952):

If there must be principles of scientific method, then surely the first to claim our attention is that one should describe phenomena faithfully and allow them to guide the choice of problems and procedures. If social psychology is to make a contribution to human knowledge, if it is to do more than add footnotes to ideas developed in other fields, it must look freely at its phenomena and examine its foundations. (p. ix)

The aim [is] to establish a psychology of social life by means of systematic observation and, where possible, of experiment. (p. viii)

In their anxiety to be scientific, students of psychology have often imitated the latest forms of sciences with a long history, while ignoring the steps these sciences took when they were young. They have, for example, striven to emulate the quantitative exactness of natural sciences without asking whether their own subject matter is always ripe for such treatment, failing to realize that one does not advance time by moving the hands of the clock. Because physicists cannot speak with stars or electric currents, psychologists have often been hesitant to speak to their human subjects. (pp. viii–ix)

Psychology must center on great and permanent problems, and psychologists should avoid the undignified posture of those whom in another connection Santayana has described as redoubling their effort when they have forgotten their aim. (p. 31)

The primacy of the social world and the implications of this primacy for scientific methods are summed up in Asch's 1987 retrospective comment on his work:

Thus a human psychology necessarily had to be a social psychology. In turn, it had to be an account of human experience, of beliefs and actions as they appeared to their human agents. This was an important step from the standpoint of method. In short, my intention was to produce, in contrast to the prevalent non-cognitive versions, a phenomenological psychology in which social facts and processes held central place. By the same token facts of culture were inseparable from this aim. . . . Not to sound too grandiloquent, I aimed for a treatise on human nature, informed by recent Gestalt strivings . . . a psychology with a human face. (1987, p. ix)

THREE CLASSIC STUDIES

Asch's first major research initiative, a series of studies of visual perception from a Gestalt perspective, was undertaken at Brooklyn College in collaboration with Herman Witkin. The results were reported in four articles on spatial orientation, all published in 1948. These experiments introduced the "rod-and-frame test." In this test people see a narrow rod surrounded by a frame of about the same width. With controls that are provided they try to set the rod to true vertical, although the enclosing frame may be tilted. These judgments pit the participants' gravitational sense of the vertical against the influence of a tilted visual frame. Asch and Witkin demonstrated that there is a tendency for people to judge the vertical as parallel to the sides of the tilted rectangle in which the rod is displayed. This work emphasized the idea of framing, a central concept in psychology some 50 years later (Rock, 1990b). Both the importance of framing and the balancing of forces—gravitational versus visual in the work with Witkin, social versus visual in Asch's later work—became central to Asch's social psychology.

In this section, we focus on Asch's three best-known and most influential studies. In order of their publication, these were "Forming Impressions of Personality" (1946), "The Doctrine of Suggestion, Prestige, and Imitation in Social Psychology" (1948), and "Studies of Independence and Conformity: I. A Minority of One Against a Unanimous Majority" (1956). Each of the three investigations joined an elegantly simple method with a question of surprising depth. Each involved a conflict of judgment that was presaged in Asch's earlier research.

Impression Formation

Asch's study of impression formation emerged from his Gestalt perspective. His concern was to show that one individual's perception of another person is a creative integration of a pattern of information about the person, rather than just a summation of the separate pieces of information. In one of his best-known procedures, college students were asked to form an impression of someone described by a list of personality traits: intelligent, skillful, industrious, warm, determined, practical, and cautious. The students wrote brief descriptions of their impressions of this person and then checked off, on a list of 18 pairs of traits, the traits most likely descriptive of the person they described.

The first and in some ways most surprising aspect of the results was that students do as they are asked. They do not complain that the task is impossible, that all they know is what the experimenter gave them in the list, that they have no idea how to say more than they were given. Rather, they write the sketch and check the traits with no signs of strain; they seem to have no trouble going beyond the given. How is this possible?

One answer to this question is suggested by the results of a comparison condition in which the task was the same except that the stimulus list of personality traits was changed by substituting *cold* for *warm* in the list. The sketches elicited were very different from those elicited by the list in which the adjective was *warm*. The impression now was of a self-centered person using positive traits to obtain advancement at the expense of others, whereas the impression from the *warm* list was of someone whose positive traits are directed at the service of others. Asch suggested that these data provide evidence that the meaning of the other traits has changed. A cold intelligence is analytical, logical, closed, whereas a warm intelligence is social, holistic, and open. One way the students could go beyond the given, then, is that the collection of traits is understood as a pattern in which the elements take on different meaning in combination than in isolation.

Further evidence came from a variation of this study in which *polite* and *blunt* were used in the stimulus list instead of *warm* and *cold*. This time the sketches and the trait checking were not very different; *polite* and *blunt* did not have the strong effect on impressions that *warm* and *cold* had had. Nor did *polite* and *blunt* have much effect on the meaning of other traits: The personality sketches did not suggest much difference between blunt intelligence and polite intelligence. Asch suggests that *warm* and *cold* should be considered *central traits*, in the sense that other impressions are organized around them to a degree that is not true of traits such as *polite* and *blunt*. Again, the organization is key to the impression of personality conveyed by the word list, but *warm* and *cold* affect that organization more than other pairs of adjectives.

Another kind of organization implied by these results is a network of trait inferences in which every trait is connected to many others, such that knowing one trait about a person makes some other traits more likely and other traits less likely. If a person is warm, he or she is more likely to be generous; if a person is cold, he or she is less likely to be generous. Asch's checklist data showed just this pattern. The network of trait inferences provides a second answer to the question of how we go beyond the given in impression formation: Even a brief list of traits implies a rich network of expectations about other, unmentioned, traits made more or less likely by the stimulus traits. This network of mutual implications among traits came to be called "implicit personality theory" and research exploring the origins and implications of this theory continues today. Of particular interest is the degree to which empirical evidence of actual correlations among traits is similar to the implicit correlations we carry in our heads.

Prestige Suggestion

Asch's research on prestige suggestion was prompted by a study by Irving Lorge (1936) that seemed to show that people evaluate opinions on the basis of who expresses them, with little regard to content. Lorge had students read a number of opinion statements, each attributed to a notable political figure. For instance, students read that Thomas Jefferson had said, "I hold it that a little rebellion, now and then, is a good thing, and as necessary in the political world as storms are in the physical." The students then rated the level of their agreement or disagreement with the statement. After rating all the statements, students rated their degree of respect for each of the political figures quoted. Some months later, when the students were unlikely to recall the statements or their ratings, the same students repeated the task but now the attribution of each statement was changed. The rebellion statement, for instance, was now said to be a quotation from Vladimir Lenin, leader of the Russian Revolution.

The results of Lorge's experiment showed that level of respect for the figure associated with the quotation has a big effect on students' agreement with the opinion expressed in it. Agreement with the rebellion quotation was much higher when it was attributed to Jefferson than when it was attributed to Lenin. In general, the greater the discrepancy in respect for the attributed sources of a quotation, the greater the discrepancy in student agreement with the quotation. Lorge concluded that students were irrationally attending to source rather than content of statements of opinion, that their evaluations were determined by blind association of source and statement.

Asch took a more positive view of the students' capacities and performance. His idea was that the students agreed more or less with a statement because the meaning of the statement changed with its attributed source. Thus, it was not the same opinion that the students evaluated differently according to its attribution; rather, they were evaluating effectively different opinions differently. Asch was able to martial two kinds of evidence in support of this interpretation. First, he reanalyzed Lorge's data to show that the attribution effect was concentrated in the opinion statements that were most ambiguous. The meaning of rebellion, for instance, can range from peaceful protest to violent insurrection. Second, he repeated the Lorge experiment using the more ambiguous quotations and asked students to write briefly how they understood each quotation. The results supported his interpretation. Students understood "rebellion" to mean rapid political change when the quotation was attributed to Jefferson, but understood the same quotation to mean violent revolution when attributed to Lenin. A certain irony attaches to the fact that Jefferson was the source of the quotation that could mean violent revolution in the context created by the name of Lenin.

For Asch, then, the differential response to a quotation depending on its source was not an indication of irrationality and blind association. Rather, the students were doing their best to organize the quotation and its source into a single coherent perception that accounted for the entire pattern of the information they were given. The fact that they were wrong about what Jefferson meant did not indicate something wrong with the inferential capabilities they brought to the task; their perception was the result of a creative effort to make sense of what they were presented with.

Independence and Conformity

Asch's studies of independence and conformity were undertaken in a context where many psychologists were claiming that human opinions are the result of the same kinds of stimulus associations, rewards, and punishments that shape nonhuman behavior. Asch wanted to show instead that human opinions are the result of an active search for interpretations of whole perceptual fields. So, he arranged a task in which social pressure was in conflict with reality. The task differed slightly in the two phases of his work, the first reported in his 1952 *Social Psychology* text and the second in his 1956 *Psychological Monographs* article. Here, we describe the first procedures.

A college student, recruited for a study of visual perception, arrive at the laboratory and is seated near the end of a row of seven seats, with five other students to the right and one to the left. The six other students are all confederates of the experimenter. The experimenter puts two cards in the chalk tray of a blackboard facing the students. One card is a "standard" card with a single vertical line on it (on different trials these lines are nine different lengths ranging from 1 in. to 9 in.). The other card is a "comparison" card with three vertical lines labeled 1, 2, and 3. Starting at the right end of the row of students, each student is asked to say out loud the number of the comparison line that matches the standard. The experimenter records each student's judgment.

There were 12 trials of this kind in which, on 7 of the 12 trials—the critical trials—the confederates unanimously gave the same incorrect judgment. Actually, the correct answer was easy to see—students making the same judgments privately were correct 93% of the time—but the confederates in the majority made errors that identified the matching line as one that differed from the standard by as little as 0.25 in. to as much as 1.75 in. The behavior of interest was the judgment of the naive students: Would they conform to the incorrect judgment of the majority or give the correct answer?

The results show surprising levels of conformity. Only 20% of the naive students gave the correct answer on every critical trial; 80% yielded to the majority at least once. Across all students and all trials, yielding to the majority occurred on 33% of the critical trials. There was considerable individual consistency in the pattern of the students' yielding. Those who yielded on the first trial or two were likely to keep yielding on succeeding trials, whereas those who were independent on the initial trails were more likely to be independent later on.

After each session, Asch interviewed the naive students, asking in particular why they had conformed. The majority said they didn't want to stick out, didn't want to be laughed at. A smaller number said they believed that the majority must be correct, must be able to see the lines better than they could. This difference defines an important distinction between *compliance* and *internalization*. Compliance is public show of conformity without true commitment—going along to get along. Internalization is a real and private conviction that the group is correct. Most of those who yielded did so only at the level of compliance, but a smaller number exhibited internalization and accepted the majority opinion as better evidence of reality than the evidence of their own eyes.

Many people who hear about these results believe that they would be among the 20% who never conformed in Asch's experiments, and that those who did conform must be inferior people. This belief is hard to maintain, however, given that Asch conducted his experiments at Swarthmore, Haverford, and St. Joseph's Colleges—all small institutions with excellent students. The naive student for each session was recruited by a friend who was one of the confederates for that session. Thus the naive student was facing, not a group of strangers, but a peer group of acquaintances and friends. It is hard to imagine a majority with more power in relation to a minority of one.

There is little doubt that Asch would have preferred to find 100% independence and 0% conformity, but he nevertheless emphasized that the majority of responses actually were independent. As mentioned previously, across all trials and participants, only 33% of the responses were conforming. Indeed he suggested (Asch, 1990, p. 54) that sensitivity to the opinions of others and the tendency to dislike public disagreement is a positive human disposition. Without this kind of sensitivity, social life would be undermined and cooperation for common goals less likely. In contrast to many subsequent interpretations— which have tended to stress the weaknesses and irrationality of people who conform to the group—Asch's own interpretation emphasized participants' efforts to make sense of conflicting information.

Replications of Asch's conformity research have been many and worldwide. In a meta-analysis of this research tradition, Bond and Smith (1996) found 133 studies from 17 countries that used Asch's line-length task to examine conformity. The analysis indicated that conformity had declined in the United States since the 1950s, that conformity is less in countries where individualism is valued more than collectivism, and that females are more likely to conform than males. From Asch's point of view, the decline in conformity may not be altogether good news, and the greater conformity of females may not be altogether bad news.

Asch's View of Human Perception and Judgment

What is common to the studies just reported is a view of human perception and judgment as creative responses to the whole array of available information. The response is a Gestalt, an organized whole in which the elements of information are interpreted rather than merely summed. An explicit version of Asch's theoretical perspective is provided by Yates (1983) in his article, "The Content of Awareness Is a Model of the World." Yates reviewed a wide array of research in cognitive psychology and argued that perceptual machinery outside awareness operates to provide awareness with the "best" interpretation of the data received. This best interpretation is one that is maximally simple (integrates the most data), univocal (only one of multiple possible interpretations is available in awareness at a given moment), and complete and consistent (missing or inconsistent information is not represented in the interpretation). Yates also argued that the interpretations we naively identify as reality go beyond immediate sense data. They represent our theories of where perceptual objects came from and anticipations of what they may lead to.

The view of perception as problem solving is the key to Asch's experiments, each of which poses a conflict for the research participants. In studies of personality impressions, the conflict is between positive and negative traits in descriptions of a person. In research on prestige suggestion, the conflict is between the content of a quotation and the source to which it is attributed. In experiments on conformity, the conflict is between perceptual and social evidence about the length of a line. These experiments are revealing because, in all of them, the stronger the conflict in the inputs, the stronger must be the creativity of the judgment that integrates the inputs. Asch had confidence in the creativity of human perception, and his studies demonstrated and supported his confidence.

ASCH'S TEXTBOOK, *SOCIAL PSYCHOLOGY*

Asch's *Social Psychology* (1952) is one of the great books in psychology, a book written by someone with an unusual gift of expression. The presentation is brilliant even as it is surprisingly close to common sense and, at the same time, surprisingly balanced. The critiques of other views—from associationism and behaviorism to psychoanalysis—are sympathetic. They aim to learn from these alternatives rather than to destroy them. There is also balance in Asch's view of the discipline of psychology. He respects human complexity and dignity while shaping a scientific approach. He acknowledges the importance of the individual in understanding social phenomena while recognizing the importance of groups and culture as more than the sum of the individuals that compose them. There is balance again in his treatment of the issues later battled over between universalists and relativists or deconstructionists. For Asch, our world and our minds are, for the most part, socially constructed, but he allows for universal aspects of human thought and nature. And on the ever-divisive nature–nurture issue, Asch again holds a middle line. As a Gestalt psychologist, and in contrast to the classical behaviorists, he accepts the idea that there is substantial genetic determination of psychological dispositions, but he also sees great opportunities for shaping of human beings by experience and culture.

Unlike most subsequent texts in social psychology, Asch (1952) confronted the fundamental issues in social psychology, such as how we know there are other minds in other persons. This realization is at the root of social psychology, and Asch described it as "the basic psychological unity among men." Our surroundings are equally accessible to all of us, as are perceptions of causality and inference, and we somehow understand this:

> To take our place with others we must perceive each other's existence and reach a measure of comprehension of one another's needs, emotions and thoughts. (p. 139)

> To naive thought nothing is less problematic than that we grasp the actions of others, but it is precisely the task of psychology to remove the veil of self-evidence from these momentous processes. (pp. 139–140)

> What we need to understand is how psychological events, which as such can never leave the individual, can nevertheless make contact with another individual. This is the heart of the problem. (p. 143)

> It is precisely the interpenetration of conscious events in individuals that is necessary for the birth of society, of language, of art, and of science. (p. 163)

Asch argued that it is impossible to understand how we acquire knowledge of other minds through experience alone, and that, just as with some of the Gestalt principles of perception, the predisposition to appreciate other minds is innate. "It is necessary to assume that there is an intrinsic correspondence between experience and action, that they are isomorphic" (p. 159). His conclusion here, and the argument that leads to it, has much in common with the later argument by Chomsky and others that we must presume a predisposition for language to understand how language is acquired.

In the last section of his text, Asch questioned the Western presumption that an independent individual is the optimal and "morally desirable" outcome that we should wish to achieve (see Markus and Kitayama, 1991, on the independent versus interdependent self). Donald Campbell (1990) realized the importance of this question in describing the "moral epistemology" of Asch. Campbell noted that conformity is really about our dependence on the report of others, and he developed three Asch-based moral norms for socially achieved knowledge:

1. Trust: It is our duty to respect the reports of others and be willing to base our beliefs and actions on them.

2. Honesty: It is our duty to report what we perceive honestly, so that others may use our observations in coming to valid beliefs.

3. Self-respect: It is our duty to respect our own perceptions and beliefs, seeking to integrate them with the reports of others without deprecating them or ourselves.

These ideas offer the prospect of a moral foundation for research on social influence.

CONCLUSION

Partly as a result of spending much of his academic life at an undergraduate institution, Asch did not sponsor a legion of doctoral candidates. Instead, he inspired many undergraduates at Swarthmore to careers in psychology and influenced numerous others who came to know him during or after their graduate education. Stanley Milgram (chap. 21, *Pioneers II*) spent a postdoctoral year with Asch, and Milgram's later studies of obedience are like Asch's classic studies in examining reactions to a situation of conflicting social pressures. More explicitly, 17 eminent psychologists who contributed to *The Legacy of Solomon Asch: Essays in Cognition and Social Psychology* (Rock, 1990a) offered individual testimonies of the range and fecundity of Asch's influence on their research.

Asch's own work—the classic studies and especially his textbook—pointed the way to a social psychology that is yet to be achieved. Fifty years later, only half of his advice has been heeded. His goal of a natural science of social psychology has been developed exquisitely in modern experimental social psychology, but his focus on the essential sociality of human beings, and the richness of the human experience, has been lost to a large extent in the urge to imitate particle physics (Rozin, 2001). Asch made this point many times in his 1952 text, and in 1987, in the preface to the reprinting of the 1952 book, looked back in distress at what had happened in social psychology in the years after his text was published:

Clearly I was swimming, often without realizing it, against the current. (p. x)

Why do I sense, together with the current expansion, a shrinking of vision, an expansion of surface rather than depth, a failure of imagination? (p. x)

Why is not social psychology more exciting, more human in the most usual sense of that term? To sum up, is this discipline perhaps on the wrong track? (p. x)

REFERENCES

Asch, S. E. (1946). Forming impressions of personality. *Journal of Abnormal and Social Psychology, 41*, 258–290.

Asch, S. E. (1948). The doctrine of suggestion, prestige, and imitation in social psychology. *Psychological Review, 55*, 250–276.

Asch, S. E. (1952). *Social psychology*. New York: Prentice-Hall.

Asch, S. E. (1956). Studies of independence and conformity. I. A minority of one against a unanimous majority. *Psychological Monographs, 70*, 1–70.

Asch, S. E. (1958). The metaphor: A psychological inquiry. In R. Taguiri & L. Petrullo (Eds.), *Person perception and interpersonal behavior* (pp. 86–94). Stanford, CA: Stanford University Press.

Asch, S. E. (1968). A reformation of the problem of associations. *American Psychologist, 24*, 92–102.

Asch, S. E. (1987). *Social psychology* (rev. ed.). New York: Oxford University Press.

Asch, S. E. (1990). Comments on D. T. Campbell's chapter. In I. Rock (Ed.), *The legacy of Solomon Asch. Essays in cognition and social psychology* (pp. 43–55). Hillsdale, NJ: Lawrence Erlbaum Associates, Inc.

Asch, S. E., & Witkin, H. A. (1948). Studies in space orientation: II: Perception of the upright with displaced visual fields and with body tilted. *Journal of Experimental Psychology, 38*, 455–477.

Bond, R., & Smith, P. B. (1996). Culture and conformity: A meta-analysis of studies using Asch's (1952b, 1956) line judgment task. *Psychological Bulletin, 119*, 111–137.

Campbell, D. T. (1990). Asch's moral epistemology for socially shared knowledge. In I. Rock (Ed.), *The legacy of Solomon Asch. Essays in cognition and social psychology* (pp. 39–52). Hillsdale, NJ: Lawrence Erlbaum Associates, Inc.

Ceraso, J., Rock, I., & Gruber, H. (1990). On Solomon Asch. In I. Rock (Ed.), *The legacy of Solomon Asch* (pp. 3–19). Hillsdale, NJ: Lawrence Erlbaum Associates, Inc.

James, W. (1902). *Varieties of religious experience*. New York: Longmans, Green.

James, W. (1950). *Principles of psychology*. New York: Holt. (Original work published 1890)

Lorge, I. (1936). Prestige, suggestion and attitudes. *Journal of Social Psychology, 7*, 386–402.

Markus, H. R., & Kitayama, S. (1991). Culture and the self: Implications for cognition, emotion and motivation. *Psychological Review, 98*, 224–253.

Rescorla, R. A. (1990). Associative learning in animals: Asch's influence. In I. Rock (Ed.), *The legacy of Solomon Asch. Essays in cognition and social psychology* (pp. 159–174). Hillsdale, NJ: Lawrence Erlbaum Associates, Inc.

Rock, I. (Ed.). (1990a). *The legacy of Solomon Asch. Essays in cognition and social psychology*. Hillsdale, NJ: Lawrence Erlbaum Associates, Inc.

Rock, I. (1990b). The frame of reference. In I. Rock (Ed.), *The legacy of Solomon Asch. Essays in cognition and social psychology* (pp. 243–268). Hillsdale, NJ: Lawrence Erlbaum Associates, Inc.

Rozin, P. (2001). Social psychology and science: Some lessons from Solomon Asch. *Personality and Social Psychology Review, 5*, 2–14.

Yates, J. (1983). The content of awareness is a model of the world. *Psychological Review, 92*, 249–284.

Chapter 16

Anne Anastasi: Master of Differential Psychology and Psychometrics

John D. Hogan
St. John's University

Anne Anastasi is known to generations of psychology students as the author of *Psychological Testing*, a textbook that she first published in 1954. She completed work on the seventh edition, more than 40 years later, at age 87. It was her last publication. Anastasi's mastery of differential psychology and psychometrics established her as an international authority on those subjects.

Anastasi was also the author of several other important books and more than 200 monographs, articles, and reviews. In 1972, she became the third woman president of the American Psychological Association, and the first woman to hold that office in 51 years. In addition to her work in differential psychology and psychometrics, she was a scholar of general psychology and contributed important writings in that area. Beyond her academic accomplishments, she had a striking personality and a sharp sense of humor. Almost everyone who knew her had a story they wanted to tell about her.

CHILDHOOD AND EARLY EDUCATION

Anne Anastasi was born December 19, 1908, to Anthony and Theresa Gaudiosi Anastasi, Italian immigrants who settled in the Bronx, the northern county of New York City. Her father worked for the New York City Board of Education. When she was a year old, her father died suddenly. She later said that his death was a pivotal point in her development. It resulted in her unusual upbringing in a household consisting of her mother, her mother's brother, and her maternal grandmother. Because of her family arrangement, she said that she was unaware of gender stereotypes until she entered college and found herself in gender-segregated classes (Anastasi, 1988). Anastasi traced her distrust of authority figures and group stereotypes to lessons learned from her grandmother.

Although Anastasi's mother and uncle were well educated in the classics and the humanities, they had not been prepared for the world of work. Her mother was energetic and resourceful, however, and soon became an effective breadwinner. Theresa Anastasi taught herself accounting and founded a piano company. When that failed, she took a series of managerial jobs and eventually became the office manager for *Il Progresso Italo-Americano*, one of the largest foreign newspapers in New York. She continued in that position until her retirement.

The family members decided that Anastasi should not attend the nearby public school because the children there were too loud and boisterous. As a result, Anastasi was home-schooled until she was 9 years old. Her grandmother, who ruled the household, was in charge of her schooling. Although Anastasi had little opportunity to interact with peers, the adults in her life always had time for her. In fact, she preferred the company of adults. Her mother frequently played word games with her and engaged in role playing, a type of learning Anne enjoyed. A regular public school teacher, Dora Ireland, was hired to conduct lessons for Anne in the afternoon. Eventually, Ireland was successful in convincing the family to let the young girl attend the public school at which Ireland regularly taught (Sexton & Hogan, 1990).

Initially, the experiment was a failure. Anastasi spent only 2 months in the third grade before her teacher decided the material was too easy for her and she was transferred to a fourth-grade class. There she was forced to sit in the last row of an already crowded classroom. She found the experience confusing and she soon returned to her home studies. Later, her family realized that Anastasi needed eyeglasses—she hadn't been able to see the school blackboard from where she was seated. When she returned to grammar school in the fall, her pace was accelerated by several grades. Eventually, she graduated from PS 33 in the Bronx at the top of her class with a gold medal for general excellence (Sexton & Hogan, 1990).

Anastasi's matriculation at Evander Childs High School presented more problems. Because of overcrowding, the entering class was assigned to temporary quarters, resulting in limited facilities and overworked teachers. Anastasi found the experience unpleasant and dropped out after only 2 months. The family held several conferences to determine what she should do next. Eventually a family friend, Ida Stadie, came to the rescue. She convinced Anastasi that she should apply directly to college. Anastasi spent 2 years taking courses at the Rhodes Preparatory School in Manhattan and then applied to Barnard College, where she was admitted in 1924 at age 15.

COLLEGE AND GRADUATE SCHOOL

Anastasi had always been fascinated with mathematics. As a teenager, she developed a program of self-study and eventually taught herself many advanced concepts, including spherical trigonometry (Goode, 2001). When she began college, mathematics was her first choice for a major. She changed her mind in her sophomore year, however, because of two separate but related events.

Anastasi took a required introductory psychology course from Harry Hollingworth (chap. 9, *Pioneers II*), the knowledgeable and witty chair of the Psychology Department, and found herself fascinated. She had never even heard of the subject of psychology before the course. Soon after completing the session, she read a paper by Charles Spearman (chap. 6, *Pioneers IV*) on correlation coefficients that convinced her she could pursue psychology but still retain her interest in mathematics. Anastasi's career path was settled. She changed her major to psychology and never regretted entering the field. The fact that psychology was a "new" field was part of the enticement—she thought she might be able to make important contributions because the field was so young (Fish, 1983).

Anastasi was admitted to the honors program in her junior year, which freed her from attending regular classes at Barnard. Instead, she enrolled in several advanced classes, including graduate classes in psychology at Columbia University and a psychology of advertising course in the Columbia School of Business Administration. As a junior, she also undertook a study on aesthetic preferences with Frederick H. Lund, then an instructor at Barnard. The resulting research became her first publication (Lund & Anastasi, 1928). Later in her career, she conducted many studies in related areas, such as art and creativity. In her senior year, she was elected to Phi Beta Kappa and was awarded a graduate fellowship. Anastasi found Barnard to be a very stimulating place intellectually, although she was not fond of the women-only classes. She received her A.B. (Bachelor of Arts) degree from Barnard in 1928 at age 19.

The following fall, Anastasi entered Columbia University to study for a doctorate in general experimental psychology—the only psychology doctoral degree then available at Columbia. She told the department chairman, Albert T. Poffenberger, that she intended to complete the program in 2 years. He told her that her goal was possible but unlikely. Anastasi was as good as her word, however. She received her doctorate 2 years later in 1930 at age 21. Later she described those 2 years as among the most stimulating in her life.

Her professors during those years were from Columbia's "golden age," and included Poffenberger, Robert Woodworth, Carl Warden, Gardner Murphy, and Henry E. Garrett. The last became her doctoral mentor. Anastasi said that Garrett was an excellent teacher and that he did a lot for his students (Fish, 1983). It was in one of his classes that she wrote her first paper on differential psychology and engaged in her first discussions on the relative contributions of heredity and environment to behavior. Garrett was strongly on the side of heredity, a position Anastasi found questionable, but Garrett refused to engage in arguments on the subject with Anastasi or anyone else. Anastasi said he always remained the Southern gentleman (Fish, 1983, p. 60). After his retirement from Columbia, however, he promoted his hereditarian views much more strongly.

In 1929, Anastasi received a summer research assistantship to study with Charles Davenport at the Carnegie Institution of Washington, in Cold Spring Harbor on Long Island, New York. Her job was to assist Davenport in devising culture-free tests. The work raised many questions for her, and she would express strong opinions on the subject later in her writing. She took summer courses at Columbia with Clark Hull (chap. 14, *Pioneers I*) and R. M. Elliott, both of whom she found inspiring, and with whom she remained in contact. Hull became a particularly close friend and she frequently sought his counsel.

In September of that year Anastasi attended the 9th International Congress of Psychology, held at Yale University, the first such congress to be held in the United States. In addition to hearing addresses by American notables such as James McKeen Cattell, James Rowland Angell (chap. 4, this volume), and E. L. Thorndike (chap. 10, *Pioneers I*), she also heard talks by European psychologists including Ivan Pavlov (chap. 3, *Pioneers I*), Henri Pieron, William Mac-Dougall (chap. 6, this volume), Charles Spearman (chap. 6, *Pioneers IV*), and Edouard Claparede. She was surprised to see Pavlov waiting on the cafeteria breakfast line one morning with a tray, just like everyone else.

By the beginning of her second graduate year, Anastasi had completed most of the basic courses and began to specialize. She took a course on intelligence testing given at Randall's Island Children's Hospital under the title "clinical psychology." (In that era, "clinical psychology" had a different meaning from what it would have in subsequent years.) She also took a course on racial differences from Otto Klineberg, who later become an important force in social psychology. She was very impressed by his findings, and she and Klineberg became lifelong friends. Finally, she worked on her dissertation, published as *A Group Factor in Immediate Memory* (Anastasi, 1930).

EARLY CAREER AND MARRIAGE

Anastasi was offered her first academic position while crossing the street near Columbia University at Broadway and 119th Street. Her former professor, Hollingworth (chap. 9, *Pioneers II*), was crossing from the other side. The transaction took only a few moments. By the time it was completed, she had accepted a position as instructor for the fall term at Barnard. Her initial annual salary was $2,400. She remained an untenured instructor at Barnard until 1939, with only one raise in salary, but it was the height of the Great Depression, and she was grateful to have a job at all (Fish, 1983, p. 9). She once wrote that she had never applied for any position that she accepted, although she applied for some positions that she did not accept (Anastasi, 1988).

In 1933, Anastasi married John Porter Foley Jr. who, at age 23, had just completed his doctoral studies in psychology, also at Columbia University. Anastasi said that her marriage gave her the benefit of two doctoral degrees because her husband's interests and background were so different from hers. While he was an undergraduate student at Indiana University, Foley had been strongly influenced by J. R. Kantor. Anastasi met Kantor and read his works. She was also impressed by Kantor's writings. Foley was interested in research on animals and was in charge of the animal laboratory at Columbia. He had also participated in research with Franz Boas, the great cultural anthropologist. Virtually all of Foley's influences would have an impact on Anastasi's writing.

A year after their marriage, Anastasi was diagnosed with cervical cancer. Radium and x-ray treatment followed. Because her treatment took place over the December holidays, she missed only two days of class. At the end of treatment, her cancer was gone, never to recur, but she was sterile and could never have children. Later, she would assess her illness with characteristic directness. She saw the cancer as one of the principal reasons for her success. Women of her generation frequently had to choose between motherhood and a career. That choice was taken from her, and she was free to concentrate on her career without conflict or guilt (Hogan, 2000).

In the early years of their marriage, the couple were frequently separated. Jobs were scarce and universities were reluctant to hire a husband and wife in the same department. While Anastasi taught at Barnard, Foley taught at George Washington University in Washington, D.C. The issue was not resolved until Foley, who found himself increasingly drawn to industrial psychology, left academic psychology in the mid-1940s and took a position with the Psychological Corporation in New York City. The couple remained in New York City for the rest of their lives.

Anastasi and Foley sometimes published together, particularly early in their careers. By the mid-1950s, they had coauthored 18 articles and reports. Foley worked closely with Anastasi on the first edition of her text *Differential Psychology*, and was coauthor with her on the second edition. He became very successful in his own right as a pioneer in the use of quantitative testing in the selection and training of industrial personnel. Eventually, he established his own consulting firm (Greenman, 1996). Anastasi always acknowledged his contribution to her work, even noting that it had become stronger as the years went by.

Anastasi left Barnard in 1939 to become chair—and the only member—of the new Department of Psychology at Queens College of the City University of New York. By 1947, the department had grown to six, but the bureaucratic demands and department infighting hampered her teaching and research. She then accepted a position as associate professor of psychology in the Graduate School at Fordham University where, in 1951, she was promoted to professor. She remained at

Fordham until her retirement in 1979. Anastasi maintained that she never had a master plan for her career; she simply followed her interests. She also wrote that, whatever her contributions to psychology, they were to be found in her writings. This last statement is true up to a point. She also made significant contributions to research, teaching, textbook writing, and organizational leadership.

RESEARCH AND WRITING

Anastasi was impressed by the writing styles of both Hollingworth and Garrett. She said that before Garrett, most statistics books were very difficult but that he had made the subject so basic and clear that the subject could be taught to all psychology students. Anastasi liked that approach and promised herself that when she wrote, she was going to take difficult concepts and make them understandable. That promise became one of her lifelong goals (Fish, 1983, p. 46). True to her early interest in mathematics, she kept current with all the innovative statistical methods, even traveling to the University of Minnesota in the early 1930s to study the new technique called "analysis of variance," then being introduced in the United States by the British statistician, R. A. Fisher.

Anastasi was an active researcher and her interests covered a wide range of topics. One of her early research emphases was on the development and measurement of traits, particularly the role of experience in trait development and measurement. In 1934, she published a monograph on the role of practice as related to trait variability (Anastasi, 1934). By 1936, only 6 years after receiving her doctorate, she was engaged in an ongoing debate with the distinguished psychologist and psychometrician, L. L. Thurstone (chap. 6, *Pioneers III*), on the subject of traits (e.g., Anastasi, 1938). This was a remarkable exchange considering the differences in their age and experience—Anastasi was in her late 20s and an unknown instructor; Thurstone was almost 50 and was already somewhat of a giant in the field.

Among her many research topics, Anastasi investigated sex differences in traits, age changes in adult performance, language development among Black and Puerto Rican children, and intelligence and family size. She pointed out that mechanical aptitudes could consist of many subabilities, and that these abilities could favor either men or women depending on a number of other variables (Anastasi, 1958). She maintained that it was not only the level of performance that is of interest in evaluations, but also the fact that individuals of different cultures or subcultures, socioeconomic levels, and types of schooling exhibit different patterns of trait organization (Anastasi, 1970). She was particularly sensitive to the importance of developing appropriate age norms for tests, and she encouraged the investigation of adult activities that might relate to changes in test scores (Anastasi, 1986). She also conducted research on test construction and evaluation, including problems related to misuse and misinterpretation.

Anastasi investigated test performance as it was related to issues such as coaching and test sophistication. She determined that the effects of coaching on test scores, based on many published studies, were ambiguous or uninterpretable because of methodological problems with the research, particularly in the failure to use comparable control groups (e.g., Anastasi, 1981a). She studied the effects of test sophistication, or test-taking practice, and demonstrated that short orientation and practice sessions were effective in equalizing test sophistication (Anastasi, 1981b). She wrote extensively on misconceptions concerning "culture-fair" and "culture-free" tests, and methodological problems related to test bias, speeded tests, and item selection. She maintained that all test results should be understood only within a specific contextual framework.

With her husband, Anastasi wrote several articles on psychological aspects of art. Their personal interest in art developed into a study of the cultural differences in artistic expression, including the investigation of children's spontaneous drawings and animal drawings by Indian children of the North Pacific Coast (Anastasi & Foley, 1938). They also investigated the relationship between artistic production and abnormality. In several of their studies they compared the artistic production of adult psychotics with that of normal control groups (e.g., Anastasi & Foley, 1944). Their work tended to debunk the notion of a relationship between artistic production and abnormality, instead implicating the causative role of such factors as education, occupation, and sociocultural background. As a result of their research, they developed an even greater appreciation for art and eventually became ardent collectors.

In 1958, Anastasi published an article titled "Heredity, Environment, and the Question 'How?' " (Anastasi, 1958). Based on her presidential address to the APA Division of General Psychology, it is her most frequently reprinted article. In it, she reconceptualized the age-old nature–nurture issue, and gave it focus and a new direction. Too much time had been spent asking the wrong question, she said. Nature and nurture never exist independently of each other. They are always inextricably bound together. Therefore, the proper question can never be which one is responsible or how much is due to either. The only proper question to ask is: How do they interact? The article became required reading for many graduate students, particularly in developmental psychology, and it remains an important contribution today.

Anastasi was a strong supporter of Oscar Buros and his work with the *Mental Measurement Yearbooks*, and was convinced that Buros and his wife had done a tremendous service to testing by publishing the series. The fact that they ran the operation virtually out of their basement made their contribution all the more impressive. Psychological tests in the early years often had little technical information available on them and Anastasi believed that the *Yearbooks* helped upgrade test construction. She was very proud of the fact that she reviewed for the first *Yearbook* in 1938 and continued as the only reviewer to have reviews appear in all eight of the original *Buros Mental Measurements Yearbooks* (Fish, 1983).

LEADERSHIP

As Anastasi's work became known, she was elected to a number of positions in the scientific community. The first office she held, a few years after receiving her doctoral degree, was that of secretary of the Psychology Section of the New York Academy of Sciences. One of the most surprising elections, she said, was her selection as president of the Eastern Psychological Association (1946–1947). She did not campaign for the office—a practice that was virtually unknown then—and she was only an assistant professor when she was selected. Later, when she served as president of the APA (1972), her election was equally free of any electioneering. She also served as president of the General Psychology Division of the New York State Psychological Association (1953–1954).

Anastasi served in the APA governance for almost 40 years, beginning in 1947 as a representative to the APA Council for Division 1 (General Psychology) shortly after the divisional structure was established. She served four terms on the Board of Directors, the first as Recording Secretary, and was elected to several other terms on the council, the last in 1982–1985, again as a representative of Division 1. She also served as president of the APA Division of General Psychology (1956–1957), the APA Division of Evaluation and Measurement (1965–1966), and the American Psychological Foundation (1965–1967).

Anastasi's election as APA president took place during a period of great turmoil in the country and in the APA. Although the office had not yet become highly politicized, it became more so shortly after. She viewed her role as that of a representative for all APA members and as a facilitator of group decision making. She did not feel it was necessary for her to take a stand on all of the issues before the organization; her role was to be available to listen to the voices of the membership. Her presidential address was given at the Eightieth Annual Meeting of APA (1972), held that year in Honolulu, Hawaii, the first time the APA meeting was held outside of the contiguous 48 states. The address was titled "The Cultivation of Diversity" (Anastasi, 1972a), and although she felt her talk had little impact (Fish, 1983), many of the points she made are just as important today as when she first spoke them.

Anastasi challenged psychologists to remain humble in pursuing and interpreting their research and to recognize the contributions of other disciplines. She stressed the importance of remaining objective and not confusing personal beliefs with science. This was a theme that appeared again and again in her work. She was critical of psychologists who presented personal values in the guise of science. Her criticism was directed, among others, at those who were trying to promote the idea that psychology could end wars and influence international understanding. She would ask: Where are the data? Most of the individuals promoting such ideas, she thought, were acting outside their areas of expertise. They were simply announcing their political preferences under the guise of psychology, and although they were well meaning, they were essentially dishonest.

She was adamant in her belief that psychologists should offer solutions to social problems only when there is adequate research evidence to support their recommendations (Denton, 1987).

Consistent with past-APA president George Miller's famous "giving psychology away" presidential address (Miller, 1969), Anastasi recommended that psychologist share "orienting concepts" with the public, that is, ideas that are widely agreed on among psychologists and corroborated in both basic research and technology. These should be simple but strong concepts that could be assimilated by the contemporary culture and used as guides to thinking about human nature and human problems.

THE UNITY OF PSYCHOLOGY

During the course of Anastasi's long career, she saw psychology begin to splinter into various groups, many with increasing levels of specialization. The result was to create a discipline in which some members had difficulty communicating with one another. A few critics even maintained that scientific psychology is not a unified discipline and that there are reasons why it could not and should not be (e.g., Koch, 1981).

Anastasi recognized the need for specialization but also believed strongly in a united discipline. She considered herself a "generalist" in psychology. For many years, the only division of the APA that she joined was Division 1: General Psychology (Fish, 1983, p. 45). She believed that all psychologists should be trained in "general psychology" and not simply in their specialties. She maintained there was a common core to psychology and that core is the scientific explanation for human behavior (Anastasi, 1972a, p. 1092). Moreover, she argued there were many unifying principles in psychology if we cared to look for them.

Early in her career, Anastasi believed—as did many others at the time—that the work of Clark Hull held the key to the unification of psychology. When his efforts failed, she realized that no "grand unifying theory" lay in the immediate future. Nonetheless, she supported attempts to unify psychology on an intermediate level. In her own area of specialization, psychometrics, she identified seven areas she believed could be used as sources of this unification. Methodologically, she defined "psychometrics" to include psychological testing and statistical analysis, and substantively to include the nature and source of individual differences (Anastasi, 1992, p. 31).

The areas of potential unification within psychometrics that Anastasi identified were: trait hierarchies, trait formation, traits and situations, cognitive and affective variables, heredity and environment, and testing in context (Anastasi, 1992). In each case, she maintained that if the concepts involved are understood properly, many of the differences among competing ways of thinking disappear. For instance, she argued that although there were many apparent differences among factor analytic solutions to trait identification, the solutions were frequently mathematically equivalent. Traits may appear to be organized differently, but they are often described at different levels of generality, depending on the purposes for which they are to be used (Anastasi, 1992).

Anastasi also noticed attempts to unify psychology outside of her specialty area. She was particularly optimistic about the trends she had observed in research in psychotherapy. Although there had been some attempts to integrate the various psychotherapies as early as the 1930s, no serious movement was apparent until the mid-1970s. By then, the number of psychotherapeutic approaches and procedures had reached well into the hundreds. Since then the number of books and professional meetings devoted to the topic of the unification of clinical psychology has continued to grow, and clinical psychologists are recognizing the benefits of such study. Just as there are clear benefits to psychotherapy, Anastasi bellieved that unification attempts, in general, could only benefit psychology as a whole (Anastasi, 1992).

TEACHER, COLLEAGUE, ROLE MODEL

Anastasi approached her teaching very seriously and took pains to keep each of her classes clearly focused and organized. Despite her many other contributions, she considered teaching to be the central activity of her professional life, and she established different classroom goals for each of her audiences—graduate students, undergraduate students, and educated nonmajors (Anastasi, 1972c, pp. 19–21). One of the stories that was shared among her students described the time she tripped and fell while teaching, spilled the coffee she was carrying, but righted herself and never lost a beat in the lecture.

Anastasi was a gifted editor, with great respect for proper grammar and punctuation. Few papers passed her discerning eye untouched, as many students and colleagues learned. Most of her own writing was accomplished in a single draft. On a personal level, she was known as a taskmaster, with high standards, but always fair. She was a student advocate long before the practice became common. She had a heightened sense of justice that, in the 1960s, led her to a strikingly generous act. A young colleague had been trying to find a down payment on a home for his new family. Anastasi thought that the university had treated him badly and asked him how much he needed. She wrote him a check for $10,000 and told him that he needn't pay it back. (He did.) The check was larger than his annual salary.

For 6 years Anastasi served as chair of the Department of Psychology at Fordham University (1968–1974). As opposed to her earlier experience at Queens College, she found the undertaking to be surprisingly satisfying. Her characteristic style of fairness, focus, and organization served her well. She was considered a good model for women for her many accomplishments, particularly as the first woman to become president of the APA in 51 years, but she was not always comfortable in that role. In fact, she made it clear that her role models had all been men—Hull, Kantor, and Hollingworth (Fish, 1983, p. 37). In a survey published in 1987, she was rated the most prominent living woman in psychology in the English-speaking world (Gavin, 1987). She was not impressed. She said that she was a "psychologist," not a "woman-psychologist."

MAJOR BOOKS

Anastasi's three major books were all favorably received and had a substantial impact on psychology. In one of her award citations, they were described as "models of clarity, comprehensiveness, and synthesis. They frame the very questions scientists in these disciplines ask and the manner in which research is conducted" (American Psychological Foundation Awards for 1984, 1985, p. 340).

Her first book, *Differential Psychology* (first edition, 1937) has been described as a major force in the development of differential psychology as a behavioral science. Before Anastasi chose that title for her book, the area was known as "individual differences." Her title was a direct translation of a term proposed by William Stern (chap. 6, *Pioneers II*) in 1900 in a German book on the subject (Anastasi, 1972c). For Anastasi, the basic problem underlying much of differential psychology was an understanding of the contribution of heredity and environment to individual differences in psychological traits. Other important questions for the specialty concerned the identification and organization of psychological traits, and the understanding of group differences in behavior.

Fields of Applied Psychology (first edition, 1964) helped to give further legitimacy to a large part of psychology that was frequently ignored by academic psychologists. She said the book appealed to her generalist tendencies and allowed her to bring together several apparently unrelated areas in psychology (Anastasi, 1972c, p. 16). These ranged from engineering and consumer psychology to clinical, counseling and legal psychology. The aim of the book was to introduce students to the world of psychology outside of the classroom and laboratory, and to show the connections among the fields.

Psychological Testing (first edition, 1954) has been Anastasi's most popular and best-selling book. It is a detailed account of the manner in which tests are constructed, validated, and interpreted. It also contains extensive information on specific tests. The book was the standard text in psychological testing for decades. When the seventh edition appeared in 1996 (this time with former student Susana Urbina as coauthor), the book was immediately translated into nine languages.

Of all of Anastasi's books, *Psychological Testing* had the greatest role in solidifying and maintaining her reputation. It was, for all practical purposes, an encyclopedia of psychological testing. In it, she covered the full range of information necessary for a sophisticated and current approach to the subject. It included information about the history, nature, and use of psychological tests; ethical considerations; relevant statistical concepts including norms, reliability, validity, and item analysis; and descriptions of a broad band of instruments from the Stanford–Binet to the Thematic Apperception Test. (She found most projective tests to be poor psychometric instruments, and she suggested they were clinical tools that often could not be evaluated apart from the clinician using them.)

Anastasi's role in writing *Psychological Testing* was not a passive one. As the literature expanded, she developed techniques to meet the new approaches to information sharing. She stopped relying only on the literature. (Until it ceased hard-copy publication, she faithfully read *Psychological Abstracts* from cover to cover each month.) Instead, she used a variety of methods to keep current on the new tests including in-house reports, preprints, and unpublished manuscripts. She supplemented that information with direct inquiries by mail, telephone and personal conferences.

For Anastasi, there was nothing mysterious about psychological tests. They were simply tools, and their effectiveness depends on the skills and integrity of the examiner. Public criticism of testing was due, at least in part, to the misuse and misinterpretation of tests, and to the failure of psychometricians to stay connected to the mainstream of psychology and to relevant behavioral research. In one of the more controversial areas of evaluation, she noted that the term "intelligence" was used with a variety of meanings among different disciplines, and even among psychologists themselves. As societies change, so will the concept. The goal of intelligence testing is not to label individuals but to help in understanding them.

Anastasi never grew blasé about accurate measurement and was always cautious about errors that might go unnoticed. She cautioned about being sensitive to influences that may have acted on normative samples, such as subtle selective factors or changing conditions in the society. She believed basic research was still needed on larger issues such as the generality of psychological constructs derived within a single culture. She maintained that to develop a valid test, multiple procedures should be employed at various levels of test construction. Validity is not simply an issue to be considered at the final stage of test development; it should be built into the test from the beginning. Her thoughts were taken very seriously by other psychologists because they came from someone who knew the field so intimately and so well.

RETIREMENT AND LATER YEARS

On her retirement from Fordham University in 1979, Anne Anastasi was awarded an honorary Sc.D. (Doctor of Science) degree. It was one of five honorary degrees she would receive. As retirement gifts she asked for, and received, a calculator and a dictionary. In 1977, she was awarded the Distinguished Service to Measurement Award, given by the Educational Testing Service. Other awards followed, including the APA Distinguished Scientific Award for the Applications of Psychology (1981), the American Educational Research Association Award for Distinguished Contributions to Research in Education (1983), the E. L. Thorndike Medal for Distinguished Psychological Contributions to Education (1984), and the American Psychological Foundation Gold Medal for Lifetime Achievement (1984; Sexton & Hogan, 1990). In 1987, President Ronald Reagan awarded her the National Medal of Science, the nation's highest award for scientific achievement. With that award, she joined several other prominent psychology recipients such as B. F. Skinner (chap. 16, *Pioneers III*) and Harry Harlow (chap. 17, this volume).

After her retirement, Anastasi remained active, preparing the sixth and seventh editions of her testing book (1990, 1996) and writing many papers. The papers were often of a summary nature, revisiting topics she had researched earlier in her career. She also continued her schedule of consultantships, committee memberships, and invited addresses. She spoke at APA conventions until she was well into her 80s.

In 1992, at the 100th anniversary meeting of the APA, Anastasi participated in a symposium on past "women-presidents" of the APA. At that convention, she also delivered a well-received "master lecture" titled "A Century of Psychological Testing: Origins, Problems and Progress." In it, she reviewed modern testing, from its beginnings in 1890 to contemporary trends that were likely to be reflected in the future of testing. As usual, her comments were succinct and as objective and science-based as she could make them. She said before the lecture that, at age 84, she had trouble standing for very long but she delivered the lengthy talk with no discernible fatigue.

Back in New York, Anastasi attended weekly luncheons with colleagues from Fordham University. Eventually, her public appearances grew less frequent. Her husband died in 1994, after almost 61 years of marriage. Even at this late stage of her career, she was concerned that the large amount of stock in a testing company that she inherited from him might have an effect on her objectivity regarding tests. She sold the stock as quickly as she could.

Anastasi died in her Manhattan brownstone on May 4, 2001. She was 92 years old. In her last years, she had counseled friends and colleagues that they should not mourn her death. She had had a full life and she was satisfied with it.

CONCLUDING REMARKS

Almost 3 weeks after her death, a memorial service was held in New York City at the Frank E. Campbell Funeral Home. The service had not been easy to arrange because Anastasi had wanted no memorial whatsoever. But before her death some of her friends convinced her that a small gathering was necessary for them, if not for her.

Jonathan Galente, Anastasi's principal caretaker in her final years, and a long-time family friend from Fordham, made the final arrangements. The memorial was scheduled for 2 hours and, for the entire time, people told stories about her. The stories were spirited and often humorous, the kind of stories she would have enjoyed. They had little to do with her professional accomplishments, as such—those were taken for granted—but many had to do with her love of scholarship. She smiled out at the gathering from a large photograph taken by Galente and flanked by two gigantic bouquets of roses (Hogan, in press).

Despite all of her remarkable accomplishments, the speakers made clear that Anastasi was not an austere or distant personality. Although she was a self-described workaholic, she enjoyed having a few drinks from time to time, usually bourbon, and she occasionally smoked a cigarette, right up until the end of her life. Her secret, she said, was to do all things in moderation. She displayed a certain indifference to the ordinary and practical aspects of daily life. For instance, she professed to be fascinated by people who regularly cook at home. She had driven a car briefly during World War II, considering it her patriotic duty to learn, but she never learned to parallel park. And although she was well traveled, she declared that her favorite spot on earth was the zoo in New York's Central Park.

Anastasi was a formidable scholar, always promoting scientific objectivity, and with a great respect for the potential of psychology to serve the public good. She never doubted her choice of psychology as a career, and she never ceased to recommend it to young scholars. She said that she did not plan her life around money or status or approval. Her strengths, she believed, were her strong task orientation and the ability to immerse herself in the material at hand.

She summarized the unifying principles in her own life as "a desire to understand the world around me; to use tough-minded rational procedures; to debunk weak, sloppy generalizations; to fight charlatanism; and to correct popular misconceptions" (Anastasi, 1988, pp. 63–64). As with most matters of assessment, there are few who could disagree with her.

REFERENCES

American Psychological Foundation Awards for 1984. (1985). *American Psychologist, 40*, 340–341.

Anastasi, A. (1930). A group factor in immediate memory. *Archives of Psychology*, No. 120.

Anastasi, A. (1934). Practice and variability. *Psychological Monographs, 45*(5, Whole No. 204).

Anastasi, A. (1937). *Differential psychology.* New York: Macmillan.

Anastasi, A. (1938). Faculties versus factors: A reply to Professor Thurstone. *Psychological Bulletin, 35*, 391–395.

Anastasi, A. (1954). *Psychological testing.* New York: Macmillan.

Anastasi, A. (1958). Heredity, environment and the question "how?" *Psychological Review, 65*, 197–208.

Anastasi, A. (1964). *Fields of applied psychology*. New York: McGraw-Hill.

Anastasi, A. (1970). On the formation of psychological traits. *American Psychologist, 25*, 899–910.

Anastasi, A. (1972a). The cultivation of diversity. *American Psychologist, 27,* 1091–1099.

Anastasi, A. (1972b). Technical critique. In L. A. Crooks (Ed.), *Proceedings of Invitational Conference on "An investigation of sources of bias in the prediction of job performance: A six-year study"* (pp. 79–88). Princeton, NJ: Educational Testing Service.

Anastasi, A. (1972c). Reminiscences of a differential psychologist. In T. S. Krawiec (Ed.), *The psychologists* (pp. 3–37). New York: Oxford University Press.

Anastasi, A. (1981a). Coaching, test sophistication, and developed abilities. *American Psychologist, 36,* 1086–1093.

Anastasi, A. (1981b). Diverse effects of training on tests of academic intelligence. In B. F. Green (Ed.), *Issues in testing: Coaching, disclosure, and ethnic bias* (pp. 5–20). San Francisco: Jossey-Bass.

Anastasi, A. (1982). *Contributions to differential psychology: Selected papers*. New York: Praeger.

Anastasi, A. (1986). Experiential structuring of psychological traits. *Developmental Review, 6,* 181–202.

Anastasi, A. (1988a). Anne Anastasi. In A. N. O'Connell & N. Felipe Russo (Eds.), *Models of achievement: Reflections of eminent women in psychology* (Vol. 2, pp. 59–66). Hillsdale, NJ: Lawrence Erlbaum Associates.

Anastasi, A. (1990). *Psychological testing* (6th ed.). Englewood Cliffs, NJ: Prentice-Hall.

Anastasi, A. (1992). Are there unifying trends in the psychologies of the 1990s? In Margaret E. Donnelly (Ed.), *Reinterpreting the legacy of William James* (pp. 29–48). Washington, DC: American Psychological Association.

Anastasi, A., & Foley, J. P., Jr. (1938). A study of animal drawings by Indian children of the North Pacific Coast. *Journal of Social Psychology, 9,* 363–374.

Anastasi, A., & Foley, J. P., Jr. (1944). An experimental study of the drawing behavior of adult psychotics in comparison with that of a normal control group. *Journal of Experimental Psychology, 34,* 169–194.

Anastasi, A., & Foley, J. P., Jr. (1949). *Differential psychology* (2nd ed.). New York: Macmillan.

Anastasi, A., & Urbina, S. (1996). *Psychological testing* (7th ed.). Englewood Cliffs, NJ: Prentice-Hall.

Denton, L. (1987, October). The rich life and busy times of Anne Anastasi. *APA Monitor,* 10–11.

Distinguished Scientific Award for the Applications of Psychology: 1981. (1982). *American Psychologist, 37,* 52–59.

Fish, J. (1983). Oral history of Anne Anastasi. Report submitted to the Board of Professional Affairs of the American Psychological Association.

Gavin, E. (1987). Promient women in psychology, determined by ratings of distinguished peers. *Psychotherapy in Private Practice, 5,* 53–68.

Goode, E. (2001, May 16). Anne Anastasi, the "test guru" of psychology, is dead at 92. *The New York Times,* C-19.

Greenman, N. L. (1996). John Porter Foley, Jr. (1910–1994). *American Psychologist, 51,* 978.

Hogan, J. D. (2000). Anne Anastasi. In A. Kazdin (Ed.), *Encyclopedia of psychology* (Vol. 1, pp. 167–169). Washington, DC: American Psychological Association and Oxford University Press.

Hogan, J. D. (in press). Anne Anastasi (1908–2001). *American Journal of Psychology.*

Koch, S. (1981). The nature and limits of psychological knowledge: Lessons of a century qua "science." *American Psychologist, 36,* 257–269.

Lund, F. H., & Anastasi, A. (1928). An interpretation of esthetic experience. *American Journal of Psychology, 40,* 434–448.

Miller, G. A. (1969). Psychology as a means of promoting human welfare. *American Psychologist, 24,* 1063–1075.

Sexton, V. S., & Hogan, J. D. (1990). Anne Anastasi. In A. N. O'Connell & N. F. Russo (Eds.), *Women of psychology: A bio-bibliographic sourcebook* (pp. 3–11). Westport, CT: Greenwood Press.

Chapter 17

Harry Frederick Harlow:
And One Thing Led to Another . . .

Helen A. LeRoy
University of Wisconsin-Madison

Gregory A. Kimble
Duke University

This chapter presents an overview of Harry Harlow's legacy derived from personal acquaintance with Harlow and his work, as well as from his research papers, extensive correspondence files, and unpublished writings. It is important to look at Harlow's contributions from a long-range perspective. They continued for more than 40 years at the University of Wisconsin and did not end when he resigned from there in 1974 or when he died in Tucson, Arizona, on December 6, 1981.

FAMILY BACKGROUND AND EARLY LIFE

Harry Harlow's father, Lon Harlow Israel, and his mother, Mabel Rock Israel, were married when Harry's father was just 1 year short of graduating from medical school. Despite their Hebrew-sounding name, the Israels were Protestants. Harry was born in Fairfield, Iowa on October 31 (Halloween night) in 1905 and named Harry Frederick Israel. He was the third of the Israels' four sons; two older brothers, Robert and Delmer, were born in 1902 and 1904. A younger brother, Hugh, was born in 1909. Harry grew up in a compatible extended family that included his paternal grandmother and two aunts, Nell and Harriet.

Harry lived in Fairfield until he was 2 years old, when the family moved to Las Cruces, New Mexico, for 2 years because his older brother Delmer had tuberculosis. Returning to Iowa, Harry attended public schools in Fairfield and graduated from Fairfield High in 1923. As a youngster, Harry showed an interest in the arts. He studied piano and occasionally created paintings and wrote poetry.

Harry's higher education began at Reed College in Portland, Oregon, in 1923 but after just 1 year there, he transferred to Stanford University. He began as an English major, switched to psychology, and received the BA degree cum laude in 1927. Harry remained at Stanford for graduate study and received a doctorate in 1930. At Stanford, one of Harry's major professors was Calvin P. Stone, who "taught me scientific techniques . . . He was always pushing back the frontier of science—as he said—step by step and stone by stone" (Harlow, 1977, p. 137). The "step-by-step, stone-by-stone" remark was a bit of Harlow irony. He preferred what he later called "golden-angel" research that sometimes results from flashes of insight, to Stone's plodding "silver-angel" approach to science.

Other influential professors at Stanford were Lewis M. Terman (chap. 8, *Pioneers IV*) and Walter R. Miles. Terman, who is best remembered for producing the Stanford–Binet Test of Intelligence and for his work with gifted children, taught scientific theory. Walter Miles employed Harry as a research assistant and served as his moral mentor. Both Miles and Terman were instrumental in getting Harry to change his name, for reasons that Miles spelled out in a letter to Harry's father (Harlow Archives),[1] dated May 28, 1930:

> At Stanford we take great pleasure in placing the men who graduate in our Department. During the last months I have written several letters of recommendation proposing your son, Harry, for this or that opening. I believe you can understand without my going into details that in practically every such letter it was necessary for me to say that the organization or institution had a right to know that this individual was not a Hebrew and that his name was quite misleading. Recently I was in the East and in different places I tried to place your son in what I thought would be a suitable position for him. In discussing such an opening with a Dean of one of the large state universities, this Dean said to me "It makes no difference about his qualifications. I simply can't take a man with that name."

A little more than a month later, Harry Israel changed his last name to "Harlow," his father's middle name.

EARLY YEARS AT THE UNIVERSITY OF WISCONSIN

Soon after he changed his name, Harlow found his first and only job, as an assistant professor at the University of Wisconsin, Madison, with a salary of $2,750 per year—fairly high in those Great Depression years—and the promise of an animal laboratory where he could do research. He spent most of his productive

---

[1]At the present time, the senior author is custodian of the "Harlow Archives."

life in Madison, rising to the level of associate professor in 1938, professor in 1944, and chair in 1949.

While Harlow was getting acquainted with the Wisconsin campus and starting his teaching career, he met Clara Mears, a new graduate student in the department of educational psychology who, coincidentally, had been a subject in Terman's gifted-children study. Mears enrolled in Harlow's first-semester course, "Psychology of the Emotions," and was so fascinated by his teaching that she signed up for his second-semester course in "Physiological Psychology" as well as an evening seminar. As the semester progressed, Harlow began escorting Mears home after the seminar. Harlow and Mears were married on May 8, 1932, in Milwaukee. They had two children: Robert, born in 1940, and Richard, born in 1943. They were divorced in 1946 and remarried in 1972. In between Harlow was married to Margaret Ruth (Peggy) Kuenne Harlow (1918–1971), a distinguished developmental psychologist who had a doctorate degree from the University of Iowa, where she studied with Kenneth W. Spence (chap. 17, *Pioneers III*). Before she married Harlow, she had served as an intern at the Western State Psychiatric Hospital in Pittsburgh, as an instructor at the University of Minnesota, and as an assistant professor at the University of Wisconsin. They also had two children: Pamela, born in 1950, and Jonathan, born in 1953.

THE BEGINNINGS OF RESEARCH
WITH PRIMATES

When Harlow joined the faculty at Wisconsin and arrived on campus, one of the first things he did was to visit his department chairman, V. A. C. Henmon. As Harlow recalled, "Almost before the amenities were completed, I asked to be shown the laboratory I had been promised with the job. The chairman's kindly face fell, 'I am so sorry,' he said, 'They tore it down last month' " (Harlow, 1977, p. 138). Henmon assured Harlow, however, that the university would find him a laboratory of some sort to house a few students and some rats, although in the meantime he would have to be patient. Actually, the university kept its promise better than some such institutions have been known to do under these circumstances. Harlow's first lab was a cramped cubicle located below the dean of men's office. Later on, the medical school lent him another small room, which had to suffice until better space could be found.

When they were courting, Harlow and Mears found that they shared an interest in playing bridge—and soon thereafter they were enjoying bridge games with chairman Henmon and his wife. One night over a game of bridge, Mrs. Henmon, who was a member of the Vilas family who had endowed Madison's Vilas Park Zoo, suggested that Harlow spend some time observing the monkeys at the zoo. She was sympathetic to his lack of research facilities and knew he found it frustrating. Mrs. Henmon accompanied Harry to the zoo the next day and introduced him to its director, Fred Winkleman, who then introduced him to the entire resident primate population. Thus began Harlow's program of primate learning research, which would develop and grow for more than 50 years.

In 1932, the university provided Harlow with a 24-ft square two-story building, recently vacated by another department. The building had been condemned and was unheated, but for the next two decades Harlow and a few dedicated graduate students pioneered a diverse and dynamic program of study of primate learning capabilities and their cortical localization, using the rhesus monkey as a primary experimental subject. It was the ingenuity, plus the physical labor provided by Harlow and his graduate students, that led to the growth and development of the facility. In an unpublished address, "My Life With Men and Monkeys," that Harlow gave in 1959 at a dinner meeting (Harlow Archives), to which diversified Wisconsin faculty were invited, he related that "Actually, a very considerable part of the material cost was paid from a special University Fund, the Harry F. Harlow monthly salary check."

Harlow went on to explain that "the first floor was a maze of reinforced concrete posts with two enormous pillars extending through the ceiling 5 feet into the second floor. . . . Two graduate students and I knocked the small ones to pieces with sledge hammers and finally rented a pneumatic hammer and cut the two big pillars to bits. No matter how abstract our research eventually became, it started out by being very concrete." They continued to remodel and expand, operating independently of the usual bureaucratic processes found on college campuses. With their own resources, they added outdoor observation chambers and were pleasantly surprised by how effective they were as all-weather test rooms. Harlow related that "a year later we received an outraged letter from the Superintendent of Buildings and Grounds saying we couldn't do what we had done, and we were pleased by this letter because it established the fact that the University now recognized these buildings as an integral part of their campus." Harlow went on to observe:

> Don't think for a minute that we didn't take this letter seriously and learn something from it. We immediately initiated our landscaping program and built a 7-ft. high wire fence around the laboratory grounds and planted a hedge of mock orange and honeysuckle bushes. We also planted two fir trees, two wisteria, an American Beauty climbing rose, and some forsythia and spirea bushes, because we wanted the University Administrators to think of the Primate Lab as a place of beauty.
>
> For better or for worse, our first try at physical plant construction proved to be so rewarding that it became habit-forming. We put a temporary observation chamber on the other side of the building . . . a little addition 30 ft. long and 15 ft. wide, holding 16 monkey cages and outside runways. We laid the reinforced concrete foundations 3.5 feet deep and built the two rooms out of concrete blocks. We did not experience any immediate trouble from the administration—I already mentioned that the landscaping program left the property surrounded by a 7 foot high fence, and it is amazing how rapidly ivy grows and you would be surprised what an impenetrable

hedge a row of honeysuckle bushes makes. . . . It is a great deal harder to see through a honeysuckle hedge than a college professor. (Harlow Archives)

In spite of the limitations of working in a zoo and a primitive research laboratory, Harlow and his students carried out more than 50 studies of learning and the effects of cortical lesions in rhesus monkeys, in the first 20 years there. These studies assessed the intellectual capabilities of a broad range of nonhuman primate species and established the basis for Harlow's later work, as well as for research by other investigators. Harlow's first paper on primate behavior compared delayed reaction test performance—the length of time animals could remember the location of an object they had watched the experimenter hide—of a group of primates (Harlow, Uehling, & Maslow, 1932). A book that Harlow and Mears put together after Harlow had retired and they moved to Tucson described their first work this way:

> The first major researches at the Wisconsin Primate Laboratory related to cortical localization of psychological functions. Through lesions in varied locations of the cortex, different intellectual functions could be related or localized to appropriate cortical areas. In the 1920s Lashley had postulated equipotentiality of all areas of the cortex for all intellectual functions. A decade or so later, Jacobsen conducted his classical studies on localization of function in the prefrontal lobe of the cortex. He showed that destruction of this area was followed by loss of immediate memory as measured by delayed response tests. . . . Since we had age-dated monkeys, comparison of intellectual loss through identical lesions at different ages could be assessed. (Harlow & Mears, 1979, p. 6)

CHALLENGES TO ACCEPTED WISDOM

Safely hidden behind the honeysuckle, Harlow and his students set about revolutionizing the field of primate learning. They soon discovered that the tasks used to test the learning abilities of traditional laboratory subjects such as pigeons, white rats, and even dogs were far too simple and too easily mastered by the monkey. So they were forced to develop new tests and invent new apparatus to present their subjects with suitable intellectual challenges. With John Bromer, Harlow invented the Wisconsin General Test Apparatus (WGTA) shown in Fig. 17.1, which has since served throughout the world as the basic monkey learning test device (Harlow, 1949; Harlow & Bromer, 1938).

Learning Sets and Error Factor Theory

As the story develops in this chapter, it will become clear that a major theme in Harlow's research was the questioning of generally accepted theories. When he was a Carnegie Fellow in Anthropology at Columbia University in 1939–1940, the neurologist Kurt Goldstein (chap. 8, this volume) was a member of the medi-

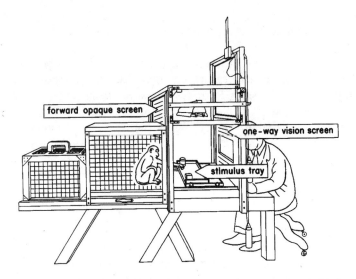

FIG. 17.1.   The Wisconsin General Test Apparatus. Picture reproduced with the permission of the Harlow Primate Laboratory.

cal faculty there. Goldstein (and indeed most scientists of that day) believed that only human beings are capable of reasoning and insight, and that subhuman animals are limited to solving very concrete problems. Returning to Wisconsin, and using the WGTA, Harlow set out to challenge this belief, by showing that monkeys could make discriminations suddenly and seemingly with insight.

In these experiments, monkeys mastered a long series (344) of discrimination problems in which they learned to choose one of two objects to get a reward of food. The discriminanda varied from problem to problem. The first problem discrimination involved a hemispherical object and a cube; the second, a circle and a rectangle; the third, a white object and a black one; and so on. Finding all the hundreds of small objects that were needed for all of these discriminations was a problem and Harlow and his graduate students scoured the local Woolworth 5-and-10-cent store looking for them. After shopping with Harlow for WGTA objects, Harlow's friend Delos Wickens put it in the words of an old pop tune, remarking that Harlow "found a million dollar baby in the five and 10 cent store" (Harlow Archives). The results of this study showed that, early on, the monkeys learned the discriminations gradually and slowly. After considerable practice, however, learning was sudden and seemingly insightful. The percentage of correct choices was 50% on the first trial with the new problems but 97% on the second trial. In almost every case, the outcome of the first trial—whether the choice was right or wrong—served, as if by insight, to inform the monkeys of the right choice.

But to say that the monkeys had improved so dramatically because they had developed insight is circular and no explanation at all. Harlow did better than that. He interpreted his results in terms of what he called "error-factor theory" (Harlow, 1949). He argued that the benefit provided over trials in these experiments was the elimination of certain error tendencies that monkeys bring with them to the laboratory. It is well known that animals of most species have definite preferences for certain shapes, colors, sizes, and spatial locations of objects, as well as strong handedness tendencies, which may determine the first choice a monkey makes on any problem. With exposure to many discrimination problems, however, these tendencies are extinguished because they go unrewarded. This unlearning of wrong reactions is all that is required to allow the monkey to make the correct ("insightful") choice after just one attempt to solve the problem. Although Harlow was to receive greater recognition for research that he did later, error-factor theory was his own most favorite contribution to the science of psychology (personal note to GAK sometime in the 1960s).

Curiosity and Manipulation Motives

In the early 1950s the theories of Clark L. Hull (chap. 14, *Pioneers I*) and Kenneth W. Spence (chap. 17, *Pioneers III*) dominated the field of learning. One of the central hypotheses of the Hull–Spence position was drive-reduction theory, the hypothesis that organisms can learn only if they have some drive or need that can be satisfied by learning the desired task. For example, responses motivated by hunger are reinforced by hunger reduction; those motivated by fear are reinforced by fear reduction. Harlow didn't buy such interpretations for reasons that were unique to his way of selecting topics for research. He loved serendipity. Informally, he had watched his monkeys learn numerous complex tasks with no more motivation than apparent curiosity and no more reward than apparent satisfaction of that curiosity.

Stimulated by such observations, Harlow sponsored several studies of learning motivated only by curiosity and a drive to manipulate objects in the world— learning that did not fit gracefully into the drive-reduction paradigm. For example, Butler (1953) tested monkeys in an enclosed box located in a large room where there usually were people engaged in one sort of activity or another. The box contained two windows with a provision for randomly putting a blue card in one window and a yellow card in the other. Pushing on the window with one color or the other opened it, allowing the monkey to look out and watch the happenings in the room. All of the animals learned to open the window with the card indicating that it could be opened—and they kept at this task with great persistence. In later studies, Butler showed that the sight of another monkey is possibly the most effective visual incentive, but the opportunity to see an empty box, to watch an electric train, to observe a tray of food, or just to hear the sound of a train running, or the noises made by other monkeys in the colony are powerful incentives (Butler, 1954, 1957a, 1957b).

In a closely related set of studies Harlow (1950) demonstrated that monkeys will master mechanical puzzles for the sheer sake of doing them. Apparently, monkeys have a motive that is satisfied by nothing more than the opportunity to manipulate objects in the environment. Harlow and McClearn (1954) added the information that monkeys will learn a discrimination on the basis of this motive. In their study, the monkey was presented with a board containing five pairs of screw eyes of different colors. Those of one color were removable; those of the other color were not. The monkeys learned which were removable and practice led to an increase in the number of screw eyes removed.

Expansion of the Primate Laboratory and Founding of the Wisconsin Primate Center

Early in the 1950s Harlow became interested in studying the development of learning capabilities in newborn infant monkeys as they grew to adulthood. But there was a problem, the lack of a sufficient number of baby monkeys to make such a program of research feasible. The establishment of a breeding colony was the only way to solve that problem. However, a breeding colony would require several times the space of Harlow's entire existing laboratory. The Wisconsin Alumni Research Foundation generously provided the funds required to purchase a deserted cheese factory and to remodel it extensively into a primate research facility.

Harlow told of his encounter with the university's supervisor of building and grounds when the latter presented him with the initial remodeling plans. Harlow recalled, "I noticed with astonishment that there was a door at the back of the building, and I asked him what it was for. 'That,' he said, 'is to give you access when you build the addition.' . . . I said, I can promise you one thing. I now have the laboratory I have always dreamed of, and there will never be a need for any addition. I don't know how he ever got such an idea!" (Harlow, 1977, p. 144). Three years later, construction began on a new addition, bringing the Primate Laboratory to its present-day size. Nine years later, in the spring of 1964, construction was completed of yet another addition—actually, an entirely new building, separate but adjacent to the laboratory. Thus, in the early 1960s, this facility became the Wisconsin Regional Primate Research Center, one of seven large primate research facilities throughout the United States established and funded by the National Institutes of Health. In recognition of his prominence in research, an award supporting the primate center was granted to Harlow in 1961.

THE DEVELOPMENT OF FILIAL ATTACHMENT

The presence of infant monkeys opened the avenue of research that made Harlow most famous. As in the case of his research on learning sets, he was convinced that drive-reduction theory could not account for the development of filial attachments in infant rhesus monkeys. Drive-reduction theory's account of why infants develop attachments to their mothers was a theory of "cupboard love." Because mothers feed their babies when those babies are hungry, drive-reduction theory held that this satisfaction of an important need leads infants to love their mothers and that this love serves as the basis for all other social relationships the individual enters into for a lifetime. In those days, even the psychoanalysts joined with the behaviorists in the acceptance of this interpretation. Harlow took exception—again because of serendipitous observations, which had suggested to him that the true basis of infants' attachment to their mother was contact comfort.

Monkey babies born in the laboratory were usually separated from their mothers at birth and reared in a nursery (similar to the hospital maternity wards of the time) to minimize the risk of disease. As Harlow described his original observations:

> Our interest in infant-monkey love grew out of a research program that involved the separation of monkeys from their mothers a few hours after birth. Employing techniques developed by Gertrude van Wagenen of Yale University, we had been rearing infant monkeys on the bottle with a mortality far less than that among monkeys nursed by their mothers. We were particularly careful to provide the infant monkeys with a folded gauze diaper on the floor of their cages, in accord with Dr. van Wagenen's observation that they would tend to maintain intimate contact with such soft, pliant surfaces, especially during nursing. We were impressed by the deep personal attachments that the monkeys formed for these diaper pads, and by the distress that they exhibited when the pads were briefly removed once a day for purposes of sanitation. The behavior of the infant monkeys was reminiscent of the human infant's attachment to its blankets, pillows, rag dolls or cuddly teddy bears. These observations suggested the series of experiments in which we have sought to compare the importance of nursing and all associated activities with that of simple bodily contact in engendering the infant monkey's attachment to its mother. (Harlow, 1959, p. 68)

Contact Comfort

In Harlow's initial experiments, infant monkeys were separated from their mothers 6 to 12 hr after they were born and were raised alone in cages with substitute or "surrogate" mothers. One of the stories Harlow related in later years concerned the creation of the mother surrogate. As he recalled it, a "vision" of the surrogate mother appeared to him in the airplane's window while he was flying over Detroit on a champagne flight—those were the halcyon days when government consultants often flew first-class at government expense—from Washington D.C. to Madison, "So I came back and tried to find a graduate student to work with me on maternal deprivation, and by God I couldn't find anyone who thought it was a researchable topic. Finally Bob

FIG. 17.2.   The power of contact comfort. The baby monkey clings to the terry-cloth mother while it nurses from a bottle on the wire mother. Photo reproduced with permission of the Harlow Primate Laboratory.

Zimmermann saw the light and joined me—he made the apparatus of the surrogate mothers" (Tavris, 1973, p. 74).

One of the surrogate mothers was a stiff bare-wire cylinder; the other was a wooden cylinder covered with soft terry cloth. In one experiment, both of these surrogate mothers were available to the infant monkeys but only one possessed a nipple from which the infant could nurse. Some infants received nourishment from the wire mother, others from the cloth mother. Even when the wire mother was the only source of nourishment, the infant spent a greater amount of time clinging to the cloth surrogate. These studies suggested, contrary to drive-reduction theory, that it is the contact comfort provided by regular mothers, rather than their association with feeding, that fosters the infant's attachment to her (see Fig. 17.2).

Harlow introduced his position in his presidential address before the American Psychological Association in Washington, D.C., in 1958. The article resulting from the talk (Harlow, 1958) contained several whimsical examples of Harlow's penchant for writing poetry. The poems featured contact comfort in several animals, including the elephant, and crocodile:

The Elephant

Though mother may be short on arms,
Her skin is full of warmth and charms.
And mother's touch on baby's skin
Endears the heart that beats within.

The Crocodile

Here is the skin they love to touch.
It isn't soft and there isn't much,
But its contact comfort will beguile
Love from the infant crocodile. (p. 678)

Surrogate Mothers Versus Natural Mothers

Inevitably, the surrogate and real monkey mothers had to be compared in their effects on the infant monkeys' overall development. Results demonstrated the superiority of the natural mothers. Although the comfort provided by the terry-cloth mothers seemed to allow normal behavioral development during infancy, the actions of the monkeys raised by surrogates and without peers became bizarre in later life. These monkeys had stereotyped patterns of behavior—they moved in circles, clutched at themselves, and rocked constantly back and forth while staring vacantly. They exhibited excessive and misdirected aggression, sometimes attacking infants or injuring themselves. They proved to be particularly deficient in their sexual and parenting behavior. Harlow colorfully described the sexual inadequacy of these monkeys:

> Sex behavior was, for all practical purposes, destroyed; sexual posturing was commonly stereotyped and infantile. Frequently when [a surrogate-raised] female was approached by a normal male, she would sit unmoved, squatting upon the floor—a posture in which only her heart was in the right place. Contrariwise, [a surrogate-raised] male might approach an in-estrus female, but he might clasp the head instead of the hind legs, and then engage in pelvic thrusts. Other [surrogate-raised] males grasped the female's body laterally, whereby all sexual efforts left them working at cross purposes. (Harlow, 1972, p. 47)

"Motherless Mothers"

Some of the surrogate-raised females were finally impregnated, either through artificial insemination or after repeated and heroic efforts by the most persuasive of normally raised males. When these females gave birth to babies of their own, the behavior of these "motherless mothers" as Harlow called them proved to be very inadequate. They met the winsome appeals of an infant monkey seeking to be cuddled either with indifference or abuse. The indifferent mothers did not nurse, comfort, or protect their young, but neither they did harm them. The abusive mothers, however, bit and otherwise injured their babies, to the point that many of them died.

The indifference and brutality of these mothers raised the question whether their infants would become attached to them. Harlow found that the babies of the motherless mothers were unceasing in their efforts to gain maternal contact. Over and over again, the infants would try to nuzzle and cuddle with the mother, despite repeated physical rebuffs. It is interesting that these persistent efforts of the baby monkeys had a rehabilitating effect on some of the motherless mothers. After several months they became less rejecting and less punishing. In fact, some of their infants established more contact with their mothers than did infants born to normal mothers. These rehabilitated mothers demonstrated their rehabilitation by becoming adequate caretakers of their later born infants. However, the motherless mothers who never warmed up to their first born babies continued to be inadequate or even brutal mothers to their later offspring (see Ruppenthal, Arling, Harlow, Sackett, & Suomi, 1976).

Following this lead, in the late 1960s Harlow's focus turned to animal modeling of human psychiatric disorders and to detailed study of phenomena associated with human-like depression in monkeys. He worked with graduate students and research staff to attain significant breakthroughs in understanding depression, the most common and widespread mental illness, as well as the development of more effective treatment strategies (McKinney, Suomi, & Harlow, 1973; Suomi, Harlow, & Novak, 1974). As Harlow's more than 40-year career at Wisconsin neared an end, he liked to think of the later research, which commenced with the mother surrogate and progressed through psychopathology to rehabilitation, as embodying the theme: "Love Created, Love Destroyed, and Love Regained" (Harlow, 1972).

PROFESSIONAL CONTRIBUTIONS

Harlow led a very busy life. He published more than 300 scholarly works, including several books. He was an active letter writer. His files contain hundreds of notes from faculty, researchers, and students at other universities, expressing interest in his research and asking his opinion about the feasibility of their own ideas for research or their explanations of behavior. He answered most of them. There are also hundreds of letters from deans, department chairs, and faculty at other colleges and universities seeking Harlow's input on potential candidates for faculty openings at their schools. He replied to letters from colleagues; academicians; authors of accepted and rejected journal articles; the general public; grade-school, high-school, and college students; individuals in prisons; and those with mental problems seeking help. A husband–wife team of university psychologists wrote to say they had added his name to their private vocabulary—"a Harlow is a hug"—and the wife wanted to obtain a surrogate mother for her husband for his birthday. A rock band wrote about wanting to name itself "Soft Monkey" in honor of the comfort offered by the cloth mother. Several artists employed the mother surrogate and contact comfort as symbols in their work (Harlow Archives).

Harlow's strong writing skills resulted in his work's being read by a wider audience than just his colleagues in the behavioral sciences. For example, shortly after the publication of a 1971 article in the *American Scientist* (Harlow, Harlow, & Suomi, 1971), Harlow received a letter of appreciation from the dean of the College of Earth Sciences at a southwestern university. The dean, who was a geologist by profession, took the time to let Harlow know: "Rarely do I read an article totally outside my own field that is so clearly written and educationally rewarding. . . . As a geologist, my professional life has been centered in the inanimate world of glaciers, rocks, and fossils. . . . Many thanks for an extremely well-written article; it can stand as a model for others who ought to 'go out and do likewise' " (Harlow Archives).

As director of both the Primate Center and the laboratory, Harlow faced enormous pressures resulting from the day-to-day business of running the operation. In spite of these demands, he made important contributions to the work of federal and state agencies and scholarly societies. He served as a consultant for the National Institutes of Health and Mental Health, and the Department of the Army, heading the Human Resources Research Office in 1952. He played an active role as a consultant for the Educational Testing Service in the design of the psychology component of the Graduate Record Examination and for the American Institute for Research in the evaluation of doctoral dissertations for national awards. He attended meetings of the National Academy of Sciences and the American Philosophical Society, the APA, the American Association for the Advancement of Science, the Society for Research in Child Development, the Psychonomic Society, the Society of Experimental Psychologists, and the International Primatological Society. He made presentations as an invited speaker at hundreds of colleges and professional conventions. He was on the editorial board of *Science*, and was a reviewer for many other journals, including *Scientific American, American Scientist*, and *Brain Research*. He was the editor of the *Journal of Comparative and Physiological Psychology* for 12 years, from 1951—when his one-time professor C. P. Stone retired as editor of that journal—to 1963. For McGraw-Hill, he also was the editor of a series of textbooks in psychology.

The following chronology only hits the highlights of Harlow's participation in the affairs of the APA and other scholarly organizations:

1939–1942—Member of the Council, Midwest Psychological Association

1946–1948—Secretary of APA Division of Comparative and Physiological Psychology

1954–1955—Chair of APA Policy and Planning Board

1950–1952—Chief of the Human Resources Research Office, U.S. Army

1954–1956—Chair, Division of Anthropology and Psychology, National Research Council

1956–1965—Consultant, U.S. Army Scientific Advisory Panel

1959—Sigma Xi Lecturer

1960—Thomas William Salmon Lecturer in psychiatry

1961—Messenger Lecturer, Cornell University

HARLOW, THE INDIVIDUAL

Harlow was a bright and very creative scientist, totally devoted to his program of research. His capacity for work was legendary. He usually arose around 6:00 a.m. and went for an early-morning walk, sometimes to get relief from the previous night's bout of drinking—his capacity for alcohol was also legendary. He might not return home until early the following morning. He spent the intervening hours with staff and students, all of whom he treated as his equals. He often had early-morning coffee with the janitors. The academic world is populated with snobbery and pomposity, but Harlow displayed neither of these. In his personal relationships, he was down to earth and unassuming. He never let his fame intrude in his dealings with those around him.

There was not a trace of the dictator in Harlow's management of laboratory personnel. He allowed his graduate students, postdoctoral students, and staff enough latitude to blossom on their own, to try out their own ideas. Many individuals below the doctoral level played major roles in research, administration, the oversight of the Primate Center, and the operation of the laboratory. The animal-care staff members were key in maintaining the successful breeding program essential for fulfilling colony and investigator requirements. Harlow's staff was a closely knit family. Some of them maintained friendships over many years.

Harlow as a Teacher

Harlow was an extremely popular teacher at the University of Wisconsin, one of the most popular professors on campus. Throughout his entire career there, he often taught the introductory course in psychology—admitting that he found the diversity in the topics covered a useful stimulus to thinking. Over that same period Harlow supervised the dissertations of about three dozen doctoral students. Abraham Maslow, who received his degree in 1934, was Harlow's first doctoral student. Maslow worked with Harlow at the zoo, writing his dissertation on dominance hierarchies in monkeys. For years, it was considered the seminal paper on the topic. Maslow would later become the famous humanistic psychologist who described the self-actualization process (Maslow, 1970). Many of the students to follow Maslow published journal articles with their mentor.

Philosophy of Research

As pointed out previously in this chapter, Harlow had strong opinions—mostly minority opinions—about the science of psychology. He opposed the then-dominant drive-reduction theory of reinforcement, and much of his research was an attack on that position. At a more general level, again in opposition to prevailing attitudes, he never displayed much interest in psychological theorizing. His only important effort of that sort was his "error-factor" theory of learning to learn in terms of "learning sets." Whereas most research in other laboratories in Harlow's day was aimed at testing the implications of one theory or another, Harlow got his research ideas from observations of the behavior of primates—or even human beings. Behind this preference there was the idea that research with primates should touch on human problems:

> I always believed that I should never do anything with monkeys that would not have significance with man. . . . I firmly believe that one should never study problems in monkeys that cannot be solved in man. . . . A question commonly asked is, "Does primate research generalize to human beings?" . . . At the Wisconsin Primate Laboratory we have approached the question in reverse. Because of the basic similarity between monkeys and men, human models may be used to plot and to plan monkey researches. . . . There is far more reason to use human data to plan and interpret monkey researches than to use monkey data to plan human studies. (Harlow & Mears, 1979, pp. 2–3)

Harlow also had a negative reaction to certain research practices that were highly regarded in his day. He disliked "parametric" experiments which looked at the effects of subjecting many groups of research participants to many different values of some independent variable. He much preferred "golden-angel" research that made its point in a single dramatic demonstration over such "silver-angel" exercises:

> Different kinds of psychologists using very different methods will do golden- and silver-angel research. . . . It is my opinion that golden-angel research will be best achieved if every psychologist feels that he is free to work on the problems which he believes are important, in the way which he thinks is appropriate, without feelings of deference. We need not worry too greatly about the techniques used or the capabilities of the men who first secure the intellectual beachheads. They will be followed by successive waves of silver-angels who will move in the heavy equipment, . . . the Monroe calculators, and even the IBM machines and digital computers if the assault on the intellectual island is worthy of such logistic support. The grains of gold which were already uprooted from the sandy beaches will then be arranged in rows and columns, combinations and permutations, and eventually re-

constructed and reassembled into intellectual coins which will be scientific legal tender for all time and all eternity. (Harlow, 1957, p. 490)

CONCLUSION: RECOGNITION AND HONORS

Harlow was one of the most renowned psychologists of the 20th century. His groundbreaking studies of monkeys shed light on the brain function, learning capabilities and intelligence of his subjects. They also added to the understanding of their development, both normal and abnormal, their social behavior, and their affectional relationships. Harlow's work had a major impact on psychology, but it was also influential in the related sciences of psychiatry, ethology, sociology, and cultural anthropology. His demonstrations of the importance of contact comfort in infancy, the role of the mother, and the significance of peer relationships and play during childhood and adolescence were assimilated into the popular views of childrearing and social practice.

The significance of Harlow's scholarly contributions did not go unnoticed. As the following summary reveals, few years went by in which he failed to receive some major recognition:

1935—Elected Fellow of the American Psychological Association

1946—Elected to the Society of Experimental Psychologists

1947—Elected President of the Midwestern Psychological Association

1950—Elected President of the APA Division of Experimental Psychology

1951—Elected to National Academy of Science

1956—Awarded the Howard Crosby Warren Medal, Society of Experimental Psychologists, one of experimental psychology's most prestigious awards. Only one Warren Medal is awarded in a given year and in some years there is none.

1957—Elected to the American Philosophical Society

1957—Elected President of American Psychological Association

1960—Distinguished Scientific Contribution Award (APA). "For his indefatigable curiosity which has opened up new areas of research in animal behavior and has helped greatly to keep comparative psychology near the center of the psychological stage. Throughout the years his vivid imagination has led to the analysis of many stimulus relationships, the exploratory and manipulatory motives, and the all-but-ubiquitous learning sets. Recently the age-old problem of love has been revitalized by his persistent concern for the facts of motivation. It is, indeed, his unswerving devotion to fact, observation, and experiment that has given his contribution an integrity of inestimable value to scientific psychology."

1961—Elected to the American Academy of Arts and Sciences

1964—Elected President of the APA Division of Comparative and Physiological Psychology

1964—Elected vice president, psychology section, of the British Association for the Advancement of Science

1965—Sigma Xi Lecturer

1968—National Medal of Science, America's highest official award for scientific achievement. The citation reads: "For original and ingenious contributions to comparative and experimental psychology, particularly in the controlled study of learning and motivations, the determinants of animal behavior, and development of affectional behavior. Dr. Harlow has shed much light on human behavior and mental development through study of the social behavior of monkeys."

1968—Listed in *Who's Who in Science*, cited for development of new hypotheses in neurophysiology, love, and motivation

1972—Named Honorary Fellow of the British Psychological Society

1972—Awarded the G. Stanley Hall Medal (APA; with Margaret K. Harlow) for the Harlows' distinctive contributions to developmental psychology

1972—Recipient of the Martin Rehfuss Award, presented for distinguished service to medicine.

1973—Recipient of the Gold Medal Award of the American Psychological Foundation "in recognition of a distinguished and long-continued record of scientific and scholarly achievements. A creative and dedicated investigator, he has enlarged the science of man through artful experimentation with monkey."

1973—Harlow himself considered it an honor to have his work recognized in connection with the award of the Nobel Prize in Medicine-Physiology to Konrad Lorenz, Karl von Frisch, and Nikolaas Tinbergen. The citation included this mention of Harlow's research: "Other researchers have gone on to show the disastrous consequences of isolation on primate infants. . . . These findings, which underscore the importance of intimate early contact between mother and child, have already been incorporated in modern theories of child rearing" (*Newsweek*, October 22, 1973). There were many psychologists, including the present authors, who believed that the prize should have gone to Harlow.

1974—Recipient of the Annual Award of the Society of Scientific Study of Sex for outstanding contributions to the knowledge and understanding of sexuality.

1975—Recipient of the Third International Kittay Award, the most prestigious award in the field of psychiatry. At the time of his award, *Science News* praised Harlow's work as "important, fruitful, imaginative, ingenious, valid, original, creative and outstanding." Theodore Lidz of Yale University Medical School called Harlow's work "of extreme significance for understanding those aspects of human behavior related to depression, aggression or sexual dysfunction, which originate in the formative years of mother–infant interaction." George Serban, medical director of the Kittay Foundation, said Harlow's work "freed clinical psychiatrists from existent speculative concepts and unverified assumptions concerning the mother-infant bond and the development of depression."

1979—Recipient of the Distinguished Scientific Contribution Award of the Society for Research in Child Development.

Day-to-day life with Harlow at his primate laboratory was challenging, rewarding, and frequently quite entertaining. Harlow's Groucho Marx–like wit kept the place humming, while his enthusiasm for his work, his creative approach to his research, and his wonderful sense of curiosity permeated the atmosphere. Harlow loved the notion of "serendipity," and his "golden-angel" approach to research took him down paths that he might not necessarily have foreseen. It just always seemed as though one thing led to another.

REFERENCES

Butler, R. A. (1953). Discrimination learning by rhesus monkeys to visual-exploration motivation. *Journal of Comparative and Physiological Psychology, 46*, 95–98.

Butler, R. A. (1954). Curiosity in monkeys. *Scientific American, 190*, 70–75.

Butler, R. A. (1957a). The effect of deprivation of visual incentives on visual-exploration motivation in monkeys. *Journal of Experimental Psychology, 50*, 239–241.

Butler, R. A. (1957b). Discrimination learning by rhesus monkeys to visual-exploration motivation. *Journal of Comparative and Physiological Psychology, 50*, 177–179.

Harlow, H. F. (1949). The formation of learning sets. *Psychological Review, 56*, 51–65.

Harlow, H. F. (1950). Learning and satiation of response in intrinsically motivated complex puzzle performance in monkeys. *Journal of Comparative and Physiological Psychology, 43*, 289–294.

Harlow, H. F. (1957). Experimental analysis of behavior. *American Psychologist, 123*, 485–490.

Harlow, H. F. (1958). The nature of love. *American Psychologist, 13*, 673–685.

Harlow, H. F. (1959). Love in infant monkeys. *Scientific American, 200*, 68–74.

Harlow, H. F. (1972). Love created—love destroyed—love regained. In *Modeles animaux du comportement humain* (pp. 13–60). Paris: Editions du Centre National de la Recherche Scientifique, No. 198.

Harlow, H. F. (1977). Birth of the surrogate mother. In W. R. Klemm (Ed.), *Discovery processes in modern biology* (pp. 133–150). Huntington, NY: Krieger.

Harlow, H. F., & Bromer, J. (1938). A test-apparatus for monkeys. *Psychological Record, 2*, 434–436.

Harlow, H. F., Harlow, M. K., & Suomi, S. J. (1971). From thought to therapy: Lessons from a Primate Laboratory. *American Scientist, 59*, 538–549.

Harlow, H. F., & McClearn, G. E. (1954). Object discrimination learned by monkeys on the basis of manipulation motives. *Journal of Comparative and Physiological Psychology, 47*, 73–76.

Harlow, H. F., & Mears, C. (1979). *The human model: Primate perspectives*. Washington, DC: Winston.

Harlow, H. F., Uehling, H., & Maslow, A. H. (1932). Comparative behavior of primates: I. Delayed reaction tests on primates from the lemur to the orangutan. *Journal of Comparative Psychology, 13*, 313–343.

Maslow, A. H. (1970). *Motivation and personality* (2nd ed.). New York: Harper & Row.

McKinney, W. T. , Jr., Suomi, S. J., & Harlow, H. F. (1973). New models of separation and depression in rhesus monkeys. In J. P. Scott & E. C. Senay (Eds.), *Separation and depression. Clinical and research aspects* (pp. 53–66). Washington, DC: American Association for the Advancement of Science, Publication No. 94.

Ruppenthal, G. C., Arling, G. L., Harlow, H. F., Sackett, G. P., & Suomi, S. J. (1976). A 10-year perspective of motherless-mother monkey behavior. *Journal of Abnormal Psychology, 85*, 341–349.

Science: Learning from the animals. (1973). *Newsweek*, Oct. 22, 1973, p. 102.

Suomi, S. J., Harlow, H. F., & Novak, M. A. (1974). Reversal of social deficits produced by isolation rearing in monkeys. *Journal of Human Evolution, 3*, 537–544.

Tavris, C. (1973, April). Harry Harlow talks. *Psychology Today, 7*.

Chapter 18

Frederick M. Lord: Measurement Theorist and Statistician

Bert F. Green
Johns Hopkins University

Fred Lord was a principal developer of the statistical theory that forms the foundation for the statistical methods used today in psychological and educational testing. With Melvin Novick, he wrote the definitive treatise on test theory, which was the culmination of the classical view of testing. The same book ushered in a new theory that has now largely supplanted the classical approach. Lord developed and extended the new theory and introduced many applications, including one to computer-based adaptive testing. He made many other contributions to the psychological measurement of individual differences in cognitive performance, and during his lifetime was viewed by his colleagues as the dean of statistical test theory.

THE PERSONAL LIFE OF FREDERICK M. LORD

Frederick Mather Lord was born on November 12, 1912, in Hanover, New Hampshire. His father taught anatomy at the Dartmouth Medical School, and his mother, Jeanette Mather Lord was a prominent suffragette. Fred graduated from Dartmouth in 1936 with a major in sociology.

In 1946, Fred married Shirley Lord. They had three sons: Steven, John, and, Eric. The marriage to Shirley ended in divorce in 1973. In 1983 he married Muriel Bessemer Lord, and acquired three stepchildren: Conrad, Robert, and Dianne Bessemer.

---

*Photo of Fred Lord by Eugene Cook. Reprinted by permission of the Educational Testing Service.

Although Lord retired officially in 1982, he continued working and consulting until a fateful trip to South Africa in 1985. There, Fred was a passenger in an automobile that was involved in a serious accident. He was hospitalized and spent several weeks in a coma before recovering sufficiently to be brought back home to Princeton, New Jersey. He recuperated for several months, but never recovered sufficiently to resume full-time activities. In the accident, Lord's eyesight was severely damaged, as was his right arm. An eye operation gave him limited vision and a fused right wrist gave him partial use of his right arm, but he was confined to a wheelchair. Even under these circumstances, Lord continued to consult with colleagues and kept abreast of current developments, but he published no further work. Eventually Fred and Muriel retired to Florida. While living there, he was able to travel, and he occasionally attended professional meetings and bridge tournaments.

Lord had two main hobbies: growing exotic plants and playing bridge. He cultivated orchids and similar flowers, and occasionally presented colleagues with the products of his green thumb. He was very serious about bridge and attained the status of life grand master. He helped to organize duplicate bridge sessions at the Educational Testing Service (ETS), where he was employed, and played in national and international tournaments. He had little interest in social bridge, but played duplicate bridge with gusto. After his accident, he resumed playing bridge with the use of a special rack to hold the cards. The move to Florida enabled him to play bridge daily.

LORD'S PROFESSIONAL LIFE

During the Second World War, Lord engaged in personnel research at the U.S. Civil Service Commission. During that same period, he enrolled in the University of Minnesota, where he earned a master's degree in educational psychology in 1943. In 1944, he moved to New York, where he worked as a research assistant in the Graduate Record Office of the Carnegie Foundation, becoming assistant director in 1946.

In 1949, the Graduate Record Office became a part of the ETS, then being pieced together in Princeton, New Jersey. Lord was head of statistical analysis for ETS. In 1950, he entered the graduate program in psychology at Princeton University, where he worked with Harold Gulliksen and Ledyard Tucker in psychometrics and with John Tukey and Sam Wilks in mathematical statistics. By the time he received his doctorate in psychology from Princeton in 1952, he had already published 10 technical papers.

Lord remained at ETS throughout his entire subsequent professional career. In 1950, he moved from statistical analysis to the research division. From 1960 until his retirement, he chaired the psychometric research group there. In 1976, ETS named him Distinguished Research Scientist.

Lord was active in the Psychometric Society, serving as its president in 1958. The Psychometric Society is a small professional group interested in developing statistical methods for analyzing psychological data and developing models of psychological processes. At one time the society was expected to become Division 4 of the APA, but finally, it chose to remain a separate entity. For many years, Lord served on the Psychometric Society's publication board and as associate editor of its publication, *Psychometrika*.

Lord was a fellow of the American Psychological Association, the American Statistical Association, and the Institute of Mathematical Statistics. In 1988, he received the American Educational Research Association's E. F. Lindquist award for outstanding research in the field of testing and measurement. In 1997, he received an award from APA's Division 5 (Evaluation, Measurement, and Statistics) for distinguished lifetime contributions in evaluation, measurement, and statistics.

Lord occasionally taught graduate courses at Princeton, where he was visiting lecturer with the rank of professor. He also taught summer courses at the University of Pennsylvania and in 1963 was visiting professor in the University of Wisconsin's School of Education. Early in his career, Lord was instrumental in inaugurating a visiting scholar program at ETS and in choosing who would be invited. Some of those invited were promising beginners who went on to have outstanding careers in psychometrics, statistics, or mathematical psychology. Others were already established. Many were from other countries.

LORD VERSUS STEVENS

Although Lord's work was mainly in the statistical analysis of educational test data, his name first became prominent in psychology when he challenged S. S. Stevens's rigid view of measurement scales. The Stevens litany, which still appears in some texts on psychological statistics, classifies measurement scales into four types: nominal, ordinal, interval, and ratio scales. According to Stevens, the way the scale uses numbers to represent psychological attributes determines its scale type and restricts the kind of statistical manipulations that are admissible. The numbers are interpretable only in terms of the properties they represent. Nominal scales use numbers as labels and support no more elaborate statistics than counts and percentages. Ordinal scales use numbers to describe the order of the elements involved. Because order does not imply equality of units, means and standard deviations of ordinal numbers have no referential meaning, although medians and ranges are permissible. Means and standard deviations have meaning only when the units of the scale are equal in some definite sense, as found in interval and ratio scales. Interval scales, such as the Fahrenheit scale of temperature, have equal units, but have an arbitrary origin. They do not allow ratio comparisons; the assertion that 80°F is twice as warm as 40° is meaningless. Ratio scales have a rational origin and permit ratio statements, such as 20 ft is twice as long as 10 ft. It was not a coincidence that Stevens's pronouncement about scales came at a time when he was promoting a ratio scaling method for psychological attributes such as brightness and loudness. Statisticians believed that Stevens's characterization of measurement scales was overly simple and knew that the choice of statistics depends on the nature of the question being asked. Some uses of numbers shade from nominal to ordinal, such as numbers used in street addresses, or from ordinal to interval, such as in the method of paired comparisons (Gulliksen, 1946), which uses ordinal comparative judgments and a statistical model to form interval scales. Scores on educational and psychological tests also had anomalous status in the Stevens hierarchy. Tests were usually scored by counting the number of items answered correctly. (In testing, questions are called items, because often the item is not in the form of a question but is a task of some kind.) Because test items could not, in general, be considered equivalent, the units of a test score scale had little or no fundamental meaning; test scores seemed to be merely ordinal measurement. It would then follow that average test scores have no meaning, whereas the flourishing field of testing had been happily computing average test scores for decades.

Lord's (1953) article, "On the Statistical Treatment of Football Numbers," attacked the rigidity of the Stevens dicta through a clever parable in which he ostensibly showed that even lowly football numbers could be averaged. In his parable, a supplier of football jerseys sold the numbers on those jerseys from a vending machine into which he had placed a very large number of two-digit numbers in a generally haphazard order and with no attention to how many of each two-digit number was stocked. One year, the sophomore team bought its numbers before the freshman team could buy theirs. The freshman team complained that the machine was not vending numbers at random, because their numbers were smaller than those doled out to the sophomores. The proprietor, a defrocked psychometrician who had been caught averaging test scores, called on the services of a statistician. To quote the article:

> So, when the problem had been explained to him, the statistician chose not to use the elegant nonparametric methods of modern statistical analysis, Instead, he took the professor's list of the 100 quadrillion "football numbers" that had been put into the machine. He added them all together and divided by 100 quadrillion. "The population mean, he said, "Is 54.3."
>
> "But these numbers are not cardinal numbers," the professor expostulated. "You can't add them."
>
> "Oh can't I?" said the statistician. "I just did. Furthermore, after squaring each number, adding the squares, and proceeding in the usual fashion, I find the population standard deviation to be exactly 18.0."
>
> "But you can't multiply 'football numbers'," the professor wailed. "Why, they aren't even ordinal numbers, like test scores."

"The numbers don't know that," said the statistician. "Since the numbers don't remember where they came from, they always behave just the same way, regardless." The professor gasped. (pp. 750–751)

The statistician in Lord's fable then used the mean and standard deviation in a statistical test that made no assumptions about the distribution of the numbers, specifically Tchebycheff's inequality (e.g., Hayes, 1994), and showed that the numbers obtained by the freshman class were very unlikely to have been a random sample from the population of numbers in the machine.

Unfortunately, the article's format disguised the serious message. Some readers were misled by the style. As later noted by Turnbull in a tribute at Lord's retirement, the paper read very much like Lewis Carroll's Alice in Wonderland.[1] Others were misled by the football numbers. Learned comments were published, intending to show that Lord had it all wrong and was merely an unsuccessful court jester. Lord (1954) then replied, giving a sober logical argument supporting the view that, in certain restricted situations, some hypotheses about ordinal data could be tested using statistical methods that use means and standard deviations. The article, the comments, and the reply have often been reprinted.

Few readers recognized that the freshmen in the parable who complained about the size of their numbers were interpreting the numbers not as nominal, but as ordinal in character. Statistical methods that use means and standard deviations can be used to test null hypotheses about such interpretations of numbers. Furthermore, if one reads "test scores" for "football numbers" and "test" for "vending machine," the parable can be read as discussing what statistics may properly be used in analyzing test scores. Those who did see this point were either quietly amused or disgruntled for having been led down the garden path.

Looking back at his argument today, I believe Lord's challenge to the hierarchy was too strong, just as Stevens's advocacy was too strong. Technically, number-right test scores provide only ordinal measurement. A person with a higher score than someone else has answered more questions correctly. However, the score can be given additional meaning by referring it to the statistical distribution of scores for the population of test takers. Intervals of test scores, measured in standard deviation units, become meaningful in terms of the score distribution. Such units are especially convenient when the distribution of test scores is approximately normal in shape. Nevertheless, for some test-score interpretations, especially score gains, units of measurement do matter. A gain from 400 to 450 on the SAT cannot be interpreted as being the same as a gain from 600 to 650. Ironically, Lord spent much of his professional life developing a mathematical model of test scores—item response theory—that provides a theoretical basis for interpreting test scores on an interval scale.

---

[1] Excerpted from comments by William Turnbull, President of ETS from 1970 to 1980, at a dinner in Lord's honor at ETS on May 22, 1982. Reprinted from a program of a memorial service for Frederick M. Lord at the Educational Testing Service, March 5, 2000.

LORD'S PARADOX

The measurement of change or growth is a perplexing problem in the fields of individual differences and personality. Typically, when *before* and *after* measures of some characteristics are compared, complications arise because of the statistical variation associated with each measure, and the imperfect correlation of the *before* and *after* measures. Lord made early contributions to this problem and called attention to a paradox that may arise in interpreting the results of the analysis of covariance.

Researchers often examine the effect of an experimental treatment by randomly assigning subjects to one of two groups, an experimental group and a control group that, respectively, receive the experimental treatment or do not. Sometimes in such research it is felt necessary to control for the effect of some related variable on which people differ. The analysis of covariance is designed for use in this situation. Occasionally, the same analysis is done for the data from experiments using preexisting groups, rather than randomly assigned groups. Lord demonstrated that this practice could lead to anomalous results (Lord, 1967). The analysis can backfire and introduce a difference in the main variable that had not been there before taking the so-called control variable into account. This effect is known in the literature as "Lord's paradox."

Lord made this point with the aid of an example in which a hypothetical researcher studied the effect of college food on the weight of college students. Expecting a gender difference, the researcher weighed groups of men and women in September and in May, the beginning and the end of a college year. The results were that the average weight in May was exactly the same as the average weight in September for both groups. This simple and straightforward comparison showed no gain in either group. Analysis of covariance, however, treats the September weights as a control variable and the May weights as the target variable. It uses regression to predict the effect of the control variable on the target variable and subtracts the prediction from the actual result for each case, presumably leaving the net effect of the treatment. Suppose the average man weighed 150 pounds both in September (weight before) and May (weight after), with $SD = 10$, and that the correlation of before and after weights was 0.8. Suppose further that the average woman weighed 110 in September (weight before) and in May (weight after) with the same variance and correlation. If there were the same number of men and women in the study, the overall mean for men and women is 130. Calculated for men and women separately, the net gain, according to the analysis of covariance, is (weight after – 0.8 weight before – 0.2 × 130). By this calculation, the average net gain is –4 pounds for women and +4 pounds for men. The imperfect correlation of September and May weights, together with the fact that, on average, the men initially weighed more than the women, caused the analysis to show that the men gained 8 pounds more than the women.

Again some readers misunderstood, saying that no one would use analysis of covariance in that situation. Lord countered by pointing out that if the control variable had been September girth rather than September weight, the simpler mean comparison would not have been available, and the apparent net advantage to the men shown by the analysis of covariance would have been anomalous. In short, with preexisting groups, the analysis of covariance can be difficult to interpret unambiguously (Lord, 1969). Lord's paradox is one of a host of regression effects that turn up in statistics to mislead the unwary (Campbell & Kenny, 1999).

TEST ANALYSIS

Most of Lord's work related to practical aspects of ability testing. Throughout his career, he worked on problems of equating test scores and establishing test norms. Equating is the process of calibrating the scores from two or more forms of the same test (such as the SAT) so that the scores from all forms are placed on the same scale, thus facilitating score interpretation. Test norms permit comparing a test score with the scores of all persons in some reference group, such as all high school seniors. Test norms are especially tedious to obtain because the test must be given to a large population of students. Lord was asked to consider ways of simplifying the process through sampling. Sampling of students is straightforward; Lord added the sampling of items, so that each sampled student would take only a small subset of the test items. Robert Hooke, a Princeton statistician, had done some theoretical work on the general problem of item sampling, but Lord was able to develop the idea into a practical method (Lord, 1962). The method is widely used today; the National Assessment of Educational Progress (NAEP) makes extensive use of the method, thereby being as unobtrusive as possible when assessing student achievement.

The technical quality of test scores is established by elaborate statistical methods that had been compiled in Gulliksen's 1950 book *The Theory of Test Scores*. Gulliksen encouraged Lord and a colleague, Melvin Novick, to bring the theory up to date and put it on a sound statistical basis. Although the result, *Statistical Theories of Mental Test Scores*, was hailed as a landmark when it appeared (Lord & Novick, 1968), their collaboration was not a happy one. Lord had a strong practical bent, whereas Novick liked formality. Novick liked Bayesian statistics; Lord hated them—they appear very briefly in the book. The style of the book is heavier and more formal than the rest of Lord's writing. It seems likely that Novick had a substantial hand in the formality. I never heard Lord say anything about working with Novick, but I certainly heard Novick being exasperated with Lord.

ITEM RESPONSE THEORY

Lord's doctoral dissertation, *A Theory of Test Scores* (1952), was a turning point in test theory, although at the time many people did not recognize it as such. It began a series of developments by Lord and several others that eventually transformed the methods used in the statistical analysis of responses to items on psychological tests. For many years, progress was slow and painful, because the application of the theory depended on intensive statistical calculations that strained the computational resources of the time. Practical interest in the theory took root when digital computers became widely available, and it grew as computers grew. Today it is supplanting the classical methods in most large testing programs. It forms the basis of computer-based adaptive testing (CAT), in which the computer selects items for each candidate that match the candidate's demonstrated level of proficiency.

Shortly after Lord's work, Allen Birnbaum, working with the Air Force Personnel laboratory, developed essentially the same theory, his "logistic model," and elaborated the considerable statistical theory surrounding the model. Novick and Lord, in their landmark book, included three chapters by Birnbaum (1968) on the logistic model.

Lord gave no name to his theory in 1952, but others, including Samejima (1973) and Birnbaum (1968), called it "latent trait theory." At the time, Lazarsfeld (1950) had just introduced his "latent structure theory." The term derives from the notion that a test is presumably measuring some underlying property or trait of the test taker. A trait signifies coherent behavior by persons with respect to a certain subject matter. There is no necessary implication that a trait has any physical or physiological basis, nor that it is in any way inherited. Nevertheless, the term "latent trait" brings to mind the neverending arguments about nature versus nurture. Lord tried using the term "item characteristic curve theory" (Lord, 1977b). Darrell Bock remembers introducing the bland term "item response theory" informally in the late 1970s. Lord quickly adopted the term (Lord, 1980); the theory is now known as IRT throughout psychometrics. Bock was less successful in proposing "proficiency" in place of "ability." Usage of those two terms is running neck and neck, with "propensity" a weak third. What's in a name? Well, in a highly public and controversial arena like testing, a name can matter a lot.

IRT provides a mathematical model that relates test scores to properties of the items comprising the test. Before this theory was introduced, most test theory was expressed in terms of test scores. In classical test theory, the unit of analysis is the test score, whereas Fred's approach made the item score the unit of analysis. IRT relates the probability of answering a given item correctly to the scale of ability underlying the test performance. The more able the test taker, the more likely that he or she would correctly answer the item. Items vary in difficulty, so the relation of the item to the ability scale differs from item to item.

The function relating the probability of a correct response to the ability scale is called the item characteristic curve.

Figure 18.1 shows some examples. In the theory, all curves have the shape of a normal ogive, but the location of the curve with respect to ability levels differs, to account for item difficulty in the test-taking population. Throughout most of its range, Item A is easier than Items B and C, because the probability of answering it correctly is higher. The item characteristic curves can also vary in slope, steeper slopes indicating stronger relationship to ability. Item B is more weakly related to proficiency than Items A and C. Items B and C represent multiple-choice items; because the probability of correctly answering an item is never as low as zero, many test takers guess when they do not know the right answer, and sometimes they guess correctly.

According to IRT, the observed interrelationships among the items is accounted for solely by the relationship of the items to the proficiency being assessed. The concept of proficiency in IRT corresponds with the concept of "true score" on a test in classical test theory. True score is a test-centered concept. A test taker's true score is defined as the average of the scores obtained on an infinite number of equivalent tests. True score has no meaning apart from the test. The notion that the test is measuring some characteristic of the test taker is implicit, at best, in classical test theory. IRT explicitly models such a characteristic, or trait, which it calls proficiency or ability, which it defines through the large

Some IRT item response functions

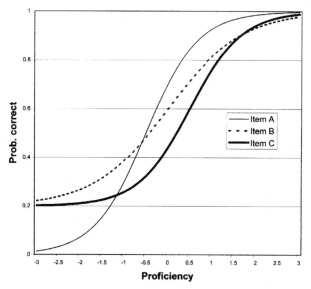

FIG. 18.1.   *Some hypothetical IRT Response Functions.* For an explanation, please see text.

set, or pool, of items that assess it. The scale of proficiency is an interval scale: It is the scale on which all the item response curves have the required shape. But the scale's zero point and the size of its units are arbitrary. For mathematical work, a mean of zero and a unit standard deviation, as shown on Fig. 18.1, are convenient but for reporting purposes the scale is generally transformed to some other convenient values—such as $M = 50$ and $SD = 10$.

In classical test theory, the test score is generally taken to be the number of items answered correctly. One correct answer counts as much as another. In IRT, a correct answer to a more difficult item implies higher proficiency than a correct answer to an easier item. Moreover, incorrect answers to items are also taken into account; answering an easy item wrong implies lower proficiency than does a wrong answer to a difficult item. IRT is formulated to provide an estimate of proficiency from the pattern of a test taker's item responses, using the known characteristics of the items. This method, known formally as proficiency estimation and informally as pattern scoring, provides added precision to the test scores.

IRT has much in common with many other models used in quantitative psychology. For example, in classical psychophysics, an observer's sensitivity to a very weak tone, or to a very dim light, is sometimes represented by a normal ogive like Item A in Fig. 18.1. In psychophysics, the abscissa represents stimulus intensity rather than proficiency; the curve shows that the probability of detecting a stimulus, such as a weak tone, increases in a regular way as the intensity of the tone increases. This idea is most clearly stated in signal detection theory, which was imported from electrical engineering into psychology (Swets, Tanner, & Birdsall, 1961). The use of probability in signal detection results from the fact that the same tone will sometimes be detected, and sometimes not, by an observer. The variation is presumed to occur because a human observer's nervous system varies slightly from time to time. In IRT, the variation is a population concept. That is, the variation is between people—test takers vary in their experiences, as well as in other irrelevant aspects of the situation, so the same item is not always answered the same way by persons of the same level of proficiency or ability.

Throughout the theoretical development of IRT, Lord was at great pains to examine the fit of the model to data. He even developed a method for estimating item response functions without assuming a logistic form and found that, with few exceptions, the curves could be very well fit by a logistic function. That was characteristic of Lord. He always sought verification in data of any theoretical development.

PRACTICAL LORD

Lord's work nearly always addressed a practical problem. Every statistical analysis, every theoretical development, was for some purpose. His important IRT book (Lord, 1980) was called *Applications of Item Response Theory to Practical*

Testing Problems. Unlike the Lord and Novick tome, this work bore the Lord stamp of clarity and neatness. It has become one of the most widely referenced works in the psychometrics of testing.

Among the practical problems Lord addressed with IRT was the charge of item bias has been leveled at academic selection tests such as the SAT and ACT. The fact that some subgroups of test takers have higher average scores than others has led some to believe the tests must be biased. Small differences are sometimes noted between males and females, and large differences are usually observed between African-Americans and Whites. Lord, along with many others, used IRT to examine these charges empirically. It is possible to obtain separate IRT response functions for the separate groups. In doing so, it is necessary to standardize on one of the groups, using a process such as that developed by Stocking and Lord (1983). If the characteristic curves for an item are nearly the same, the item is functioning about the same for each group, not being biased toward either group. If the items have different response functions for different groups, the item is measuring something different for the various groups and is a candidate for removal from the test. The main outcome of this work has been that very little evidence for item bias has been found, and when it is found, it is usually inexplicable. Nevertheless, empirical techniques for assessing item bias, some using IRT, some based on other premises, have become common practice in professional test development.

A corollary of Lord's practical orientation was his interest in statistical computation. His interest in computing was shared by his mentor and colleague at ETS, Ledyard Tucker. In the mid 1950s, when digital computers were first becoming available, they journeyed to Massachusetts Institute of Technology (MIT) to look into the possibility of doing the calculations for test score analysis on the MIT computer, Whirlwind. They were disappointed to find that Whirlwind had a very limited storage capacity (only about 8 kilobytes, in today's terminology) and could not begin to hold either their (pre-Fortran) computer program or their test-score data. They were about 10 years too soon. In the next decade, computer power and capacity expanded greatly, so that behavioral and social scientists could begin to use computers effectively for large problems.

IRT is impractical without extensive calculations. Unlike classical test theory, which obtains scores by counting the number of correct answers and needs nothing more elaborate than means, standard deviations, and correlations, IRT needs to solve intricate equations by iterative calculation. Lord and his assistants used Fortran to develop computer programs to do the job. Their work resulted in the well-known computer program LOGIST, which is still in use, although it has undergone many revisions and improvements (Wood, Wingersky, & Lord, 1976).

According to Marilyn Wingersky, his long-time computer associate, Lord was a stickler for accuracy and a fuss-budget about details. When he needed a new data analysis done, one that required writing a computer program, he would sometimes do it himself, but more often give the problem to his computer experts. Generally, with a new procedure, he wanted two independent programs to be written and would be seriously concerned if the results differed in any way. Any lack of correspondence had to be explained in detail.

TAILORED TESTING

During the early 1960s, minicomputers appeared in psychological laboratories. The immense range of computer applications was still ahead, but laboratory computers quickly became a great help in running psychological experiments. Display screens and response keys were developed, along with more specialized interfaces. Computer hardware and software were developed so that stimuli could be displayed and responses recorded, by computer. These developments made it possible to give psychological tests by computer, but the advantages were not obvious at first. Why use a huge machine when paper and pencil do just as well?

One reason was the possibility of tailoring the difficulty of a test to the proficiency of the test taker. There is little value in asking a high-scoring test taker a lot of easy questions, nor does it help much to ask a low-scoring person very difficult questions. Psychometricians therefore began to consider ways to make testing more efficient for the test giver and less onerous for the test taker, by selecting items that match the examinee's ability. Early work focused on procedures in which a short "routing test" was used to select a subsequent test of appropriate difficulty. Reasonable ways were devised to provide equable test scores, and the method was shown to improve testing efficiency. However, the administrative complications made the schemes unfeasible for conventional tests that are routinely given to large assemblages of examinees.

The idea of matching the test to the test taker was not new; it had been used routinely with the Stanford–Binet Intelligence Test, which is individually administered. With a computer at hand to administer the tests, tailored testing became feasible for ability tests generally. Moreover, instead of two stages of testing, the computer could select items one at a time. The problems were to devise suitable ways to select the items and to score the test.

Lord saw that IRT could do both jobs. IRT is formulated at the item level; it follows that examinees' proficiency can be estimated from their responses to any subset of items. If the theory holds, it is not necessary that everyone take the same test items. It is only necessary to have a large supply of items that have been all been calibrated together, with reference to a single reference population of test takers. With different test takers taking different items, their scores cannot be based on the number of items they answered correctly. After looking at several scoring methods that involved other methods, Lord settled finally on IRT. He described some of his results on tailored testing at a conference in 1968 hosted by Wayne Holtzman at the University of Texas (Lord, 1970). I was a discussant and voiced skepticism because I thought the very poor and the very able students would be shortchanged. Lord knew this was a misinterpretation and was not deterred.

The U.S. Civil Service Commission, which does a great deal of testing, saw many advantages in computer-based adaptive testing (CAT). They developed a complete CAT system to replace their then-current procedures. In 1976, they organized a conference to explain their results to selected psychometric professionals. Lord presented a paper (Lord, 1977a), and I commented again, this time much more positively. The system was ready to go when Jimmy Carter, in one of his last acts as president of the United States, killed the project, having been convinced by some of his political advisors that ability tests were biased and were keeping deserving minority applicants from government service.

Carter's dictum did not extend to the military services, where the Armed Services Vocational Aptitude Battery (ASVAB) continued to be used for selecting recruits for military service. The Office of Naval Research had sponsored much of Lord's work, and many other developments in CAT and IRT. David Weiss, another early worker in the field, held conferences on CAT at the University of Minnesota in 1977 and 1979. One practical outcome of all this work was a project to prepare a CAT version of the ASVAB. The work began in 1984, and the system became operational in 1995. Lord was one of the advisors of the project (Green, Bock, Linn, Lord, & Reckase, 1983).

LORD'S STYLE

Lord's style of writing was terse, but very clear. There was no pretension nor any excessive formality in his papers. He was only interested in informing his readers, not in impressing them. I served on a few committees with Lord (e.g., Green et al., 1983). He was quiet and did not participate very much in the give-and-take that often happens when a bunch of experts are trying to brainstorm a problem. But whenever he did offer something, the room got very quiet. All of us knew that Lord's discussion of any aspect of the problem would be carefully reasoned and especially important. Lord got special, well-deserved respect.

Lord also was a quiet and unassuming colleague. Some people found him disconcerting, or even frightening, perhaps because his style in professional discussion was deliberate and soft-spoken. When someone approached Lord with a problem, he would listen, and sometimes ask insightful questions, but sometimes he would think quietly, making no effort to keep the conversation going. Lord would sometimes be silent for many moments before answering a question or delivering an opinion. This is unnerving to people for whom talking is a sign of thinking. One coworker told of going to see Lord with a proposal for a line of research. After describing the problem in considerable detail, he asked if Lord would be interested in working on the project. Lord sat quietly for what seemed like a very long time, and then replied, "No."

Turnbull, at a dinner in honor of Lord's retirement from ETS, described Lord's typical style of interaction thus:[2]

> As a long-time Lord-watcher I have tried to analyze how he approaches the problems that people bring him—not the kind entailed in developing a whole new theory but the merely intricate kind having to do with questions that can be solved more or less on the spot if you happen to be or know Fred Lord. Essentially, he seems to proceed by asking just enough questions to allow him to pare away the erroneous and the extraneous. He is a practitioner *par excellence* of the technique of excluding false assumptions and blind alleys of deductive illogic until he has left a nugget of truth. You can almost see him shaving your fuzzy ideas with Occam's Razor.
>
> Incidentally, for a man who is sparing in his verbal communications, Fred has a remarkably rich and clear body language, when his mind is in its processing mode. Not when he's in his input mode. While you are presenting your problem, Fred rivets his attention on you and what you want to say for as long as you want to keep on saying it. This he does without moving a muscle. But while he processes, he becomes silently expressive. A lifted eyebrow. Perhaps a smile and nod as if complimenting the problem on its complexity. Sometimes a shake of the head in apparent despair—or to shake away cobwebs of confusion with which the stated problem is festooned. Possibly standing for a while in his favorite pose of contemplation, which sometimes involves looking out a window while assuming his best problem-solving configuration—a stance in which he achieves from the waist up a backward slant of alarming proportion, as if he is keeping his head clear of the intellectual underbrush he sees before him while he fixes his gaze on the higher planes of logic. Then sitting down and producing the answer in a few sentences. It's quite a procedure.

Likewise, his style when commenting on the work of others was diplomatic and gentle. Instead of saying, "You're wrong," he would be more likely to say, "You may want to take thus and so into consideration." And, in general interaction he was generally pleasant and cheerful, although usually reserved. His reserve was not always apparent in bridge tournaments. Muriel Lord said that on occasion he would startle the other players by calling loudly, "Madam Director" because some bridge irregularity had occurred.

CONCLUSION

Lord had a large influence on the major developments in test theory and practice during the past half century. His work touched all aspects of the technical analysis of test data. Of course, many others also contributed to these developments, and Lord had no wish to be considered in any way extraordinary. He led the way

---

[2]Op. cit.

toward the switch to the IRT model and CAT and contributed useful methodology in other arenas. Quietly, and carefully, he made a difference.

ACKNOWLEDGMENTS

I gratefully acknowledge the help of the Educational Testing Service and many of Fred's family, friends, and colleagues, especially Darrell Bock, Eleanor Horne, Shirley Lord, Muriel Lord, Robert Mislevy, Fumiko Samejima, Martha Stocking, the late William Turnbull, and Howard Wainer.

REFERENCES

Birnbaum, A. (1968). Some latent trait models and their use in inferring an examinee's ability. In F. M. Lord & M. R. Novick (Eds.), *Statistical theories of mental test scores* (pp. 397–479). Reading, MA: Addison-Wesley.

Campbell, D. T., & Kenny, D. A. (1999). *A primer on regression artifacts.* New York: Guilford.

Green, B. F., Bock, R. D., Linn, R. L., Lord, F. M., & Reckase, M. D. (1983). A plan for scaling the computerized adaptive ASVAB. Research Report 83-1. Baltimore, MD: The Johns Hopkins University, Department of Psychology, 1983. Also MPL TN 85-2 (1985). San Diego, CA: Manpower and Personnel Laboratory, Naval Personnel Research and Development Center.

Gulliksen, H. (1946). Paired comparisons and the logic of measurement. *Psychological Review, 53,* 199–213.

Gulliksen, H. (1950). *Theory of mental tests.* New York: Wiley.

Hayes, W. L. (1994). *Statistics* (5th ed.). New York: Harcourt Brace.

Lazarsfeld, P. F. (1950). The logic and mathematical foundation of latent structure analysis. In S. Stouffer, L. Guttman, E. A. Suchman, P. F. Lazarsfeld, S. A. Star, & J. A. Clausen (Eds.), *Studies in social psychology in World War II. Vol IV. Measurement and prediction* (pp. 362–412). Princeton, NJ: Princeton University Press.

Lord, F. M. (1952). A theory of test scores. *Psychometric Monograph, 7.*

Lord, F. M. (1953). On the statistical treatment of football numbers. *American Psychologist, 8,* 750–751. Reprinted in Mason, R. O., & Swanson, E. B. (Eds.). (1981). *Measurement for management decision* (pp. 52–55). Reading, MA: Addison-Wesley. Also in Maranell, G. H. (Ed.). (1974). *Scaling: A sourcebook for behavioral scientists* (pp. 402–405). Chicago: Aldine. Also in Haber, A., Runyon, R. P., & Badia, P. (Eds.). (1970). *Readings in statistics* (pp. 30–33). Reading, MA: Addison-Wesley. Also in Vanderplas, J. M. (Ed.). (1966). *Controversial issues in psychology* (pp. 399–402). Boston: Houghton Mifflin.

Lord, F. M. (1954). Further comments on "football numbers." *American Psychologist, 9,* 264–265. Reprinted in Vanderplas, J. H. (Ed.). (1966). *Controversial issues in psychology* (pp. 405–407). Boston: Houghton Mifflin.

Lord, F. M. (1962). Estimating norms by item sampling. *Educational and Psychological Measurement, 22,* 259–267.

Lord, F. M. (1967). A paradox in the interpretation of group comparisons. *Psychological Bulletin, 68,* 304–305.

Lord, F. M. (1969). Statistical adjustments when comparing preexisting groups. *Psychological Bulletin, 72,* 336–337.

Lord, F. M. (1970). Some test theory for tailored testing. In W. H. Holtzman (Ed.), *Computer-assisted instruction, testing, and guidance* (pp. 139–183). New York: Harper & Row.

Lord, F. M. (1977a). A broad-range tailored test of verbal ability. *Applied Psychological Measurement, 1*, 95–100.

Lord, F. M. (1977b). Practical applications of item characteristic curve theory. *Journal of Educational Measurement, 14*, 117–138.

Lord, F. M. (1980). *Applications of item response theory to practical testing problems.* Hillsdale, NJ: Lawrence Erlbaum Associates, Inc.

Lord, F. M. & Novick, M. R. (1968). *Statistical theories of mental test scores.* Reading, MA: Addison-Wesley.

Samejima, F. (1973). A comment on Birnbaum's three-parameter logistic model in the latent trait theory. *Psychometrika, 38*, 221–233.

Stocking, M. L., & Lord, F. M. (1983). Developing a common metric in item response theory. *Applied Psychological Measurement, 7*, 201–210.

Swets, J. A., Tanner, W. P., & Birdsall, T. G. (1961). Decision processes in perception. *Psychological Review, 68*, 301–340.

Wainer, H. (2000). *Computerized adaptive testing: A primer* (2nd ed.). Mahwah, NJ: Lawrence Erlbaum Associates, Inc.

Wood, R. L., Wingersky, M. S., & Lord, F. M. (1976). LOGIST—A computer program for estimating examinee ability and item characteristic curve parameters. Research Memorandum 76-6. Princeton, NJ: Educational Testing Service.

Chapter 19

Mary Ainsworth: Insightful Observer and Courageous Theoretician

Inge Bretherton
University of Wisconsin–Madison

Mary Ainsworth's pioneering work has changed conceptions of infant–mother relationships, and by extension, conceptions of human relationships more generally. As John Bowlby's major collaborator in the development of attachment theory, she is commonly credited with providing supporting empirical evidence for the theory whereas Bowlby is regarded as creating its basic framework. This view is too simple. Ainsworth's innovative approach to studying the development of relationships not only made it possible to put some of Bowlby's ideas to empirical test, but her insights expanded the theory itself in fundamental ways. Among her major contributions are the concept of the attachment figure as a secure base from which an infant can explore the world, the identification of patterns of infant–mother attachment as indicators of relationship quality, and the concept of parental sensitive responsiveness to infant signals as precursor to secure attachment. Without this work, attachment theory and research would not have attained the importance they currently hold in developmental and social psychology.

That Ainsworth and Bowlby became collaborators was the result of a series of fortunate coincidences, although their thinking about personality development had developed along congenial lines before they met. Their first encounter took place when both were in midlife, after their professional careers had been interrupted by military service during the Second World War, and when their most creative and original contributions still lay ahead.

BIOGRAPHICAL SKETCH

Mary Dinsmore Salter, born on December 1, 1913, in Glendale Ohio, was the eldest daughter of Charles and Mary Salter. She grew up in Toronto, Canada, where her father was transferred by his company in 1918. Mary had fond memories of her father, who was the parent who tucked the children into bed at night and sang to them. Her relationship with her mother was less warm. She was a precocious child with a strong desire for knowledge, who learned to read at the age of 3. Her interest in psychology was sparked by William McDougall's (chap. 6, this volume) *Character and the Conduct of Life* (McDougall, 1927), which she discovered during her final year in high school. "It had not previously occurred to me that one might look within oneself for some explanation of how one felt and behaved, rather than feeling entirely at the mercy of external forces. What a vista that opened up" (Ainsworth, 1983, p. 202). Thus, when she entered the University of Toronto as a 16-year-old, Mary had already decided to become a psychologist. As one of only five students, she was admitted to the challenging and intensive Honours Course in Psychology. There was, she said, a "messianic spirit that permeated the department—a belief that the science of psychology was the touchstone for great improvements for the quality of life" (Ainsworth, 1983, p. 201). It was a spirit in which Mary shared.

When she obtained her bachelor's degree in 1935, her parents "went along" with her wish to pursue a doctorate in psychology, even though her father had initially suggested that she work as a stenographer for a while before getting married. Mary's doctoral mentor was the founder and first director of the Institute of Child Study at the University of Toronto, William Emet Blatz (chap. 14, *Pioneers II*), whom some considered the Doctor Spock of Canada. Blatz's research program in which Mary had become interested during her undergraduate years focused on his "security theory."

According to Blatz's theory, "secure dependence" on parents enables infants and young children to muster the courage to explore the unfamiliar, and thus to develop toward "independent security" (or self-reliance). Because pure independent security is unattainable, however, the "immature dependent security" of childhood must be replaced with a more mutual "mature secure dependence" on age peers, and eventually, a sexual partner. Where such a relationship develops each partner can find security in the skills, knowledge, and emotional support of the other. However, not all individuals succeed in achieving mature (mutual) dependence. Some remain immaturely dependent whereas others rely on defensive maneuvers to overcome their feelings of insecurity. Those familiar with attachment theory will recognize the similarity of some of these formulations to Ainsworth's concept of the parent as secure base for a child's exploration and her ideas about individual differences in patterns of attachment.

After completing her dissertation (Salter, 1940), based on Blatz's security theory, Mary stayed on as as lecturer at the University of Toronto. In 1942, wishing to contribute more directly to the war effort, she joined the Canadian Women's Army Corps, in which she attained the rank of major. Through participation in officer-selection procedures, she gained extensive expertise in clinical interviewing, history taking, test administration, and counseling. These skills served her well when she was hired as assistant professor of psychology at the University of Toronto in 1946 and asked to offer a course in clinical assessment. To bolster her clinical skills further, she sought training in the Rorschach Test with the well-known interpreter of this projective test, Bruno Klopfer. Klopfer was so impressed by a manual about the Rorschach that Mary prepared for her students, that he asked her to coauthor a volume "Developments in the Rorschach Technique," which was later published under her married name (Klopfer, Ainsworth, Klopfer, & Holt, 1954).

In addition to teaching, Mary codirected a research team headed by Blatz. Members of this team developed a variety of paper-and-pencil scales to assess familial and extrafamilial aspects of adult security (see Ainsworth & Ainsworth, 1958). In 1950 she married a member of the team, Leonard Ainsworth, a World War II veteran who had just completed his master's thesis.

RESEARCH ON ATTACHMENT AND SECURITY

To continue as married professor and graduate student in the same department made the Ainsworths uncomfortable, so they moved to London where Leonard had been accepted into a doctoral program. Mary had not been able to line up a job before leaving Canada, but a London friend from war days drew her attention to an announcement in the *Times* that called for a researcher with diagnostic skills who could assist with a study on early personality development, specifically the effects of separation from the mother in early childhood. The research was directed by the psychoanalyst and child psychiatrist John Bowlby at the Tavistock Clinic. Ainsworth joined Bowlby's team, not realizing at the time that this decision would reset the whole direction of her research career (Ainsworth, 1983; Bretherton, 1992).

Research in London

Ainsworth's closest colleague at the Tavistock was James Robertson, who had been charged by Bowlby with observing young children before, during, and after being hospitalized or institutionalized. In those days, parental visiting in hospitals was severely restricted, and children's obvious distress at separation was barely acknowledged. One of Ainsworth's tasks was to assist Robertson with the analysis of his detailed observational notes. She was so impressed with the quality of Robertson's data that she made up her mind to adopt his methods should she ever have the opportunity to conduct a study of her own. It is interesting that Robertson had obtained his training in observation while working at Anna Freud's wartime residential nursery for evacuated children where all members of the staff, no matter what their job description, were required to write their observations on cards to be used in subsequent discussions of the children's development.

In addition to gaining experience in the analysis of observational data, Ainsworth became intrigued with Bowlby's quest to find a more compelling explanation for young children's distress in response to enduring separation from parents than the then-current view. This view, shared by psychoanalysts and learning theorists alike, was that babies become attached to their mothers because they feed them and fulfill the babies' other basic needs. Ainsworth, who held this view herself, became quite uneasy when Bowlby began to toy with ethological explanations of infant–mother attachment, inspired by Konrad Lorenz's studies of imprinting. She even warned Bowlby that publishing these ideas might ruin his reputation.

The Move to Uganda

After Leonard Ainsworth completed his doctorate in 1953, he applied for a job at the East Africa Institute of Social Research in Kampala, Uganda. Mary was not at all enthusiastic about going to Africa. Once in Uganda, however, she saw an opportunity to fulfill her dream of conducting an observational study modeled on Robertson's work with hospitalized children. The director of the institute managed to "scrape together" funds (Ainsworth, 1983, p. 208) for a study of mother–infant separation at weaning when—Ainsworth had been told—infants were traditionally sent away to relatives for a few days to "forget the breast." After the study had begun, Ainsworth quickly discovered that most mothers no longer followed this custom and that her study design was therefore unworkable. Instead of giving up, she decided to document normative developmental changes and individual differences in patterns of mother–infant interaction. The study participants were 26 polygynous, monogamous, and separated Christian and Muslim mothers and their infants who lived in six villages surrounding Kampala. Ainsworth's appreciation for the families she studied is best conveyed by her description of one of the infants and his mother:

> His father . . . was posted so far away that he could get home only rarely. William was the youngest of 10 children, and there was also a foster child. The mother, single-handed, had reared all of these children, grown their food and prepared it, made many of their clothes, and looked after a large mud and wattle house which was tastefully decorated and graced by a flower garden. She was a relaxed, serene person, who could talk to us in an unhurried way, devote time to playful, intimate interchange with William, and also concern herself with the other children according to their needs. . . . She used a wheelbarrow as a pram, and there lay William, nested amid snowy white cotton cloths. The wheelbarrow could be moved from place to place—out to the garden where his mother worked, or under the shade tree

where the other children were playing, and never out of the earshot of some responsible person. (Ainsworth, 1963, pp. 85–86)

Unlike others who maintain that studies in non-Western societies should only be undertaken by members of that society, Ainsworth (1982, p. 228) felt that "it is easier to be objective when viewing another society, and then, as I discovered later, it is easier to take a fresh, unbiased view when later undertaking research in one's own society."

Although she had some notion of what she was looking for, Ainsworth was primarily on an exploratory, hypothesis-generating missison. In addition to frequent home observations, most of them lasting over two hours, she conducted detailed interviews with the help of a local social worker who served as interpreter and collaborator. She also made a serious effort to learn enough of the local language to engage in simple conversation. As a result of this experience, she later commented in an autobiographical sketch (Ainsworth, 1982 , p. 228): "It is a pity that one cannot require field work in another society of every aspiring investigator of child development."

Not long after beginning her observations of mother–infant interactions in Uganda, Ainsworth realized that Bowlby's emerging framework about the origins of attachment provided a much more useful theoretical basis for studying infants' growing attachment to their mothers (and other family members) than the theory of "cupboard love" proposed by classical psychoanalysis and learning theory. Somewhat surprising, however, she did not immediately let Bowlby know about her "volte-face" (Ainsworth, 1982, p. 228). Thus the first developmental study examining infant–mother attachment from an evolutionary perspective was not only conducted in a non-Western culture, but several years before Bowlby himself was to present his first formal account of attachment theory to the British Psychoanalytical Society where it stirred up a storm of controversy in 1958.

It is during the Uganda study that Ainsworth rediscovered the secure base phenomenon which she had first described in her dissertation with Blatz:

The behavior pattern to which I have referred as "using the mother as a secure base" highlights the fact that there can be a sound development of close attachment at the same time that there is increasing competence and independence. It is the insecure child who clings to his mother and refuses to leave her. The secure child, equally closely attached, moves away and shows his attachment by the fact that he wants to keep track of his mother's whereabouts, wants to return to her from time to time, and in his occasional glances back to her, or in his bringing things to show her, he displays his desire to share with her his delight in exploring the wonders of the world. So in reply to one question from parents I reply that attachment does not normally or necessarily interfere with the development of competence and self-reliance but rather supports this development. (Ainsworth, 1967, pp. 447–448)

The Johns Hopkins University

The Ainsworths' next move, in late 1955, was to Baltimore where Leonard had found a position as forensic psychologist. Mary explored employment possibilities at The Johns Hopkins University with the result that a lecturer position in clinical psychology was "patched up" for her (Ainsworth, 1983, p. 210). She also held a part-time clinical appointment at the Sheppard and Enoch Pratt Psychiatric Hospital and conducted a small private practice in the diagnostic assessment of children with emotional problems. This experience, added to her earlier expertise, proved to be invaluable for her later research methodology, but it did delay the analysis of her observations in Uganda for several years.

In 1958, Ainsworth was offered a permanent position as associate professor of developmental psychology at The Johns Hopkins University. In the same year, Bowlby sent her a preprint of his seminal article on attachment theory, "The Nature of the Child's Tie to His Mother" (Bowlby, 1958). In 1960, Bowlby was able to visit Ainsworth in Baltimore after he had spent the year at the Stanford University Institute for Advanced Study. This offered her an opportunity to give him a detailed account of her study in Uganda, and initiated the second phase of their collaboration. While Ainsworth was a member of Bowlby's research team in London, he had mostly played the role of mentor, but during this second phase of their joint work, they became equal partners who deeply influenced each others' thinking through frequent correspondence and exchanges of draft articles and book chapters for detailed comment and critique as well as through intermittent transatlantic meetings.

In 1961, a year after a stressful divorce, Ainsworth made her first public presentation of findings from her Uganda study at a meeting of Bowlby's Tavistock Mother–Infant Interaction Study Group in London. The reception of her work by the participants—distinguished developmentalists and ethologists from Britain, France, and the United States—was somewhat lukewarm (Ainsworth, 1963, transcription of subsequent discussion, pp. 104–112). One developmental psychologist commented: "I am not really happy about the application of words like security and anxiety as applied to early infancy." Another queried: "They were reinforced for crying, yet they did not cry?" and later cautioned: "I think the word 'attachment,' like the terms 'intelligence' and 'perception,' is much too broad or abstract to serve as a label for a domain of scientific interest." The question: "How do you know that the child was attached?" was useful, however, because it led Ainsworth to "scrutinize the decision-making processes involved in such a judgment" (1977, p. 51). As a result she constructed a catalogue of behaviors (crying when the mother left the room, following her, greeting her on return with smiling, vocalization, excited bouncing, reaching or approach behavior) that might serve as a set of criteria for attachment if differentially shown to a specific individual. This catalogue and other insights from the Uganda study informed plans for a second observational study of infant–mother attachment during the first year of life, but this time in an industrialized society. After obtaining funds from the William T. Grant Foundation, the study was begun in 1963.

The Baltimore Study

The 26 families who participated in the Baltimore study were recruited through pediatricians before the infant was born and visited until the child was 1 year old. Monthly home visits lasted several hours to encourage mothers to behave naturally while following their normal child-care and household routines.

Ainsworth never used checklists to record observations. Observers trained with the help of findings from the Uganda study noted interactive behavior in shorthand, interspersed by time markers every few minutes and then dictated a detailed narrative based on these notes into a tape recorder immediately after the visit ended. This technique, inspired by Ainsworth's expertise in clinical observation, was designed to capture the meaning and pattern of maternal and infant behaviors within their situational and social context, something that mere frequency counts, even if reliably recorded, cannot do. The transcribed narratives served as the basis for data analysis, including the construction of scales. Data collection was completed in 1966, just before the publication of the book *Infancy in Uganda* in 1967 on which Ainsworth had worked with Bowlby's encouragement.

Several influential journal articles about the Baltimore Study and a book that summarizes the findings, *Patterns of Attachment* (Ainsworth, Blehar, Waters, & Wall, 1978), appeared over the next decade or so. Analyses of mother–infant interaction sequences during feeding, close bodily contact, face-to-face play, and crying yielded clear evidence that when a mother responded to her infant with sensitive responsiveness during the first 3 months of life, the pair had a more harmonious relationship during the last quarter of the first year. The finding (Bell & Ainsworth, 1972) that a mother's prompt and appropriate responsiveness to her infant's crying during the early months was associated with less crying later in the first year was greeted with disbelief, especially by learning theorists. The latter were convinced that attending to a baby's crying necessarily served as a reinforcer to crying and would definitely not foster advanced preverbal gestural and vocal communication. Eventually, however, Ainsworth's results led to changes in recommended parental practice.

The final observation of each infant–mother pair in the Baltimore study took place when the infant was 12 months old. Together with her assistant Barbara Wittig, Ainsworth had devised a laboratory procedure for assessing infants' use of the mother as a secure base for exploration (Ainsworth & Wittig, 1969). The idea for this was, in part, inspired by Harlow's (chap. 17, this volume) study showing that infant rhesus monkeys, placed in an unfamiliar environment were able to engage in exploration while their "cloth mother" (a wire frame covered with cloth) was present, but not when only a "wire mother" (a wire frame fitted out with a bottle) was available. Infants would run to the cloth mother and cling to her tightly. After a while, still maintaining a tight grip, they would visually explore the novel cage and potentially frightening toy, and then break contact. They would manipulate the novel object, but intermittently scamper back to the cloth mother. By contrast, in the presence of the wire mother, the infant monkeys curled into a ball and screamed rather than engaging in exploration (Harlow, 1961).

Ainsworth's analogous 20-minute procedure, termed "The Strange Situation," took place in a playroom furnished with appealing toys to encourage infants to explore. In addition, they encountered a stranger and were twice briefly separated and then reunited with their mothers. A majority of infants behaved during this procedure as Ainsworth had expected. While the mother was gone, they stood near the door and many cried. When the mother returned, they approached her and requested contact by holding up their arms. Once comforted, they fairly quickly returned to play. Not all infants showed the expected pattern, however. Some, later termed "avoidant," snubbed the mother when she came back into the room by looking and even turning away or refusing to interact with her if she tried to engage them in play. A third and smaller group of infants protested loudly when the mother left, but seemed angry at her when she returned even though they also indicated a desire for contact. These "resistant" or "ambivalent" infants did not "sink in" when the mother picked them up. Not only were they difficult to calm, but they often pushed away from the mother when she did pick them up or angrily brushed away toys she offered (Ainsworth & Wittig, 1969). The behavior of the avoidant and ambivalent infants reminded Ainsworth of extreme versions of similar patterns that Robertson had described among somewhat older children when reunited with the mother following a long, traumatic separation (Robertson & Bowlby, 1952). Using the transcripts of dictated descriptions concurrently made by two side-by-side observers wearing earphones and watching through a one-way mirror, Ainsworth created a classification system and several behaviorally anchored rating scales for the Strange Situation that could be applied to infant behavior patterns in subsequent studies using this procedure. In doing so she was able to draw on her experience with developing manuals for interpreting clinical diagnostic tests, such as the Rorschach.

To help her interpret the meaning of the three different reunion patterns, Ainsworth checked the Strange Situation classifications of secure, avoidant, and ambivalent infants against home-observation analyses. This comparison revealed that mothers of secure infants had behaved most sensitively with them at home during the first 3 months of life, while mothers of avoidant infants had shown more rejection, especially of close bodily contact. Mothers of ambivalent infants had responded very inconsistently in response to their infant's attachment behaviors, behaving sensitively at times, but ignoring or rejecting their infants on many other occasions. Later in the first year, secure infants had the most harmonious interactions with their mothers, whereas those of the avoidant and ambivalent infants were more problematic (summarized in Ainsworth et al., 1978).

The documentation of links with home observations led to the widespread use of the Strange Situation as a tool for assessing the quality of infant–mother attachment, but home observations were relatively neglected. Ainsworth repeatedly expressed regret about this turn of events: "I have been quite disappointed that so many attachment researchers have gone on to do research with the Strange Situation rather than look at what happens in the home or in other natural settings—like I said before—it marks a turning away from field observations and I don't think it's wise" (Ainsworth & Marvin, 1995, p. 12).

Given that the Baltimore findings were based on a relatively small sample,· Ainsworth planned a replication study. However, when she applied for funds, federal review panels "while respectful of her research capabilities, replied that there was no point in replicating something of so little value" (Karen, 1994, p. 172), and her proposal was turned down.

AINSWORTH AS TEACHER AND AS MENTOR

Despite extensive controversies aroused by attachment research, the late 1960s and the 1970s were an exciting time in the psychology department at Johns Hopkins. Ainsworth's innovative approaches to the study of infant–mother relationships attracted many graduate students (among them Silvia Bell, Mary Blehar, Inge Bretherton, Alicia Lieberman, Mary Main, and Sally Wall and—for 1 year until he left for Yale—Michael Lamb).

As a mentor, Ainsworth was exacting and caring. She was Dr. Ainsworth, not Mary, to her students until they were close to completion of the doctoral dissertation, but at the same time she conveyed a deep personal interest in her advisees' accomplishments. Unlike many doctoral advisors, Ainsworth required that students plan independent projects and encouraged them to develop new measures rather than rely on her own substantial database and limit themselves to well-established methods. She preferred written statements as a prelude to oral discussions of research topics over open-ended brainstorming. At the same time, she was an extremely thoroughgoing and helpful reader of what her students produced. Mary Main (2000) remembers spending many late afternoons and early evenings on the pleasant screened porch that surrounded Ainsworth's home in Baltimore, discussing revisions of her doctoral dissertation.

Believing in hands-on training, Ainsworth encouraged beginning graduate students to assist their more advanced peers who were already collecting and analyzing their own data. She also insisted that participant families be made to feel valued. To establish rapport with families, all students were therefore required to make home-visits to explain their study before embarking on data collection.

In addition, Ainsworth was a challenging but inspiring classroom teacher. Her courses in developmental psychology were attended by both undergraduate and beginning graduate students. At a time when learning theory was still the dominant paradigm, the required readings for her introductory developmental psychology course were Freud's (1923/1961) "The Ego and the Id," Piaget's (1951) *The Origins of Intelligence in Children,* and Bowlby's new volume *Attachment* (1969). The last included extensive summaries of concepts and findings derived from the Uganda study and preliminary findings from the Baltimore study, without which Bowlby's book would probably have been much less influential.

Ainsworth's classroom teaching made a deep impression on a number of undergraduates who later became academics (among them Mark Cummings, Saul Feinman, Mark Greenberg, Milton Kotelchuck, Robert Marvin, Everett Waters, and Rob Woodson). Some also served as Ainsworth's undergraduate research assistants and thus gained expertise in the creation and analysis of home-observation narratives. After entering graduate programs at other universities, these students based their doctoral research on attachment theory. One of these was Robert Marvin, who had served as observer for the Baltimore study and who went on to conduct the first study of attachment in the preschool years at the University of Chicago, supervised by the distinguished evolutionary psychologist and human ethologist, Daniel Freedman (Marvin, 1972). In 1973, Everett Waters was admitted to graduate study at the University of Minnesota, where he aroused Alan Sroufe's interest in attachment research, particularly the Strange Situation. The outcome was a classic coauthored article "Attachment as an Organizational Construct" (Sroufe & Waters, 1977) and a very influential and still ongoing longitudinal study whose participants are now young adults.

In 1974, Ainsworth accepted an offer from the University of Virginia, where she trained a second cohort of productive researchers (among them Jude Cassidy, Deborah Cohn, Virginia Colin, Patricia Crittenden, Carolyn Eichberg, Rogers Kobak, and Ulrike Wartner). Ainsworth's effectiveness in attracting and training attachment scholars who became influential investigators, theoreticians, and clinicians was responsible for the tremendous growth of attachment research beginning in the late 1970s. Mary Blehar conducted the first attachment study of daycare, Main investigated the attachment–exploration balance in toddlers and began a longitudinal study, Lamb and Main each conducted Strange Situation studies with fathers, and Alicia Lieberman became senior supervisor of the late Selma Fraiberg's clinical Parent–Infant Program and infused it with attachment theory. Further new ground was broken with the 1985 volume "Growing Points of Attachment Theory and Research" (Bretherton & Waters). Waters, with his student Deane, presented a new Q-sort to help observers describe infants' "secure base behavior" at home. Main and colleagues moved "attachment to the level of representation" with their analysis of the Adult Attachment Interview (Main, Kaplan, & Cassidy, 1985). The volume also presented international findings from attachment research in Germany, Israel, and Japan. A few years later Kobak conducted the first attachment study with adolescents (Kobak & Sceery, 1988). The volume *Attachment in the Preschool Years* (Greenberg, Cicchetti, & Cummings, 1990) began to focus on the period beyond infancy and created links to developmental psychopathology.

Attachment research also proliferated because Ainsworth provided unusually generous help to many other investigators who had read her published work or heard about it at professional meetings. Some consulted her only by correspondence or telephone, others came to Baltimore. Klaus Grossmann visited in 1973 to learn more about the Strange Situation and home-observation strategies. Together with his wife, Karin Grossmann, and their numerous students he subsequently replicated many aspects of the Baltimore study in Germany, but then extended the study of attachment into young adulthood. Others who regularly consulted Ainsworth were Joan Stevenson-Hinde in England who was interested in the relation of attachment to temperament and Abraham Sagi in Israel who studied attachment in kibbutzim. In the late 1970s, Philip Shaver sought Ainsworth's advice while developing a self-report inventory he had designed with Cindy Hazan, which was designed to capture adult-attachment styles inspired by descriptions of secure, avoidant, and ambivalent infant attachment patterns in the Strange Situation. Their measure brought attachment theory into social psychology.

ACTIVE RETIREMENT

After reluctantly retiring as Professor Emerita in 1984 at the required age of 70, Ainsworth remained professionally active until 1992. During this period, she became highly engaged in workshops of the Attachment Group of the MacArthur Research Network on Early Childhood Transitions headed by Mark Greenberg, and collaborated in the development of a coding system appropriate for separation–reunion procedures for children over 2 years of age (Cassidy, Marvin, & the MacArthur Attachment Group, 1991). Her greatest enjoyment, however, came from opportunities to return to hands-on involvement in research, which her growing administrative duties—including election as President of the Society for Research in Child Development—had increasingly precluded. She helped many current and former students with the coding of Strange Situations videotapes and gave detailed and thoughtful advice when they consulted her about new measures they were creating. She also became highly involved in both learning and teaching the painstaking analytic procedures developed for the Adult Attachment Interview (AAI) by Main and her colleagues. With one of her graduate students, Carolyn Eichberg, she coauthored her last empirical study linking maternal AAIs with the Strange Situation (Ainsworth & Eichberg, 1991). Last, but not least, she proposed extensions of attachment theory to friendship, mentor–student, and spousal relationships (Ainsworth, 1991).

To her chagrin, Ainsworth did not have biological children. Instead, she repeatedly referred to her former students as her academic family (Ainsworth, 1982). In an interview (Ainsworth & Marvin, 1995, p. 21), she noted: "The most extraordinary thing in my life has been seeing so many people become interested in the concept of attachment and dedicating themselves to developing it further. . . . I think of them as my extended family." When a series of strokes began to interfere with her professional life during the 1990s, a former student and thereafter lifelong friend Robert Marvin, together with his wife Cheri, acted as her primary caregivers until her death in 1998, but she also cherished continued links by visit, letter, and telephone with many other members of her extended family from across the globe.

COURAGE, CRITICISM, AND ACCLAIM

An account of Ainsworth's contributions would not be complete without discussing her intellectual courage. Whereas psychologists are enjoined to examine phenomena dispassionately, this is difficult when the focus is on attachment. Because it touches so closely on personal experience, it is a topic that tends to arouse deep emotions. Findings that upset previous notions about parent–child relationships—even if well supported—were therefore not easy to present and publish, and were quite often received with hostility or even ridicule by established figures in the field. In public, at meetings and during her lectures in university classes, Ainsworth consistently responded to criticisms, even attacks on her work, with astonishing equanimity and grace. In private, she could show her impatience, irritation, frustration, and sometimes hurt when the negative comments came from individuals who had not read her work (or Bowlby's) carefully and who attributed ideas to her that she did not hold. At one point she wrote:

> The almost immediate popularity of the concept of attachment as a basis for research testifies to its filling a need long felt by students of early social development, and yet many who have appealed to its authority have misunderstood it and, I believe, misused it. Attachment theory is part of a new paradigm (Kuhn, 1962) that is not readily assimilated. . . . Consequently contemporary literature on attachment is chaotic and controversy is active about points that I would consider to be phantom issues. (Ainsworth, 1977, pp. 49–50)

Ainsworth wrote several articles and gave numerous talks attempting to put what she called phantom issues to rest. Many of these turned either on interpretations of the Strange Situation or on maternal responsiveness to crying. Her method of identifying relationship patterns rather than counting behavior frequencies was considered to be problematic by some. Terminology was a problem for others. Ainsworth was frequently asked to dispense with value-laden "nonscientific" descriptions of maternal behavior such as "tender, careful" or "inept" holding. Instead of "sensitive responsiveness," colleagues suggested "contingent responsiveness," which they considered to be a more objective label. She listened to questions and doubts, replied politely, and performed additional analyses of her own where she felt comments to be helpful, but she persevered.

Initially, journal articles proved difficult to publish; hence, some of Ainsworth's important work has appeared in the form of book chapters. That attachment research was still highly controversial in the late 1970s is illustrated by the fate of her presidential address at the plenary session of the biennial meetings of the Society for Research in Child Development (SRCD) in 1977. The written version of her speech (a summary of her life's work) was rejected by reviewers of the society's journal, *Child Development*. It therefore appeared in 1982, in a book honoring John Bowlby. As past SRCD president, however, Ainsworth saw to it that all subsequent presidents of the society would have their addresses printed in *Child Development* without peer review.

The tide turned as further studies, particularly long-term longitudinal and cross-cultural studies, replicated and supported much of Ainsworth's work. Some of the earlier controversies abated, and the originality of her work began to be more widely appreciated. By the mid-1980s she became the recipient of major awards, including the G. Stanley Hall Award from Division 7 (Developmental Psychology) of the APA in 1984. In 1985, the Society for Research in Child Development honored her with its Award for Distinguished Contributions to Child Development. Many other honors followed. She was especially pleased to be the first recipient of the newly established Mentoring Award of the APA's Division of Developmental Psychology. The culmination was the APA Gold Medal Award for Lifetime Achievements in the Science of Psychology in 1998, some months before her death. The citation for this award (Anonymous, 1998, p. 869) reads:

> Mary Ainsworth stands out as one of the major figures of the 20th century in the study of the relations between young children and their caregivers. Her work on the nature and development of human security, her exquisite naturalistic observations of attachment–caregiving interactions, her conceptual analyses of attachment, exploration and self-reliance, and her contributions to methodology of infant assessment, are cornerstones of modern attachment theory and research. The patterns of attachment that she identified have proven robust in research across diverse cultures and across the human life span. Her contributions to developmental psychology, developmental psychopathology, and ultimately to clinical psychology, as well as her teaching, colleagueship, and grace, are the secure base from which future generations of students can explore.

REFERENCES

Ainsworth, M. D. S. (1963). The development of infant–mother interaction among the Ganda. In B. M. Foss (Ed.), *Determinants of infant behavior* (pp. 67–104). New York: Wiley.

Ainsworth, M. D. S. (1967). *Infancy in Uganda: Infant care and the growth of love*. Baltimore, MD: The Johns Hopkins University Press.

Ainsworth, M. D. S. (1977). Attachment theory and its utility in cross-cultural research. In P. H. Leiderman, S. E. Tulkin, & A. Rosenfeld (Eds.), *Culture and infancy* (pp. 49–67). New York: Academic.

Ainsworth, M. D. S. (1982). Attachment: Retrospect and prospect. In C. M. Parkes & J. Stevenson-Hinde (Eds.), *The place of attachment in human behavior* (pp. 3–30). New York: Basic Books.

Ainsworth, M. D. S. (1983). Mary D. Salter Ainsworth. In A. N. O'Connell & N. F. Russo (Eds.), *Models of achievement: Reflections of prominent women in psychology* (pp. 201–219). New York: Columbia University Press.

Ainsworth, M. D. S. (1991). Attachment and other affectional bonds across the life cycle. In C. M. Parkes, J. Stevenson-Hinde, & P. Marris (Eds.), *Attachment across the life cycle* (pp. 33–51). New York: Routledge.

Ainsworth, M. D. S., & Ainsworth, L. H. (1958). *Measuring security in personal adjustment*. Toronto: University of Toronto Press.

Ainsworth, M. D. S., Blehar, M. C., Waters, E., & Wall, S. (1978). *Patterns of attachment: A psychological study of the strange situation*. Hillsdale, NJ: Lawrence Erlbaum Associates, Inc.

Ainsworth, M. D. S., & Eichberg, C. G. (1991). Effects on infant–mother attachment of mother's experience related to loss of an attachment figure. In C. M. Parkes, J. Stevenson-Hinde, & P. Marris (Eds.), *Attachment across the life cycle* (pp. 160–183). New York: Routledge.

Ainsworth, M. D. S., & Marvin, R. S. (1995). On the shaping of attachment theory and research. In E. Waters, B. E. Vaughn, G. Posada, & K. Kondo-Ikemura (Eds.), *Caregiving, cultural, and cognitive perspectives on secure-base behavior and working models. Monographs of the Society in Child Development, 60*(2–3, Serial No. 244), 3–21.

Ainsworth, M. D. S., & Wittig, B. A. (1969). Attachment and the exploratory behaviour of one-year-olds in a strange situation. In B. M. Foss (Ed.), *Determinants of infant behaviour* (Vol. 4, pp. 113–136). London: Methuen.

Anonymous. (1998). Gold medal award for life achievement in the science of psychology. *American Psychologist, 53*, 869–871.

Bell, S. M., & Ainsworth, M. D. S. (1972). Infant crying and maternal responsiveness. *Child Development, 43*, 1171–1190.

Bowlby, J. (1958). The nature of the child's tie to his mother. *International Journal of Psychoanalysis, 29*, 1–23.

Bowlby, J. (1969). *Attachment and loss. Vol. 1: Attachment*. New York: Basic Books.

Bretherton, I. (1992). The origins of attachment theory: John Bowlby and Mary Ainsworth. *Developmental Psychology, 28*, 759–775.

Bretherton, I., & Waters, E. (Eds.). (1985). Growing points of attachment theory and research. *Monographs of the Society for Research in Child Development, 50*(1–2, Serial No. 209), 41–65.

Cassidy, J., Marvin, R. S., & the MacArthur Attachment Work Group. (1991). *Attachment organization in preschool children. Coding guidelines*. Unpublished manuscript, University of Washington, Seattle.

Freud, S. (1961). The ego and the id. In J. Strachey (Ed. and Trans.), *The standard edition of the complete works of Sigmund Freud* (Vol. 20, pp. 1–59). London: Hogarth Press. (Original work published 1923)

Greenberg, M. T., Ciccetti, D., & Cummings, E. M. (1990). *Attachment in the preschool years: Theory and intervention*. Chicago: University of Chicago Press.

Harlow, H. F. (1961). The development of affectional patterns in infant monkeys. In B. M. Foss (Ed.), *Determinants of infant behaviour* (pp. 75–97). London: Methuen.

Karen, R. (1994). *Becoming attached: First relationships and how they shape our capacity to love*. New York: Oxford University Press.

Klopfer, B., Ainsworth, M. D. S., Klopfer, W. F., & Holt, R. R. (1954). *Developments in the Rorschach technique* (Vol. 1). Yonkers-on-Hudson, NY: World Book.

Kobak, R. R., & Sceery, A. (1998). Attachment in later adolescence: Working models, affect regulation, and representations of self and others. *Child Development, 59,* 135–146.

Kuhn, T. S. (1962). *The structure of scientific revolutions.* Chicago: University of Chicago Press.

Main, M. (2000). Mary D. Salter Ainsworth: Tribute and portrait. *Psychoanalytic Inquiry, 19,* 582–736.

Main, M., Kaplan, K., & Cassidy, J. (1985). Security in infancy, childhood and adulthood: A move to the level of representation. In I. Bretherton & E. Waters (Eds.), *Growing points of attachment theory and research, Monographs of the Society for Research in Child Development, 50*(1–2, Serial No. 209), 66–104.

Marvin, R. S. (1972). *Attachment and communicative behavior in two-, three-, and four-year-old children.* Unpublished doctoral dissertation, University of Chicago.

McDougall, W. (1927). *Character and the conduct of life.* London: Methuen.

Piaget, J. (1951). *The origins of intelligence in children.* New York: International Universities Press.

Robertson, J., & Bowlby, J. (1952). Responses of young children to separation from their mothers. *Courier of the International Children's Center, Paris, 2,* 131–140.

Salter, M. D. (1940). *An evaluation of adjustment based upon the concept of security. Child Development Series.* Toronto: The University of Toronto Press.

Sroufe, L. A., & Waters, E. (1977). Attachment as an organizational construct. *Child Development, 48,* 1184–1199.

Waters, E., & Deane, K. E. (1985). Defining and assessing individual differences in attachment relationships: Q-methodology and the organization of behavior in infancy and early childhood. In I. Bretherton & E. Waters (Eds.), Growing points of attachment theory and research, *Monographs of the Society for Research in Child Development, 50* (Serial No. 209, 1–2), 41–65.

Chapter 20

Floyd Ratliff and the Neural Foundations of Perception

John S. Werner
University of California, Davis

Lothar Spillmann
University of Freiburg, Germany

There were two golden eras during which scientists were able to forge links between visual perception and the brain mechanisms responsible for them. The first era was in the 19th century during the life and times of the Austrian physicist and philosopher, Ernst Mach. Together with Ewald Hering and others, Mach showed that how we perceive the world can reveal a great deal about the code used by the brain. The second era was in the 20th century during the life and times of Floyd Ratliff. It was during this time that the neural networks themselves were studied directly and related to phenomena of visual perception.

Based on our perception of contrast at borders or edges of visual stimuli, Mach observed that the activity in one region of the visual field influences perception of neighboring regions. His proposal that this demonstrates reciprocal inhibitory interactions among neighboring points in the retina was one of the first attempts to link psychophysics to physiology using the tools of mathematics. Direct evidence for this idea was not reported until about 100 years later through the electrophysiological investigations of retinal neural circuitry in the horseshoe crab, *Limulus polyphemus*, carried out by Hartline and Ratliff (1954). Later, in his 1965 book, *Mach Bands: Quantitative Studies on Neural Networks in the Retina*, Ratliff wrote that "Mach recognized no boundaries dividing the scientific disciplines" (p. 1). This view characterized Ratliff himself, as he used the tools of mathematics, biophysics, and psychophysics to study neural circuits in the visual pathways. He then went on to demonstrate elegantly how neural networks in the retina can help us better understand phenomena of brightness, color and form, and how they have been exploited in the visual arts at least since the Sung dynasty in China.

EARLY YEARS

Ratliff did not plan on a career in science. He was born near La Junta, Colorado on May 1, 1919, the youngest of the 12 children of Alice Hubbard Ratliff and Charles Frederick Ratliff. Three of the children died between the ages of 1 and 2 so Floyd grew up with seven older brothers and one sister. His father was a blacksmith and rancher who stressed the importance of a strict ethic of hard work, thrift, and honesty. Floyd was very fond of his mother, a hardworking and intelligent woman who encouraged him in his schoolwork and other endeavors. Life was not easy and his graduate student colleague, Tom Cornsweet, a distinguished vision scientist himself, recounted Ratliff's story about how difficult it was growing up in Colorado in the mid-1930s. For example, there was a knothole in the door of his family's cabin and the wind was so strong that he and his father both had to put all their weight against the bear skin covering the hole to keep the dust out during the many dust storms of that era. The topsoil blew away, waterfowl disappeared, and Ratliff then recognized that all things are interconnected. Without realizing it, Ratliff began to ponder deep philosophical issues.

> I would watch the freight train passing by on a branch of the Santa Fe Railroad a quarter of a mile or so away. I could see the steam from the whistle and then, later, I'd hear the whistle. I could feel the vibrations in the ground. These sensations were disjointed, and I would wonder where the train ended and I began, which part of the experience belonged to the train and which to me. I must have been around eight or ten when I started thinking about these things. I couldn't realize then, of course, that I was struggling with one of the most intractable problems in science and in philosophy—the delineation of the border between mind and matter and how one interacts with the other. I'm still struggling. (quoted in Bradossi & Schwartz, 1981–1982, p. 2)

Later, Ratliff would show how the methods of psychophysics and neuroscience can render these issues tractable.

Young Ratliff was quiet and loved to read, especially government bulletins that, at the time, provided detailed instructions on how to carry out a wide variety of projects. In the second grade he was advanced a year, but he disliked being the youngest in his class. He remedied that situation by dropping out of school for a year when he reached the seventh grade. He was a Lone Scout and especially enjoyed long camping trips by himself in the Piñon Canyon country south of La Junta. Ratliff was interested in Indian lore and this area is an important source of Indian artifacts and pictographs. He maintained this interest throughout his life. Some of these experiences may also have been pivotal in forming his long-time interest in the border between mind and matter. In an interview he described his budding interests in visual phenomena: "I can remember lying next to a haystack wearing a straw hat and noticing the effects of the sun through the holes" (Goodrich, 1992, p. 21). In addition to earning an associate of arts degree in 1940 from Pueblo Junior College, Ratliff obtained a taxidermist's license. His one ambition was to become a forest ranger, but World War II changed all that.

Ratliff enlisted in the U.S. Army in 1941 and, having already completed officer's training as an extension of his service in the National Guard, he was sent to the European front at the rank of second lieutenant. There, he served in Normandy, northern France, the Rhineland, and central Germany. He was decorated with the Bronze Star in 1945. The horrors that Ratliff saw during the war, including those he witnessed in the liberation of a concentration camp, stimulated his interest in human behavior and led him to a career in psychology. Later, his 1992 book on the artist Paul Signac would be dedicated to the memory of his "Comrades in the United States Army and in The French Forces of the Interior who fell in France, 1944–45."

With the support of his wife, Orma Vernon Priddy Ratliff, whom he had met on a train while on leave from the Army to visit his dying mother, the GI bill, a football scholarship, and part-time work in a bakery, Ratliff managed to complete his bachelor's degree at Colorado College in 1947. The Psychology Department at Colorado College had a strong tradition in sensory and physiological studies so it was natural for him to undertake graduate training at Brown University in Providence, Rhode Island, under Lorrin Riggs. Only 7 years younger than Riggs, and with a similar demeanor and appearance, Ratliff and Riggs became known as the "Bobsey twins." Ratliff's classmates included John Armington, Robert Boynton, and Tom Cornsweet, all of whom would become major figures in the field. During this time, Ratliff began a series of studies on the importance of eye movements for sustaining visual perception.

After completion of the doctorate degree in psychology at Brown in 1950, Ratliff worked with H. Keffer Hartline at The Johns Hopkins University from 1950 to 1951 on a National Research Council fellowship. After that, he spent 3 years at Harvard University, initially as an instructor and then as an assistant professor in psychology, where he worked with Georg von Békésy. Békésy and Ratliff shared similar scientific interests as well as a passion for art.

At Harvard, Ratliff and his first graduate student, Donald Blough, began a series of behavioral studies of vision in the pigeon. In contrast to the focus on behavioral control then prevailing at Harvard—largely because B. F. Skinner (chap. 16, *Pioneers III*) was a member of the faculty there—Ratliff and Blough wanted to study the sensory processes of nonhuman animals. They demonstrated successfully that pigeons respond to brightness contrast, by showing that for pigeons the brightness of a central disk is influenced by the intensity of the light surrounding it. During the summer months Ratliff continued research at Brown on the topic that he had begun as a graduate student.

EYE MOVEMENTS AND PERCEPTION

When we want to view, or fixate, an object of interest, we move our head and eyes to position the image of the object on a portion of the retina called the fovea. This is the region of the retina that has the maximum density of photoreceptors and is sampled with highest resolution at subsequent stages of processing in the brain. In natural viewing, even when the eye is intently fixating an object, small contractions of the eye muscles keep it moving to some extent. These tiny eye movements, known as physiological nystagmus, include tiny drifting movements as well as small ballistic movements called microsaccades. These movements can be demonstrated by recording the eye movements of someone who is looking at a picture (Yarbus, 1967). The eye fixates on one point momentarily and then jumps to another point of interest. Much of our fixation occurs to features, areas of abrupt light–dark change. Homogeneous areas normally do not evoke prolonged inspection.

Ratliff and other scientists working in Riggs's laboratory at Brown wondered what would happen if the visual stimulus is stabilized on the retina, by canceling the effects of involuntary eye movements. To answer this question, Riggs, Ratliff, Cornsweet, and Cornsweet (1953) designed an apparatus in which observers wore a contact lens with a mirror attached to it. A stimulus delivered by a projector was reflected by this mirror and projected as an image of the stimulus on a screen. This image was viewed through an optical path so that the movement of the stimulus corresponded exactly to the movement of the eye. When the eye moved, the mirror moved and, of course, so did the visual stimulus projected by the mirror. As a consequence, the retinal image always fell onto the same region, and the retinal image was said to be stabilized. The visual experience with a stabilized image is startling. Observers are amazed to discover that borders of a stabilized image fade away and the entire visual image disappears after a few seconds. In other words, when stimulation of the retina does not change in time—even though it changes in space—the observer becomes blind to the image. Small movements of the eye destabilize the retinal image and make vision possible by sustaining perception of borders and surfaces over time.

This finding is related to earlier observations by Metzger (1929, chap. 11, this volume) using a *Ganzfeld* (German for "total field"). A Ganzfeld is created by having observers look into a completely uniform sphere encompassing the entire visual field. The interior of the sphere is coated with some substance such as magnesium oxide that produces a field of uniform color, brightness, and texture. Sometimes, for research purposes, the Ganzfeld may be illuminated with a uniform light that appears red or some other color (Khan & Spillmann, 1996). What participants report when placed in such a Ganzfeld is quite surprising. After several minutes of being completely surrounded by a bright red field, the red disappears, and the subject does not "see" anything but a uniform gray. The discoveries of what happens in a Ganzfeld and what happens with stabilized images both demonstrate the importance of contrast for visual perception. The visual system has evolved not to extract information about absolute light levels, but about changes in light over space and time—that is, contrast.

LATERAL INHIBITION

Ratliff rejoined Hartline at the Rockefeller University in 1954 as an associate in the Laboratory of Biophysics and rose through the professorial ranks there. He was appointed professor in 1966 and held that rank until he became professor emeritus in 1989. Ratliff was a close friend and colleague of Nobel laureates von Békésy and Hartline, to whom he dedicated his 1965 book on Ernst Mach, *Mach Bands: Quantitative Studies on Neural Networks in the Retina*. This book combined the history and philosophy of science espoused by Mach in the 19th century with data and modeling of the neural circuitry of the "horseshoe crab," *Limulus polyphemus*.

Each eye of *Limulus* contains about 1,200 ommatidia, separate photoreceptive elements that can be individually stimulated and monitored electrophysiologically. The measurement of the electrical activity of the optic nerve was initiated by Adrian and Matthews (1927), but their measurements included the discharge of the whole nerve rather than individual optic nerve fibers. The latter was first accomplished at the Marine Biological Laboratory at Woods Hole, Massachusetts, by Hartline and Graham (1932; chap. 18, *Pioneers II*). It was expected that each ommatidium would send a signal to the next neural cell that coded faithfully a representation of the energy or number of quanta of light that were absorbed. This expectation, although reasonable, turned out to be wrong. Hartline and Ratliff (1954; Ratliff & Hartline, 1959) discovered that the activity of each ommatidium was inhibited when neighboring ommatidia were stimulated. The reduction of response that occurs when neighboring ommatidia are concurrently stimulated is called *lateral inhibition* because the opposition derives from the lateral, or crossing, elements of the retina. Lateral inhibition refers to the reduction of activity in one region of a sensory surface that results from stimulating a neighboring region of the sensory surface. Lateral inhibition diminishes in strength with increasing distance between any two ommatidia.

Hartline and Ratliff (1957) quantified the reciprocal inhibitory interactions between two ommatidia in the eye of *Limulus*, using a pair of simultaneous equations. These equations, which became known as the "Hartline–Ratliff equations," provided the first mathematical description of a neural network. Later, they extended their mathematical description based on empirical data to encompass a larger number of interactions in the network. For example, activity in a third ommatidium may inhibit the second, which reduces the inhibition of the first, a phenomenon called *disinhibition*, by analogy to the disinhibition of Pavlov (chap. 3, *Pioneers I*). This phenomenon was thought to be unique to *Limulus*, but is now recognized as a general neural principle that applies to other species of animal.

Each ommatidium of *Limulus* is connected with its neighbors so that the entire retina is functionally interconnected. In later work, Ratliff and his colleagues moved from characterizing response in the steady state to its dynamic organization. The spatial and temporal organization of the retina was modeled in terms of a set of linear filters by use of a spatiotemporal transfer function (Brodie, Knight, & Ratliff, 1978). This permitted retinal responses to be predicted for any arbitrary stimulus. This mathematical approach was extended to neurophysiological studies of neural networks in the vertebrate retina, and then to human visual processing assessed by the visually evoked cortical potential (Ratliff, 1980). The linear models developed for *Limulus* provided an excellent starting point, but Ratliff encouraged other techniques in his laboratory as the importance of functionally significant nonlinearities in visual processing emerged in these more complex visual systems.

The discovery of lateral inhibition reveals the importance of understanding the activity of single cells in isolation, as well as their responses when cells with which they are functionally connected are active. The important principle revealed by the phenomena of lateral inhibition and stabilized retinal images is that, although the visual system is relatively insensitive to uniform stimulation, neural circuitry is capable of sharpening responses to edges and borders. This is a fundamental property not only of visual systems, but of many other sensory systems (Békésy, 1967).

BORDER AND CONTRAST PHENOMENA
IN THE VISUAL ARTS

Ratliff had a deep and abiding interest in the visual arts and was a respected collector of Chinese ceramics, especially the Sung dynasty celadon ware, a grassy-to-sea-green porcelain ware. His appreciation of art was informed by his knowledge of the physiological mechanisms underlying visual perception. In articles written for a general audience (e.g., Ratliff, 1972), he demonstrated how principles acquired from studies of the horseshoe crab can help explain the delicate border and contrast effects attained by early Chinese artists. Bringing together his early work on eye movements, his later studies of lateral inhibition and the filtering properties of retinal visual processing, and studies of contour interactions at the cortical level, Ratliff expanded into analyses of how artists achieved many of their effects, combining edge enhancement, contrast, and color assimilation.

An important example of such an analysis is the Craik–O'Brien–Cornsweet effect (Ratliff, 1985), in which the perceived brightness of an area is higher (or lower) than a surrounding area of the same light level, when the two portions of the image are separated by a double-sawtooth edge, a border that ramps up (or down) in intensity on the inside. It is as though the brightness in each area is "assigned" according to the brightness at the surrounding edges with the gradual luminance change rectified. Although the neurophysiological basis of the Craik–O'Brien–Cornsweet effect is still not fully understood, it was exploited by artisans in ink painting, underglaze painting on ceramics and incised decorations on ceramics of the Sung and Tang dynasties of China in about the year 1,000 (Ratliff, 1985).

Ratliff was particularly enamored of the neo-impressionist painter Paul Signac (1863–1935), and especially Signac's use of border effects in paintings such as *Le Petit Déjeuner* (*The Breakfast*), painted in 1886. Edges and borders are produced by discontinuities in the physical image based on a change in reflectance of the pigment on canvas. What is normally perceived, however, does not correspond completely to the distribution of light in the image. The perceived pattern is an exaggeration of the abrupt light–dark transitions at edges and borders. Thin light and dark bands appear at the light and dark edges, respectively. These light and dark bands are illusory in the sense that they do not correspond to the physical distribution of light, but are so striking that many people believe they are due to physical phenomena such as multiple shadows or light diffraction. Instead, they are attributable to the reciprocal antagonistic interactions (lateral inhibition) within the visual pathways. They are called Mach bands, and Mach (1865; translation in Ratliff, 1965) provided a prescient account of them in terms of lateral inhibitory interactions in the visual system. Ratliff showed how Signac, who was not familiar with Mach's work, exaggerated perceptual borders to good effect on canvas. The origin of these effects in lateral inhibitory processes underlying Mach bands can be linked to similar processes observed by Ratliff in *Limulus*. These border effects, however, do not explain area contrast such as the Craik–O'Brien–Cornsweet effect in which the appearance of an entire area is affected by what surrounds it (Békésy, 1968). The latter seems to require long-range connections in the human visual cortex (Spillmann & Werner, 1996).

Ratliff continued his analysis of the works of Signac and in 1992 published *Paul Signac and Color in Neo-Impressionism*, the definitive treatise on the physiological basis for fundamental aspects of "divisionism," a technique that evolved from the Pointillism of Georges Seurat and others, in which dots of paint, of varying sizes, are placed side by side to enhance the color and brightness of the canvas. These effects occur because the physical mixture of light within the eye is *additive*. Traditionally, the light reaching the eye from a painting is based on a mixture of pigments on the canvas to produce *subtractive* mixture. Subtractive mixture is familiar to most people through playing with paints;

the mixture of blue and yellow paint typically appears green. In this example, the blue pigment absorbs many of the long-wave quanta and the yellow pigment absorbs many of the short-wave quanta. What reaches the eye is primarily middle wavelengths, the band that is reflected by both pigments. This is analogous to passing a white light with all wavelengths through two successive filters, a blue and a yellow. The blue filter transmits quanta primarily of short and middle wavelengths whereas the yellow filter transmits primarily the middle- and long-wavelength quanta. Light of specific wavelengths is subtracted out at each stage and all that reaches the eye is that which both filters transmit, the middle wavelengths, which we usually call green. In subtractive color mixture the result is always a loss of light compared with that which would be transmitted (reflected) by either filter (pigment) alone. In additive mixture, the same blue and yellow paints are used but are not mixed on the canvas. Instead, small dots of each pigment are placed side by side. If the dots are too small to be resolved at the normal viewing distance, the mixture of the reflected light will take place in the eye in an additive manner and there will be no loss of light. When the dots are larger, there is no additive mixture of them. Instead, the light reflected from the dots may initiate neural responses that produce contrast, with blue enhancing the yellow and vice versa. This simultaneous color contrast effect has been exploited by many artists for centuries and is the basis for dark colors such as brown and black (Werner & Ratliff, 1999).

Hering (1874, 1920) articulated the probable physiological basis for contrast not only in the spatial, but also in the temporal domain on the hypothesis that reciprocal antagonistic interactions occur between blue and yellow, red and green, and black and white mechanisms of color vision. Ratliff (1976) pointed out that these six fundamental colors, forming three pairs in the opponent-color theory of Hering, are deeply rooted in the language of color. It has been suggested that these six color names may have been the first to appear in the evolution of language, and Ratliff argued that this, like border contrast effects, is due to the organization of the nervous system.

A major complication for neo-impressionism is that the appearance of a painting depends critically on the viewer's distance. At one distance, blue and yellow dots may produce contrast, rendering a more vivid blue and yellow than would be possible with either pigment alone. At a greater distance, however, the dots will be too small to be resolved and the additive mixture will appear gray because of the cancellation of blue and yellow. Signac emphasized that the best technique practiced by neo-impressionists was "Divisionism" not "Pointillism," by which he meant that the paint should be applied with small distinctive strokes, not tiny points. Signac wrote: "The Neo-Impressionist does not paint with dots, he divides" (Ratliff, 1992, p. 207). Unfortunately, this does not eliminate the dependence of a painting on viewing distance, but only defines a new set of distances at which one has hue cancellation versus contrast. In anticipation of this problem, Signac referred to Rembrandt:

"A painting is not to be sniffed," said Rembrandt. When listening to a symphony, one does not sit in the midst of the brass, but in the place where the sounds of the different instruments blend into the harmony desired by the composer. Afterwards one can enjoy dissecting the score, note by note, and so study the manner of orchestration. Likewise, when viewing a divided painting, one should first stand far enough away to obtain the impression as a whole, and then come closer in order to study the interplay of the colored elements, supposing that these technical details are of interest. (Signac, in Ratliff, 1992, p. 264)

Ratliff's book included a careful "dissection of the score," an explication of the physical and physiological principles underlying these and other effects in this important period of Western art history. He showed how the history of research in this area evolved from a misconception that color is a property of light to our current understanding of color as activity in the brain. As an appendix, he included the first English translation of Signac's (1921) book, *D'Eugène Delacroix au Néo-Impressionnisme*.

LATER YEARS

Throughout his career, Ratliff's scientific contributions were widely appreciated, and he received numerous awards including election to the Society of Experimental Psychologists (1957), the National Academy of Sciences (1966), the American Academy of Arts and Sciences (1968), and the American Philosophical Society (1972). He also received the Warren Medal of the Society of Experimental Psychologists (1966); an honorary doctorate of science from his alma mater, Colorado College (1975); the Edgar D. Tillyer Award of the Optical Society of America (1976); the Medal for Distinguished Service of Brown University (1980); the Pisart Vision Award of the Lighthouse, New York Association of the Blind (1983); and the American Psychological Association Distinguished Scientific Contribution Award (1984).

From 1983 to 1989, Ratliff served as the president of the Harry Frank Guggenheim Foundation. In that capacity, he provided direction for the foundation's program of research on violence. This research involved anthropologists, historians, political scientists and sociologists, as well as biologists and ethologists. Ratliff continued to pursue related work when he retired to Santa Fe, New Mexico, serving as a member and president of the board of Esperanza (Spanish for "hope"), a shelter for families who have suffered from domestic violence.

Ratliff's retirement to Santa Fe allowed him to indulge his love of the arts. He died there on June 13, 1999. His scientific advances have stood the test of time. Ratliff is remembered by his friends and colleagues for his gentility, intellectual acumen, his historical scholarship, and his creative bridging of the chasm that sometimes exists between the arts and sciences.

ACKNOWLEDGMENTS

The helpful comments of Israel Abramov, Walter Ehrenstein, James Gordon, Edith Johnson, Merry Muraskin, and Jonathan Victor are gratefully acknowledged. Supported by a Senior Scientist Award from the Alexander von Humboldt Foundation to JSW.

REFERENCES

Adrian, E. D., & Matthews, R. (1927). The action of light on the eye: 1. Discharge of impulses in the optic nerve and its relation to the electrical changes in the retina. *Journal of Physiology, 63*, 378–414.

Békésy, G. v. (1967). *Sensory inhibition.* Princeton, NJ: Princeton University Press.

Békésy, G. v. (1968). Mach- and Hering-type lateral inhibition in vision. *Vision Research, 8*, 1483–1499.

Bradossi, F., & Schwartz, J. N. (1981–82). Particles of light, webs of interaction. *Rockefeller University Research Profiles.* Winter, No. 7. New York: Rockefeller University Press, pp. 1–6. *The Rockefeller University Archives.*

Brodie, S. E., Knight, B. W., & Ratliff, F. (1978). The response of the *Limulus* retina to moving stimuli: A prediction by Fourier synthesis. *Journal of General Physiology, 72*, 129–166.

Goodrich, C. (1992). Rockefeller Press looks to trade audience. *Publishers Weekly, 239*, 21–22.

Hartline, H. K. & Graham, C. H. (1932). Nerve impulses from single receptors in the eye. *Journal of Cellular and Comparative Physiology, 1*, 277–295.

Hartline, H. K. & Ratliff, F. (1954). Spatial summation of inhibitory influences in the eye of *Limulus*. *Science, 120*, 781.

Hartline, H. K. & Ratliff, F. (1957). Inhibitory interaction of receptor units in the eye of *Limulus*. *Journal of General Physiology, 40*, 357–376.

Hering, E. (1874). Zur Lehre vom Lichtsinne. VI. Grundzüge einer Theorie des Farbensinnes [On the theory of the light sense, VI. Outlines of a theory of the color sense]. *Sitzungsberichte. der Akademie für Wissenschaften, Wien, Mathematische und Naturwissenschaftliche Klasse, Abteilung, 70*, 169–204.

Hering E. (1920) *Outlines of a theory of the light sense.* (English translation of *Zur Lehre vom Lichtsinne* by L. M. Hurvich & D. Jameson, 1964). Cambridge, MA: Harvard University Press.

Khan, H., & Spillmann, L. (1996). Failure of brightness and color constancy under prolonged Ganzfeld stimulation. *SPIE Proceedings, 2657*, 19–29.

Mach E. (1865). Über die Wirkung der räumlichen Vertheilung des Lichtreizes auf die Netzhaut, I [On the effect of the spatial distribution of the light stimulus on the retina]. *Sitzungsberichte der mathematisch-naturwissenschaftlichen Classe der kaiserlichen Akademie der Wissenschaften, 52*, 303–322.

Metzger, W. (1929). Optische Untersuchungen am Ganzfeld. II. Mitteilung: Zur Phänomenologie des homogenen Ganzfelds [Optical investigations of the Ganzfeld. II. Report on the phenomenology of the homogeneous Ganzfeld]. *Psychologische Forschung, 13*, 7–29.

Ratliff, F. (1965). *Mach bands: Quantitative studies on neural networks in the retina.* San Francisco: Holden-Day.

Ratliff, F. (1972). Contour and contrast. *Scientific American, 226*, 90–101.

Ratliff, F. (1976). On the psychophysiological bases of universal color terms. *Proceedings of the American Philosophical Society, 120*, 311–330.

Ratliff, F. (1980). Form and function: Linear and nonlinear analyses of neural networks in the visual system. In *University of Texas Symposium on Neural Mechanisms in Behavior* (pp. 73–138). New York: Springer-Verlag.

Ratliff, F. (1985). The influence of contour on contrast: From cave painting to Cambridge psychology. *Transactions of the American Philosophical Society, 75,* 1–19.

Ratliff, F. (1992). *Paul Signac and color in neo-impressionism.* New York: Rockefeller University Press.

Ratliff, F., & Hartline H. K. (1959). The responses of *Limulus* optic nerve fibers to patterns of illumination on the receptor mosaic. *Journal of General Physiology, 42,* 1241–1255.

Riggs, L. A., Ratliff, F., Cornsweet, J. C., & Cornsweet, T. N. (1953). The disappearance of steadily fixated visual test objects. *Journal of the Optical Society of America, 43,* 495–501.

Signac, P. (1921) *D'Eugène Delacroix au Néo-Impressionnisme.* (Paris: H. Floury). [trans. and ed. by W. Silverman in F. Ratliff (1992) *Paul Signac and color in Neo-Impressionism* (pp. 193–285). New York: Rockefeller University Press.

Spillmann, L., & Werner, J. S. (1996). Long-range interactions in visual perception. *Trends in Neurosciences, 19,* 428–434.

Werner, J. S., & Ratliff, F. (1999). Some origins of the lightness and darkness of colors—In the visual arts and in the brain. *TECHNE—La Science au Service de L'histoire de L'art et des Civilisations, 9–10,* 61–73.

Yarbus, A. L. (1967). *Eye movements and vision.* New York: Plenum.

Index